BIBLICAL
HERMENEUTICS

BIBLICAL HERMENEUTICS

A Comprehensive Introduction To Interpreting Scripture

Bruce Corley

Steve Lemke

Grant Lovejoy

BROADMAN
& HOLMAN
PUBLISHERS

Nashville, Tennessee

4211–47
0–8054–1147–X

Dewey Decimal Classification: 220.6
Subject Heading: BIBLE—CRITICISM, INTERPRETATION, ETC.
Library of Congress Card Catalog Number: 95–46615

Unless otherwise stated Scripture citations are from the following: The King James Version . The HOLY BIBLE, NEW INTERNATIONAL VERSION®. Copyright© 1973, 1978, 1984 by International Bible Society. Used by permission of Zondervan Publishing House. All rights reserved. The New American Standard Bible. ©The Lockman Foundation, 1960, 1962, 1963, 1968, 1971, 1972, 1973, 1975, 1977. Used by permission. The New King James Version. Copyright ©1979, 1980, 1982, Thomas Nelson, Inc., Publishers. The Revised Standard Version of the Bible, copyrighted 1946, 1952, ©1971, 1973. The New Revised Standard Version of the Bible, copyright ©1989 by the Division of Christian Education of the National Council of Churches of Christ in the United States of America. Used by permission. All rights reserved. The New English Bible. Copyright ©The Delegates of the Oxford University Press and the Syndics of the Cambridge University Press, 1961, 1970. Reprinted by permission. The Good News Bible, the Bible in Today's English Version. Old Testament : Copyright © American Bible Society 1976; New Testament: Copyright © American Bible Society 1966, 1971, 1976. Used by permission. The Jerusalem Bible, copyright ©1966 by Darton, Longman and Todd, Ltd., and Doubleday and Company, Inc. Used by permission of the publisher.

Acquisitions and Development Editor: John Landers
Page Design: Steve Boyd

Library of Congress Cataloging-in-Publication Data
Biblical Hermeneutics : a comprehensive introduction to interpreting Scripture / Bruce Corley, Steve Lemke, Grant Lovejoy, editors.
    p. cm.
  ISBN 0–8054–1147–X
  1.Bible—Hermeneutics. 2.Baptists—Doctrines.
I. Corely, Bruce. II. Lemke, Steve, 1951– III. Lovejoy, Grant, 1958–
BS476.B494   1996
220.6—dc20   95–46615
                                                                      CIP

1 2 3 4 5 6 01 00 99 98 97 96

Contributors

Robert W. Bernard, Consultant, Doctoral Research and Writing; Director, Modern Language Studies Program, Southwestern Baptist Theological Seminary

Thomas V. Brisco, Associate Professor of Biblical Backgrounds and Archaeology; Associate Dean of Special Masters Degrees, Southwestern Baptist Theological Seminary

James A. Brooks, Professor of New Testament, Bethel Theological Seminary

Bruce Corley, Professor of New Testament and Greek, Southwestern Baptist Theological Seminary

Lorin L. Cranford, Professor of New Testament, Southwestern Baptist Theological Seminary

E. Earle Ellis, Research Professor of Theology, Southwestern Baptist Theological Seminary

Millard J. Erickson, Distinguished Professor of Theology, Western Seminary, Portland, and Truett Seminary of Baylor University

Harold Freeman, Associate Dean, Ph.D. Program; Ralph and Bess Smith Chair of Preaching; Professor of Preaching, Southwestern Baptist Theological Seminary

R. L. Hatchett, Associate Professor of Christianity and Philosophy at Houston Baptist University

Rick Johnson, Associate Professor of Old Testament, Southwestern Baptist Theological Seminary

Wm. David Kirkpatrick, Professor of Systematic Theology, Southwestern Baptist Theological Seminary

Thomas D. Lea, Dean, School of Theology; Professor of New Testament, Southwestern Baptist Theological Seminary

Steve W. Lemke, Associate Professor of Philosophy of Religion, Southwestern Baptist Theological Seminary

Grant Lovejoy, Assistant Professor of Preaching, Southwestern Baptist Theological Seminary

H. Leon McBeth, Distinguished Professor of Church History, Southwestern Baptist Theological Seminary

Calvin Miller, Professor of Communication and Ministry Studies; Writer in Residence, Southwestern Baptist Theological Seminary

Carey C. Newman, Formerly Assistant Professor of New Testament at The Southern Baptist Theological Seminary

John P. Newport, Emeritus Vice President for Academic Affairs & Provost and Distinguished Professor of Philosophy of Religion, Southwestern Baptist Theological Seminary

B. Keith Putt, Associate Professor of Philosophy of Religion, Southwestern Baptist Theological Seminary

Rodney R. Reeves, Pastor, Central Baptist Church, Jonesboro, Arkansas, formerly Chairman of the Department of Philosophy and Religion at Williams Baptist College in Arkansas

Daniel R. Sanchez, Vernon and Jeanette Davidson Professor of Missions; Director, Scarborough Institute for Church Growth, Southwestern Baptist Theological Seminary

Robert B. Sloan, President and CEO of Baylor University

Jim Spivey, Associate Professor of Church History, Southwestern Baptist Theological Seminary

William B. Tolar, Distinguished Professor of Biblical Backgrounds, Southwestern Baptist Theological Seminary

Contents

PART TWO
Implications of Authority, Inspiration, and Language

PART THREE
Applying the Grammatical-Historical Method

Preface

Questions about the interpretation of the Bible have been with the Christian faith from its beginning. Jesus' confrontations with the Pharisees, for example, often had to do with the interpretation of Scripture. On one occasion Jesus chided them, "Is this not the reason you are mistaken, that *you do not understand the Scriptures*, or the power of God?" (Mark 12:24, NASB—emphasis added). Consequently, Christians have worked through the centuries to develop and follow principles of sound biblical interpretation. After all, people committed to living under the authority of Scripture want to be sure that they grasp its teaching. Many Christians have heeded Paul's instruction: "Be diligent to present yourself approved to God as a workman who does not need to be ashamed, handling accurately the word of truth" (2 Tim. 2:15). Those of us working in theological education know how crucial it is that we equip students to interpret Scripture accurately.

Interpreting the Bible faithfully has been a chief concern at the school where the three of us have taught for the last several years, Southwestern Baptist Theological Seminary in Fort Worth, Texas. In courses as diverse as church history, philosophy of religion, Old Testament, New Testament, Christian ethics, missions and preaching, questions of appropriate interpretation have been raised and addressed. Yet, several years ago the faculty in Southwestern's School of Theology sensed a growing need for students to study biblical hermeneutics more systematically. The piecemeal approach was not adequately meeting students' needs. Many of them were coming to seminary with little or no background in the liberal arts. Some, having become Christians only a few years before, had only limited knowledge of Scripture and its interpretation. Thus, Southwestern decided to begin requiring all students in its basic theological degree programs to take a course in biblical hermeneutics.

Faculty members carefully planned the course content. They wanted it to cover four basic areas: philosophical presuppositions, the history of biblical interpretation, the actual practice of interpretation, and the use of the resulting insights in ministry tasks such as preaching and missions. This breadth of scope made teaching the course a challenge, since it cut across academic disciplines. Indeed, faculty members did extensive cross-disciplinary study and discussion in preparation for teaching the new course.

In due time it was necessary to select a textbook for the course. The breadth of the course, however, made selecting a textbook a challenge. A number of very fine books on biblical hermeneutics have been written in recent years; yet none of them met our needs. Some are too technical for entering students. Other books deal with one or two, perhaps even three, of the major areas marked out for the course; but none covers all four areas. It is difficult, for example, to find a biblical hermeneutics book that shows how exegesis leads to a sermon that is faithful to the text. Often the books are strong in describing different types of biblical criticism but give little or no guidance in actually doing exegesis.

Those who have taught biblical hermeneutics at Southwestern have used combinations of textbooks in an effort to cover all these bases. This approach has several inadequacies. Thus it seemed advisable that we should attempt to put together the type of book needed. Conversations at professional meetings revealed that we were not alone in wanting a textbook that is written for beginning students and that introduces them to biblical hermeneutics within a philosophical and historical context, yet with a practical goal in mind: actually to study the text in a systematic fashion that produces insights which will be lived and proclaimed in and through the church.

As the three of us discussed this book, we decided to draw on the expertise of colleagues in various fields. We recognize the inherent challenges of such an approach, but we believe the advantages to be worth the risks. Whether the decision was the correct one will of course be each reader's right to judge. Because all the contributors have a connection with Southwestern as a former student or as a current or former faculty member, the volume does have a common perspective. The contributors share a commitment to the inspiration and authority of Scripture and its centrality in the life and mission of the church.

In preparation of the volume we have had much assistance. Our colleagues in the theology faculty at Southwestern Seminary encouraged us to undertake the project. Later they reviewed an initial outline of the book and gave constructive feedback. Our contributors worked within the limitations we imposed on them and produced some excellent chapters. Our support staff gave crucial assistance in the preparation of the book. Danny Wilson, a graduate assistant in our Ph.D. program, edited and proofread the bibliography. A husband and wife team were invaluable to us: Laverne Smith, a secretary at Southwestern, updated several drafts of most of the material as we sought consistency in method of citation and a style suitable for introductory students; her husband, Fred Smith, a Ph.D. student, worked on the glossary, the index, and also proofread the manuscript. In each case he improved the book by his efforts. Their efficiency and attention to detail were a blessing.

We are also indebted to others in Southwestern Seminary's faculty, administration, and staff who encouraged us in the preparation of this book. Their friendship and support make our work a joy. Additionally, we owe a debt of gratitude to our students. Their commitment to Christ makes teaching them a source of deep satisfaction. Their questions keep us growing and searching the Scriptures ourselves. Their future contributions to the life of the church make our efforts immeasurably worthwhile. To the Lord who has called both them and us, we express gratitude for life and strength and the indwelling of the One who leads us into truth.

Bruce Corley
Steve Lemke
Grant Lovejoy

Introduction

A Student's Primer for Exegesis

Bruce Corley

In the first class of my first semester in seminary, the professor wrote the word *exegesis* on the chalkboard and told us that one of these research assignments was due in two weeks. I had no idea what he meant. As it turns out, not many others have claimed to know what he meant and those who have seem to disagree. *Exegesis,* like its well-traveled partner *hermeneutics,* "is a word that is forever chasing a meaning" (Frei, 16). The scholarly debate has featured a baffling array of linguistic insights, philosophical critiques, and competing theories of interpretation—all about the "meaning of meaning."

Meanwhile, theological students everywhere, still working to produce acceptable papers, continue to enter the strange world of exegesis and hermeneutics. The puzzled looks and bewildering talk that usually follow are reminiscent of an oft-repeated story, the dispute between Alice and the contemptuous Humpty Dumpty, who with delight turned "meaning" on its head (Lewis Carroll, *Through the Looking Glass* [1872], chap. 6):

"When *I* use a word," Humpty Dumpty said, in rather a scornful tone, "it means just what I choose it to mean—neither more nor less."

"The question is," said Alice, "whether you *can* make words mean so many different things."

"The question is," said Humpty Dumpty, "which is to be master—that's all."
Alice was too much puzzled to say anything.

Like Alice who did not know the language games of a nonsense world, the alert student could wish for a bit of help in grasping what words really mean, especially when their masters stretch them beyond recognition.

Here, then, is a short primer for beginning students—a field guide for those who are "too much puzzled"—along the fundamental lines of "How to Write an Exegetical Paper." From the viewpoint of the ever-growing literature on this subject, it is a pretentious venture, written at the risk of slighting important issues and technical jargon (that will appear in later chapters) but in search of a clear reward, namely: an approach to exegesis and how to do it in plain and simple terms.

The Aims of Biblical Exegesis

What is exegesis, and how is it related to hermeneutics? Although both words appear in other fields of academic study, they mainly belong to the classical disciplines of theology, where both exegesis and hermeneutics refer to the interpretation of the Bible. Hermeneutics probably first emerged as a name for this biblical discipline in J. C. Dannhauer's *Hermeneutica Sacra* (Strasburg, 1654); whereas exegesis had already appeared in the title of Papias's five-volume work in the early second century, *Exegesis of the Lord's Sayings*, an exposition of Gospel teachings known to us only by fragments quoted in later authors. For Papias, like other ancient writers, exegesis and hermeneutics were overlapping concepts; the preface to the *Exegesis* describes Jesus' sayings themselves, collected and handed down, as "interpretations" (Greek *hermēneiai*; see Eusebius, *Ecclesiastical History* 39.1, 3). The skills of interpretation taught in Greco-Roman education had long before shaped the popular coinage of both terms, and we must first look there to define their meanings.

Classical Definitions

The Greek word groups related to the nouns *exēgēsis* and *hermēneia*, which gave us the English counterparts, denote an understanding or meaning derived from an object of reflection and study such as an event, a speech, or a law. In the area of our interest—literary usage—both nouns refer to an "explanation, interpretation, or meaning" of a written text, and the corresponding verbs *(exēgeomai* and *hermēneuō*) describe the act by which meaning is found, "to expound, to explain, to interpret" the text. When applied to texts in foreign languages, *hermēneuō* means "to translate."

Usage that reaches back to classical Athens (fourth century B.C.) shows the closeness of the two word groups. According to Plato, a *hermēneutēs* could be an "interpreter" of the sacred law (*Laws* 907d) or a poet expounding divine utterances as a "spokesman" for the gods (*Ion* 534e; *Statesman* 290c), one practicing the "art of interpretation" (cf. *Symposium* 202e; *Theaetetus* 209a; *Statesman* 260d). Plato's *exēgētēs* had similar skills (cf. *Cratylus* 407a), whether an "expounder" of ancestral law (*Laws* 631a; 759c; 775a), or the famous Delphic oracle entrusted as the "interpreter *[exēgētēs]* of religion to all mankind" (*Republic* 4.427c). This functional linkage between exegesis and hermeneutics persisted in Greek literature, specifically in the Jewish writings of the Second Temple period (LXX, Philo, and Josephus), down to the New Testament itself.

A wordplay found in the Acts account of Paul and Barnabas at Lystra (Acts 14:8–18) provides an instructive example. After the crowd saw a lame man healed, they acclaimed Paul and Barnabas as miracle workers, shouting "the gods have come down to us in human form" (14:11, REB). Likely echoing local knowledge of a legendary visit of Zeus and Hermes to the Phrygian hill country, Paul was "called Hermes because he was the chief speaker" (14:12, NIV). Hermes was the spokesman for the gods who invented language and its uses, and according to Plato's etymology of his name, Hermes meant "interpreter" *[hermēneus]* whose gift was the hermeneutical art (*Cratylus* 408a). On the other hand, the description of Paul as the "chief speaker" (literally, "the one who leads in speaking") hints at the exegetical skill. The Greek word used of Paul, *ēgeomai*, ("to lead"), is the verbal root behind exegesis, which in its compound form (*ex* + *ēgeomai*) means "to lead, bring out [the meaning]."

Biblical Images

More than two dozen terms in the Hebrew and Greek Scriptures make up the vocabulary domain related to interpretation (see the references in Thiselton, 574–82). However the noun *exēgēsis*, used sparingly in the Old Testament, does not occur in the New Testament and its cognate verb is used only six times (John 1:18; Luke 24:35; Acts 10:8; 15:12, 14; 21:19). The "hermeneutics" word group dominates the biblical usage (cf. Ezra 4:7; Gen. 42:23; Sir. 47:17;

Matt. 1:23; Mark 4:41; 15:22, 34; John 1:38, 41–42; Acts 4:36; Heb. 7:2). Notable instances of *hermēneia* are Joseph's gift for the interpretation of dreams (Genesis 40–41) and Paul's instruction concerning the interpretation of tongues (1 Corinthians 12–14). As for interpretation of the Scriptures, the Old Testament has little to say, but we get memorable images of the biblical perspective in four New Testament passages.

1. Opening up the Scriptures. Along the Emmaus road, Jesus spoke with Cleophas and a despondent companion, helping them to understand the Scriptures: "And beginning with Moses and all the Prophets, he explained *[dia + hermēneuō]* to them what was said in all the Scriptures concerning himself" (Luke 24:27, NIV). Later in the evening, after they had recognized Jesus, the two recounted their experience with a parallel term; they said to one another that their hearts had been set on fire as Jesus had "opened up" (*dianoigō*, 24:32) the Scriptures to them. Interpetation opened up the closed text, inspiring the mind and heart to a new understanding.

2. Guiding through the Scriptures. When Philip came upon a chariot on the desert road south of Jerusalem, he heard an Ethiopian eunuch reading aloud from the prophet Isaiah. Philip asked him whether he understood what he was reading. "How can I," he said, "unless someone explains *[hodēgeō]* it to me?" (Acts 8:31, NIV). The eunuch wanted a pathfinder to lead or guide, to strike a trail to a chosen place; interpretation was a guide along the right path of meaning.

3. Cutting Straight with the Scriptures. Paul enjoined Timothy to be an unashamed workman "handling accurately the word of truth" (2 Tim. 2:15, NASB). The verb *orthotomeō* conveys the picture of cutting a straight line, for example, cutting a straight road through a dense forest or plowing a straight furrow in a field. Timothy was to expound the word of truth along a straight line without being turned aside by wordy debates or impious talk. Such interpetation cut straight through the issues with the unswerving truth.

4. Unlocking the Scriptures. In warning against "cleverly devised tales" used by false teachers, 2 Peter cautions against an arbitrary reading of prophecy: "But know this first of all, that no prophecy of Scripture is a matter of one's own interpretation *[epilysis]*" (2 Pet. 1:20, NASB). The noun *epilysis* ("solution, explanation") touches the area of inquiry and problem solving, particularly the unlocking of a mystery or secret. The confirmation (1:19) of the Scriptures was not located in personal whim; rather its meaning was secured and unlocked by the Spirit's activity (1:21).

Contemporary Models

The cases of exegesis and hermeneutics we have surveyed indicate that interpretation aims at the appropriate meaning of a text, that is, a meaning judged to be accurate, responsible, or faithful to a specified goal. How can an accurate meaning be found? This question gave rise to the development of "rules" for interpretation both in Judaism and Christianity, such as the seven rules of Rabbi Hillel (see the description of *Middoth* in chap. 2) and the seven rules of Tyconius that were appropriated by Augustine (see *On Christian Doctrine* 3. 42–56). Rule-governed procedures were handy controls on the possible meaning(s) of a biblical text; therefore, the rationale and enumeration of such principles were subjects of paramount importance in the history of biblical interpretation. The church's quest for the rules by which to understand the Bible gave hermeneutics its modern definition: the *theory of interpretation*. When theory was applied and put to work in the text, it was then called exegesis: the *practice of interpretation.*

Moreover, the traditional aim of exegesis was retrospective, that is, to understand *what the text originally meant* by discovering the historical meaning intended by the ancient author. The prospective aim, *what the text means now* for the contemporary reader, was usually called *exposition*, an application based on exegesis but not part of it. The traditional model can be sketched as follows:

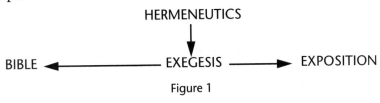

Figure 1

This sequential model, hermeneutics–>exegesis–>exposition, has all but collapsed under the weight of literary criticism with its dual insistence upon the autonomy of the text and the centrality of the reader (see Morgan and Barton, 167–263). The customary distinction between hermeneutics as theory and exegesis as practice, while helpful in some ways, has proven to be artificial. Much hermeneutical theory is distilled from the experience of reading the biblical text; its principles are reshaped and verified by how they work in the text. Hermeneutics and exegesis may be distinguished but not divided; they form a seamless continuum wherein the one constantly informs the other (Ramm, 11). The line between exegesis and exposition, never a clear one, has also faded with the recognition that meaning is shaped by the reader's presuppositions and interests.

Modern theory of written communication involves an author who creates (encodes) a text and a reader who interprets (decodes) a text. Therefore, "the process of discovering the 'meaning' of a written utterance has three foci: the author, the text and the reader" (Osborne, 366). A satisfactory model for exegesis should take account of the "trialogue" among the biblical author, the scriptural text, and the contemporary reader. Exegesis in this model (fig. 2) attempts to maintain an author-text orientation with a formal integration of text-reader concerns (for a careful analysis of the issues see Osborne, 366–415, and relevant chapters in parts 2 and 3 below). On the one hand, a reader's tendency to create biased and fanciful meanings is under the restraint of historical investigation; on the other, a dry-as-dust historical account, however tediously factual, is under the constraint of theological relevance. We are suggesting that the aims of exegesis must be balanced so that both the past and the present get a proper hearing.

Figure 2

The aims we are proposing may be construed in terms of three interpretive stances with regard to the biblical text :

1. *Behind-the-text Aim*. Exegesis has and should approach the biblical text as a window to see into the world of the author. Questions that go behind the text typically probe the circumstances of a writing, such as its date, sources, and terminology: When did the Exodus occur? How were the Synoptic Gospels composed? What did the term "righteousness" mean in the Old Testament? In the New Testament? The required studies are diachronic ("through time"), moving through the text to a point of time in the past; the results are historical in nature. Historical-critical methods were fashioned to achieve this goal, and when freed from the tyranny of Enlightenment skepticism ("the historical-critical method"), they still offer the best promise of finding the world and intention of the author (cf. Maier, 376–79, 386–93).

2. Within-the-text Aim. The literary world of the text itself is a second focal point for exegesis. While still dependent on historical data, the textual aim is primarily literary-critical, giving attention to prominent words, markers, and structures that convey meaning. How does the narrative of Genesis 1–11 set the themes for the rest of the book? Do certain aspects of poetic parallelism in the Psalms signal different meanings? What about the allegorical details of some Gospel parables? Why are they significant? Such within-the-text explorations are synchronic ("together in time"), studying the side-by-side literary features of the text in comparative and contrastive fashion. This generation's fervor for literary criticism has the salutary effect of requiring an exegesis that reads the Bible in a holistic, integrative manner. The word splintering and arid historicism that often passed for exegesis have long needed the enrichment of literary topics such as genre, style, narrative, plot, semantics, discourse, and rhetoric.

3. Before-the-text Aim. The stance before the text brings us to the role of the reader, and this focal issue has raised the distinctive question for contemporary exegesis: Is not interpretation, after all, subjective and relative? Is it not the reader, armed with a preunderstanding that seeks only certain kinds of knowledge, who finds and creates meaning? Some will argue that the role of the reader is the only thing that matters, and specimens of exegesis from ideological and sociological viewpoints provide ample evidence of this claim. Yet the facts of the author and the text exist prior to and apart from the reader; the reality of the written communication is not created by a reader's response, but its significance is. The reader focus teaches us the importance of prior commitments or the legitimating values that we bring to the text (cf. Kaiser and Silva, 240–47; and Vanhoozer, 301–24).

Among the commitments a reader brings to the Scriptures, commitment to one basic conviction is essential: God has spoken. God's self-revelation, both in word and deed, called forth a written record from the hearts and hands of human authors who worked in a wide variety of circumstances. The Bible, the whole of the Old and New Testaments, is truly a human book; but because God also worked in it from beginning to end, this book is just as truly the inspired Word of God. The fact of revelation leads us a step farther. The warrant for interpreting the Bible in a plain, straightforward manner, the so-called literal sense, comes from the desire to understand what God said and says. The Bible is not a jumble of religious opinion or a mystical cryptogram that the contemporary reader sorts out according to whim or fad. On the contrary, God purposed to speak through human language and to be understood. So exegesis puts a premium on what the Bible says, using the best of linguistic and historical research to interpret meaning properly.

For the interpreter before the Scriptures, we have come to the heart of the matter: the Bible is God's Word, and thus what it says must be taken as trustworthy and true. To stand before the text is to be called to live under its authority (Black, 65). Exegesis takes seriously the actual words of the text and seeks the truth they affirm in order that the reader may hear and obey. True understanding proceeds under the conviction that the reliability and truthfulness of the Bible are vouchsafed in its divine character.

Exegetical Strategies and Tools

Because we have no English verb "to exegete" (though many insist on coining it in speech and writing), the noun *exegesis* must do double duty, standing for both the process and the product of interpretation. In short, biblical exegesis embraces the "how to" (critical methods) and the "what is" (valid results) of interpreting the Scriptures. In this section we will develop the three aims we have just defined—historical, literary, and theological—in terms of practical "strategies," the application of critical methods that yield valid results.

The tasks suggested are neither exhaustive in scope nor outlined with the advanced student in mind. The lack of ability to study firsthand the Hebrew and Greek Scriptures obviously limits exegetical competence, but it is often the case that students are asked to do exegesis before they gain any language skills. No interpretive skill can substitute for a working knowledge of the biblical languages, but we have chosen to describe an entry-level model to help the English-only reader get started. For guidance in the exegesis of the Hebrew and Greek texts, we recommend the student manuals by Douglas Stuart, *Old Testament Exegesis*, and Gordon Fee, *New Testament Exegesis*, which illustrate many of the points in our discussion.

"Cubing" the Text

We may visualize the exegesis of a text as a six-sided cube; through six exegetical strategies that touch each other like the sides of a cube, we get a complete perspective on the text. These six strategies, outlined in the diagram (fig. 3) integrate the components of meaning related to the author, text, and reader. The top and bottom strategies (setting and significance) address respectively the issues of author and reader, while the middle strategies (structure, syntax, semantics, and summation) correspond more closely to the textual focus. No one strategy can be practiced in isolation from the others. Each strategy, as the arrows in the diagram indicate, interacts with the others and creates a hermeneutical "spiral," opening up one side of meaning and shaping it in light of the other viewpoints. The technique of "cubing" is to read and think (spiral carefully) through a given text, looking at all six sides where they are applicable, in order to bring out meaning.

Six Strategies for Biblical Exegesis

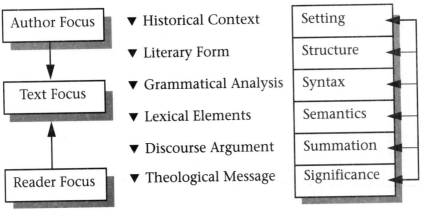

Figure 3

Using Strategies (Six "S's") and Tools

The strategies themselves are familiar methods of biblical criticism that are discussed in following chapters; in technical detail they go far beyond our purposes here. We will define the six "S's" in a limited way and indicate the resources available to make them user-friendly.

1. Setting. What is the historical context? Every text has a birthplace, some better known than others, that tells us important things about it. The matters of authorship, date of the composition, and original readers frame the historical context of a writing. When persons, places, and events are named in a passage, they point to a background that provides essential information for the interpreter. The phrase "in the year that King Uzziah died" (Isa. 6:1, NIV) sets the stage for Isaiah's prophetic call. What was important about this event? The so-called "Romans debate" has turned upon competing proposals for the setting and purpose(s) of the letter. How did Paul's intention that he was "eager to preach the gospel also to you who are at Rome" (Rom. 1:15, NIV) shape the contents of the Letter to the Romans?

The search for the setting of a passage may engage several areas of biblical backgrounds: chronology, archaeology, geography, culture, literature, society, and political institutions. In addition to biblical commentaries and introductions, the primary tools to be consulted are biblical atlases, dictionaries, and histories (see the resources listed in the bibliography and in Stuart, 99–105; Fee, 115–23; and Danker, 203–81).

2. Structure. What is the literary form? A significant portion of meaning is carried by the written form that the author chose to use. Even the major genres such as law, narrative, poetry, wisdom, prophecy, parable, and epistle present obvious challenges, to say nothing of smaller literary figures such as repetition, parallelism, and chiasm. For example, the first four chapters of Lamentations are separate lament psalms with verses arranged in a progressive, acrostic format, but the final poem of the book (chap. 5) has no acrostic pattern. It marks the end of a discourse that "peaks with intensity" and then "diminishes to a whimper" (Stuart, 55).

Form analysis makes both literary and historical comparisons. An epistolary structure like the Galatian letter may be compared to other letters of Paul as well as examples of rhetoric in classical literature. The Old and New Testaments are replete with macro-structures (e.g., a rhetorical genre) and micro-structures (e.g., a figure of speech). The "literary analysis" sections in larger biblical commentaries treat these matters in detail. For guidance in analyzing different literary forms the student should consult the major contributions of three handbooks: Klein, Blomberg, and Hubbard, 215–374; Osborne, 149–260; and Kaiser and Silva, 69–158.

3. Syntax. What is the grammatical rule? Grammatical analysis deals with the smallest units of meaning in a language (morphemes) and how they function together in sentences and discourses. The foundation of exegesis is that part of grammatical analysis called syntax: the study of the arrangement of words, phrases, and clauses to form sentences (from Greek *syntaxis*, "[words] drawn up together, arranged in order"). What is the main verb? The subject? Is the participial phrase a modifier of the verb? How are the subordinate clauses in the sentence related to the main clause? Syntax interprets the parts of speech in Hebrew and Greek, especially the functions of case, tense and mood, phrase, and clause. Although integrally related, larger units of meaning (above the level of the sentence) may be reserved for discourse analysis (cf. summation below).

The reference grammars for Hebrew and Greek (see Stuart, 114–16; and Fee, 170–71) will be of little use to the English-only student; however, special editions of the Hebrew and Greek Scriptures will permit some grammatical analysis to be done (read the suggestions by Danker, 89–147). Interlinear editions print the biblical texts with an English equivalent immediately above (or below) each Hebrew or Greek word so that an English translation can be compared to the original word order. Similarly, analytical editions print grammatical tags for each word, allowing a student to pinpoint its form and make a judgment about how it is translated. The most effective way to make grammatical observations is by a comparison of translations. More literal, formally-equivalent versions (KJV, RV, ASV, NASB, RSV) should form the baseline for comparison with more idiomatic, dynamically-equivalent translations (NIV, REB, NJB, NRSV, GNB).

4. Semantics. What do the words mean? Lexical semantics, the study of word meanings, is the world of the dictionary. Entries for Hebrew and Greek words in standard lexicons are based on usage, the conventional senses of a term found in previous documents and in passages contemporary with the text being studied. "The lexical meaning is the range of senses of a word that may be counted on as being established in the public domain" (Cotterell and Turner, 140). A word's shade of meaning in a given text may depart from the lexicon's "range of senses," but the immediate context must make that meaning clear. The lexical debates concerning terms like Hebrew *ḥesed* ("lovingkindness, faithfulness, mercy") or Greek *kephalē–* ("head, authority, source") demonstrate the importance of established usage as a criterion for meaning in an ambiguous context.

Word studies done correctly are invaluable, but beware of those that load words with too much baggage and make overly subtle distinctions (see the cautions in Osborne, 65–75; and Cotterell and Turner, 106–28). The best index to established usage is the concordance. It should have first place among the word-study tools and be consulted alongside the lexicons and theological dictionaries (on their use, see the bibliography and Danker, 1–21).

5. Summation. What argument has the text made? The term "summation" implies a review of particulars that gathers them up into a meaningful whole. Having dealt with various details in the biblical text, good exegesis goes on to ask how these findings fit together: What is the overall thrust—the persuasive logic—in this passage? This strategy is the newest of the exegetical methods and the most difficult to define because it borrows from various linguistic disciplines: rhetorical criticism, semantic structure analysis, and discourse analysis. Simply put, summation traces the argument of a discourse in terms of its linguistic markers and logical propositions. It restates the separate features of literary structure, syntax, and lexical stock in terms of an integrated, logical meaning.

Tracing the argument of a few verses, or a section comprising several paragraphs or chapters, or even an entire book is not only rewarding but necessary for exegesis. Whether in narrative, poetry, or letter, no individual word, sentence, or paragraph stands alone; meaning is contextual, bound to what precedes and follows in a discourse. What are we to make of colliding statements like "the doers of Law will be justified" (Rom. 2:13, NASB) and "by the works of the Law no flesh will be justified" (Rom. 3:20, NASB) if the linking argument in Paul's discourse is neglected? Summation can be done very well by the English reader in a formal translation. The best student guides to structural and propositional analysis are Cotterell and Turner, 188–229; Osborne, 19–40, 93–126; and Schreiner, 97–126.

6. Significance. What message is there for us? "Significance is the relationship of meaning between authorial meaning and the world of a reader, or some aspect of that world" (Cotterell and Turner, 57). Although one could imagine several motives for a reader's interest in the Bible (e.g., aesthetic appreciation), our goal with this strategy is theological significance. The premise that the Scriptures—as the Word of God—are theological documents obliges exegesis to address faith's warrants and convictions. Theological exegesis asks how the diverse particulars of the biblical text are understood as a unified revelation.

The axiom "Scripture is its own best interpreter" reflects the inner-textual search for significance that points to the classical role of biblical theology. Biblical theology is a synthetic method that both informs and derives from exegesis. Whether a theology of Paul, the Psalms, or the Gospels, a similar procedure is used: Scripture interpreting Scripture in order to find a coherent message. The basic paradigm for biblical theology, which in the past was a word-study approach to theological concepts, has shifted to broader canonical issues—the New Testament's interpretation of the Old Testament. The exegesis of an individual passage is not complete until its place in the biblical self-witness has been evaluated. The primary resources are biblical theologies, theological dictionaries, and the "message" sections in larger commentaries (for various approaches to significance, see Klein, Blomberg, and Hubbard, 377–426).

Seven Concise Steps to an Exegesis

How do the aims and strategies we have proposed actually work in the preparation of an exegesis? The move from theory to practice is more often than not a difficult one for the student; and most assignments in exegesis require a finished paper, not a collection of research notes. Let's take a passage and walk through the steps leading to an acceptable paper. An attractive example to consider is Eph. 1:3–14, a highly-structured text laden with theological concepts that will illustrate our suggestions. A formal translation of Eph. 1:3–14 (resembling the KJV, RV, or NASB) is printed in the accompanying display of the text (fig. 4).

Epistolary materials like Ephesians are easier to handle because of their rhetorical sentence style (called *hypotaxis* = main clauses with dependent clauses, subordinated modifiers, etc.). Their surface features yield patterns of thought that can be readily followed and outlined. Other genres such as narrative stories in the Pentateuch or the Gospels are more difficult to analyze, but the steps we are going to take in Ephesians 1 can be applied to them as well. You should set a goal of working with all the types of biblical writings and, by practice, developing your skills with the strategies that match each of them (see the chapters by Rodney Reeves and Grant Lovejoy).

To get started, locate yourself in a work space with ample room for your books and paper (or computer). Scatter the resources about you within easy reach so they can be read at a glance.

Step 1. Read the passage several times in various translations.

Secure at least six different translations of the passage and make photocopies that you can mark. Choose the KJV, NASB, and NIV as a baseline and three other modern translations for comparison (e.g., GNB, RSV/NRSV, NEB/REB, Phillips, JB/NJB).

STRUCTURAL ANALYSIS OF EPHESIANS 1:3-14

[3] Blessed [be] the <u>God</u> and <u>Father</u> of our Lord Jesus Christ,
     <u>who</u> blessed us
         with every spiritual blessing
         in the heavenlies *in Christ,*

----

[4]   **Ia**   <u>inasmuch as</u>
        he chose us *in him*
           before the foundation of the world,
           <u>that</u> we should be holy and blameless before him, in love
[5]   **Ib**   <u>having predestined</u> us
            to adoption as sons through Jesus Christ to himself,
            according to the kind intention of his will,
[6]   **to the praise of the glory** of his <u>grace</u>,
                  <u>which</u> he kindly gave us *in the <u>beloved</u>.*

----

[7]   **IIa**   *<u>In whom</u>*
        we have redemption through his blood,
            =the forgiveness of our trespasses,
            according to the riches of his <u>grace</u>,
[8]   <u>which</u> he lavished upon us
                in all wisdom and insight,
[9]   **IIb**   <u>having made known</u> to us the mystery of his will,
            according to his good <u>plan</u>
            <u>which</u> he purposed beforehand *in him*
[10]   for carrying out in the fullness of the times,
                =to sum up all things *in Christ,*
                  =things in the heavens
                  and things upon the earth *in <u>him</u>.*

----

[11] **IIIa** *<u>In whom</u>* also
        we have obtained an inheritance,
     IIIb   <u>having been predestined</u>
            according to <u>his</u> purpose
            <u>who</u> works all things after the counsel of his will,
[12]   that <u>we</u> should be **to the praise of his glory.**
            <u>who</u> were the first ones to hope *in <u>Christ</u>.*

----

[13]   *<u>In whom</u>* also,
            <u>having heard</u> the message of truth,
     IVb   =the gospel of your salvation,
         in whom also,
            <u>having believed</u>,
     IVa   you were sealed with the <u>Holy Spirit</u> of promise,
[14]   <u>who</u> is a pledge of our inheritance,
                until the redemption of God's own possession,
                to the praise of his glory.

Figure 4

1.1. *Record the substantive differences among the translations* by marking the copies and making a full list. These are preliminary pointers to exegetical issues. Minor stylistic differences are negligible but not wide variations in wording.

1.2. Are any of the differences due to Greek manuscript variants that stand behind the text preferred by a translation? *Check marginal notes in the translations* for evidence of such readings.

Step 2. Map the boundaries of the passage by observing format markers in the translations.

Format markers are the headings, paragraphing, and punctuation used in modern editions and translations of the text. Sections, paragraphs, and sentences provide important clues to structure and syntax.

2.1. *Observe the paragraphing and sentences* for Eph. 1:3–14 in the baseline translations. It is construed as one paragraph and thus carries a single theme or topic. There are three sentences in the KJV (vv. 3–6, 7–12, 13–14), but the NASB has six (vv. 3–4b, 4c–6, 7–8a, 8b–10c, 10d–12, 13–14) and the NIV eight (vv. 3, 4a–b, 4c–6, 7–8, 9–10, 11–12, 13a, 13b–14).

2.2 *Check the punctuation of an interlinear.* Note that the KJV is closest to the Greek clause structure (UBS^4 and NA^{27} have four sentences: vv. 3–6, 7–10, 11–12, 13–14). In fact Eph. 1:3–14 is a single, undulating sentence, the longest in the Greek New Testament. Note the comma with the phrase "in love" (v. 4c). Does it belong with what precedes or what follows?

Step 3. Construct a structural analysis of the passage, and display it in graphic form.

In order to grasp the content of the passage, it is very important to visualize the flow of thought in the sentences. A schematic showing how sentences relate to each other is called a sentence flow or block diagram. A display similar to figure 4 should be made. Your knowledge of English grammar must now be put to work arranging main clauses and their modifiers.

3.1. *Follow the word order of a formal translation* like the NASB. Begin with scratch paper, arranging and revising, then settling on a final structure; you may wish to use other conventions for marking and arranging the text.

3.2. *Mark off the sentence divisions with horizontal lines and tag them with Roman numerals.* We have made four major divisions in our display: I—vv. 4–6; II—vv. 7–10; III—vv. 11–12; IV—vv. 13–14.

Verse 3 is the introductory main clause that heads the rest of the paragraph.

3.3. *Coordinate by lining up and subordinate by indentation.* Note in the display that the main clauses—tagged "a" (vv. 4, 7, 11, 13)—are vertically aligned; their modifying participles—tagged "b" (vv. 5, 9, 11b, 13a)—are indented to aligned positions.

3.4. *Underline connections and color code repetitions* (italics and bold face in the display). All the underlined words and phrases point to grammatical links; e.g., since "who" in verse 3 refers to "God and Father," both are underlined. Key repetitions are best highlighted with color: the "in Christ" motif recurs eleven times (in italics); and the phrase "to the praise of his glory" three times (in boldface). A graphic display takes time. Ponder the text—read it again—wait for insight.

Step 4. Adapt an outline for the paper from the structural analysis of the passage.

The mechanics and format of an exegetical paper adhere to the same general standards found in manuals of English style and composition. A biblical exegesis should be well written, just as readable and persuasive as a prose essay in any other literary field. Steps 4 through 7 sketch one way to proceed effectively, but they are no substitute for basic writing skills.

You should develop the parts of the paper to reflect the logic of the text; this is the heart of expository writing.

4.1. *Restate the displayed text as brief topics in outline form.* Taking a cue from the main divisions of the display, our passage can be restated as follows:

Praise to God for Spiritual Blessings (Eph. 1:3–14)

1. The Full Blessing in Christ (v. 3)
2. God's Eternal Choice (vv. 4–6)
    1) Chosen in Christ Before the Creation (v. 4a–b)
    2) Destined to Sonship in Love (vv. 4c–5a)
    3) Ordained by His Gracious Disposition (vv. 5b–6)
3. Redemption through the Cross (vv. 7–12)
    1) Forgiveness of Sins (v. 7)
    2) Gift of Wisdom and Understanding (vv. 8–10)
        a. What God Planned from Eternity (v. 9)
        b. The Summing Up of All Things in Christ (v. 10)
4. A Share in the Heritage of God's People (vv. 11–12)

1) The Role of His People (v. 11)
2) The Hope of His People (v. 12)
5. The Promise of the Holy Spirit (vv. 13–14)
   1) Inclusion by Proclamation and Faith (v. 13a)
   2) The Sealing and Pledge of the Inheritance (vv. 13b–14)

4.2. *Fashion the theme and headings of the paper after the outline.* "Praise to God for Spiritual Blessings" is an appropriate title for the exegesis. Use the main points in the outline as section headings for the body of the paper and the subsidiary ones as topics for paragraph development.

Step 5. Develop the sections of the paper with a focus on syntax, semantics, and summation.

The bulk of the research and writing comes here. Turn to the resources that help you elaborate aspects of grammar, lexical sense, and logical argument. Concentrate the paragraphs you write on the following activities.

5.1. *Describe main verbs and their phrase/clause modifiers.* The primary assertion "Blessed be God" is grounded in the fact of his blessing us in Christ (v. 3); the extent and manner of that blessing is described in the series of affirmations that follows: "chosen for sonship in Christ" (vv. 4–6), "redeemed by his blood" (vv. 7–10), "obtained a heritage in him" (vv. 11–12), and "sealed by the Spirit in him" (vv. 13–14). Verbs strike at the nerve center of the grammar.

5.2. *Define key words and repeated themes.* Lexical elements in this passage fairly bristle with interest. A short list includes "heavenlies," "adoption," "predestined," "mystery," "plan," "sum up," "inheritance," and "pledge." Explore the function of the repeated phrases "in Christ" and "to the praise of his glory."

5.3. *Trace the argument from one paragraph to another.* Do not leave the thoughts hanging in the air; summarize the logic of election, salvation, and hope as you move through the exegesis.

Step 6. Introduce the paper with a focus on setting and structure.

After you have finished the body of the paper, you are better prepared to write an introduction for the exegesis. In the opening paragraphs, present an overview of the passage and the issues that you will discuss.

6.1. *Raise the reader's interest in the text.* Briefly characterize its importance from a theological perspective.

6.2. *Give attention to the historical context.* Do not rehearse in detail a general introduction to the Ephesian letter; rather treat aspects of setting that shed light on the origin and function of 1:3–14.

6.3. *Sketch the literary form.* This strategy will pay rich dividends in our passage. The structure is reminiscent of benedictions found in Israel's worship (cf. Ps. 103); it is the overture to a prayer theme that pervades the first three chapters of Ephesians (cf. 3:1).

Step 7. Conclude the paper with a focus on significance.

The closing paragraphs should review the discourse argument and highlight its theological message. What is the thrust of the passage, and how is it to be applied? We suggest two levels of explanation.

7.1. In a few sentences, *summarize the truth claims and indicate their role in biblical theology.*

7.2. Then briefly *indicate the faith issues and their role in historical and systematic theology.*

Epilogue

Approach exegesis with expectancy. The Spirit is our guide in the Word that "we might know what God has graciously given us" (1 Cor. 2:12). Gifted exegesis is the practice of criticism in its best sense, as it was before the modern scientific era, the positive art of making an intelligent judgment about the form and meaning of a given text. A purely rational criticism that excluded the supernatural from the Bible got negative results and treated the text as nothing more than a human word. You can aspire as a Christian exegete to join a growing number of "believing critics" (see Mark Noll's *Between Faith and Criticism*) who bring the best tools and methods of research to the study and understanding of the Scriptures. Value the study of the Bible as a high commitment to the Word of God, and therein labor with no occasion to fear the truth.

▼

For Further Study

Black, David Alan. *Using New Testament Greek in Ministry: A Practical Guide for Students and Pastors.* Grand Rapids: Baker, 1993.

Klein, William W., Craig L. Blomberg, and Robert L. Hubbard Jr. *Introduction to Biblical Interpretation.* Dallas: Word, 1993.

Cotterell, Peter, and Max Turner. *Linguistics & Biblical Interpretation.* Downers Grove, Ill.: InterVarsity, 1989.

Danker, Frederick W. *Multipurpose Tools for Bible Study.* Rev. and expanded ed. Minneapolis: Augsburg Fortress, 1993.

Fee, Gordon D. *New Testament Exegesis: A Handbook for Students and Pastors.* Rev. ed. Louisville: Westminster/John Knox, 1993.

Frei, Hans W. *Types of Christian Theology.* Edited by George Hunsinger and William C. Placher. New Haven: Yale University Press, 1992.

Kaiser, Walter C. Jr. *Toward an Exegetical Theology: Biblical Exegesis for Preaching and Teaching.* Grand Rapids: Baker, 1981.

Kaiser, Walter C. Jr., and Moisés Silva. *An Introduction to Biblical Hermeneutics: The Search for Meaning.* Grand Rapids: Zondervan, 1994.

Morgan, Robert, with John Barton. *Biblical Interpretation.* Oxford Bible Series. Oxford: Oxford University Press, 1988.

Maier, Gerhard. *Biblical Hermeneutics.* Translated by Robert W. Yarbrough. Wheaton, Ill.: Crossway Books, 1994.

Noll, Mark A. *Between Faith and Criticism: Evangelicals, Scholarship, and the Bible in America.* 2d ed. Grand Rapids: Baker, 1991.

Osborne, Grant R. *The Hermeneutical Spiral: A Comprehensive Introduction to Biblical Interpretation.* Downers Grove, Ill.: InterVarsity, 1991.

Ramm, Bernard. "Biblical Interpretation." In *Hermeneutics,* ed. Bernard Ramm, 7–28. Grand Rapids: Baker, 1987.

Schreiner, Thomas R. *Interpreting the Pauline Epistles.* Guides to New Testament Exegesis 5. Grand Rapids: Baker, 1990.

Stein, Robert H. *Playing by the Rules: A Basic Guide to Interpreting the Bible.* Grand Rapids: Baker, 1995.

Stuart, Douglas. *Old Testament Exegesis: A Primer for Students and Pastors.* 2d ed., rev. and enlarged. Philadelphia: Westminster, 1984.

Thiselton, Anthony C. "Explain, Interpret, Tell, Narrate." In *The New International Dictionary of New Testament Theology,* ed. Colin Brown, 3 vols., 1:573–84. Grand Rapids: Zondervan, 1975–78.

Vanhoozer, Kevin J. "The Reader in New Testament Interpretation." In *Hearing the New Testament: Strategies for Interpretation,* ed. Joel B. Green, 301–28. Grand Rapids: Eerdmans, 1995.

PART ONE

Biblical
Hermeneutics
in History

▼

Chapter One

Ancient Jewish Hermeneutics

Robert B. Sloan and Carey C. Newman

What ancient Jews did with their scriptures spoke volumes: it announced who they were (covenant believers in the one true God, Yahweh) and it told of their innermost dreams (that Yahweh had a purposeful future for his people in this world). While a study of various Jewish groups and their differing visions for Jewish life could happily occupy our time, this study is devoted solely to the *methods* used by Jews to read/interpret their sacred texts during the Greco-Roman period (roughly 400 B.C. to A.D. 200).

The survey which follows does not present an exhaustive taxonomy of interpretive strategies—a goal reaching far beyond the confines of this space and the objectives of this volume (see Patte, *Early Jewish Hermeneutics,* for the most complete recent attempt). Furthermore, the best—certainly the most provocative—example of Jewish interpretation from the period in question, the New Testament's use of the Old Testament, will not receive major attention here; the next chapter in the present volume addresses this question in detail. While this survey is by no means exhaustive, it will, by presenting several actual examples, seek to show some of the various imaginative possibilities open to Jews during this period.

Some Preliminaries

The subject "ancient Jewish hermeneutics" is a large and unwieldy one. Each of the three words is problematic: the word *ancient* connotes clear boundaries, but in determining where to be-gin and end a study of this sort one must grapple with the com-plexities of Jewish history. One searches with difficulty for a uniquely "Jewish" method of interpretation, since, in some cases, both Jews and Greeks used the same or similar reading strategies. Finally, discerning a recognizable "hermeneutic" in the mass of Jewish literature is akin to looking for the proverbial needle. Several words of caution are therefore in order as this survey begins.

1. Since the word *hermeneutics* presumes a "text" upon which an interpreter reflects, the first word of caution concerns the assump-tion that there was universal agreement on what constituted the "Bible" during the Greco-Roman period. While it may be argued that by the first-century A.D. a pragmatic consensus had been reached on nearly all of what we now call the Old Testament, a complete and final agreement on a fixed and authoritative list of sacred books would have to wait. Thus, the luxury of easily detect-ing the line where Scripture stops and those works which are based upon Scripture begin, a luxury which Christians enjoy today, should not be taken for granted. The boundary between holy, in-spired revelation and a work based upon Scripture was sometimes a very fuzzy one in the Greco-Roman period. Furthermore, the pro-found commitment to an exclusive brand of monotheism and an attempt to make sense of Yahweh's covenant purposes for Jews unite all Jewish writings into something of a seamless whole. From this perspective, the history of interpretation really turns into a study of the different *kinds* of literature.

2. One should also be wary of studying the methods of Jewish in-terpretation in isolation from the history of the Jewish people. The oppression of Jews by Assyria, Babylon, Persia, Alexander, the Ptolemies and the Seleucids, and Rome, along with the Hellenistic spirit that infused the Greco-Roman world, provided the context against which any Jewish attempt to make sense of their scriptural traditions took its shape. There is a positive correlation between the complexities of Jewish history during the Greco-Roman period and the multiplicity of (and often inventive) interpretive strategies adopted by Jews.

3. There are four principal "collections" of Jewish documents from the Greco-Roman era—the Apocrypha, the Pseudepigrapha, the Dead Sea Scrolls, and the Mishnah. To these collections the works of individual authors, like Philo and Josephus, must surely be add-ed. One should always bear in mind that, with the exception of the

Mishnah, these are all "modern" collections and not ancient. Documents within each of these collections—and even within an individual document—can represent wildly different perspectives and methods of interpretation.

4. These "collections" represent many different kinds (or genres) of literature. There are apocalyptic works, testaments, expansions, wisdom, philosophical works, prayers, psalms, history—and plenty of "mixed" genres. The generic diversity is almost as great as the number of documents. Since genre establishes an interpretive contract between the text and reader (i.e., genre announces ahead of time what the reader should expect and even clues the reader on how to read), such diversity certainly complicates the job of reading and, by extension, makes the job of coming to grips with how a document is interpreting another text doubly difficult.

5. Finally, a word of caution about "hermeneutics." Until a few years ago among biblical scholars hermeneutics denoted "the science of interpretation." Hermeneutics typically entailed a comprehensive study of the *rules* or *principles* by which interpretation occurred. More recently, hermeneutics has taken a decidedly philosophical turn: it has come to denote the study of communication generally, the philosophy of language, epistemology (i.e., the way in which we know what we say we know), and complex theories of textuality. With a couple of exceptions, Jews during the Greco-Roman time period did not reflect on their interpretive activities and did not write handbooks on interpretation. Simply stated, the hermeneutical discussions and exegetical practices of today were virtually unknown in the period. (This is not to imply, however, that Jewish interpretation was somehow unsophisticated; indeed, many of the most erudite—and sometimes incomprehensible!—hermeneutical theories embraced today find substantive precursors in this time period.) To import our modern expectations of hermeneutics to the study of ancient Jewish interpretive methods not only does an injustice to ancient Jews but it will also lead to our frustration as well.

With these observations in hand, we now turn to look at some of the various ways Jews interpreted their sacred traditions.

Intertextual Exegesis

Various portions of the OT commend—even command—the reading, meditation upon and application of Scripture (e.g., Josh. 1:7–8; Ps. 1). By the early postexilic period there had developed the office of a scribe whose job description, among other things, included the interpretation of Scripture (see Eccles. 39:1–8). Probably the most famous scribe was Ezra. His public reading of Scripture (Neh. 8:1) included interpretation and application: he "helped the people understand the law" because he read from the law of God "clearly" (Neh. 8:7–8; all passages are RSV unless otherwise noted). The process of scriptural interpretation should not be restricted, however, to a guild of professionals. The interpretation of Scripture began *with* and *within* the Old Testament itself.

Intertextual (or innerbiblical) exegesis is the imbedding of fragments, images, and echoes of one text within another one. Later biblical authors demonstrated their love for and allegiance to their tradition by strategically reworking a scriptural subtext. Much more than simple citation, innerbiblical exegesis represents a very strong prophetic and poetic stance, sometimes extending a subtext to the very limits of its possible horizon of meaning. A prime example can be found in Isa. 61:1–3. Here one text washes itself thoroughly in the river of images which flow from its subtext.

> The Spirit of the LORD God is upon me, because the LORD has anointed me to bring good tidings to the afflicted; he has sent me to bind up the brokenhearted, to proclaim liberty to the captives, and the opening of the prison to those who are bound; to proclaim the year of the LORD's favor, and the day of vengeance of our God; to comfort all who mourn; to grant to those who mourn in Zion—to give them a garland instead of ashes, the oil of gladness instead of mourning, the mantle of praise instead of a faint spirit; that they may be called oaks of righteousness, the planting of the LORD, that he may be glorified.

The initial glance at this text may miss the vast textual quarry standing behind it. Isa. 61:1-3 resonates with several subtexts— Leviticus 25; Exod. 21:2-6; 23:10–12, Deut. 15:1–8 and 31:9–13. Of special importance is Lev. 25:8–12:

> And you shall count seven weeks of years, seven times seven years, so that the time of the seven weeks of years shall be to you forty-nine years. Then you shall send abroad the loud trumpet on the tenth day of the seventh month; on the day of atonement you shall send abroad the trumpet throughout all your land. And you shall hallow the fiftieth year, and proclaim liberty throughout the land to all its inhabitants; it shall be a jubilee for you, when each of you shall return to his property and each of you shall return to his family. A jubilee shall that

fiftieth year be to you; in it you shall neither sow, nor reap what grows of itself, nor gather the grapes from the undressed vines. For it is a jubilee; it shall be holy to you; you shall eat what it yields out of the field.

Ready at hand for the prophet was imagery involving the levitical year of Jubilee. Specifically, what ties the two texts together are the relentless repetition of the words "year" (twelve times in Leviticus 25) and "forgiveness"/"liberty" (fourteen times in Leviticus 25). Any Jew familiar with the jubilary legislation would have heard the two texts speaking to each other.

The intertextual connections between Leviticus and Isaiah are strengthened by examining the effects of Isaiah's use of the levitical provisions for his theological agenda. The jubilary code to return all property, to release all Jewish slaves, to cancel debts, and to allow the land to lay fallow all emphasize reversal. Isaiah, too, pictures dramatic reversal— good news to the afflicted; binding of the brokenhearted; liberty to captives; comfort to those who mourn; strength to the faint in spirit.

Isaiah also exploits the theological foundations of the levitical jubilary announcement. Yahweh's ownership of the world, his choice of, unique relationship with, and purpose for Israel, along with the expectation of Israel's singular devotion to Yahweh, all unite in Isaiah's vision. God is not finished with Israel and this bit of "good news" gives hope, not only for Israel; but also for the whole world.

But the eschatological tone in which Isaiah speaks is the most provocative feature of Isaiah's intertextual conversation with Leviticus. By baptizing the jubilary theology of Leviticus in his eschatology, the prophet envisions a day in which society and humans undergo a powerful, quite singular, and final transformation. The jubilee of Isaiah's dream renders obsolete all other (previous) jubilees: there awaits but one more climactic jubilee.

It may be argued that Isaiah's eschatological commentary on Leviticus 25 runs the risk of undoing what Leviticus had done. The (re)visionary power of Isaiah's echo does create a new figure, and, admittedly, does so in ways certainly not stated in Leviticus 25. However, this new figuration neither violates nor destroys the larger narrative foundations (the story of God's dealings with the world through his special agent, Israel) which inform both the text and the subtext, even if the web of meaning generated by the intertextual connections forces both text and subtext to be viewed differently.

Isaiah's text was not the only one daring enough to enter into conversation with Leviticus. A document found among the Dead Sea Scrolls, *11QMelchizedek*, also employed the jubilary legislation in creative ways. A three-way conversation can be found in Luke 4:16–30, where the Gospel cites Isaiah 61 (and through it Leviticus 25). That Isaiah 61 plays such a prominent role in Luke's Gospel should alert us to the way in which the New Testament requires a dialogue partner to have meaning. In fact, the New Testament can be viewed as nothing short of a sustained intertextual commentary on Israel's sacred and holy Scripture.

Although Christians certainly are not creating Scripture today, intertextual connections abound. All of our preaching, writing and hymnody is, by definition, an intertextual act. When a certain text inspires a prayer, a short devotion, when we mix technical interpretation with application to create a brand new figure, we are engaging in intertextual exegesis, even if what we produce is not sown into the canon.

Allegorical Exegesis

Allegory can refer to (1) a *kind* of literature or (2) a *method* of interpretation. As a kind of literature, an allegory, like Bunyan's *Pilgrim's Progress*, is a story in which hidden meanings are built into the characters, places, and events of the narrative.   An allegory *must be read* allegorically if it is to be understood properly. Allegorical interpretation is the act of understanding a text, *any* text (be it an allegory or not), to be referring primarily—though not exclusively—to something else other than the "literal" meaning. Allegorical interpretation construes the surface text of a document as a set of codes which *can be read* as possessing "deeper," "hidden" meaning(s).

Allegorical interpretation has a venerable history. When the Hellenistic Cynic-Stoic philosophers sought to modernize the ancient Greek myths, they did so by allegory. The first hints of Jewish allegorical interpretation can be found in the Septuagint and in the Wisdom of Solomon. The first Jew (whose work survives) to employ the method extensively was Aristobulus (3rd–2nd century B.C.), an Alexandrian philosopher. But it is the prodigious exegetical activity of yet another Alexandrian Jewish philosopher, Philo (20 B.C.–A.D. 45), which demands our attention here.

Philo sought to reconcile his Greek Bible with his surrounding Hellenistic culture. Specifically, Philo tried to square the Pentateuch with Greek philosophy. (Though a committed monotheist, one is never quite sure if Philo is pouring Hebrew theology into Greek molds or the other way around.) Philo argued that the literal meaning was immature; the full and mature significance of a text was reached only through allegorical means.

Philo engaged in allegorical interpretation whenever there was something in the text which said something unflattering about God.

> "The Lord went down to see that city and that tower" [Gen. 11:5] must be listened to altogether as if spoken in a figurative sense. For to think that the divinity can go towards, or go from, or go down, or go to meet, or, in short, that it has the same positions and motions as particular animals, and that it is susceptible of real motion at all, is, to use a common proverb, an impiety deserving of being banished beyond the seas and beyond the world. But these things are spoken, as if of man, by the lawgiver, of God who is not invested with human form, for the sake of advantage to us who are to be instructed, as I have often said before with reference to other passages. (*Conf. Ling.* 134–36).

God's character and nature are to be preserved at all costs. "The Lord came down to see the city and the tower" cannot be taken literally for two reasons: because (1) God is not like a human (Philo abhorred anthropomorphisms) and (2) God never leaves a part of the universe devoid of his presence. Thus, the passage must be interpreted "figuratively."

Philo also allegorized when the biblical text presented an unexplained difficulty.

> And God says, he "who slays Cain shall suffer sevenfold" [Gen. 4:15]. But I do not know what analogy this real meaning of this expression bears to the literal interpretation of it, "He shall suffer sevenfold." For he has not said what is to be sevenfold, nor has he described the sort of penalty, nor by what means such penalty is excused or paid. Therefore, one must suppose all these things are said figuratively and allegorically; and perhaps what God means to set before us here is something of this sort. The irrational part of the soul is divided into seven parts, the senses of seeing, of smelling, of hearing, of tasting, and of touch, the organs of speech, and the organs of generation. If, therefore, any one were to slay the eighth, that is to say, Cain,

the ruler of them all, he would also paralyze all the seven (*Det.* 166b–168b).

The text leaves no clue as to what a "sevenfold" punishment may be; Philo thus finds a pretext for his primitive anthropology.

Philo discovered a textual invitation to allegorize when the sense of the text contradicted another part of Scripture (or something that was known to be true outside of Scripture).

There is also another expression in the Psalms, such as this, "The course of the river makes glad the city of God." [Ps. 46:6] What city? For the holy city, which exists at present, in which also the holy temple is established, at a great distance from any sea or river, so that it is clear, that the writer here means, figuratively, to speak of some other city than the visible city of God.

Having rejected the plain sense of the text—because of the tension it would create with geographical facts—Philo then opts for an allegorical reading of the "river" as "the divine word" and the "city of God" as the "world."

For, in good truth, the continual stream of the divine word, being borne on incessantly with rapidity and regularity, is diffused universally over everything giving joy to all. And in one sense he calls the world the city of God, as having received the whole cup of divine draught, . . . and being gladdened thereby, so as to have derived from it an imperishable joy, of which it cannot be deprived forever" (*Som.* II. 246–48).

Almost any textual peculiarity encouraged Philo's eagerness to interpret a text allegorically. In Philo's defense, it must always be kept in mind that he did not deny the historicity of the text. In fact, Philo had something of a two-level approach, a literal *and* an allegorical reading, even if the latter was the much preferred. Further, Philo's approach to Scripture did not develop in a vacuum. He positioned himself between two camps. On the right were those who adopted *only a literal* reading and on the left those who wished for *only an allegorical* one. Philo effectively stood in the middle in his use of literal and allegorical methods.

For the last one hundred years or so Christian interpreters have expressed some reluctance to practice allegorical interpretation. Several reasons can be cited: (1) The lack of New Testament precedent for the practice of this method—the two chief exceptions being Jesus' allegorical interpretation of the parable of the sower (Mark

4:1–20) and Paul's treatment of Hagar and Sarah (Gal. 4:24–31). (2) The abuses and excesses of this method throughout nearly nineteen hundred years of Christian theology. And (3) the popularity of privileging the/a (so-called) literal reading.

These reasons, among others, should certainly caution about imposing willy-nilly an allegorical meaning upon texts which were never intended to possess one. But allegorical interpretation does have its place. Craig Blomberg (*Interpreting the Parables*) argues that the parables of Jesus do invite (limited) allegorical decodings, as do certain apocalyptic sections of Old Testament books (e.g., Daniel 7; Zechariah 1–2) and the Book of Revelation in the New Testament. Allegorical readings require the audience/listeners to suspend their prejudices and, with full sympathy, join the world of the text. When properly applied, an allegorical interpretation can engender consent without (necessarily) endangering literalism.

Charismatic Exegesis

Among the scrolls discovered in caves near Khirbet Qumran (and known as the Dead Sea Scrolls) were found copies of Old Testament texts, rules for the community, liturgies, poetry, calendars, horoscopes and, most importantly for the purposes at hand, fifteen manuscripts devoted entirely to Scripture interpretation. They are known as *pesharim* (sing., *pesher*—lit. "its interpretation/solution is").

Although the *pesharim* share some striking similarities with other Jewish interpretive strategies (and thus some scholars simply see the Qumran *pesharim* as another form of non-legal midrash), the *pesharim* do betray a distinguishing exegetical feature: whereas the other methods of interpretation move from text to life (that text has relevance for this situation), *pesher* exegesis moves the other way, from current event to text (this event is what that text is speaking about). This exegetical move represents some of the boldest handling of sacred text in the period under discussion.

The first example comes from the longest and best preserved *pesher* of Qumran, a *pesher* on the Book of Habakkuk.

> I will take my stand to watch and will station myself upon my fortress. I will watch to see what He will say to me and how [He will answer] my complaint. And the Lord answered [and said to me, "Write down the vision and make it plain] upon the tables, that [he who reads] may read it speedily." (Hab. 2:1–2)

and God told Habakkuk to write down that which would happen to the final generation, but He did not make known to him when time would come to an end. And as for that which he said,

That he who reads may read it speedily: (Hab. 2:2b)

Interpreted [*pesher*] this concerns the Teacher of Righteousness, to whom God made known all the mysteries of the words of his servants the Prophets.

For there shall be yet another vision concerning the appointed time. It shall tell of the end and it shall not lie. (Hab. 2:3a)

Interpreted [*pesher*], this means that the final age shall be prolonged, and shall exceed all that the prophets have said; for the mysteries of God are astounding.

If it tarries, wait, for it shall surely come and shall not be late. (Hab. 2:3b)

Interpreted [*pesher*], this concerns the men of truth who keep the Law, whose hands shall not slacken in the service of truth when the final age is prolonged. For all the ages of God read the appointed end as he determines for them in the mysteries of His wisdom (1QpHab vi 12b-vii 14).

The most striking formal feature of this commentary on Hab. 2:1-3 is the line-by-line and sometimes word-by-word interpretation. All the *pesharim* follow this structure—a bit of Scripture is given and then its exposition; a bit of Scripture, and then its exposition.

Three times the text employs the "this is that" pattern—twice concerning persons and once concerning activities—with all three using the verb *pesher* (lit., "its interpretation is"). The "Teacher of Righteousness" is identified as the one who reads "speedily"; the "final age" in which the community found itself is the "appointed time" of Habakkuk; and the "men of truth who keep the law" (i.e., the community who was reading and studying this document) are those who should "wait" for the final age.

The commentary singles out the Teacher of Righteousness for particular honors. Even though Habakkuk authored this prophecy, he did not understand its full implications. God reserved that privilege for the Teacher. Only he, as an inspired and anointed interpreter, possesses the proper charisms to render the secrets of God intelligible. Only he "understands all the mysteries."

4QFlorilegium (*florilegium,* Latin for "a gathering of flowers"; used here to designate an "anthology") represents a second kind of *pesharim*. Instead of following the text, the *pesher* exegesis is governed by a theme around which various texts are arranged.

> . . . *[I will appoint a place for my people Israel and will plant them that they may dwell there and be troubled no more by their] enemies. No son of iniquity [shall afflict them again] as formerly, for the day that [I set judges] over my people Israel. (2 Sam. 7:10–11a)*

This is the House which [He will build for them in the] last days, as it is written in the book of Moses,

> *In the sanctuary which Thy hands have established, O Lord, the Lord shall reign for ever and ever. (Ex. 15:17b–18)*

This is the House into which [the unclean shall] never [enter, not the uncircumcised,] nor the Ammonite, nor the Moabite, nor the half-breed, nor the foreigner, nor the stranger, ever; for there shall My Holy Ones be. [Its glory shall endure] forever; it shall appear above it perpetually. And strangers shall lay it waste no more, as they formerly laid waste the sanctuary of Israel because of its sin. He has commanded that a sanctuary of men be built for Himself, that here they may send up, like the smoke of incense, the works of the Law.

> . . . *The Lord declares to you that He will build you a House I will raise up your seed after you. I [will be] his father and he shall be my son. (2 Sam. 7:11b)*

He is the Branch of David who shall arise with the Interpreter of the Law [to rule] in Zion [at the end] of time.

As it is written, *I will raise up the tent of David that is fallen (Amos 9:11)*

That is to say, the fallen tent of David is he who shall arise to save Israel (*4QFlor 1–7, 10–13*).

Several issues are noteworthy. (1) In this document (only a short excerpt of which is printed above), many passages are brought together: they include (in order) 2 Sam. 7:10b–11a; Exod. 15:17–18; 2 Sam. 7:11b; 2 Sam. 7:11c–14a; Amos 9:11. (2) *4QFlorilegium* links these various texts together with "catchwords." In lines 1–7 "place" is linked with "house" by the catchword "sanctuary"; while in lines 10–13 the "seed" of David is linked to the

"Branch" by the catchwords "raise up," "tent" and "shoot." (3) Although many texts are incorporated into this short document, 2 Sam. 7:10–14 is the principal text, and thus Davidic messianism is the primary theme exerting a controlling theological force. (4) *4QFlorilegium* develops messianic hope in an unique way. Nathan's prophecy for a "Branch of David" is linked with an "Interpreter of the Law"—two messianic figures and not just one (cf. 4QpIsa[a] 7–10; 4QPartrBless 3; CD 7:16). (5) It is these two who will usher in the eschatological age of blessing.

The bold exegetical moves of the Qumran *pesharim* reflect a very profound sense of community identity (the community of interpreters were the only true people of God), of eschatology (the end of the ages is already here), and spirit inspiration (God has given to the leader[s]/community the exclusive right to read the scriptures accurately). *Pesher* exegesis is anything but dispassionate about the text and its significance for life.

In the New Testament we find this kind of Spirit-inspired interpretation from day one. Peter begins his explanation of the extraordinary events of Pentecost with the phrase, "this is what was spoken by the prophet Joel" (Acts 2:16). Under the Spirit's guidance, Peter, like the *pesher* commentaries of Qumran, was moving from current event (the outpouring of God's Spirit) to text (Joel 2). What was hidden from previous generations—the true significance of Joel 2—was now revealed. Although the New Testament rarely employs the formula "this is that," its bold, Spirit-inspired, eschatological treatment of the Old Testament is often *pesher*-like: the cross and resurrection of Jesus created a new situation which (finally) explains the Old Testament promises.

One should be extremely reluctant to emulate the New Testament apostles in this method. Iraq's invasion of Kuwait in the early '90s spawned any number of sermons. Saddam Hussein, almost overnight, in the hands of Christian preachers was transformed into a biblical figure—but not just any figure, he most assuredly was the Antichrist. The event (invasion) was viewed as the true reading of that text (Revelation). The dangers here are obvious. While Christians do possess Spirit-inspired insight into the salvific mysteries surrounding the death and resurrection of Jesus, we must exercise exegetical humility when it comes to the way in which current history relates to the biblical record. We are on much safer ground when we use the gifts of the Spirit to apply the gospel to our life situations.

Applied Exegesis

Like all other Jews during this period, the rabbis revered the biblical record. The Bible served as the starting point, the baseline, and the object of reflection. But the Bible was only one voice among others, even if it remained the most important voice. Alongside the written law there had grown up a tradition of oral law (believed to have been delivered to Moses at Sinai). When this oral law was memorialized in writing (c.a., A.D. 200, called the *Mishnah*) and accorded an authoritative status within Judaism, it touched off a process of exposition which has yet to stop. Just how does this oral law relate to the written Torah? To answer this question required all the exegetical ingenuity that the rabbis could muster.

The rabbinic term for exegesis was *midrash*, derived from the Hebrew word *darash* meaning "to seek out," "to find out." Like allegory, *midrash* can refer to a kind or a form of literature, the particular shape an interpretation of a biblical text takes (i.e., a commentary); or it can refer to an exegetical method, a strategy for reading a biblical text. As a method *midrash* can be what Gese Vermes ("Bible and *Midrash*," in *Post-Biblical Jewish Studies*) calls "pure exegesis" (the explanation of a curious phrase or word; a verse which lacks sufficient detail; a verse which apparently contradicts another verse; a verse whose apparent meaning is unacceptable)— or be termed "applied exegesis" which was concerned "with the discovery of principles of providing a non-scriptural problem with a scriptural solution" (62). It is by these principles, *middot*, that the rabbis sought to reconcile their oral tradition about what is legally acceptable and the written Torah.

Rabbinic literature preserves three lists of *middot* for interpreting Scripture: the 7 rules of Hillel, which were subsequently subdivided into the 13 rules of Ishmael, which, in turn, were expanded to the 32 rules of Eliezer. (It is highly improbable that these three rabbis were responsible for creating or practicing all the rules attributed to them.) Below is printed the list of Hillel (see L. Jacobs, "Hermeneutics," for documentation and a fuller discussion).

1. Qal wahomer—An argument from the minor (*qal*) to the major (*homer*). If something applies in a less important point, it will certainly apply in the major.

2. Gezerah shawah—By comparing similar expressions in two different verses it is reasoned that whatever applies in one of the verses is equally applicable in the other.

3. *Binyan ab mikathub 'ehad*—When the same phrase is found in a number of verses, then what is found in one verse applies to them all.

4. *Binyan ab mishene kethubim*—A principle is established by relating two verses together; once established, this principle can be applied to other verses.

5. *Kelal upherat*—If a law is stated in the general and then followed by a specific statement, the general law only applies in the specific statement. The reverse is also true: if the particular instances are stated first and are followed by the general category, instances other than the particular ones are included.

6. *Kayoze bo bemaqom 'aher*—a difficulty in one text may be resolved by comparing it with another similar text.

7. *Dabar halamed me'inyano*—a meaning established by its context.

Of the seven, the first two of the *middot* can be singled out as the most important. An example of *qal wahomer* reasoning can be found in the Mishnah Sanh. 6:5. The background for the comment is Deut. 21:22-23 which reads: "And if a man has committed a crime punishable by death and he is put to death, and you hang him on a tree, his body shall not remain all night upon the tree, but you shall bury him the same day, for a hanged man is accursed by God; you shall not defile your land which the LORD your God gives you for an inheritance." It is recorded that Rabbi Meir said:

> "When a person is distressed, what words does the Presence of God say? As it were: 'My head is in pain, my arm is in pain.' If thus the Omnipresent distress on account of the blood of the wicked when it is shed, how much more so on account of the blood of the righteous!" If God is troubled by the death of a criminal how much more, then, will God be certainly troubled by bad things befalling the good.

An example of a *gezerah shawah* can be found Besah 1:6. The background for this *Mishnah* saying is Num. 15:17–21:

> The LORD said to Moses, "Say to the people of Israel, When you come into the land to which I bring you and when you eat of the food of the land, you shall present an offering to the LORD. Of the first of your coarse meal you shall present a cake as an offering; as an offering from the threshing floor, so shall you

present it. Of the first of your coarse meal you shall give to the Lord an offering throughout your generations."

And Deut. 18:3: "And this shall be the priests' due from the people, from those offering a sacrifice, whether it be ox or sheep: they shall give to the priest the shoulder and the two cheeks and the stomach."

The problem: should a Jew carry these offerings to the temple on a feast day? Two of the first-century Jewish groups split on the question. The followers of Hillel permitted the two gifts to be brought, while the Shammaites said "no." The rationale: "The House of Shammai say, 'They do not bring dough offering and priestly gifts to the priest on the festival day, whether they were raised up the preceding day or on that same day.' And the House of Hillel permit. The House of Shammai said to them, 'It is an argument by way of analogy [*gezerah shawah*]. The dough offering and priestly gifts are a gift to the priest, and heave offering is a gift to the priest. Just as [on the festival day] they do not bring heave offering [to a priest], so they do not bring these other gifts [to a priest].'"

Both of these examples underscore the legal character of early midrash. The rabbis were intensely interested in clarifying specific behavior in light of both oral and written law. The middot were helpful in developing an elaborate system for determining what counted as a good argument. But the *middot* are simply possible ways to interpret a text or specific set of texts. Nothing in the rules themselves instructed a rabbi on how and when to apply the specific rules. This hermeneutical ambiguity has contributed in no small way to the vitality of Jewish literature and tradition.

In the NT we find Paul employing *qal wahomer* to answer his Corinthian detractors.

Do I say this on human authority? Does not the law say the same? For it is written in the law of Moses, "You shall not muzzle an ox when it is treading out the grain." Is it for oxen that God is concerned? Does he not speak entirely for our sake? It was written for our sake, because the plowman should plow in hope and the thresher thresh in hope of a share in the crop. If we have sown spiritual good among you, is it too much if we reap you material benefits? (1 Cor. 9:8–11).

Paul defended his apostolic rights by appealing to the law: if God's law made provision for animals to receive something for their labors, then how much more Christian workers should enjoy the same benefit.

The logical and analogical character of *middot* anticipate some of what Christians now know as grammatical-historical criticism. Specifically, the way in which inaugurated eschatology governs the discussion of Old Testament citations in the New Testament is very reminiscent of the *qal wahomer*. Also: the Reformational principle of allowing a clearly understood text to interpret an obscure one is a first cousin to the *gezerah shawah*. A careful study of the Mishnah and its interpretive methods would pay rich dividends for a Christian interpreter today.

Conclusion

The Jews of the Greco-Roman era were a people of the text. It is because Jews so fervently believed that the words of the text were God's words that we have so much and so varied scriptural interpretation. Another reason might be that the story of Israel as recorded in sacred Scripture is a story that alternatively begged for an ending and demanded some sort of practical application. The various ways that Jews interpreted their book witnesses to this fact: they were trying to find the proper end of the story and were attempting to live out that text in this world. And yet, for all their efforts the text was not exhausted without remainder. For ancient interpreters the text was a treasure trove into which they could run their exegetical hands time and time again without ever emptying the text of its jewels. If it were true for ancient interpreters, how much more for modern ones?

▼

For Further Study

Blomberg, Craig L. *Interpreting the Parables*. Downers Grove, Ill.: IVP, 1990.

Brooke, George J. *Exegesis at Qumran: 4QFlorilegium in Its Jewish Context.* JSOTSS 29. Sheffield: JSOT, 1985.

Bruce, F. F. *Biblical Exegesis in the Qumran Scrolls*. Grand Rapids: Eerdmans, 1959.

Charlesworth, James H., and Craig A. Evans, eds. *The Pseudepigrapha and Early Biblical Interpretation*. JSPSS 14 / SSEJC 2. Sheffield: JSOT, 1993.

Dimant, Devorah. "Pesharim, Qumran" in *Anchor Bible Dictionary*. Edited by D. N. Freedman, 5:244–51. Garden City, N.Y.: Doubleday, 1992.

Ellis, E. Earle *Prophecy and Hermeneutic in Early Christianity*. WUNT 1/18. Tübingen: Mohr-Siebeck, 1978.

Hays, Richard B. *Echoes of Scripture in the Letters of Paul.* New Haven: Yale University Press, 1989.

Horgan, Maurya P. *Pesharim: Qumran Interpretations of Biblical Books.* CBQMS 8. Washington: CBA of America, 1979.

Juel, Donald. *Messianic Exegesis: Christological Interpretation of the Old Testament in Early Christianity.* Philadelphia: Fortress, 1988.

Kugel, James L. and Rowan A. Greer. *Early Biblical Interpretation.* LEC 3;. Philadelphia: Westminster, 1986.

Longenecker, Richard. *Biblical Exegesis in the Apostolic Period.* Grand Rapids: Eerdmans, 1975.

Neusner, Jacob. *A Midrash Reader.* Minneapolis: Fortress, 1990.

Patte, Daniel. *Early Jewish Hermeneutic in Palestine.* SBLDS 22; Missoula, Mont.: Scholars Press, 1975.

Porton, Gary G. *Understanding Rabbinic* Midrash: *Text & Commentary.* Hoboken, N. J.: KTAV, 1985.

Vermes, Géze. "Bible and *Midrash*: Early Old Testament Exegesis." *Post-Biblical Jewish Studies.* SJLA 8. Leiden: Brill, 1975.

Chapter Two

The New Testament's Use of the Old Testament

E. Earle Ellis

The Character of New Testament Usage

Old Testament phraseology in the New Testament occurs occasionally as a part of the writer's own patterns of expression that have been influenced by the Scriptures (1 Thess. 2:4; 4:5). Most often, however, it appears in the form of citations or intentional allusions. Professor Lars Hartman ("Exegesis," 134) suggests three reasons for an author's citation of another: to obtain the support of an authority (Matt. 4:14), to call forth a cluster of associations (Mark 12:1f.), and to achieve a literary or stylistic effect (Titus 1:12). He rightly observes that an allusion to the Old Testament sometimes can be discerned only after the total context of a passage has been taken into account.

As might be expected in Greek writings, citations from the Old Testament are frequently in agreement with the Septuagint (LXX "70"), the Greek version commonly used in the first century. But they are not always so, and at times they reflect other Greek versions, Aramaic paraphrases (targums) or independent translations of the Hebrew text. Apart from the use of a different text-form, they may diverge from the LXX because of a lapse of memory. However, this explanation is less probable than has been supposed in the past (Ellis, *Paul's Use*, 11–16, 150ff.). More frequently, as will be detailed below, citations diverge from the LXX because of deliberate alteration, that is, by a free translation and elaboration or by the use of a different textual tradition, to serve the purpose of the New Testament writer. The textual variations in the quotation, then, become an important clue to discover not only the writer's interpretation of the individual Old Testament passage but also his perspective on the Old Testament as a whole.

Introductory Formulas

Formulas of quotation, which generally employ verbs of "saying" or "writing," correspond to those found in other Jewish works, such as the Old Testament (e.g., 1 Kings 2:27; 2 Chron. 35:12), the Qumran scrolls (e.g., 1QS 5:15; 8:14), Philo and the rabbis (e.g., Philo, *de migr.* 118; *m. Abot* 3:7; Ellis, *Paul's Use*, 48f.). They locate the citation with reference to the book or writer or less frequently to the biblical episode, such as "in Elijah" (Rom. 11:2) or "at the bush" (Mark 12:26). At times they specify a particular prophet (Acts 28:25), a specification that on occasion may be important for the New Testament teaching (e.g., Mark 12:36; France, 101f.). When one book is named and another cited, the formula may represent an incidental error that is no part of the teaching or, more likely, the cited text may be viewed as an interpretation (Matt. 27:9) or elaboration (Mark 1:2) of a passage in the book named.

Introductory formulas often underscore the divine authority of the Old Testament, not in the abstract but within the proper interpretation and application of its teaching. Thus, the formula "Scripture (*graphē*) says" can introduce an eschatological, that is "Christianized," summation or elaboration of the Old Testament (John 7:38; Gal. 4:30), and *graphē* can be contrasted to traditional interpretations (Matt. 22:29). That is, it implies that the revelational, "Word of God" character of Scripture is present within the current interpretation. In the words of Renée Bloch (109), Scripture "always involves a living Word addressed personally to the people of God and to each of its members." B. B. Warfield (148) put it similarly: "Scripture is thought of as the living voice of God speaking in all its parts directly to the reader." The formula "it is written" can also have the intended connotation of a specific and right interpretation of Scripture (Rom. 9:33; 11:26) even though the connotation may not always be true (Matt. 4:6).

Sometimes an explicit distinction between reading Scripture and knowing or hearing Scripture may be drawn. It is present in the story of the Ethiopian eunuch (Acts 8:30) and, implicitly, in Jesus' synagogue exposition at Nazareth (Luke 4:16–21). It may be presupposed, as it is in rabbinical writings (Daube, 433–36), in the formula "have you not (*ouk*) read?" That is, "you have read but have not understood." This formula is found in the New Testament only on the lips of Jesus and usually within a Scriptural debate or exposition (e.g., Matt. 12:3, 5; 19:4; cf. Doeve, 105ff.).

A few formulas are associated with specific circles within the Christian community (Ellis, *Old Testament*, 79–82). The nine *legei kyrios* ("says the Lord") quotations probably reflect the activity of Christian prophets. The *hina plērōthē* ("that it might be fulfilled") quotations, found especially in the Gospels of Matthew and John, may have a similar origin. Both kinds of quotations contain creatively altered text-forms that facilitate an eschatological reapplication of the Old Testament passages, similar to that found in the Qumran scrolls (Ellis, *Paul's Use*, 139–47), to the experiences and understanding of the early church. This is a kind of activity recognized in first century Judaism to be appropriate to prophets as well as to teachers (Ellis, *Prophecy*, 55–60, 130ff., 182–87).

Somewhat similar are the *pistos ho logos* ("faithful is the word") passages in the Pastoral letters (1 Tim 1:15; 4:9; 2 Tim 2:11a–3:1a; Ellis, "Pastoral," 664). They appear to be instructions of Christian prophets (cf. 1 Tim. 4:1,6, *tois logois tēs pisteōs*) and/or inspired teachers, used by Paul in the composition of the letters. Although they do not contain Old Testament quotations, some of these "faithful sayings" may refer to the exposition of the Old Testament (e.g., 1 Tim. 2:13–3:1a; Titus 1:9, 14; 3:5–8; cf. Ellis, *Old Testament*, 82f.). They appear to arise out of a prophetic circle engaged in a ministry of teaching.

Forms and Techniques in Quotation

1. Combined Quotations. Combined quotations of two or more texts appear frequently in a variety of forms: a chain of passages (Rom. 15:9–12), a commentary pattern (John 12:38–40; Romans 9–11) and composite or merged citations (Rom. 3:10–18; 2 Cor. 6:16–18). With the exception of the last type these patterns were commonly employed in Judaism and in classical writings (Johnson, 92–102). They serve to develop a theme and perhaps exemplify the principle in Deut. 19:15 that two witnesses establish a matter. Sometimes (e.g., Rom. 10:18–21), in the fashion of the rabbis, they bring together citations from the Law, the Prophets and the Writings. Such combinations usually were formed in conjunction with catchwords important for the theme (e.g., "stone," "chosen" in 1 Pet. 2:6–9).

2. *Testimonia.* Citations "testifying" to the messiahship of Jesus were of special interest to the early church. Sometimes they appear as combined quotations (Hebrews 1), combinations that possibly lie behind other New Testament citations (Ellis, *Old Testament,* 70ff.). Such "testimonies" were primarily thematic combinations for instructional and apologetic purposes and, as the *testimonia* at Qumran indicate (4QTestim), some may have circulated in written form during the apostolic period. However, the hypothesis that they were collected in a precanonical "testimony book," used by the church in anti-Jewish apologetic, is less likely.

The "testimonies" apparently presuppose a worked-out christological understanding of the particular passages and are not simply proof texts randomly selected. The earliest Christians, like twentieth-century Jews, could not, as we do, simply infer from traditional usage the "Christian" interpretation of a biblical word or passage. Proof texts standing alone, therefore, would have appeared to them quite arbitrary if not meaningless.

According to a thesis of C. H. Dodd (78f., 107f.), the "testimony" quotations were selected from and served as pointers to larger Old Testament contexts that previously and as a whole had been Christologically interpreted. For example, Matt. 1:23 in citing Isa. 7:14 probably has in view the total section, Isa. 6:1–9:7, as the additional phrase "God with us" (Isa. 8:8, 10 LXX) and the frequent use of the section elsewhere in the New Testament indicate. Dodd (126) correctly perceived that the *testimonia* were the result of "a certain method of biblical study." But what precisely was that method? It may well have included, as Dodd thought, a systematic Christological analysis of certain sections of the Old Testament. Beyond this, however, the method probably corresponded to a form and method of scriptural exposition used in contemporary Judaism and known to us as midrash.

Quotation and Midrash

1. *Midrash.* The Hebrew term "midrash" has the meaning "commentary" (cf. 2 Chron. 13:22; 24:27), and in the past it has usually been associated primarily with certain rabbinic commentaries on the Old Testament. Recently it has been used more broadly to designate an activity as well as a literary genre, a way of expounding Scripture as well as the resulting exposition (Ellis, *Prophecy,* 188–92). Thus, "the house of midrash" (Sirach=Ecclus. 51:23) was a place where such exposition was carried on (and not a library of commentaries). According to Bloch (32f.) the essence of the

midrashic procedure was a contemporization of Scripture in order to apply it to or make it meaningful for the current situation. This contemporizing of Scripture takes two basic forms. *Implicit* midrash is sometimes evident in renderings of the Hebrew text into Greek (LXX) or Aramaic (targums). For example, the LXX changes "Arameans and Philistines" in Isa. 9:11(12) to "Syrians and Greeks" to give a contemporary application to the text. The contemporizing also occurs in *explicit* midrash. Explicit midrash takes the more formal pattern of a text plus exposition of the text. Explicit midrash is what one typically finds in the rabbinic commentaries. Both kinds of midrash appear in first-century Judaism in the literature of the Qumran community.

2. *Implicit Midrash.* Implicit midrash appears in double entendre, in interpretive alterations of Old Testament citations and in more elaborate forms (Ellis, *Old Testament*, 92–96). The first type involves a play on words. Thus, Matt. 2:23 cites Jesus' residence in Nazareth as a "fulfillment" of prophecies identifying the Messiah as a *Nazōraios* (= ?Nazirite, Judg. 13:5,7 LXX) or a *netzer* (= branch, Isa. 11:1; cf. 49:6; 60:21; Betz, 399ff.). Possibly the double meaning of "lift up" in John 3:14; 12:32–36, i.e. hang and exalt, alludes to an Aramaic rendering (*zeqaph*) of Isa. 52:13, which carries both meanings; the terminology is clarified in the Synoptic Gospels where Jesus prophesies that he is to "be killed and rise" (Mark 8:31; cf. Luke 18:33). A similar double entendre may be present in Acts 3:22–26 where "raise up" apparently is used both of Messiah's pre-resurrection ministry and of his resurrection.

The second type can be seen in Rom. 10:11: "For the Scripture says, 'Everyone (*pas*) who believes on him shall not be put to shame.'" The word "everyone" is not in the Old Testament text; it is Paul's interpretation woven into the citation and fitting it better to his argument (Rom. 10:12–15). Similarly, in the citation of Gen. 21:10 at Gal. 4:30 the phrase "son of the free woman" is substituted for "my son Isaac" in order to adapt the citation to Paul's application. More elaborate uses of the same principle will be discussed below.

More complex forms of implicit midrash occur (1) in making a merged or composite quotation from various Old Testament texts, altered so as to apply them to the current situation, and (2) in the description of a current event in biblical phraseology in order to connect the event with the Old Testament passages. Contemporized composite quotations appear, for example, in 1 Cor. 2:9;

2 Cor. 6:16–18. The use of scriptural phraseology to describe and thus to explain the meaning of current and future events is more subtle and reflects a different focus: the event appears to be of primary interest and the Old Testament allusions are introduced to illumine or explain it. This kind of midrash occurs, for example, in the Lucan infancy narratives, in Jesus' apocalyptic discourse (Matt. 24:15 *parallels in 2 other Gospels,* abv. parr) and his response at his trial (Matt. 26:64 parr) and in the Revelation of John where about seventy percent of the verses contain allusions to the Old Testament.

In the infancy narratives the Annunciation (Luke 1:26–38) alludes to Isa. 6:1–9:7—for example, to Isa. 7:13f. (27, *parthenos, ex oikou David*); 7:14 (31); 9:6f. (32, 35)—a section of Isaiah that C. H. Dodd (78–82) has shown to be a primary source for early Christian exegesis. It probably also alludes to Gen. 16:11 (31); 2 Sam. 7:12–16 (32, 35, *huios theou*), Dan. 7:14 (33b); and Isa. 4:3; 62:12 (35, *hagion klēthēsetai*). The Magnificat (Luke 1:46–55) and the Benedictus (Luke 1:68–79) appear to be formed along the same lines. It is probable that family traditions about the events surrounding Jesus' birth were given this literary formulation by prophets of the primitive Jerusalem church (Ellis, *Luke,* 27ff., 67f.).

The response of our Lord at his trial (Mark 14:62 par) is given by the Gospels in the words of Ps. 110:1 and Dan. 7:13. It probably represents a summary of Jesus' known response, a summary in biblical words whose "messianic" exegesis either had been worked out in the Christian community or, more likely, had been taught to the disciples by Jesus. That Jesus made use of both Ps. 110:1 and Dan. 7:13 during his earthly ministry is highly probable (cf. France, 101ff.).

The apocalyptic discourse (Matt. 24 parr), which also includes the use of Dan. 7:13, consists of a midrash of Jesus on certain passages in Daniel, a midrash that has been supplemented by other sayings of the Lord and reshaped by the evangelists and their predecessors "into something of a prophetic tract" linked to the church's experiences. In the course of transmission the midrash "lost many of its once probably explicit associations with the OT text" (Hartman, *Prophecy,* 242). If this reconstruction is correct, it shows not only how teachings of Jesus were contemporized in a manner similar to the midrashic handling of the Old Testament texts but also how our Lord's explicit midrash was modified so that the Old Testament references, although not lost, were largely assimilated to the current application. The process is much more thoroughgoing than is the case in the composite quotations cited above.

These examples suggest that implicit midrash sometimes presupposes or develops out of direct commentary on the Old Testament, that is, explicit midrash. We may now turn to that form of the early Christian usage.

3. *Explicit Midrash*. Explicit midrash in the New Testament has affinities both with the *pesher* midrash at Qumran and with certain kinds of midrash found in rabbinic expositions. The ancient expositions of the rabbis are preserved in sources that are dated several centuries after the New Testament writings. However, in their general structure they provide significant parallels for early Christian practice since it is unlikely that the rabbis borrowed their methods of exposition from the Christians and since similar patterns may be observed in the first-century Jewish writer, Philo (e.g., *de sacrif. Abel.* 76–87; cf. Ellis, *Old Testament*, 96–101). They probably originated not only as "sermon" or "homily" but also as "commentary," that is, not only as the complement of the synagogue worship but also as the product of the synagogue school. The type of discourse that finds most affinity with New Testament expositions is the "proem" midrash. As used in the synagogue, it ordinarily had the following form:

- The (Pentateuchal) text for the day
- A second text, the proem or "opening" for the discourse;
- Exposition containing additional Old Testament citations, parables or other commentary and linked to the initial texts by catch-words
- A final text, usually repeating or alluding to the text for the day

The New Testament letters frequently display, with some variation, the general outline of this pattern (cf. Ellis, *Prophecy*, 155ff.). The structure appears specifically in Rom. 9:6–29:

6f.–Theme and initial text: Gen 21:12

9–A second, supplemental text: Gen 18:10

10–28–Exposition containing additional citations (13, 15, 17, 25–28) and linked to the initial texts by the catchwords *kalein* and *huios* (12, 24ff., 27)

29–A final text alluding to the initial text with the catchword *sperma*.

At Gal. 4:21–5:1 the initial text of the commentary is itself a summary of a Genesis passage, an implicit midrash introducing the key word *eleuthera*. It is probably Paul's summation, but it might have been drawn from a Genesis midrash similar to Jubilees or to the Qumran Genesis Apocryphon (cf. Ellis, *Prophecy*, 190f., 224ff.).

21f.–Introduction and initial text; cf. Gen. 21;

23–29–Exposition with an additional citation, linked to the initial and final texts by the catchwords *eleuthera* (22, 23, 26, 30), *paidiskē* (22, 23, 30, 31) and *ben/huios = teknon* (22, 25, 27, 28, 30, 31)

30ff.–Final text and application, referring to the initial text; cf. Gen. 21:10

2 Peter 3:3–13 is similar (cf. Ellis, *Old Testament*, 99).

The above examples show how a composite, interpreted citation and an interpretive summary of a larger section of Scripture may serve as the "text" in a midrash. The use of short, explicit midrashim as "texts" in a more elaborate commentary-pattern is only an extension of the same practice (e.g., Rom 1:17–4:25; cf. Ellis, *Prophecy*, 217f.). One instance of this appears in 1 Cor. 1:18–3:20, which is composed of the following sections, all linked by catchwords, such as *sophia* and *mōria*:

1:18–31–Initial "text"
2:1–5–Exposition/Application
2:6–16–Additional "text"
3:1–17–Exposition/Application
3:18–20–Concluding texts: Job 5:13; Ps. 94:11

The synoptic Gospels also display exegetical patterns similar to those in the rabbis (cf. Ellis, *Prophecy*, 157ff., 247–52). Matt. 21:33–44 corresponds to an ancient form of a synagogue address:

33–Initial text: Isa. 5:1f.

34–41–Exposition by means of a parable, linked to the initial and final texts by a catchword *lithos* (42, 44, cf. 35; Isa. 5:2, *saqal*); cf. *oikodomein* (33, 42)

42–44–Concluding texts: Ps. 118:22f.; Dan. 2:34f., 44f.

In Luke 10:25–37 appears a somewhat different pattern, called in the rabbinic writings the *yelammedenu rabbenu* ("let our master teach us"), in which a question or problem is posed and then answered. Apart from the interrogative opening it follows in general the structure of the proem midrash:

25–27–Dialogue including a question and initial texts: Deut. 6:5; Lev. 19:18

28–A second text: Lev. 18:5

29–36–Exposition (by means of a parable) linked to the initial texts by the catchwords *plēsion* (27, 29, 36) and *poiein* (28, 37a, 37b)

37–Concluding allusion to the second text (*poiein*).

Matt. 19:3–8 is similar. (cf. Ellis, *Old Testament*, 97f.).

As the Gospels uniformly attest, debates with scribes, that is, theologians, about the meaning of Scripture constituted an important part of Jesus' public ministry. They were certainly more extensive than the summarized Gospel accounts although they may have followed the same general arrangement. In any case a *ye-lammedenu* pattern known and used by the rabbis is the literary form often employed by the Gospel traditioners. In the rabbinical writings the pattern is usually not a dialogue but the scriptural discourse of one rabbi. In this respect the exegetical structure in Romans 9–11 is closer to the rabbinic model than are the Gospel traditions (Ellis, *Prophecy*, 218f.).

Four differences between rabbinic and New Testament exegesis should also be noted. First, the New Testament midrashim often do not have an initial text from the Pentateuch, that is, they do not employ the sabbath text of the synagogue lectionary cycle. The New Testament midrashim also differ in that they often lack a second, proem text. Third, they often have a final text that does not correspond or allude to the initial text. Finally, they have an eschatological orientation (cf. Ellis, *Prophecy*, 163ff.).

Nevertheless, in their general structure the New Testament patterns have an affinity with the rabbinic usage that is unmistakable and too close to be coincidental.

4. Pesher Midrash. A kind of exposition known as the pesher midrash appears in the Qumran writings, for example, the commentary on Habakkuk (3:1ff.). It receives its name from the Hebrew word used in the explanatory formula, "the interpretation (*pesher*) is." This formula and its apparent equivalent, "this is" (*huah*), sometimes introduce the Old Testament citation (CD 10:16) or, more characteristically, the commentary following the citation. Both formulas occur in the Old Testament, the latter translated in the LXX by the phrase *houtos estin* (cf. Isa. 9:14f.; Zech. 1:9f.; Dan. 5:25f.; 4QFlor 1:2f.; Ellis, *Prophecy*, 160, 201–205).

Besides the formula, the Qumran *pesher* has other characteristics common to midrashic procedure. Like the midrashim discussed above, it apparently uses or creates variant Old Testament text-forms designed to adapt the text to the interpretation in the commentary. It also links text and commentary by catchwords. It is found, moreover, in various kinds of commentary patterns: anthology (4QFlor), single quotations (CD 4:14) and consecutive commentary on an Old Testament book (1QpHab).

More significantly for New Testament studies, the Qumran *pesher*, unlike rabbinic midrash but very much like early Christian practice, is both charismatic and eschatological. As *eschatological exegesis*, it views the Old Testament as promises and prophecies that have their fulfilment within the writer's own time and community, a community that inaugurates the "new covenant" of the "last (*'aharit*) days," and constitutes the "last (*'aharôn*) generation" before the coming of Messiah and the inbreaking of the kingdom of God (cf. Jer. 31:31; 1QpHab 2:3–7; 7:2).

This characteristic feature, the *pesher* formula combined with an eschatological perspective, appears in a number of New Testament quotations:

"'In Isaac shall your seed be called' [Gen. 21:12]. That is [*tout' estin*] . . . the children of the promise are reckoned for the seed. For this is [*houtos*] the word of promise. '. . . for Sarah there shall be a son'" [Gen. 18:10] (*Rom. 9:7–9*).

"'On account of this shall a man leave father and mother and be joined to his wife, and the two shall be one flesh' [Gen. 2:24]. This is [*touto . . . estin*] a great mystery . . . for Christ and the Church" (*Eph. 5:31–32*).

"It is written, 'Abraham had two sons . . .' [cf. Gen. 21]. These are [*hautai . . . eisin*] two covenants . . ." (*Gal. 4:22–24*).

"They were all filled the Holy Spirit and began to speak in other tongues . . . . This is [*touto estin*] what was spoken by the prophet Joel, 'I will pour out my spirit . . .'" [Joel 2:28] (*Acts 2:4, 16*).

The Qumran *pesher* was regarded by the community as *charismatic exegesis*, the work of inspired persons such as the Teacher of Righteousness and other wise teachers (*maskilim*). The Old Testament prophecies were understood, as they are in the book of Daniel (9:2, 22f.; cf. 2:19, 24), to be a "mystery" (*raz*) in need of interpretation (*pesher*), an interpretation that only the *maskilim* can give. (cf. 1QpHab 7:1–8; 1QH 12:11ff.).

(5) *Testimonia.* From midrash to testimonia: "Words lifted from their scriptural context can never be a testimonium to the Jewish mind. The word becomes a testimonium for something or other after one has brought out its meaning with the aid of other parts of Scripture." With this perceptive observation J. W. Doeve (116) goes

beyond the thesis of C. H. Dodd, mentioned above, to contend that "testimony" citations in the New Testament are derived from midrashim, that is, from expositions of those particular Old Testament passages.

In support of Doeve are several examples of a "Christian" interpretation of a text that is established in an exposition and presupposed elsewhere in a "testimony" citation of the same text (cf. 1 Cor. 1:18–31, with 2 Cor. 10:17; Ellis, *Prophecy*, 192–97, 213–18). For example, the exposition in Acts 2:17–35 and that underlying Mark 13 apply Ps. 110:1 and Dan. 7:13, respectively, to Jesus. This interpretation is presupposed in the use of the verses at Mark 14:62. Similarly, Heb. 2:6–9 establishes by midrashic procedures that Psalm 8 is fulfilled in Jesus; in 1 Cor. 15:27 and Eph. 1:20, 22 this understanding of Psalm 8 (and Psalm 110) is presupposed. The same pattern is evident in Acts 13:16–41, which is probably a (reworked) midrash in which 2 Sam. 7:6–16 is shown to apply to Jesus. This interpretation of 2 Samuel 7 is presupposed in the *testimonia* in Heb. 1:5 and 2 Cor. 6:18.

The midrashic expositions in these examples are not, of course, the immediate antecedents of the cited *testimonia* texts. But they represent the kind of matrix from which the "testimony" usage appears to be derived. They show, furthermore, that the prophets and teachers in the early church were not content merely to cite proof texts but were concerned to establish by exegetical procedures the Christian understanding of the Old Testament.

We may proceed one step further. Rabbinic parables often are found in midrashim as commentary on the Old Testament texts. Christ's parables also occur within an exegetical context, for example, in Matt. 21:33–44 and Luke 10:25–37. Elsewhere, when they appear independently or in thematic clusters, they sometimes allude to Old Testament passages (Mark 4:1–20 to Jer. 4:3; Luke 15:3–6 to Ezek. 34:11). Probably such independent and clustered parables originated within an expository context from which they were later detached. If so, their present context represents a stage in the formation of the Gospel traditions secondary to their use within an explicit commentary format.

The Presuppositions of New Testament Interpretation

To many Christian readers, to say nothing of Jewish readers, the New Testament's interpretation of the Old appears to be exceedingly arbitrary. For example, Hos. 11:1 ("Out of Egypt I called my son") refers to Israel's experience of the Exodus; how can Matt. 2:15 apply it to Jesus' sojourn in Egypt? In Ps. 8:4ff. the "son of man" (*ben-'adam*) given "glory" and "dominion" alludes to Adam or to Israel's king; how can Heb. 2:8f. and 1 Cor. 15:27 apply the text to Jesus? If Gen. 15:6 and 2 Samuel 7 are predictions of Israel's future, how can New Testament writers refer them to Jesus and to his followers, who include Gentiles as well as Jews?

As has been shown above, the method used to justify such Christian interpretations of the Old Testament represents a serious and consistent effort to expound the texts. The method itself, of course, may be criticized. But then, our modern historical-critical method also is deficient: although it can show certain interpretations to be wrong, it cannot achieve an agreed interpretation for any substantive biblical passage. "Method" is inherently a limited instrumentality and, indeed, a secondary stage in the art of interpretation. More basic are the perspective and presuppositions with which the interpreter approaches the text (cf. Ellis, *Prophecy*, 163–72; and *Old Testament*, 101–21).

The perspective from which the New Testament writers interpret the Old is sometimes stated explicitly; sometimes it can be inferred from their usage. It is derived in part from contemporary Jewish views and in part from the teaching of Jesus and the experience of the reality of his resurrection. Apart from its Christological focus, it appears to be governed primarily by four factors: a particular understanding of history, of man, of Israel and of Scripture.

Salvation as History

Jesus and his apostles conceive of history within the framework of two ages, this age (*aiōn*) and the age to come (e.g. Matt. 12:32; Mark 10:30; Luke 20:34f.; Eph. 1:21; Heb. 9:26). This perspective appears to have its background in the Old Testament prophets, who prophesied of "the last (*'aharit*) days" and "the day of the Lord" as the time of an ultimate redemption of God's people and the destruction of their enemies (e.g., Isa. 2:2; Dan. 10:14; Mic. 4:1). It becomes more specific in the apocalyptic writers, who underscored the cosmic dimension and (often) the imminence of the redemption and, with the doctrine of two ages, the radical difference between the present time and the time to come. This point of view is clearly present in the message of the Baptist that "the kingdom of God is at hand" and that the one coming after him, Jesus, would accomplish the final judgment and the redemption of the nation (Matt. 3:2, 10–12).

The *twofold* consummation of judgment and deliverance that characterized the teaching of apocalyptic Judaism becomes, in the teaching of Jesus and his apostles, a *two-stage* consummation. As "deliverance" the kingdom of God that Judaism expected at the end of this age is regarded as already present within this age in the person and work of Jesus (Matt. 12:28; Luke 10:9; Rom. 14:17; Col. 1:13). As "judgment" (and final deliverance) the kingdom awaits the second, glorious appearing of the Messiah. This perspective may be contrasted with that of Platonism and of apocalyptic Judaism as follows:

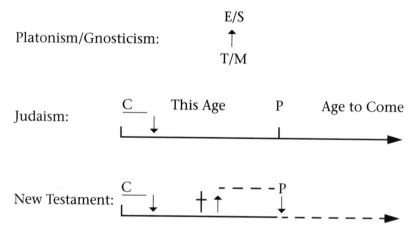

Platonic and later Gnostic thought anticipated a redemption from matter (M) and an escape from time (T) and history to eternity (E) and spirit (S) at death. The biblical, Jewish hope was for a bodily resurrection, a redemption of matter within time: The present age, from the creation (C) and the Fall ($-\downarrow$) to the coming of Messiah (P), was to be succeeded by a future age of peace and righteousness under the reign of God. The New Testament's modification of Jewish apocalyptic rested upon the perception that in the mission, death and resurrection of Jesus the Messiah, the age to come, the future kingdom of God, had become present in hidden form in the midst of the present evil age, although its public manifestation awaited the parousia (P) of Jesus. Thus, in the words of O. Cullmann, for Jesus "the kingdom of God does not culminate a meaningless history, but a planned divine process" (233). Equally, for the New Testament writers faith in Jesus means faith in the story of Jesus, the story of God's redemptive activity in the history of Israel that finds its high point and fulfilment in Jesus.

For this reason the mission and meaning of Jesus can be expressed in the New Testament in terms of a *salvation history* "consisting of a sequence of events especially chosen by God, taking place within an historical framework" (Cullmann, 25). Although the concept of *oikonomia* ("plan," "arrangement") as used in Eph. 1:10 represents this idea, that is, a divinely ordered plan, the term "salvation history" does not itself occur in the New Testament. The concept is most evident in the way in which the New Testament relates current and future events to events, persons, and institutions in the Old Testament. That relationship is usually set forth as a typological correspondence.

Typology

Typological interpretation expresses most clearly the basic approach of earliest Christianity toward the Old Testament. It is not so much a system of interpretation as a historical and theological perspective from which the early Christian community viewed itself. As a hermeneutical method it must be distinguished from *typos* ("model," "pattern") as it is widely used in the Greek world.

The New Testament uses the term *typos* only occasionally, but typological interpretation appears often. Broadly speaking, it appears either as *covenant typology* or *creation typology*. The latter may be observed in Romans 5 where Christ is compared and contrasted with Adam, "a type (*typos*) of the one who was to come" (5:14). The former appears in 1 Cor. 10:6, 11, where the Exodus events are said to be "types for us," to have happened "by way of example" (*typikōs*) and to have been written down "for our admonition upon whom the ends of the ages have come." Covenant typology accords with the Jewish conviction that all of God's redemptive acts followed the pattern of the Exodus; it is, then, an appropriate way for Jesus and his apostles to explain the decisive messianic redemption. More generally, covenant typology approaches the whole of Old Testament as prophecy. Not only persons and events but also its institutions were "a shadow of the good things to come" (Heb. 10:1).

New Testament typology is thoroughly *christological* in its focus. Jesus is the "prophet like Moses" (Acts 3:22–23) who in his passion and death brings the old covenant to its proper goal and end (Rom. 10:4; Heb. 10:9f.) and establishes a new covenant (Luke 22:20, 29). As the messianic "son of David," that is, "son of God," he is the recipient of the promises, titles and ascriptions given to the Davidic kings (e.g. 2 Sam. 7:14; Ps. 2:7; Amos 9:11–12; cf. John 7:42; Acts 13:33; 15:16–18; 2 Cor. 6:18; Heb. 1:5).

Because the new covenant consummated by Jesus' death is the occasion of the new creation initiated by his resurrection, covenant typology may be combined with creation typology: As the "eschatological Adam" and the "Son of man," that is, "son of Adam" (Ps. 8:4, 6–9; cf. 1 Cor. 15:27, 45), Jesus stands at the head of a new order of creation that may be compared and contrasted with the present one. This combination in Paul and Hebrews finds its immediate background in the resurrection of Jesus. But it is already implicit in Jesus' own teaching, for example, his temple saying (Mark 14:58), his promise of "Paradise" to the robber (Luke 23:42f.) and his teaching on divorce based on Gen. 2:24 (cf. Matt. 19:3–9). It is probably implicit also in his self-designation as the Son of man (Mark 14:62), a designation that is derived from Dan. 7:13–14, 27 with allusions to Psalm 8 and Ezek. 1:26ff. The Son of man in Psalm 8 refers not only to Israel's (messianic-ideal) king but also to Adam; likewise the Son of man in Dan. 7:13–14 is related not only to national restoration but also to the "dominion" and "glory" of a new creation. In apocalyptic Judaism also Israel was associated with Adam and the new covenant with a renewed creation (T. Levi 18; 1QS 4:22f.). Jesus and his followers shared these convictions and explained them in terms of the mission and person of Jesus.

The Old Testament type not only corresponds to the new-age reality but also stands in antithesis to it. Like Adam, Jesus is the representative headman of the race; but unlike Adam, who brought death, Jesus brings forgiveness and life. Jesus is "the prophet like Moses" but, unlike Moses' ministry of condemnation, that of Jesus gives justification and righteousness. Similarly, the law as an expression of God's righteousness "is holy, just and good" and its commandments (Exodus 20), actuated by an ethic of love (Lev. 19:18), are to be "fulfilled" by the believer (Rom. 7:12; 13:8; Gal. 5:14). However, the (works of) law was never intended as a means of man's salvation and, as such, it can only condemn him.

One may speak, then, of "synthetic" and of "antithetic" typology to distinguish the way in which a type, to one degree or another, either corresponds to or differs from the reality of the new age. For example, Abraham represents synthetic typology (i.e., his faith) but not antithetic (i.e., his circumcision; Galatians 3). Moses and the Exodus can represent both (Heb. 11:28f.; 1 Cor. 10:1–4, 6–10; 2 Cor. 3:9); so can Jerusalem (Gal. 4:25f.; Rev. 11:8;

21:2). The old covenant, that is, the law, more often represents antithetic typology.

Since the history of salvation is also the history of destruction (Cullmann, 123), it includes a judgment typology. The flood and Sodom (Luke 17:26–30; 2 Pet. 2:5f.; Jude 7), and probably the prophesied A.D 70 destruction of Jerusalem (Matt. 24:3), become types of God's eschatological judgment. The faithless Israelite is a type of the faithless Christian (1 Cor. 10:11–12; Heb. 4:11); the enemies of Israel a type of the (Jewish) enemies of the Church (Rev. 11:8; Rom. 2:24) and, perhaps, a type of the Antichrist (2 Thess. 2:3–4; Rev. 13:1–10).

In a brilliant and highly significant contribution to New Testament hermeneutics, Leonard Goppelt's *TYPOS* (1982) has set forth the definitive marks of typological interpretation. First, unlike allegory, typological exegesis regards the words of Scripture not as metaphors hiding a deeper meaning (*hyponoia*) but as the record of historical events out of whose literal sense the meaning of the text arises (17f., 201f.). Second, unlike the "history of religions" exegesis, it seeks the meaning of current, New Testament situations from a particular history, the salvation history of Israel. From past Old Testament events it interprets the meaning of the present time of salvation and, in turn, it sees in present events a typological prophecy of the future consummation (194–205). Third, like rabbinic midrash, typological exegesis interprets the text in terms of contemporary situations; but it does so with historical distinctions that are lacking in rabbinic interpretation (28–32). Fourth, it identifies a typology in terms of two basic characteristics, historical correspondence and escalation, in which the divinely ordered prefigurement finds a complement in the subsequent and greater event (202).

In a masterly essay (*Exegetica*, 1967, 369–80) Rudolf Bultmann rejected Goppelt's conclusion that salvation history was constitutive for typological exegesis and sought to show that the origin of typology lay rather in a cyclical-repetitive view of history (cf. *Barn.* 6:13). Although Judaism had combined the two perspectives, the New Testament, for example, in its Adam/Christ typology, represents a purely cyclical pattern, parallels between the primal time and the end time. However, Professor Bultmann, in interpreting the New Testament hermeneutical usage within the context of the traditional Greek conception, does not appear to recognize that the recapitulation element in New Testament typology is never mere repetition but is always combined with a change of key in which some aspects of the type are not carried over and some are intensified. Exegetically Goppelt made the better case and established an important framework for understanding how the New Testament uses the Old.

Other Presuppositions

In agreement with the Old Testament conception, the New Testament views *man as having both individual and corporate existence.* It presents the corporate dimension, the aspect most difficult for modern Western man to appreciate, primarily in terms of Jesus and his church (e.g. Mark 14:22–25; Col. 1:24). For the New Testament, faith in Jesus involves an incorporation into him: It is to eat his flesh (John 6:35, 54), to be his body (1 Cor. 12:27), to be baptized into him (Rom. 6:3), or into his name (1 Cor. 1:13; Acts 8:16), to be identified with him (Acts 9:5–6), to exist in the corporate Christ (2 Cor. 5:17) who is the "tent" (Heb. 9:11) or "house" (2 Cor. 5:1) in the heavens, God's eschatological temple.

Corporate existence can also be expressed as baptism "into Moses" (1 Cor. 10:2), existence "in Abraham" (Heb. 7:9–10) or "in Adam" (1 Cor. 15:22) and, at its most elementary level, the unity of husband and wife as "one flesh" (Matt. 19:5; Eph. 5:29–32). It is not merely a metaphor, as we are tempted to interpret it, but an ontological statement about who and what man is. The realism of this conception is well expressed by the term "corporate personality" (cf. Ellis, *Old Testament*, 110ff.).

The corporate extension of the person of the leader to include invividuals who belong to him illumines the use of a number of Old Testament passages. It explains how the promise given to Solomon (2 Sam. 7:12–16) can be regarded as fulfilled not only in the Messiah (Heb. 1:5) but also in his followers (2 Cor. 6:18) and, similarly, how the eschatological temple can be identified both with the individual (Mark 14:58; John 2:19–22) and the corporate (1 Cor. 3:16; 1 Pet. 2:5) Christ. It very probably underlies the conviction of the early Christians that those who belong to Christ, Israel's messianic king, constitute *the true Israel* (cf. Ellis, *Paul's Use*, 136–39). Consequently, it explains the Christian application to unbelieving Jews of Scriptures originally directed to Gentiles (Acts 4:25–27; Rom. 11:9f.) and, on the other hand, the application to the church of Scriptures originally directed to the Jewish nation (2 Cor. 6:16ff.; 1 Pet. 2:9f.).

Corporate personality also offers a rationale whereby individual, existential decision (Mark 1:17; 2 Cor. 6:2) may be understood within the framework of a salvation history of the nation or of the race. These two perspectives are considered by some scholars to be in tension or to be mutually exclusive. However, in the words of Oscar Cullmann (248), the "now of decision" in the New Testament is not in conflict with the salvation-historical attitude but subordinate to it: "Paul's faith in salvation history creates at every moment the existential decision." For it is precisely within the context of the community that the individual's decision is made: Universal history and individual history cannot be isolated from one another.

The history of salvation often appears in the New Testament as the history of individuals—Adam, Abraham, Moses, David, Jesus— yet they are individuals who also have a corporate dimension embracing the nation or the race. The decision to which the New Testament calls men relates to them. It is never a decision between the isolated individual and God but is, rather, a decision to "put off the old man" Adam and to "put on the new man" Christ (Eph. 4:22ff.), to be delivered from the corporeity "in Moses" and "in Adam" (1 Cor. 10:2; 15:22) and to be "immersed in" and to "put on" Christ (Gal. 3:27), that is, to be incorporated into the "prophet like Moses" and the eschatological Adam of the new creation in whom the history of salvation is to be consummated (1 Cor. 15:45; cf. Acts 3:22–24).

The early Christian prophets and teachers explain the Old Testament by what may be called *charismatic exegesis*. Like the teachers of Qumran (see above), they proceed from the conviction that the meaning of the Old Testament is a "mystery" whose "interpretation" can be given not by human reason but only by the Holy Spirit (1 Cor. 2:6–16; cf. Matt. 13:11; 16:17). On the basis of revelation from the Spirit they are confident of their ability rightly to interpret the Scriptures (Matt. 16:17; Mark 4:11; Rom. 16:25f.; Eph. 3:3ff.; 2 Pet. 3:15–16). Equally, they conclude that those who are not gifted cannot "know" the true meaning of the word of God (Matt. 22:29; 2 Cor. 3:14–16).

This view of their task does not preclude the New Testament writers from using logic or hermeneutical rules and methods. However, it does disclose where the ultimate appeal and authority of their interpretation lie. Correspondingly, an acceptance of their interpretation of Scripture in preference to some other, ancient or modern, also will rest ultimately not on the proved superiority of their logical procedure or exegetical method but rather on the conviction of their prophetic character and role.

For Further Study

Betz, Otto. *Jesus Der Herr der Kirche*. Tübingen: Mohr, 1990.

Bloch, Renee. "Midrash." In *Approaches to Ancient Judaism I*, ed. W. S. Green, 29–50. Missoula, Mont.: Scholars, 1978.

Bultmann, Rudolph. *Exegetica*. Tübingen: Mohr, 1967.

Cullmann, Oscar. *Salvation in History*, trans. Sidney G. Sowers. New York: Harper & Row, 1967.

Daube, David. *The New Testament and Rabbinic Judaism*. London: Althone, 1956; reprint, Peabody, Mass.: Hendrickson, 1994.

Dodd, C. H. *According to the Scriptures*. London: Nisbet, 1952.

Doeve, J. W. *Jewish Hermeneutics in the Synoptic Gospels and Acts*. Assen: Van Gorcum, 1954.

Ellis, E. Earle. *The Gospel of Luke*. Rev. ed. New Century Bible. London: Oliphants, 1974; 6th reprint, Grand Rapids: Eerdmans, 1996.

———. *The Old Testament in Early Christianity*. Tübingen: Mohr, 1991; reprint, Grand Rapids: Baker, 1992.

———. "Pastoral Letters." In *Dictionary of Paul and His Letters*, ed. Gerald F. Hawthorne, 658–66. Downers Grove, Ill.: InterVarsity, 1993.

———. *Pauline Theology: Ministry and Society*. Grand Rapids: Eerdmans, 1989; reprint, 1990.

———. *Paul's Use of the Old Testament*. Grand Rapids: Eerdmans, 1957; 5th reprint, Grand Rapids: Baker, 1991.

———. *Prophecy and Hermenuetic in Early Christianity*. Tübingen: Mohr, 1978; 3rd reprint, Grand Rapids: Baker, 1993.

France, R. T. *Jesus and the Old Testament*. London: Tyndale, 1971.

Gooding, D. W. *Relics of Ancient Exegesis*. Cambridge, 1976.

Goppelt, Leonard. *TYPOS*. Grand Rapids: Eerdmans, 1982.

Gundry, Robert H. *The Use of the Old Testament in St. Matthew's Gospel*. Leiden: Brill, 1967.

Hartman, Lars. "Scriptural Exegesis in the Gospel of Matthew and the Problem of Communication." In *L'evangile selon Matthieu*, ed. M. Didier, 131–52. Gembloux: Duculot, 1972.

———. *Prophecy Interpreted*. Lund: Gleerup, 1966.

Johnson, Franklin. *The Quotations of the New Testament from the Old*. Philadelphia: American Baptist Publishing Society, 1896.

Warfield, B. B. *The Inspiration and Authority of the Bible*. Philadelphia: Presbyterian and Reformed, 1948.

Chapter Three

The Hermeneutics
of the Early Church Fathers

Robert W. Bernard

The end of the first and the beginning of the second centuries A.D. marked also an end and a beginning for the Christian church. The Apostolic Age was drawing to a close; in its place a new era was dawning in which the church would trace the outlines of the faith proclaimed in the New Testament. The new era, designated in this chapter as the patristic era (from the Latin word *patres* or "fathers"), came to full flower in the fourth and fifth centuries of the present era with such "fathers" of the faith as Athanasius, Augustine, and Jerome. It was during the patristic era that the church formulated basic statements on the nature of the Triune God and the person and work of Christ. All subsequent theology finds its foundations in this period.

The formulation of theology in the patristic era took place in arenas of conflict; then as now, Christians were not unanimous. The same held true for the interpretation of Scripture. To present all aspects of that interpretation in this chapter would be an impossible task; the discussion, therefore, will focus on the schools of Alexandria and Antioch. The discussion of each school will begin with an introduction to the school, proceed to an examination of major aspects of the foundations for each school's theology, and then present very briefly the thoughts of a major representative of each school. The chapter will conclude with a comparison of the exegesis done by those representatives, Origen and Theodore of

59

Mopsuestia, of the account in the Gospel of John of Christ's cleansing of the temple.

School of Alexandria

The school of Alexandria, established originally to train converts to Christianity, found itself in one of the leading cities of the Roman Empire. Founded by Alexander the Great in the late fourth century B.C., Alexandria held a position on the eastern Mediterranean coast which soon made it a major center of commerce. Along with trade, moreover, Alexandria became a center of learning; in the third century B.C. the Ptolemies, the Greek rulers of Egypt, made the city their capital and established a library that developed into one of the greatest centers of learning in the ancient world. In that city, a number of schools of thought combined to form a foundation for the allegorical interpretation for which the Alexandrian school became famous. One finds two major sources for that foundation in the philosophical schools of Platonism and Stoicism.

It is obviously beyond the scope of this chapter to portray fully Platonic philosophy; what is essential is to understand those elements which played a role in patristic hermeneutics. Platonism presented an emphasis upon an ideal and incorporeal reality, of which this world was a shadowy copy. For Plato (429-347 B.C.), the world seen by humans was a mere reflection of ultimate reality. To understand the true nature of reality, one had to turn one's gaze away from the visible world and begin an ascent to the ideal world, in which Plato believed one would find the "forms" or patterns upon which this world was modeled. The contrast was basically one of this world, which is material, subject to change, and a shadow of reality, with the world of the "forms," which was not material at all, changeless and eternal, and truly real.

If Platonism provided a philosophical framework for comprehending reality, then Stoicism provided the interpretive framework for analyzing that reality. Begun in the late fourth century B.C., Stoicism differed from Platonism by denying a gulf between the intelligible and visible worlds; for the Stoics, all that existed was material. Furthermore, ultimate reality, which was essentially rational, was itself material and permeated the entire universe. Stoicism was thus a pantheistic system; in this respect, it would obviously not have had any effect at all upon the Alexandrian Jews and Christians, whose worldview was more like that of Plato. Critical to Stoicism, however, and of fundamental importance to Alexandria, was the insistence that the universe is governed by natural law and is rationally organized. Human beings as rational creatures could understand the natural laws which governed their universe. This insistence led, among other things, to the development of allegorical interpretation.

How allegorical interpretation arose is a complex subject, only the outlines of which can be traced here. To understand the appearance of such interpretation, one must begin by understanding that the Homeric epics, the *Iliad* and *Odyssey*, were believed by the ancient Greeks to be inspired. They were, furthermore, poems that united the Greeks in literature, if not in politics. The epics were considered as teachers of conduct and virtue. In reading the two poems, however, one encounters descriptions of both humans and gods which are quite uncomplimentary. In particular, the Homeric gods are very human; jealous, subject to emotion, quarrelsome, and prone to immorality, they were an embarrassment to their worshipers. Founded upon the conviction that the epics were inspired, and upon the belief that the inspired poet would write nothing unworthy, Greeks before the Stoics began to interpret Homer in a manner that one might call allegorical. The gods were taken as symbols for the natural elements; Hera, the jealous and very human queen of the gods, was taken as symbolizing air (her name, Hera, was connected to the Greek *aer*, or "air"). The Stoics took those earlier attempts to understand Homer rationally and systematized them. Their philosophy emphasized a rational order permeating all reality; thus, human words could be inspired by that order to express truth. It was as if the divine message were "encoded" into human words so that it might be accessible to human beings. If the literal meaning of words did not convey rationality, then the true meaning had to lie underneath the literal meaning of the words. The Stoics referred to such meaning as *hyponoia* ("the thought underneath"). They also gave the world the word "allegory," from the Greek *allegoria*: "expressing one thing (i.e., the true meaning) in terms of another (i.e., the literal word)."

Ancient peoples tended to view their world more symbolically than moderns, a factor that helps to explain how allegory could be so popular—and even understandable—to the ancient world, yet so foreign at first glance to us. When one also considers that symbols are found throughout Scripture (such as the vineyard as a symbol for Israel), as well as symbolic narratives (such as parables), one may begin to realize how Greek allegory could also appeal to Christians.

For the Alexandrians the combination of Platonism and Stoicism formed a framework for interpreting the Scriptures. Platonism presented this world as a shadow of reality differing entirely from what is experienced by human senses. One had to go beyond what was seen to the unseen, spiritual reality. Yet there had to be a bridge between the two worlds. The first interpreter of Scripture to enter into this worldview was Philo (30 B.C.–A.D. 40), a Jew who had a profound influence upon the later Christian Alexandrians, especially Clement and Origen. For Philo, as for the Greek interpreters before him, that bridge could be found in an inspired text. For such interpreters, inspiration meant the infusion of meaning which differed at times as radically from the literal meaning as the true world differed from this world of shadows. The inspired text was the bridge in which the true reality was expressed symbolically; human beings had to ascend from what was accessible to their senses to what was accessible only to the highest levels of their intellect—the true reality, entirely spiritual, eternal, unchanging. From Stoicism, the Alexandrians gained the confidence that the message encoded in the symbols of Scripture was coherent, rational, and accessible through non-literal interpretation of the text.

The outstanding exponent of Alexandrian exegesis was Origen (A.D. 185/186–254/255), one of the foremost scholars, biblical commentators, and preachers of the ancient church. Much of his work is lost, but enough is known about him to give an idea of the vast scope of his activity. One of the few ancient Christians to learn Hebrew, Origen compiled the *Hexapla*, a comparison of the Hebrew text of the Old Testament with several Greek versions. Like his fellow Alexandrians, Origen engaged in textual criticism of the Scriptures. He was also one of the first in Western thought to compose a systematic theology, entitled *On First Principles*, which includes an exposition of his hermeneutics.

School of Antioch

The other major exegetical school in the patristic church was in Antioch in Syria. Founded by one of Alexander the Great's generals in the early third century B.C., the city became the capital of a vast empire which stretched from modern Iran and Afghanistan in the east to Syria, Lebanon, and Palestine in the west. By the time of the Roman conquest of the Near East in the first century B.C., Antioch had become one of the greatest cities of the ancient world, rivaled only by Alexandria and Rome herself. Like Alexandria, furthermore,

Antioch became a center of learning and a center of commerce where many schools of thought met; it had a Jewish community which may have had a profound influence on the Christians, and schools of philosophy flourished in which the thought of Aristotle as well as Plato may have been found. In the midst of this cauldron of ideas arose an exegetical school which claimed such leaders as Lucian, Diodore of Tarsus, Theodore of Mopsuestia, and, perhaps the best known, John Chrysostom, the "Golden-Mouthed" (Greek *chrysostomos*) preacher of the ancient church.

Tracing the exegetical theories of the Antiochene school is, unfortunately, a difficult task. The Antiochenes became embroiled in a controversy over the person and work of Christ; the names of many Antiochene Christians became connected with Nestorianism, the view that Jesus had two separate persons and natures. Condemned as a heresy, Nestorianism cast a shadow over those associated with it; in the sixth century, many works by Antiochene theologians, particularly those of Theodore of Mopsuestia, were banned and were largely lost to the Christian community. What has survived of those works, however, demonstrates how different Antioch was from Alexandria. The exegetical work of Theodore especially sets him apart as the foremost exegete from Antioch.

What one can learn from the extant Antiochene writings is that their writers had no use for Alexandrian allegorical interpretation. The school of Antioch founded its approach on consideration of the literal text: its literal meaning, grammar, and historical context. Theodore, for example, saw the prophets as speaking primarily to their own times and circumstances, although he allowed that one might find statements concerning the future. Furthermore, although the Antiochenes also had an emphasis upon insight or *theoria* into spiritual truth to be gained from Scripture, they insisted that such insight be rooted in the literal meaning of the text.

One may understand an exegetical school best by examining where that school begins in its search for truth. Alexandria began with the divine reality expressed symbolically by Scripture, the truth "from above." On the other hand, Antioch began with the literal sense of Scripture as a foundation "from below" to gain spiritual insight. As with Alexandria, the sources from Antiochene hermeneutics may be found at least in part in both Judaism and Greek philosophy. The Jewish community in Antioch was of considerable size and importance. Unlike their kindred in Alexandria, the Jews of Antioch were not influenced at all by Philo and were perhaps much closer to a more literal hermeneutic. As for Greek philosophy, the Antiochene approach "from below" is similar to that of Aristotle (384–322 B.C.), Plato's most brilliant and famous pupil. Unlike his teacher, Aristotle denied that one could know anything of the world apart from the things that are available to our senses. For Plato, truth was gained from insight into the ideal world; Aristotle's insight was gained by finding properties common to a group of objects available to our senses. To know the definition of "human being," for Plato, was to have the thought of an ideal "form" in one's mind; for Aristotle, one must study real human beings to discover what they share in common. Besides being the father of modern systems of classification, Aristotle may well have given some of the philosophical underpinnings for Antiochene exegesis of Scripture. The blending of Aristotelian elements and a more literal approach from Judaism appears to have produced the Christian exegetical school in Antioch.

Theodore of Mopsuestia (350–428), one of the most striking of the exegetes from Antioch, was another outstanding scholar of the ancient church. Born in Antioch, he studied with one of the foremost orators of the ancient world, Libanius, in preparation for a career in law and government. Theodore, however, gave up a promising secular career in order to serve the church. He eventually became bishop of Mopsuestia in Asia Minor. Like Origen, Theodore became an unparalleled commentator upon Scripture; generations following him simply referred to him as "The Interpreter" without having to give any further identification.

Comparing Origen and Theodore on John 2:13–22

Origen and Theodore are the outstanding proponents of their respective schools; not all Christians who held to allegorical interpretation went as far as Origen, and such Antiochenes as John Chrysostom were not as suspicious of symbolic interpretations as was Theodore. In their exegesis, therefore, these two early Christians set most clearly in focus the approaches of their schools. To show those approaches and the difference they reveal, one should turn to commentaries by both in which they interpret the same book of Scripture. Due to the loss of both men's works, however, it is difficult to find such commentaries. Fortunately, portions of the Greek text of Origen's commentary on John survive, as well as a Syriac translation of Theodore's work on that same Gospel. To illustrate their approaches, the exegesis by Origen and Theodore, respectively, of Christ's cleansing of the temple (John 2:13-22) is the next, and last, topic for discussion.

Origen

In order to understand Origen's approach to Scripture as well as to John's account of Christ's entry into Jerusalem and cleansing of the temple, one needs to turn to a passage found early in Book X of his commentary on John. Noting differences between John and the other three Gospels, Origen warns his reader not to seek the truth in the literal sense alone, especially when accounts of the same event differ among the Gospels: "The truth about these matters lies in intelligible realities [those found by non-literal exegesis] . . . . If there are those who receive the four Gospels but do not think that the apparent inconsistency is solved through non-literal exegesis, let such people tell [how else to solve it]" (10.3.10)." (The translations are by the present writer following the text and numbering of the *Sources Chrétiennes* edition listed in the "For Further Study" section.) Two points need noting here. The first is Origen's sensitivity to the difficulties found in reconciling accounts of the same event found in the Gospels. The second is his reference to an "apparent inconsistency" that arises when one compares accounts of the same event in several Gospels. Origen's expression suggests that for him, such discrepancies are merely apparent, not real; the reality of Scripture is found by going beyond difficulties in the literal sense to the truth which is real, spiritual in nature, and which unites Holy Scripture. In this regard, one may see the combination of Platonic insistence upon a higher reality with the Stoic confidence that such reality may be perceived by proper interpretation of the visible world.

Further on in his commentary on John (X.4.15-17), Origen presents a defense of Scripture based upon an argument that an omnipotent God can reveal his purposes in different ways to different people. A critical element in his argument, however, is a phrase found in the beginning of the section now under consideration; not only do the writers of Scripture have different perspectives, but they also see God in the spirit. Truth, therefore, may be communicated directly to the human mind; this is a contribution of Platonism to Origen's exegesis. Differences in the Gospel accounts, therefore, are not merely the result of human elements; they arise as well from divine purposes. Purely historical accounts are rooted in the human realm of time and space, but the accounts found in the Gospels have their foundation both in time and space and in the purposes of God which transcend all limitations. Such purposes are revealed not to human physical senses but to the mind, which alone can perceive them.

As a result of his view of God and the inspiration of Scripture, Origen sees in the Gospels a complex interweaving of historical narrative and truths accessible only to the human spirit (X.4.18). In some places, indeed, the Gospel writers have changed some details of what actually happened in order to serve the deeper meaning of their message (X.4.19). For Origen, the transcendent importance of the spiritual realm is such that one may alter accounts of physical realities in order to serve that realm (X.4.20). It is spiritual exegesis that reveals the true harmony of the gospel message (X.6.27).

The theory established by Platonic and Stoic thought enables Origen to turn from a literal to a non-literal treatment of Christ's cleansing of the Temple. In X.23.131 he begins by alluding to statements in Matthew and Luke about seeking, asking, and knocking; he sees the words of Christ as a call to seek the Lord's help in opening things that lie hidden in Scripture. Origen then focuses on John's account of the cleansing of the temple. Turning from literal to symbolic meaning, he finds one element of truth when one compares Jerusalem to the church; both have citizens who still live in sin (X.33.131-32). A second approach interprets the Lord's cleansing of the temple as the announcement that the sacrifices performed by the Jews in the temple are about to pass away. Origen's vocabulary in this second exegesis is striking. He calls the sacrifices "perceptible to the senses" (X.24.138), indicating that he sees them as belonging to the world of sense experience and not to spiritual reality. Furthermore, the Jews are called "bodily Jews"; for Origen, the term "body" is connected with the literal understanding of the Scriptures.

To understand Origen's terminology in X.24.138, one must turn to a central passage in *On First Principles*. Following the Greek text of Prov. 22:20-21, which advises the reader to gain wisdom "in a threefold way," (Greek *trissōs*), Origen connects his anthropology of body, soul, and spirit to the interpretation of Scripture (*On First Principles* IV.ii.4). The "body" is the literal sense; the soul and spirit represent successively higher understandings of Scripture. The sacrifices in the temple, therefore, are of a lower order than that established by Christ.

Even in his consideration of the possibility of a literal interpretation, Origen shows the predominance which the spiritual meaning of Scripture has for him. To make sense of the passage literally, one must appeal to Christ's divine power, which enabled him to transcend his obscurity and perform a mighty act in the temple (X.25.148). In the midst of this discussion, however, Origen appears to dismiss the event on a literal level with the clause "if it really has occurred." Origen thus shows that fidelity to the literal meaning is not necessary for finding the truth of the passage. Whether the event occurred or not, the priority is not what is accessible to the senses but what is accessible to the mind.

Theodore

When one turns to the commentary by Theodore of Mopsuestia on John, one enters into a radically different approach. While Origen can spend page after page on one verse, or even one phrase, Theodore's work (in its surviving form) is short and to the point. The differences, however, go beyond matters of style. Origen seeks the spiritual sense that raises the soul to contemplate divine reality; while also holding to divine reality, Theodore nevertheless roots his exegesis as much as possible in the literal sense. Where there are difficulties, Origen tends to seek the truth outside the literal sense. The Alexandrian finds the chronologies of the Gospels hard to reconcile, and that Christ's exploits in the temple are difficult to understand literally; such perplexities suggest to Origen that the truth lies in something other than the letter of the text. Concerning the same difficulties, however, Theodore says the following (*Commentary on John*, 43):

> As I said before, the evangelist seems to be giving his account not in the order in which the events occurred; he seems rather to omit a number of things that took place in the intervening time. For the Lord would not have immediately approached such a great task if he had not made himself known already by miracles; nor would those carrying out commerce in the temple have allowed themselves to be cast out if it had been some obscure man who was doing the deed. (The translations are by the present writer following the text and page numbers of the Latin translation by Vosté listed in the "For Further Study" section.)

In this passage, the Antiochene explains that Jesus' ability to do what he did presupposes certain events that John has omitted and which, by implication, may be read in the other Gospels.

There is no appeal to a deeper meaning, but rather an explanation based upon a common practice of omitting certain points in order to promote one's message.

Theodore insists on staying as close as possible to a literal understanding of the text, and he understands the text as being written in a certain context by certain rules that are well known to human writers. His insistence upon a historical context for passages has as a remarkable result that passages taken as messianic prophecies in the Old Testament by other exegetes are not so taken by Theodore. An excellent example of this approach is found in his treatment of John's account under consideration (*Commentary on John*, 42):

> His disciples remembered that it had been written, "Zeal for your house has consumed me"[John 2:17]. This had not been said of him [i.e., Christ] in prophecy; rather, he was doing in suitable fashion what was fitting for the temple. For it is a characteristic of the righteous to have zeal for the house of God and to keep from it all that is unsuitable. The quotation from Ps. 69:9 in John is not understood as prophetic by Theodore, and his comments give insight into the way in which he treats the Old Testament. That portion of Scripture is sufficiently explained by its own context; one need not spiritualize it to make sense of it. Its use in the New Testament in reference to Christ is not one of prophetic fulfillment but rather one of suitability, in much the same way that modern Christians might speak of someone as having the patience of Job or the faith of Abraham. To make such comparisons in no way implies that Abraham and Job are symbols of which the person spoken of is a fulfillment; it is simply a matter that the comparison seems apt, but it was not the intention of the writers recording accounts of Abraham or Job.

To conclude, however, that Theodore sees no symbolic language in Scripture would be a serious error. Like his counterpart in Alexandria, Theodore seeks knowledge of divine reality, but that knowledge must be based upon the literal meaning of Scripture. Where it is clear to Theodore that Scripture is to be understood symbolically, however, he does so; he sees much of the account of Christ's discussion of the temple as symbolic. Much like Origen, Theodore sees Christ referring symbolically to the end of the Jewish sacrificial system in the temple, an end heralded by Christ's resurrection. Theodore goes on to say (*Commentary on John*, 43):

> Yet our Lord said these things rather obscurely and in a mystical way, just as he was doing those things with a symbolic goal, foreshadowing by allusion his meaning rather than acting openly. For he judged that his hearers were not yet able to understand what he was saying . . .

Theodore's understanding of the Lord's words as symbolic, however, is not based upon his own interpretation but that of John, who in 2:21 makes clear that Jesus is referring to his own body, thus explaining the symbolic meaning of the Lord's words. Theodore thus shows that, wherever possible, spiritual exegesis must find explicit warrant in Scripture itself.

Conclusion

One may see, therefore, that the patristic church had several approaches to the interpretation of Scripture. One, found in Alexandria and typified by Origen, placed the greater priority on the spiritual or non-literal understanding of Scripture. The Alexandrian approach drew from both the Scriptures and philosophy to form a hermeneutic that saw the spiritual realm as the true explanation of the world accessible to physical sense-perception. The other, found in Antioch and typified by Theodore of Mopsuestia, emphasized the literal sense of Scripture and placed greater priority on the world which one could perceive with one's senses; while drawing from Scripture, the Antiochenes were also influenced by Greek philosophy that stressed a view that truth could be found in this world rather than outside of it. Many exegetes, such as Augustine, could be found somewhere in-between the two approaches, although non-literal exegesis, as found in Alexandria, tended to predominate in patristic exegesis. The wide spectrum of hermeneutics, bounded by Alexandria and Antioch, brought forth interpretations often quite different from those of modern interpreters. In their use of other exegetes, both Jewish and Christian, and their employment of philosophy, however, the church fathers laid a foundation upon which later generations could build.

▼

For Further Study

Saint Augustine [Augustine of Hippo, 354-430]. *On Christian Doctrine,* trans. with an introduction by D. W. Robertson Jr. New York: Library of Liberal Arts, 1958.

Burrows, Mark S., and Paul Rorem, eds. *Biblical Hermeneutics in Historical Perspective: Studies in Honor of Karlfried Froehlich on His Sixtieth Birthday.* Grand Rapids: Eerdmans, 1991.

Froehlich, Karlfried, trans. and ed. *Biblical Interpretation in the Early Church.* Sources of Early Christian Thought, ed. William G. Rusch. Philadelphia: Fortress, 1984.

Grant, Robert M., with David Tracy. *A Short History of the Interpretation of the Bible.* 2d ed., revised and enlarged. Philadelphia: Fortress, 1984.

Greer, Rowan A. *Theodore of Mopsuestia: Exegete and Theologian.* London: Faith Press, 1966.

Hanson, R. P. C. *Allegory and Event: A Study of the Sources and Significance of Origen's Interpretation of Scripture.* Richmond: John Knox, 1959.

Origen. *On First Principles.* Trans. G. W. Butterworth, with an Introduction by Henri de Lubac. New York: Harper & Row, Harper Torchbooks, 1966.

―――. *Commentary on the Gospel According to John,* Books 1–10. Trans. Ronald F. Heine. Vol. 80, The Fathers of the Church, ed. Thomas P. Halton. Washington, D.C.: The Catholic University of America, 1989.

Origène [Origen]. *Commentaire sur Saint Jean* [Commentary on the Gospel of John], trans. [into French] by Cécile Blanc. 4 vols. Paris: Sources Chrétiennes, 1966-1982.

Theodori Mopsuesteni [Theodore of Mopsuestia]. *Commentarius in Evangelium Iohannis* [Commentary on the Gospel of John]. Trans. [from Syriac into Latin] by J. M. Vosté. Corpus Scriptorum Christianorum Orientalium. Scriptores Syri, Series Quarta, Tomus III. Louvain: Ex Officina Orientali, 1940.

Torjesen, Karen Jo. *Hermeneutical Procedure and Theological Method in Origen's Exegesis.* New York: de Gruyter, 1986.

Trigg, Joseph W. *Biblical Interpretation.* Vol. 9, Message of the Fathers of the Church, ed. Thomas Halton. Wilmington, Del.: Glazier, 1988.

Zaharopoulos, Dimitri Z. *Theodore of Mopsuestia on the Bible: A Study of His Old Testament Exegesis.* Theological Inquiries, ed. Lawrence Boadt. Mahwah, N.J.: Paulist, 1989.

▼

Chapter Four

The Hermeneutics of the Medieval and Reformation Era

Jim Spivey

Augustinian Hermeneutics

The first Latin guidebook for interpreting the Bible was written by the Donatist theologian Tyconius. His *Book of Rules* listed seven mystical principles for unlocking hidden scriptural treasures by seeking bipolar themes in the text. His goal was ecclesiological: to explain the biblical message to and about the church. He became influential throughout the West because of the impression he made on Augustine, the Donatists' staunchest opponent. In *On Christian Doctrine* Augustine modified Tyconius's rules and so unwittingly commended them to medieval scholars for a thousand years. Augustine's own exegesis bears Tyconian ecclesiological, bipolar, and mystical emphases.

Augustine held a high view of Scripture: divinely inspired, it is without error and of supreme authority in matters of faith. With respect to its purpose, to bring salvation, the message is simple; but beyond that it is sublimely suprarational. Because unaided human reason cannot penetrate its profound truths, one must come to the Bible first in faith. It is faith which informs understanding, not vice versa. He said the goal of Bible study should be to learn how to love God and one's neighbor. Therefore he guided interpretation by the two-fold law of love: glean from it the principles of a pure life, which teach how to love God and one's neighbor; and learn sound doctrine, which gives true knowledge about God and humankind.

Augustine also held a high view of the church. Attributing to it authority secondary only to Scripture, he said there is no salvation apart from the church. Only within the church is the law of love truly operable: it mediates the knowledge for salvation, and a pure life cannot be maintained outside of it. God saves by grace: first by the drawing power of the Holy Spirit, then by the witness of the church which leads to faith in the truthfulness of Scripture. To guard true doctrine and to guide the believer, the church developed the *regula fidei*, the rule of faith based on apostolic teaching, patristic writings, decisions of church councils, and creeds. Consequently, Augustine opposed private interpretation because he said it encouraged speculation beyond the rule of faith and led to heresy. Thus he developed a hermeneutical scheme based on three principles: come to the Bible in faith, stay within the *regula fidei*, and apply the law of love.

On Christian Doctrine listed specific interpretive rules: know and use the original languages; remember that words do not mean the same thing in all contexts; explain obscure passages by clear ones; understand numerology; apply secular knowledge and experience when appropriate; and determine the literal and the figurative senses. The last two points were particularly important. Viewing the arts and sciences as tools for enhancing biblical hermeneutics, Augustine integrated grammar, rhetoric, logic, and natural studies into his interpretive scheme. Regarding the literal and the figurative senses, he blended the Alexandrian and the Antiochene approaches. By grammatical-historical analysis he first determined the author's intent and then subjected it to the law of love. He allowed the literal (Antiochene) meaning to stand if it reflected purity and sound doctrine. Otherwise, he searched for the figurative (Alexandrian) sense. Before his conversion from Manichaeism, Augustine had struggled with this issue. His dualistic, literal views of the Old Testament caused him to reject Christianity until Ambrose showed him how allegory and progressive revelation could harmonize it with the New Testament. Afterward, Augustine warned that legalistic literalism could lead to heresy, but he still emphasized the value of determining the literal sense. To avoid fanciful spiritualism, the figurative had to be built upon the literal and kept within the boundary of the rule of faith.

Augustine analyzed words according to four categories of classical rhetoric: history, showing what was done; aetiology, telling why it was done; analogy, confirming harmony between the two testaments; and allegory, giving the figurative sense. He did not, however, use the medieval "four sense" method of interpretation. He interpreted only two ways: literally and figuratively. Still, his use of allegory was extensive: he aimed at unlocking biblical symbols in order to unveil metaphysical reality. Recognizing a qualitative difference between the two testaments, he argued for the essential unity of the message, to which he applied the principle of progressive revelation. Though Augustine believed every part of Scripture to be true, he did not treat it as a technical guide to science or history. Instead, he said that God had accommodated to humankind by communicating through imperfect men and in inconsistent human languages. More than the form, what really mattered to Augustine was the content of the message: the Bible is thoroughly true, without any deception, and its message infallibly accomplishes its purpose of salvation.

Augustine's influence on medieval interpretation was pervasive. During most of that period *On Christian Doctrine* was the most complete outline of Christian teaching, and his *City of God* was the most popular book after the Bible. Both of these works transmitted elements of Neoplatonism, classical learning, and ecclesiasticism. His fervent, mystical Neoplatonistism and preference for allegory encouraged the rise of monasticism and the development of a figurative school of interpretation. His emphasis on classical studies influenced three periods of scholarly renaissance: ninth century Carolingians revived the liberal arts; dialectics (logic) motivated twelfth century Scholastics to refocus theological enquiry; and fourteenth century humanists rediscovered the value of grammatical-rhetorical criticism in hermeneutics. Conversely, Augustine's rule of faith, his submission to churchly authority, and his use of ecclesiastical motifs to define reality encouraged acquiescence to ecclesiological uniformity and contributed to the ossification of hermeneutics.

Early Medieval Hermeneutics

By the sixth century, the relation between revelation and reason had not been clarified and scholars hardly used natural theology. Instead, they used the Bible as a guide to explain every natural and supernatural circumstance. They considered the Bible to be filled with many meanings. Influenced by Platonism, which viewed the visible world as a typology of metaphysical reality, they said that the words of the Bible symbolized God's truth. To understand that truth, the word symbols had to be interpreted. Later Latin fathers had done this by adding a fourth category to Origen's triple meaning of Scripture. Using this model John Cassianus influenced all later interpreters with his monastic study guide, *Conlationes*, which dealt with four senses of the text: literal, moral (how to live the daily Christian life), allegorical (symbolic of Christ), and anagogical (applied to ultimate salvation).

The Fathers had constructed theology exegetically, directly upon biblical interpretation. However, early medieval scholars such as Pope Gregory I and the Venerable Bede compiled their theology by borrowing from those patristic sources and from comments of successive generations of editors. Step by step their editorial theology distanced itself from Scripture. Gregory's hermeneutic was tropological, looking beyond the literal for the moral sense: how to love God and one's neighbor. For common believers, Gregory said the Bible appealed to the heart in order to effect moral development. But the Bible was also a book of faith which trained the clergy in theology. Gregory relied heavily on the *regula fidei* and a distillation of commentaries for his hermeneutical and theological presuppositions. Doing the same, Bede further tried to explain difficulties in the text by using literary and grammatical rules. The editorial theologians interpreted Scripture like they constructed theology, excessively spiritualizing the text and piecing together patristic citations in a chain of exegesis known as the *catena*. Though adept at collating massive materials, they contributed little to creative hermeneutics.

The purpose of Bible study in the early middle ages was to develop the spiritual life. This depended on the use of the spiritual reading, the *devotio lectio*, developed by monastic schools using Alexandrian allegory. Monks believed that it required special training to unlock the true meaning of Scripture. This did not begin as a conspiracy to keep the truth from the people, but eventually it led to theological elitism and the sacerdotal elevation of clerics as privileged holders of esoterica.

By the year 800, Bible study was conducted in two ways: the spiritual approach of the monastic schools; and the systematic approach of the cathedral schools, which had emerged in response to Charlemagne's educational decrees initiating the Carolingian renaissance. A leader in this revival was the royal tutor Alcuin. As abbot of Tours he renewed the use of the liberal arts and revised the

Vulgate, which had become corrupted through errors in copying. Two hermeneutical approaches flowed from this revival. The monastic schools followed the figurative paradigm of Alcuin's student, the mystical abbot of Fulda, Rabanus Maurus. Taking a more systematic approach, Gerbert of Aurillac, later Pope Sylvester II, revived the use of dialectics in the cathedral schools. Using Aristotle's two elementary works on logic and Boethius's three treatises on argument, he launched an intellectual revival that transformed hermeneutics, philosophy, and theology.

As archbishop of Canterbury, Lanfranc introduced this logical and grammatically precise style to England. Treating hermeneutics as a teaching discipline, he became a leading proponent of the gloss: the marginal or interlinear notes copied by students during lectures based on the "rule of faith" and editorial theology. As lecture notes were distilled by successive generations of students, the gloss developed into a commentary which set a new standard for interpretation. Lanfranc also used the "disputed question," another teaching method of the cathedral schools. By posing and answering questions from the gloss as they worked through the biblical text, students constructed a biblical theology. But in contrast to patristic biblical theology, which was exegetical, this method continued the editorial practices of Gregory and Bede.

In the twelfth century, Abelard and other systematic theologians affected hermeneutics by beginning a process which gradually separated theology from the study of Scripture. In *Sic et Non* Abelard reformulated theology by challenging traditional dotrine in a dialectical, skeptical fashion. He also took a critical look at Scripture. He distinguished the Word of God from the Bible and discriminated between its more and less important parts. He focused on the literal sense, but recognizing that the literal could have figurative imagery within it, he allowed allegorical interpretation. His approach was different from that of Anselm, who believed in order to understand; Abelard understood (and doubted) in order to believe. He applied his critical dialectical method of questioning to Scripture also because he said that even the Bible could be corrupted by scribal errors. *Sic et Non* proved that creative proof-texting could make the Bible say mutually contradictory things. The implication was that it is important to read the Bible in context. Abelard's rational, dialectic method produced two responses: the rationalism of Peter Lombard and the mysticism of Bernard of Clairveaux.

Lombard systematized Abelard's approach in his *Four Books of Sentences*, a dogmatic theology of patristic tradition which became the standard theological textbook until Aquinas's *Summa Theologica*. The most important hermeneutical controversy during this period, however, was between Bernard and Abelard. Bernard was a conservative monk who studied the Bible to learn how to love God. He interpreted by use of the *regula fidei* and accepted church tradition by faith. Abelard was a progressive, skeptical philosopher-monk. His disputational method suggested that the link between the Bible and church tradition was not always so obvious. He said logic was a more effective tool than dogmatic faith for establishing that link. Therefore he subjected traditional dogma to rational, dialectical analysis in order to substantiate its validity. As a result, he simultaneously separated theology from the study of Scripture and bridged the gulf with rationalism. This influenced the universities, which gradually shifted the focus of theological studies from the Bible to rhetoric, logic, and dialectic.

Another difference between Bernard and Abelard was how philosophy affected their hermeneutics. Bernard viewed the Bible as a Platonist: God's truth, or universals, was expressed in symbols. When that truth was unclear, the symbols had to be explained by using allegory. Influenced by Aristotle, Abelard discovered truth from the literal meaning by using logical deduction. Abelard's method was rational and empirical; Bernard's was mystical and allegorical. Bernard's was not an anti-intellectual method; he also used enlightened methods of criticism and served as one of Lombard's patrons. What bothered him was Abelard's skepticism. Though Abelard's hermeneutic prevailed, the "four senses" and Bernard's spiritual method were so embedded in the gloss that the allegorical method remained an integral part of medieval hermeneutics, even when later Scholastic theologians refined the deductive process.

Meanwhile, monks of the Abbey of St. Victor near Paris struck a hermeneutical compromise. The Victorines blended the contemplative and the scholastic approaches by teaching systematic theology and maintaining monastic spirituality. Influenced by Jewish scholars, they developed an interest in Hebrew studies which drove them to rediscover the literal sense of the Old Testament. Hugh of St. Victor looked for the deeper sense, but he began with the literal intent of the author. Following the Antiochenes, he tried to understand biblical prophecy both in historical context and in light of messianic fulfilment. He approved of Abelard's dialectic inquiry, but he said the path to truth only began there: such "cogitation" should lead to "meditation" (going beyond sense experience) and then to "contemplation" (knowing God by intellect, love, and grace). While some western scholars were influenced by Jewish Kabbalists, with their esoteric symbols and numerology, others were more concerned with parrying the attacks on Christianity made by Jewish literalists. Christians used three approaches. Ralph of St. Germer interpreted the Pentateuch figuratively in order to show the relevancy of the Law to the Gospel. Others, influenced by the Jewish Aristotelian philospher Maimonides, adopted a literal hermeneutic. John of LaRochelle blended principles from the literal and the figurative schools.

Late Medieval Hermeneutics

Six factors affected the development of hermeneutics after the twelfth century: university scholarship, literalism, scientific inquiry, religious dissent, the mendicant orders, and Aristotelian studies. The universities became centers of scholasticism: Schoolmen who applied logical deduction to propositions from the *regula fidei* and the glosses invented a systematic theology that the church wielded authoritatively in every realm of life. They integrated the liberal arts into hermeneutical studies and devoted more attention to discrepancies between the Vulgate and Greek witnesses found in patristic commentaries. Dividing the Vulgate into chapters and verses made passages easier to find and encouraged the development of concordances, lexicons, and Bible dictionaries. They also interjected new sections of gloss known as "postilla" (additions) between the lines of text. These postillae became the basis for the first printed biblical commentaries.

The Victorine method of literal interpretation was popularized by Thomas Aquinas and Nicholas of Lyra. Nicholas placed special emphasis on historical studies. Opposing the literalistic trend was the apocalyptist, Joachim of Fiore. Interpreting names and numbers symbolically, he derived a three-phase dispensational scheme of history from the Bible which anticipated the imminent advent of the "spiritual church." He believed that the purpose of Bible study was not to undergird Roman Catholic doctrine; Scripture was a coded prophecy of current and future events, a divine message which brought the church of his day under criticism.

The writings of Robert Grosseteste and Roger Bacon, plus a general renewed interest in Aristotle, stimulated scientific inquiry. Thus encouraged to rely on reason in search of empirical evidence, some biblical scholars rejected the Platonistic method of searching a text for countless subjective meanings.

Two dissenting groups with unique hermeneutical styles arose to challenge the status quo. The Cathari, a dualistic sect which interpreted all the Bible allegorically, opposed the church for its literalism. The Waldenses, however, advocated literalism. Opposing both the Catharists and the worldly Roman church, the Waldenses called for a simple lifestyle and reform based on the plain gospel message. What made them such a threat was that they spread vernacular texts of Scripture which popularized their views and gained them widespread support.

The mendicant orders, religious groups whose members originally lived on what they obtained by begging, affected both hermeneutics and theology. The mendicants called Franciscans embraced poverty based on a simple hermeneutic: obey the literal mandates of New Testament discipleship. Though Francis himself opposed the elaborate systems of scholastic theologians, eventually his followers were drawn into the university setting in order to prepare for the preaching ministry. The Dominicans felt more comfortable in the schools than the Franciscans, for there they developed the requisite tools to fulfil Dominic Guzman's vision of evangelizing the heathen and fighting heresy. Though both orders were trained in a literal hermeneutic, they also learned the spiritual meaning in the glosses because it conveyed traditions of the church which helped them fight heresy.

The introduction of the rest of Aristotle's works on logic into the West influenced hermeneutics in several ways. Since Abelard, theologians had been separating theology further from biblical study. Because Aristotle's pagan philosophical ideas were inconsistent with Christian doctrine, this gulf widened and led to three responses. Bonaventura, preserving Augustine's pure doctrine and Bernard's mysticism, rejected philosophic ideas opposing faith. Latin 'Averroists' accepted much of Aristotelianism opposing Christian doctrine on the basis that both could be true while being in apparent conflict. Thomas Aquinas contended that both theology and philosophy contained truth and that they did not conflict: natural truth can be explained by philosophy, but supernatural truth comes only by revelation. Where Aristotle disagreed with

Christian doctrine, Aquinas argued against him with both reason and revelation. So Aquinas combined the rationalism of one school and the faith of the other.

Aristotle's precise logic caused commentators to sharpen their critical examination of the text. His materialistic philosophy encouraged scholars like Albert Magnus and Aquinas to focus on the literal meaning. Regarding most of the allegorical glosses as illogical, Albert said a true spiritual sense could be determined only by properly deducing from the literal meaning. Aquinas added that when biblical authors used metaphors, it was wrong to derive spiritual meaning beyond the author's obvious intent: the moral sense of a text often was the literal sense. Regarding the Law, he charted a middle course between literalism and spiritual exegesis. While allowing for allegory, this approach also laid a foundation for research in literal interpretation. For devotional Bible study Aquinas allowed allegorical exegesis. In his commentaries, he used spiritual interpretations from the Fathers to expand the glosses. But in theological research he focused on the literal meaning. While he cited more Scripture than any other Scholastic theologian, Aquinas did this in the form of proof-texting to show that Roman dogma agreed with the Bible. Then, as a typical Dominican he used Aristotelian deduction to prove this consistency and to develop an elaborate, systematic theology. Though the Franciscans depended more on mysticism and allegorical exegesis, both Mendicant orders relied on a common hermeneutical base: that the Bible and church doctrine were in total agreement.

This view began to change in the thirteenth century. Scholars began challenging the apparent consistency between dogma and Scripture. In trying to integrate Aristotelian methods with spiritual interpretation, Henry of Ghent suggested it was possible for doctrine and Scripture to disagree. In fact they differed greatly, but this was not readily apparent because theologians had divorced theology from Bible study. Aquinas's followers, the Thomists, could lay only tenuous claim to scriptural support for their doctrine because their doctrine was derived ultimately from dogmatic presuppositions confirmed by deductive logic. Theirs was a philosophical theology, not a biblical one. Once William of Occam began to challenge the philosophic link, inconsistencies between their doctrine and Scripture became apparent. Holding that theological truth could not be demonstrated fully by pure reason, Occam and the nominalists argued that theological truth could be discerned only by faith in response to revelation. This led to renewed inductive Bible study and to further discoveries of incompatibility between the text and Roman dogma. Some scholars responded by accepting the Bible and the pope as independent and equal sources of authority. By disallowing the Thomist philosophical link, these scholars completed the separation of theology from Bible study.

Other scholars, like John Wycliffe, did the opposite. Influenced by the teachings of Thomas Bradwardine, Wycliffe was drawn away from nominalistic skepticism toward Platonistic realism and Augustinian theology. For him the Bible was an all-sufficient guide without contradictions; mirroring the truth of God, it gave access to metaphysical reality. Wycliffe not only insisted on the primacy of Scripture; he also refused to separate theology from the Bible and laid a foundation for reform by calling for church doctrine and practice to line up with Scripture. Using Augustine's principles, Wycliffe believed that the law of love should guide interpretation, that faith precedes understanding, and that the essential message of Scripture is plain to those who submit humbly to illumination by the Holy Spirit. Though colored by allegory, his preaching and his theological works were always built upon the grammatical-historical sense of Scripture, and he said all allegory should have a Christological focus. Wycliffe stood for the priesthood of the believer: individuals could work out their own salvation with the help of the gospel and without the church being the essential mediator of grace. Since this called for a Bible in the common language, he began translating the Vulgate into English. This work was completed after his death, probably by Nicholas of Hereford and John Purvey.

Renaissance Hermeneutics

Wycliffe's hermeneutic reflected Renaissance thinking. During this period intellectual renewal and rising humanism, with its premium on individual worth, began undercutting medieval philosophy, theology, and ecclesiology. While Scholastic philosophers built elaborate, subtle systems of logic upon layers of sources, humanists appealed directly to ancient writings mainly for their rhetorical, literary value. Interest in classical literature naturally encouraged the study of Greek, and the hermeneutical implications were profound. Scholars who studied the Greek New Testament for its linguistic value were both shaped by its message and motivated to examine its text critically.

These Renaissance emphases led to four key hermeneutical developments.

- Christian humanists employed textual criticism to determine the authorship, dating, and quality of texts. Foremost among the early critics were Lorenzo Valla and Desiderius Erasmus. Valla disproved the validity of the Donation of Constantine, challenged the traditional authorship of the Apostles' Creed and the works of Dionysius the Aereopagite, and pointed to mistakes in Scholastic theology derived from erroneous texts in the Vulgate. Influenced by Valla's *Annotations*, Erasmus used critical principles to identify spurious texts and to reveal errors of the Schoolmen.

- Christian humanists emphasized literal interpretation as the primary means of finding the essential meaning.

- Christian humanists translated the Bible directly, without the aid of glosses, and developed a tradition of private judgment which the church criticized.

- Christian humanists studied the Bible in the original languages and published printed editions of the Bible in the original languages.

The first printed Hebrew Bible was produced in 1488. In 1506, Johannes Reuchlin set the standard for Hebrew scholarship by publishing a comprehensive grammar-lexicon. His friend Erasmus assumed the same role in Greek studies. He was in a race with Cardinal Francisco Ximenez, who had called for the first printed Greek New Testament in 1514. Erasmus won the contest in 1516. His first desire was to produce a truly reliable Greek text, but in his haste to beat Ximenez he depended on inferior sources. Though it took him two more editions to produce a truly reliable version, his first edition circulated widely and became one of the most significant influences leading to the Reformation. His second desire was to publish a Latin version superior to the Vulgate which would be more accessible to common people. He translated this from the Greek version and published it in 1519. Believing that Bible study was rooted in rhetoric and grammar, not in dialectics, he maintained that theology should be exegetical not philosophical. He said sound exegesis could be done only from the original languages, by using textual criticism, and by understanding the circumstances of the writer. Though he focused on the literal sense, he also enjoyed the allegory of the Fathers.

Renaissance hermeneutics challenged theological dogmatism in three areas: reason, doctrine, and spirit.

- Christian humanists following Augustine and Occam's *via moderna*, abandoned deductive reasoning in favor of faith. They said the biblical message was simple, and it could be grasped more fully by faith than by convoluted reason.

- Christian humanists under Occam's sway rejected the medieval union of theology and philosophy which had obscured true doctrine. Far from being a complicated science, they said theology should explain plain truths given to the early church, such as the simple message of salvation and how to live practical Christian lives.

- Neoplatonism renewed interest in contemplative hermeneutics which initiated a new era of mystical literature and a school of devotional theology.

Mystical works were most prevalent in Germany and England; key authors were Meister Eckart, Henry Suso, John Tauler, Julian of Norwich, Walter Hilton, and Thomas à Kempis. But it was a protege of the Flemish mystic, Jan van Ruysbroeck, who developed this approach into a school of thought. Gathering a semi-monastic community in Deventer, the Dutch monk Gerhard Groote taught a blend of critical and contemplative Bible study. Beginning with the literal sense, he rejected abstract speculation and used meditation to strengthen personal morality and spirituality. His Brethren of the Common Life spread this hermeneutic throughout northern Europe in the fifteenth and sixteenth centuries, and it became one of the most decisive catalysts of the Reformation.

The grip of ecclesiastical tradition loosened during the Renaissance. Its feudal base eroded, powerful kings usurped its prerogative, humanistic scholars impugned its doctrinal authority and moral integrity, and populist movements arose against it. The last two factors were rooted partly in hermeneutical soil. Much of the scholarly opposition came from grammatical-historical interpreters who urged the church to reform itself according to the clear mandates of Scripture. Some popular resistance was influenced by the apocalyptic hermeneutic of groups such as the Joachimites and the Fraticelli. Populism was partly the consequence of humanists emphasizing the worth of individual persons and enabling the common folk to read the Bible in their own language. A first step in that direction was the invention of the printing press and the production of the first printed text, the Latin Gutenberg (Mazarin) Bible, in 1456. Though Wycliffe and others had translated versions into their own language, it was not until the Reformation that copies in the vernacular were printed and distributed in large quantities.

Reformation Hermeneutics

Renaissance trends encouraged early Protestant reformers to push biblical interpretation full circle. The *via moderna* led them to develop an inductive, faith-oriented hermeneutic similar to Augustine's, and to recover the patristic method of constructing theology exegetically. The *devotio moderna* imbued them with a pietism which emphasized the illuminatory role of the Holy Spirit, while humanism drew them to a critical study of ancient texts in the original languages. They inverted the Scholastic formula that gave reason priority over faith, and they returned to Augustine: they believed in order to understand. This priority of faith and a reexamination of the simple message of Scripture caused them to formulate four hermeneutical principles which challenged Roman Catholic tradition: the focus of Scripture was on Christ, not on the church and man; the ultimate purpose of the Bible was salvation, not knowledge; the basis for Christian doctrine and practice was the Bible, not ecclesiastical tradition; and the authority for interpreting Scripture rests with individuals illumined by the Holy Spirit, not in a dogmatic, priestly hierarchy. These shifts profoundly affected Protestant hermeneutics and theology concerning the issues of authority, faith, clarity, and the analogy of faith.

Regarding authority, Protestants followed Luther in proclaiming *sola scriptura*. They affirmed the Bible as the ultimate source of truth and authority in matters of faith, sufficient to stand alone. They held a high view of biblical inspiration which virtually mirrored Augustine's position. While Scripture is authoritative and infallible in its saving purpose, Luther and Calvin said it was not designed to be scientifically precise. It was communicated incarnationally through human authors: their human words may have been inconsistent and their historical settings may have limited their perspectives, but they never deceived at any point; and their message never erred regarding doctrine and practice. Therefore, the Bible is superior in authority to ecclesiastical tradition.

The shift to a faith-oriented hermeneutic began with Luther's *sola fide*: faith alone justifies. This soteriological principle undergirded an epistemological emphasis on faith. He and Calvin said that biblical truth is inaccessible to human reason unless the interpreter's mind first is informed by faith and illumined by the Holy Spirit. Such faith has two sources. First, it is rooted in an intuitive knowledge of Christ, God's Word revealed personally to the believer by the Holy Spirit. Second, it derives from a confidence that the Bible is the self-authenticating word of God: the message itself and the Holy Spirit's influence convince the believer of this fact. Protestants said this spiritual intuition and confidence enabled individual believers to understand Scripture by exercising their private judgment apart from hierarchical control. So their view of Scripture gave rise to their concept of the sufficiency of the believer. This was fundamental to Luther's doctrine of the priesthood of the believer, which he employed with devastating effect against sacerdotalism. Criticizing the pope for arrogating to himself the sole right of interpretation, Luther said this erected a wall around Scripture which hid the truth.

The Protestant Reformation was unrelenting in its hermeneutical quest for clarity: to penetrate beyond human authority and to peel away layers of tradition in search of plain scriptural meaning. Luther and Calvin did this by rejecting the fourfold sense and adopting Chrysostom's grammatical-historical method of interpretation. Weighing the writer's circumstances, they interpreted the message according to his obvious intent. Though these principles improved scholarly hermeneutics, they were irrelevant to parishioners unskilled in Latin, Greek, and Hebrew. This forced the issue beyond clarity to perspicuity: the Scripture is self-evidently clear, but only to those who can understand its words. Motivated to put the Bible into the hands of the common folk, Luther, Tyndale, and Lefevre published popular translations of the New Testament in German, English, and French in the 1520s. During the 1530s whole Bibles in all three languages achieved wide circulation.

Though advocating the priesthood of the believer, mainstream Protestants realized that private judgment could become excessive and dangerous. They warned against apocalyptic spiritualism and new prophecies claiming extrabiblical authority. So, in steering a middle course between Scholasticism and Spiritualism they used the following rules, collectively known as the "analogy of faith":

- Scripture interprets Scripture by explaining obscure passages in light of clearer ones.

- Exegesis must remain faithful to the context of all Scripture.
- There is an essential, organic Christological unity to the Bible.

They said doctrine should be judged by its measure of consistency with the purpose (salvation) and focus (Christ) of Scripture. Thus presuming the existence of an objective body of essential biblical truth similar to Augustine's *regula fidei*, early Protestant reformers wrote confessions as polemical hedges against heresy. However, by the end of the sixteenth century, Reformed and Lutheran theologians began using them as determinative creeds. While giving tacit assent to *sola scriptura*, in fact these theologians developed a neo-scholastic hermeneutic resembling Roman Catholic methodology, except for Protestant dogmatic presuppositions.

Roman Catholics accurately warned that dissent would produce further schism. Protestants laid claim to ecclesiastical and theological freedom on the basis of a liberated hermeneutic. As they expanded this license, they made new discoveries which elicited more reform, gave birth to new movements, and further altered their hermeneutic. Before the age of neo-scholasticism, the principles of Protestant interpretation were dynamic and highly diverse. This was evident in the way reformers applied biblical law, grammatical-historical interpretation, and *sola scriptura*.

Luther and Calvin differed in their opinions about the relationship between the two testaments. Calvin retrogressively recovered Old Testament themes and gave the law new significance. This led him and Heinrich Bullinger to develop a covenant theology which was further systematized by the federal theologians Zacharius Ursinus, Caspar Olevianus, and Johannes Cocceius. Luther emphasized the progressive development of the testaments, sharply distinguished between the law and the gospel, and diminished the authority of the law over Christians. While Calvin's scheme could be exaggerated into legalism, Luther's view could be distorted into antinomianism. The most radical expression of this came from the millennial rebels of Munster (1533–1535), who were wrongly labelled "Anabaptists." Milder forms of antinomianism later surfaced in several Protestant groups: under Lutheran Johann Agricola, Anglican Tobias Crisp, Presbyterian Joseph Hussey, Congregationalist Ann Hutchinson, and the Quakers. A balanced hermeneutic of the covenants was expressed by the Anabaptist, Pilgram Marpeck. He said the Old Testament was a promise fulfilled by the New Testament, and it was not equally authoritative with the gospel as a norm for the Christian life.

An implicit goal of the grammatical-historical method was to discover original circumstances and meaning. While magisterial reformers such as Luther and Calvin employed this as an exegetical technique, they also gave significant attention to patristic sources, especially in ecclesiological matters. Radical reformers such as the Anabaptists were more consistent. They searched for the primitive doctrine of the New Testament church with a view toward following it as closely as possible. Commitment to this hermeneutical principle drove them to abandon patristic support for the state church, which was not the New Testament model, and to advocate universal freedom of religious conscience. These principles became foundations of the free church movement.

With *sola scriptura* came freedom from extrabiblical authority. At the same time, some radical reformers went so far as to undermine biblical authority itself. In their literalistic, reductionistic zeal to discover the primitive message, humanistic skeptics discarded any doctrine they could not find explicitly articulated in the Bible. Using reason as their final authority, they departed from the analogy of faith and became Socinians, Unitarians, Universalists, or Deists. Spiritualists did the opposite. Embellishing New Testament prophecy with new revelations they said were from the Holy Spirit, they established themselves as prophets of mystical, apocalyptic sects. Examples of those who made the "spirit" their final authority were the Zwickau Prophets, the Swedenborgians, followers of Jacob Boehme, and the Quakers. Anabaptists and Baptists belong to a third tradition of radical reformers who employed a literal, primitivistic hermeneutic but always appealed to Scripture as the final authority.

▼

FOR FURTHER STUDY

Burrows, Mark S., and Paul Rorem, eds. *Biblical Hermeneutics in Historical Perspective.* Grand Rapids: Eerdmans, 1991.

Farrar, Frederic W. *History of Interpretation.* New York: E. P. Dutton, 1886; reprint, Grand Rapids: Baker, 1961.

Froehlich, Karlfried, ed. and trans. *Biblical Interpretation in the Early Church.* Philadephia: Fortress, 1984.

Gallacher, Patrick J., and Helen Damico, eds. *Hermeneutics and Medieval Culture.* Ithaca: State University of New York Press, 1989.

Grant, Robert M. *A Short History of the Interpretation of the Bible.* London: Black, 1965.

Rogers, Jack B., and Donald K. McKim. *The Authority and Interpretation of the Bible: An Historical Approach.* New York: Harper and Row, 1979.

Rogerson, John, Christopher Rowland, and Barnabas Lindars. *The Study and Use of the Bible.* The History of Christian Theology, ed. Paul Avis, vol. 2. Grand Rapids: Eerdmans, 1988.

Smalley, Beryl. *The Study of the Bible in the Middle Ages.* Oxford: Blackwell, 1952.

Steinmetz, David C., ed. *The Bible in the Sixteenth Century.* Durham: Duke University Press, 1990.

Walsh, Katherine, and Diana Wood. *The Bible in the Medieval World: Essays in Memory of Beryl Smalley.* Oxford: Blackwell, 1985.

Chapter Five

Early Baptist Hermeneutics

H. Leon McBeth

"Wee proffess and believe the Holy Scriptures, the Old and New Testament, to be the word and reveled mind of God" (White, 18). Since that statement of the Midlands Association in 1658, Baptists have updated their spelling; but they maintain the same confident faith in the Bible as God's true word to mankind.

The Bible has always been central in the Baptist faith. It was largely a new wave of intense Bible study that brought Baptists into existence as a distinct group in the early seventeenth century. Even before the nickname "Baptist" was tagged on them, this group appealed to the Bible as the basis for every teaching; they cited Scripture to justify their belief and behavior. They would accept no teaching not attested by Scripture. It would be impossible to understand Baptists, in the seventeenth century or the twentieth, apart from their convictions about Scripture.

The purpose of this article is to explore the Baptists' views of the authority, interpretation, and application of Scripture. For the sake of brevity the major emphasis will fall upon early Baptists during the formative era when their primary convictions were hammered out in an environment of opposition and turmoil. These early convictions about Scripture have largely shaped the Baptist witness ever since.

The Authority of Scripture

The Baptists emerged as a separate group in England in the midst of an extensive public debate about the role and teaching of the Bible. The heroic efforts of pioneer translators like Wycliffe, Tyndale, and Coverdale had made the English Bible increasingly available. Rising literacy rates had brought the biblical message to common folk to whom it was new and powerful. The question "What does the Bible teach?" became a crucial public as well as personal concern. No explanation of Baptist origins can neglect the impact of this intense rediscovery of the Bible in seventeenth-century England. It is no wonder that the early Baptist confessions emphasized the Bible.

Early Confessions

To explain their faith to outsiders, and to clarify issues among themselves, the Baptists issued a number of confessions early in their pilgrimage. One of the earliest specifically Baptist confessions was "A Declaration of Faith of English People," put out by the Thomas Helwys group while still in exile in Amsterdam. Under the heading "Wee beleeve and confesse," they said "That the scriptures off the Old and New Testament are written for our instruction, 2. Tim. 3.16 & that wee ought to search them for they testifie off CHRIST, Jo. 5.39. And therefore to bee vsed withall reverence, as conteyning the Holie Word off GOD, which onlie is our direction in al thinges whatsoever."

This pioneer statement affirms the authority of Scripture for every area of the Christian life. It reveals a Christocentric understanding of the Bible, and implies the need for interpretation in the statement that Christians must search the Scriptures. In this statement both testaments are accepted as authoritative, and the Bible is accepted as the basic guide for Christian faith and practice. In accepting the Bible as "conteyning the Holie Word off God," these early Baptists certainly did not imply that only parts of the Bible are true or authoritative.

The famous London Confession of 1644 is rightly regarded as one of the most important Baptist doctrinal statements of all time. Noted for its moderate Calvinism, its emphasis upon evangelism, religious freedom, and believer's baptism by immersion, this confession also includes a strong statement on the authority of Scripture. Article VII says "The Rule of this Knowledge, Faith, and Obedience, concerning the worship and service of God, and all other Christian duties, is not mans inventions, opinions, devices, lawes, constitutions, or traditions unwritten, whatsoever, but onely the word of God contained in the Canonicall Scriptures."

This pointed statement addresses both mystical spiritualism ("mans inventions, opinions, devices") and state church traditionalism ("lawes, constitutions, or traditions"), both prevalent in England. It rules out all forms of human authority in religion in favor of divine authority expressed in Scripture. Only canonical Scripture is accepted. Article VIII goes on to say that the Bible is not only *authoritative*, but also *adequate* in that it reveals to us all that God "thought needfull for us to know, beleeve, and acknowledge." The key to Scripture is Jesus Christ, who is "the Yea and Amen" of God's revelation.

Other confessions continued this theme. A confession in 1651 urged pastors to preach nothing "which is not to be heard or read of in the record of God," and Baptists who issued the *True Gospel Faith* of 1654 said "it's the Scriptures of the Prophets and Apostles that we square our faith and practice by."

Early Challenges

In the seventeenth century Baptists faced a severe challenge from the Quakers, and other mystical types, who rejected the outward Scripture along with outward ordinances such as baptism and the Lord's Supper. This was more than a debate about religious authority, for along with a "spiritual word within" to replace the Bible, many of these mystics also rejected the historical Christ in favor of a "mystical Christ within." These views sometimes led to extremes of subjectivism. Samuel Fisher, a Baptist turned Quaker, wrote that "The believer is the only book in which God now writes his New Testament" (Hill, 208). He would have agreed with another who wrote, "The Bible without is but a shadow of that Bible which is within." In his youth even John Bunyan had briefly considered the Scriptures only "a dead letter, a little ink and paper" (Hill, 210).

This tendency to reject the outward Scriptures also showed up in cases of Baptist church discipline, especially those dealing with Baptists who became Quakers. When reproved by leaders of the Fenstanton church for her views of Scripture, Mrs. William Austin said "she looked upon the scriptures as nothing, she trampled them under her feet." Three years later the same church excluded John Ward for repudiating water baptism and "affirming the scriptures to be a dead letter" (McBeth, *Sourcebook*, 57–60).

Problems like these led the Baptists of London to issue a pamphlet in 1650 with the quaint title of *Heart Bleedings for Professors Abominations.* Apparently some Baptists were leaving the fold, moving on to the Quakers and other radical spiritualists who rejected the need for the written Scriptures. One strand of Baptist life, especially among the General Baptists, seemed vulnerable to this view. Even John Smyth, founder of the earliest Baptist church, later said in "Propositions and Conclusions," a true Christian "needeth not the outwoard scriptures creatures or ordinances of the church." Smyth, somewhat like later Quakers who provided Baptists so much competition, rejected water baptism, literal Lord's Supper, and the need for written Scriptures. Some of these "super-spiritualists" contrasted the *history* (written Scriptures) with the *mystery* (the direct inner light illumination of the Spirit). They valued the *mystery,* but downgraded the *history.*

Heart Bleedings addressed these concerns in 1650 by affirming that the Scripture "is not a bare outward Relation, History, or carnal Letter, but a spiritual and substantial truth and Mystery, containing the whole Minde, Will, and Law of God for us." It went on to say that "the Scriptures which do declare this great mystery of Jesus Christ and his gospel, be the holy Scriptures, and the infallible Word of God" (McBeth, *Sourcebook,* 69).

This was a very important statement, made by baptized believers before they got the nickname "Baptist." It emphasized the importance of the written Scriptures and warned against the dangers of extreme subjectivism. *Heart Bleedings* argues that the Bible is *adequate* and needs no modern supplement; that it is *timely* and not outdated; and that it was given as an *abiding* and not a temporary guide for Christians. This is also the very first Baptist statement of record to use the term "infallible" to describe the Bible. Probably the Baptists picked up the word from the Westminster Confession.

Later Confessions

By far the longest and most elaborate Baptist statement on Scripture came in the second London Confession, issued in 1689. This confession is noted for its rigid Calvinism, its extensive (and sometimes pedantic) doctrinal statements, and a statement on Scripture that is longer than most entire Baptist confessions of the time. It is the first Baptist confession to put the article on Scripture first, and the first formal confession adopted by a group of Baptists to use the term "infallible" to describe the Bible. Article I begins, "The Holy Scripture is the only sufficient, certain, and infallible rule of all saving Knowledge, Faith and Obedience." The confession then lists the books of both Testaments and describes them as "infallible truth" (Lumpkin, 241–295).

From these and other sources, it is clear that early Baptists depended upon the Bible for their religious authority. While they issued confessions, they never elevated these to the status of creeds. They remained leery of all human statements, including those of bishops, ecclesiastical councils, and especially of government authorities who tried to pronounce in areas of religion. The Baptist attitude is summed up in the response of William Kiffin and others during the public debate with the esteemed Daniel Featley held in Southward in 1642. When Featly brought forth his logic, syllogisms, analogies, inferences, and conclusions, the Baptists brushed them aside and said, "Master Doctor, we are not here to discuss those matters. We are here to ask, 'What does the Bible say?'" Then and now, that is the question Baptists want to answer with regard to religious faith.

Interpretation of the Bible

A prominent character in John Bunyan's *Pilgrim's Progress* is Interpreter. Interpreter played a large role in Pilgrim's effort to find his way to the celestial city, and Interpreter's House was a vital place of guidance and renewal for the besieged traveler.

So it was for all the Baptists. For all their emphasis upon the authority of Scripture, the early Baptists realized that the Bible does not yield up its message without careful study and the proper use of the principles of interpretation.

Role of Human Learning

Not all the early Baptists agreed upon the role of human learning in the interpretation of the Bible. As early as 1639 Samuel How, Baptist pastor in London, published a pamphlet with a title so long that one might, by reading the title carefully, skip the treatise: *The Sufficiency of the Spirit's Teaching without Humane Learning: or, a Treatise Tending to prove Humane Learning to be No Help to the Spiritual Understanding of the Word of God.* How and others who agreed with him were no doubt reacting to the elite Anglicans who ridiculed the Baptists as "a mean ministry," made up of husbandmen, haulers, brewers and tinkers who "could not turn over Arabique" much less "dispute sylogistically." Even Hercules Collins, who argued in *The Temple Repair'd* (1702) that every Baptist church should function as a ministerial training center, admitted that "tho it be granted that human Literature is very useful for a Minister, yet it is not essentially necessary; but to have the Spirit of Christ to open the Word of Christ is essentially necessary." No amount of human learning, said Collins, could clarify the spiritual message of the Bible; without the Holy Spirit we are "as ignorant as a wild ass's colt."

However, Deacon Edward Terrill provided in his will for the Broadmead Church to call a pastor who was "well skilled in the tongues" (Hebrew and Greek). This emphasis upon an educated ministry led to the establishment of Bristol College in 1679, the oldest Baptist college in existence and still flourishing today. A later pastor of the Bristol Church, Hugh Evans, preached a sermon entitled "The Able Minister," based on 2 Cor. 3:5–6, in which he said, "The able minister needs to possess a tolerable share of endowments . . . and he needs the improvements of human learning. No profession needs this more than the ministry, when such learning is sanctified and humbly devoted to the service of God" (Moon, 15).

Heart Bleedings, cited above, warned Baptists that the mere quoting of biblical verses and phrases, without interpretation, was of little value. The writer notes that some false teachers quote Scripture but twist it so that it comes out as "swelling words of vanity, . . . a great mystery of nothing but emptiness." This pamphlet also points out the dangers of "vain allegorizings" of Scripture and laments that many are thus led away from the true message of the Bible. In a warning that seems equally relevant today, this pamphlet warns Baptists that "many poor souls knowing such expressions to be Scripture Phrases, do greedily embrace them without a true, distinct, and cleer understanding the sense of what is spoken."

In *The Temple Repair'd*, Hercules Collins emphasized the importance of careful study in understanding the Bible. Citing 2 Tim. 3:16, he said even devout believers should not expect to understand the Bible without diligent study. He also noted that proper Bible study takes time; the preacher who waits until Saturday to prepare his Sunday sermon is likely to have "but a lean Discourse." He concluded that "it is their Sin that preach and neglect Study."

Collins insisted that laymen have both the ability and the right to interpret Scripture for themselves, thus setting Baptists free from the "tyranny of the experts." He said the teachings of Old and New Testaments, while they may differ in their interest and immediate relevance, are "equally authentick" and "have the same Authority over Mens Consciences." Collins emphasized that biblical interpretation should follow the "analogy of faith." He said, "Never interpret one Text so as to thwart another; abandon all private Opinions, tho they are never so taking."

Principles of Interpretation

Citing 2 Pet. 1:20, Collins set out one of the most important principles of hermeneutics for early Baptists. This pioneer Baptist leader pointed out in *The Temple Repair'd* (27-28) that "Peter saith, No scripture is of any private Interpretation; that is, no particular Scripture differs from the whole, or any part of it. No Man, nor no Company of Men, no Church or publick Officers are to interpret the Scriptures of their own heads, according to their own Minds, so as to make their private sense the sense of the Scripture, but to seek the understanding of it from God, who shews the meaning of the Word by the Word itself, . . . the more obscure places being expounded by the more clear." The Scriptures then are their own best expositors: "No Man, nor no Church, can explain God's Word better that it doth itself" (26).

In interpreting a Scripture passage, Collins taught, one should first examine the background. In a passage that could easily come from a modern work on hermeneutics, Collins said one must first determine the author, date, occasion and overall scope of the passage studied. Those who know the biblical languages should use them, along with lexicons and dictionaries, for word studies. Collins also recommended the use of commentaries, and listed some of those considered helpful in his day.

Though Collins warns against excessive use of "Metaphors and Similitudes," he is himself not immune to similar problems. Like other Baptists of the time (and most other Protestants as well), Collins interpreted the Song of Solomon as "the sweet Conference between Christ and his Church" (45). Collins also refused to take an overly literal interpretation of 1 Tim. 3:12 ("Let the deacons be the husband of one wife"). He attested in *The Temple Repair'd* (53–54): "It is not absolutely necessary that he should be a married Man, but supposing him so, he must be the Husband of one Wife: The meaning of the Apostle is, he must not be a lover of Poligamy (sic), i.e. to have more Wives than one at a time, as many of the Jews and Ethnicks of the Eastern Nations."

The Baptists of 1689 admitted their need for help in understanding the Bible. They said, "We acknowledge the inward illumination of the Spirit of God to be necessary for saving under-standing" and observed that "All things in Scripture are not alike plain in themselves, nor alike clear unto all." They said also that "the infallible rule of interpretation of Scripture is the Scripture it-self: And therefore when there is a question about the true and full sense of any Scripture . . . it must be searched by other places that speak more clearly."

A Theology of Scripture

One of the earliest Baptist statements on a theology of Scripture was made by Thomas Collier in 1651. Collier was an energetic pas-tor, church planter and theologian in the West of England. During his long life he published over thirty books, established a number of Baptist churches, led in forming an association, and served as a "messenger" of that association (somewhat like a director of mis-sions in modern times). Collier is also known for his middle-of-the-road theology which tried to overcome the sharp differences be-tween General and Regular Baptists. Collier probably could be called the first systematic theologian among Baptists.

In 1651 Collier published *A General Epistle to the Universal Church of the First-Born.* Chapter ten of this major book deals with the doctrine of Scripture. In this chapter Collier reacted both to the rationalists on the right who, he thought, almost deified the text of Scripture; and the radical mystics on the left who downgraded the written Scripture. He said, "Scripture is abused by most in making too much of it [setting it up in the place of God], so it is [also abused] by many in making too little of it, looking on it as a thing of nought" (McBeth, *Sourcebook*, 53–54). Collier emphasized the importance of Scripture, and considered no doctrine acceptable unless it was supported by Scripture. He was careful to show that these abuses were not due to any defect in Scripture itself: "Not that I say the fault's on Scripture, but on mens Idolatrous and lying and perfidious hearts to abuse it, in making that use of it for which it was never written" (*General Epistle*, 248). Collier also distinguished between the Word of God Incarnate (as in John 1:1–18) and the Word of God Written (the Bible). He affirmed that *worship* of the Word Incarnate is proper, but worship of the Word Written is idol-atry.

Collier sought to refute the Quakers, who at that time and place were making severe inroads upon Baptists. The Quakers felt they must outgrow the written Scriptures, which were literal and ele-mentary, mere words on paper, "a carnal letter" as they called it.

They preferred the direct illumination of the Holy Spirit through the "inner light." Collier sought to show that the Holy Spirit *does* work through the Scripture. The same Spirit who inspired the writing of Scripture also guides the believer in understanding and applies the message of Scripture to the individual heart. The Baptist theologian rejected the idea that by depending upon the written Word, one was thereby rejecting the presence and power of the Holy Spirit. Collier said of Scripture (*General Epistle*, 248): "That it is not sufficient in it self as it is a Letter, or word written, to teach or bring any man to the knowledge of God; although God be declared in it, yet that declaration without God powerfully working in the declaration of himself, to and in the spirits of men, they never by this or any other means come to the true and saving knowledge of him."

When the Baptists of the early seventeenth century appealed to the authority of Scripture, some sought to dismiss their claims by saying that Baptists had never read the Scripture. Only the original manuscripts in Hebrew and Greek are *really* Scripture, they said, and since most Baptists did not read these languages, the Scripture was a closed book to them. Collier said, "Many of those who are both Scholars, and, as they say, Teachers in England, affirm that Englishmen never reade the Scripture, because they never reade it in the Original." The Baptist theologian strongly rejected these arrogant claims. He asserts that an English translation can and does convey the authentic message of Scripture; that laymen as well as scholars may read and interpret; and that textual variations in Scripture texts form no barrier to its faithful transfer of truth.

"I cannot judge that the Scripture was ever written according to the strict rules of Grammar," said Collier, unless "poor Fishermen . . . were as well furnished with the Smoak of the bottomless pit as university men" (249). The fact that the "divine Originalls" of Scripture are no longer available did not trouble Collier at all, nor did the fact that extant Hebrew and Greek manuscripts have variant readings at places. He said "Neither that I am ignorant of the possibility, nay the probability of corruption in it [variant readings in Scripture manuscripts], and in the Greek and Hebrew too, commonly called the Original; although it be true, no man ever living saw the Original Copies. . . . not that it is any Article of my Faith to believe every word or circumstance there written; but what Truth God hath made known in me, that I must acknowledge" (*General Epistle*, 250).

To those who contended that truth could be found only in the original copies of Scripture, Collier affirmed that "there is a way by which the Saints may come to judge of Scripture, and that according to the Original too, that is by the Spirit, which is the Original of all Truth" (250).

Clearly the early Baptists saw the need for interpretation of Scripture and, for the most part, they followed good principles of hermeneutics. If they fell occasionally into allegory and "spiritualizing" of texts, as Benjamin Keach did, they did so less than most of their day. Baptists were fortunate to have such sane and solid interpreters as William Kiffin, Thomas Collier, Thomas Grantham, Hercules Collins, and others to lead by precept and example in biblical interpretation.

The Application of Scripture

The early Baptists not only *accepted* and *interpreted* the Bible, they also sought to *apply* its teachings to themselves and the issues of their day. Whether in Benjamin Keach's *Exposition of the Parables*, John Bunyan's *Justification by Imputed Righteousness*, or Andrew Fuller's *Gospel Worthy of All Acceptation*, the Baptists sought to discover not only what the Bible *said* in the past, but also what it *says* to us in the present.

For Baptists, Bible study was more than a mere academic exercise. They wanted to discover where the Bible touched their lives, where its message impacted them personally. They wanted to know what the Bible *said*, what it *says*, and what *response* they should make. To the Baptists, Bible study was intensely practical. If we today find fault with some of their applications, we must at least credit them with an honest effort to go beyond a mere historical understanding of the Bible's message.

The early Baptists frequently used a phrase, to "improve the text" of Scripture. By this they did not mean they could make the text better. By this phrase they meant *applying* the text to themselves, to their own local situation and experience. The Baptists often used current events, especially calamities, as a vehicle for expressing biblical truth. They asked, "What is God saying to us in this event? What Scripture passage best explains or makes sense of this event?" They would find a biblical passage that seemed to describe or fit a current happening and apply the Scripture to that event. They usually stopped short of saying that any current event was what the Bible was speaking about; they knew that most biblical accounts were first directed to situations in an earlier time.

However, they often said that the Scripture truths *applied* to the current event, that some current event *elucidated* or *illustrated* or *reinforced* Scripture truths. Many Baptists were adept at "improving the Scripture," that is, showing how some current event expressed the truths of Scripture.

In that day before modern newspapers, to say nothing of television, the preacher served a role now taken over by newspaper columnists and television reporters: that is, offering a *commentary* on the news to show its meaning and relevance. While the Baptist preachers then would hardly appear in the pulpit with the Bible in one hand and a newspaper in the other, seeking to correlate the two, they certainly did more than most Baptists today in seeking to interpret the message of God in current events.

Summary

Baptists today still hold the basic views of the Bible that were hammered out early in the Baptist pilgrimage. The firm conviction that the Bible is God's authoritative word to us abides. When Baptists are at their best, they follow the same principles of interpretation that early Baptists hammered out in the seventeenth century. And, like the Baptists of old, Baptists still try to discern not only what the Bible *said*, but also what it *says* to us today.

▼

For Further Study

Collier, Thomas. *A General Epistle to the Universal Church of the First-Born.* London: N.p., 1651.

Collins, Hercules. *The Temple Repair'd.* London: N.p., 1702.

Hill, Christopher. *The World Turned Upside Down: Radical Ideas During the English Revolution.* London: Temple Smith, 1972.

Lumpkin, William L., ed. *Baptist Confessions of Faith.* Valley Forge: Judson, 1959.

McBeth, H. Leon. *Four Centuries of Baptist Witness.* Nashville: Broadman, 1987.

———. *A Sourcebook for Baptist Heritage.* Nashville: Broadman, 1990.

Moon, Norman. *Education for Ministry: Bristol Baptist College, 1679-1979.* Bristol: Bristol Baptist College, 1979.

Smyth, John. *Propositions and Conclusions.* 1612. Reprint, edited by W. T. Whitley. *The Works of John Smyth*, 2:743-44. Cambridge: Cambridge University Press, 1915.

White, B. R., ed. *Associational Records of Particular Baptists of England, Wales and Ireland to 1660.* London: Baptist Historical Society, 1971.

Chapter Six

Modern Old Testament Interpretation

Rick Johnson

When John the Baptist appeared proclaiming the advent of the kingdom of God, he directed the attention of the people to Old Testament promises. He warned, "Therefore bring forth fruit in keeping with your repentance" (Matt. 3:8 NASB), and he promised, "After me One is coming who is mightier than I, and I am not even fit to stoop down and untie the thong of His sandals" (Mark 1:7b). The call to repentance is reminiscent of the prophets (cf. Jer. 3:12-14; 4:1-4; Joel 2:12-14). His expectation of a future mightier person cannot be understood without reference to the Jewish hopes for a Messiah and for a prophet like Moses (Deut. 18:15, 18).

These words are characteristic of all the New Testament proclamation about Jesus. It uses the language and concepts of the Old Testament. The Gospels of Matthew, Mark, and John begin by drawing on its texts. Luke's Gospel does not begin with a citation, but it presents Jesus as inaugurating his public ministry by reading a passage from Isaiah and declaring the words to be fulfilled in that moment (Luke 4:16-21). On the day of Pentecost, Peter interpreted the strange phenomena by reference to Joel's promise of God's Spirit (Joel 2:28-32). The New Testament frequently quotes the Old Testament or alludes to it. Even the Book of Revelation, which does not quote the Old Testament, constantly appropriates its language and concepts.

When John the Baptist, Jesus, and the New Testament itself can present the gospel only by referring to the Old Testament, it demonstrates the necessity for Christians to give attention to a proper reading of it. But the difficulty of this task has been recognized ever since the first century. Jesus argued with the Pharisees about the laws of purity. The early church debated the importance of circumcision. In the second century, Marcion claimed that the God revealed in Jesus Christ was not the same as the God of Israel. Consequently, he did not accept the Old Testament as inspired. Although the dominant tradition has always rejected his position, many Christians through the centuries have largely ignored the Old Testament anyway because it seems so foreign to their piety. Those who have attempted to use it have resorted to many different methods to demonstrate its meaning and relevance for the present.

This chapter will survey the most important disciplines and approaches which are helpful in determining the proper understanding of Old Testament texts. Some of these methods are ancient, but many of them have been developed only in the modern period. Especially in the last thirty years there has been an explosion in the number of different approaches to reading texts in general and biblical texts in particular. Most of them offer helpful insights for interpretation, but some are very specialized and require advanced knowledge in particular fields. For this reason, only those methods that have proved to be the most fruitful and important will be dealt with here.

Hermeneutical Clues to the Old Testament

The first consideration in determining the proper way to read the Old Testament is to ask why one wants to read it. People read the Bible for many reasons. The kind of truth one seeks in it inevitably shapes the questions the reader asks of it. Students of *history* can read it for information about political history, ancient social and cultural development, and the birth of Judaism, from which Christianity emerged. Students of *literature* may be interested in the beauty of its prose and poetry. It is safe to say, however, that most people who read the Bible, and hence the Old Testament, do so because they expect to hear God speaking to them through its words.

Yet even this goal does not specify in what way God is thought to address the reader in connection with the text. Where does one meet God through contact with the book? In the past, some interpreters have reasoned that the meeting point is the *mighty deeds* which God has done, such as the creation, the exodus, the miraculous events, and the resurrection of Jesus. These Christians may view the Bible as a record of God's revelation. They would read it to recover the history of those events. This approach would lead one to use the methods of the historian for some passages. Others conclude that the important aspect of the Old Testament is its *theology*. They would ask what it teaches about God, the world, mankind, sin, salvation, ethics, and similar topics. But before they can appropriate these beliefs themselves, they would have to pay attention to what New Testament writers teach on the same subjects. This kind of reading requires the use of logic and analysis, the tools of philosophy.

A variety of methods is demanded, therefore, both by the range of material in the Old Testament and by the variety of interests Christians bring to the text. It will be convenient to discuss first the methods that study the historical dimensions of the text and then to treat those that examine its relevance to later ages.

Source Criticism

Basic Principles

The first modern discipline developed to answer historical questions was source criticism, known for many years as literary criticism. It seeks to determine what written documents (sources) a writer or editor used to produce a book. Several factors motivated scholars to try to study this problem. First, the Old Testament itself names many sources that were used in its compilation. The Book of Jashar (Josh. 10:13: 2 Sam. 1:18), the Book of the Wars of Yahweh (Num. 21:14), the records of various kings (1 Kings 11:41; 14:19, 29; 22:39, 45; 2 Kings 1:18; etc.), and the records ascribed to various prophets (1 Chron. 29:29; 2 Chron. 9:29; 12:15; etc.) are some of the documents used by the writers of the historical books. Although these books are apparently lost forever, the mention of them shows that biblical writers appropriated material from earlier texts.

Secondly, certain peculiarities in some stories raised the question of whether their present arrangement is their original one. On two different occasions Jacob is said to have named the town of Bethel (Gen. 28:19; 35:15). Likewise, Jacob's name is twice changed to Israel (Gen. 32:28: 35:10). In Exodus 19–20, the place where Moses received the Ten Commandments is called Mt. Sinai, but in Deut. 5:2 it is called Horeb. Moses' father-in-law is called Reuel in

Exod. 2:18, but later he is called Jethro (Exod. 18:1). These factors might be explained by saying the author drew on different texts that were already in somewhat fixed form.

Thirdly, the Enlightenment in the eighteenth century promoted the development of modern historiography. Historians seeking to explain the past look for the earliest documentation of a series of events. When they looked at the Pentateuch, traditionally ascribed to Moses, they found stories about individuals purportedly living centuries earlier than his time. They surmised that he compiled these books from earlier records and that a clearer understanding of those stories might be attained by identifying his sources. Accordingly, scholars attempted to reconstruct them on the basis of the material in Genesis.

The earliest proposed solution rested on the variations in the names for God in Genesis. Chapter one refers to him as God (*Elohim*), but in Gen. 2:4b–4:26 he is named Lord (*Yahweh*) or Lord God (*Yahweh Elohim*). This phenomenon of extended passages using one designation almost exclusively continues throughout Genesis. Early source critics concluded that Moses had used two documents to compile the book, one referring to God as Elohim and the other referring to him as Yahweh. Later scholars supported their argument by pointing out the so-called doublets (items told twice) and the differences in the literary style, vocabulary, and theology of various passages. Finally, in 1878, Julius Wellhausen argued that there were four sources used in the composition of the Pentateuch. The earliest was from the tenth century B.C., and the latest was from the sixth century B.C. These were combined and put in their final form by about the year 400 B.C.

Evaluation

The advantages of Wellhausen's newer documentary hypothesis were numerous. It appeared to solve the problems mentioned above concerning the variations in names of God, people, and places. It also offered explanations for apparent doublets and conflicts within stories. Dating legal material late in the history of Israel explained why the earlier narratives show little knowledge of the worship regulations attributed to Moses. For example, Deuteronomy required sacrifices to be offered only at the central sanctuary; but prophets and kings before Hezekiah seem ignorant of this provision.

Wellhausen's theory explained so many facets of the text so well that by the early twentieth century almost all Old Testament scholars had accepted it. Some tried to find continuations of his sources in the Books of Joshua, Judges, Samuel, and Kings. Others tried to identify independent sources behind these books. For example, in the account of the beginning of the monarchy in 1 Samuel 8–12, some passages present strong objections to the institution while others seem to present it in a positive light. The use of source criticism might lead to the conclusion that an anti-monarchy source has been combined with a pro-monarchy one to yield the present story.

Analyzing ancient texts in this fashion offers the possibility of recovering the earlier written documents. If the results are valid, scholars can then examine them and try to determine the purposes of these earlier works. They would then have a clearer view of both the interests of the authors and the events which they recounted, allowing them to describe the history of Israel and the development of Old Testament thought more precisely.

On the other hand, this discipline has always had its critics. In the field of Old Testament studies, it has mainly been used in analyzing the Pentateuch. First, it must be noted that no copies of any of the conjectured sources have been found. All the manuscripts of the Pentateuch contain basically the same form of the text as is found in modern Bibles. The separation of the four documents depends on such arguments as the use of names, differences in literary style and theology, repetitions or doublets, and apparent inconsistencies in the narratives. Yet other explanations have been given for these phenomena. Israelite storytellers loved repetition. A doublet may therefore not be evidence for multiple sources. What appears to be an inconsistency to modern readers may not have seemed so to ancient people. Before judgments about literary style, theology, and narrative consistency can be made, the reader must have a thorough understanding of the conventions of Israelite literature.

A second problem with Wellhausen's hypothesis concerns the historical implications he derived from it. He concluded that since the four sources were written long after the events they purport to describe, their historical worth was minimal. The patriarchs were not historical characters. In contrast to the traditional view, the laws came after the prophets, not before.

Later study, however, led most scholars to revise Wellhausen's conclusions considerably. The progress in archaeology allowed historians to reconstruct the history of the ancient Near East. Much archaeological evidence fits the picture presented in the Pentateuch. Texts recovered from various sites show that the personal names, the customs, and the political context of the stories fit the general period in which they are set. One cannot prove that the biblical accounts happened, but one must explain how later writers could have told stories that in many ways fit earlier periods better than their own. Scholars who continued to use the fourfold division of the text began to argue that the separate strands were better described as traditions preserved from earlier generations rather than as written documents produced *de novo* (firsthand).

Although Wellhausen's theory has dominated the study of the Pentateuch in this century, and his separation of four strands of material is still the dominant view, it is currently under serious attack by several recognized scholars. It is not yet clear whether it will maintain its dominance in the study of the Pentateuch or will be replaced by some other model. Students should be aware of both the benefits and the weaknesses of the method when evaluating the conclusions of authorities in the field.

Form Criticism

In contrast to source criticism, which seeks to uncover written documents, form criticism operates on the assumption that most of the Old Testament was passed on orally for a lengthy period before it was written down. The literature grew out of the life of the people. When it was finally recorded, the writers were preserving and reshaping the traditions, not creating new material.

The validity of this assumption can be supported by several arguments. First of all, the literature is obviously religious in orientation and purpose, and religion is a very conservative phenomenon in ancient societies. Complete novelty in this sphere was rarely accepted. To gain an audience for their texts, writers had to make use of the authoritative traditions of the people. Sometimes they were probably recording the material to insure its preservation.

The recognition of an oral prehistory of the writings also helps account for the similarities between Old Testament passages and literature from the ancient Near East. The creation and flood stories in Genesis resemble the Enuma Elish, the Gilgamesh Epic, and other stories from Mesopotamia. Many of the laws in the Pentateuch are similar to those in the law collections of Hammurabi and other Near Eastern rulers. These are only a few of the many examples that could be given, and in most cases the ancient Near Eastern writings are much older than the Old Testament counterparts. It is very unlikely that direct borrowing occurred in most instances, but the similarities strongly suggest that the material in the Old Testament was transmitted for a long time before being written down.

In order to study this period of oral transmission, Hermann Gunkel promoted the use of form criticism. The goal was to identify the earliest oral form of a *pericope*, the smallest unit of text that constitutes a coherent whole. He would then try to determine how this piece was used in the life of the people. That occasion was called the situation in life (*Sitz im Leben*). By identifying these contexts, Gunkel hoped to recover the earliest significance of the various parts of the Old Testament. As in source criticism, the results would be fruitful for understanding the history and religious development of Israel.

Form criticism has been applied to the whole Old Testament. It has been especially helpful in the study of Psalms. Since Gunkel's foundational work on that book, all scholarly work has been dominated by his approach. A brief survey of his conclusions will illustrate the benefits of the method.

Gunkel found four dominant classes of songs in the Psalter: hymns, community laments, individual songs of thanksgiving, and individual laments. The main characteristic of *hymns* is their praise to God. They frequently begin with an expression of praise which is followed by a statement about God's nature or activities which elicits such worship. Psalm 8 is a classic example. It opens and closes with the words "O LORD, our Lord, how majestic is Thy name in all the earth." The body of the song expresses awe at the attention and prominence God has given to a creature such as mankind.

Community and individual *laments* were used in occasions when groups or individual persons were experiencing some crisis. Those involved would voice their distress and plead with God for deliverance. Sometimes they end with statements of confidence that God will act. Psalm 22 is a full expression of an individual lament. The psalmist is threatened by physical afflictions and by human attacks, but the descriptions of these circumstances are too general to allow specific identification. This allowed the song to be appropriated by almost anyone experiencing any kind of threat. Such a song might be sung during rituals connected with sickness or with cleansing from sin, or it might involve some kind of attestation of innocence showing

the worshiper has been faithful to God. In either case, it expresses the grounds upon which a request for salvation is given. The
individual song of *thanksgiving* resembles the lament in describing the distress of the worshiper. The difference is that it is a
song offered after the deliverance. The individual gives public
testimony of how God heard his cry and rescued him. Psalm 116
is an excellent example of this genre.

Evaluation

By examining how such songs were used in the life of the
people, the modern student can derive a picture of various parts
of worship in Israel and of the faith voiced on those occasions.
In the Book of Psalms, the goal of interpretation is not so much
to determine the specific circumstances or events in the psalmist's own life that he might have had in mind, but how they were
used in the worship of Israel. The modern use of hymns in worship is a good guide here. When a congregation sings a well-
known hymn, it makes the words of the songs its own without
regard to what the hymn writer might have intended. Just so,
form criticism asks what the psalms meant when they were used
in Israel's worship. Another parallel is the use of different types
of songs for different parts of a worship service. Anthems or calls
to worship are used at the beginning, songs of commitment at
the end. Depending on the season of the year or the needs of the
moment, many different types of songs might be used in the service. Likewise, the Psalter contains songs for use with offerings
(100), royal psalms for rituals involving the king (2; 18; 20; 45;
110), songs for confessions (51), and songs for other purposes.
Form criticism attempts to identify what these occasions (situations in life) were, helping the modern reader gain a better grasp
of how they might speak to the present.

Tradition History

One of the factors motivating source and form criticism was the
interest in the earliest evidence behind the Bible. Source criticism
sought the earliest written documents, and form criticism sought
the earliest oral material. Those parts of the text which were considered to have been added by later editors or compilers were often
disregarded. A full understanding of the present state of the books,
however, demanded some explanation of all the pieces in the puz-
zle. In terms of historical understanding of the text, it is important

to explain all of the stages of its production. In terms of a theological interpretation of it for the believing community, inspiration can be judged to have been operative in the whole process from the beginning to the end. Accordingly, scholars began to study the history of the traditions of the Old Testament, reconstructing the whole process of transmitting and collecting the material from the earliest oral stages to the written ones.

This kind of examination was inherent in the exercise of source criticism and form criticism, but now greater attention was given to the interests of those who joined the large complexes of literature together. The two scholars most noted for their work in this field were Gerhard von Rad and Martin Noth. Von Rad explained the growth of the Hexateuch, the books from Genesis to Joshua, on the basis of a series of short passages (credos), each containing a brief summary of the story of the nation Israel from the ancestors to the entrance into Canaan. In his view, the credo originated early in Israel's history, and the four traditions of the Pentateuch grew up as different people retold and expanded various parts of the story. Von Rad's *Old Testament Theology* treats all of the traditions of the Old Testament according to this method.

Martin Noth's main contributions dealt with the Pentateuch and the Deuteronomistic history. He argued that the Pentateuch grew as various stories were collected around five themes: the exodus, the entrance into Canaan, the patriarchs, the wilderness wandering, and the giving of the law at Sinai. One of his most enduring contributions was his thesis that the Books of Joshua, Judges, Samuel, and Kings were compiled by historians under the influence of the theology of Deuteronomy. Writing during the exile, these historians explained the destruction of Israel and Judah as the result of disobedience to the Sinai covenant. He showed that many of the theological judgments in these history books were derived from Deuteronomy, hence the designation Deuteronomistic history. These writers drew on earlier traditions for information about bygone centuries, but they interpreted the fortunes of the people on the basis of their faithfulness to the requirements in Deuteronomy.

Evaluation

Clearly, von Rad and Noth emphasize the contributions of the later writers in the tradition process. Yet they used the results of source criticism and form criticism in their work. This shows both the ambition and the weakness of tradition history. It employs all of the other methods of study, but practitioners have not been able to agree on a clearly defined set of rules to study traditions. Furthermore, since source criticism and form criticism leave a large measure of uncertainty in their results, tradition history necessarily shares the same faults.

On the other hand, when tradition critics focus on the later stages of the writing process, they have firmer ground on which to stand, because they are trying the explain the present shape of the texts, not oral or written sources no longer available. This interest in the later stages of writing has led biblical scholars to turn to what is now called literary criticism.

Literary Criticism

Basic Principles

In the last twenty years the term "literary criticism" has more and more been used to designate the kinds of analysis used in reading any written work in a university literature course. Questions about how a work came to be written are less important than examining its nature as it presently exists. The reader asks about the genre in order to know what kinds of other questions to ask. Anyone who picks up a newspaper automatically reads it with different expectations than he or she would have in reading a billboard or an instruction manual. Likewise in reading a book, people ask what kind of literature it is. If it is non-fiction, is it biography, autobiography, history, or perhaps a science textbook? If it is fictional literature, is it a novel, an epic, a play, or poetry?

The Old Testament contains many different genres and subgenres. Narrative makes up a large portion, but many books are poetry. Further, the narrative sections contain many smaller passages belonging to other categories, such as laws, poems, prophecy, and sermons. This variety challenges the reader to be skilled in interpreting a wide range of genres.

Although the critical study of world literature has been around a long time and is well developed, the use of these methods in biblical studies has not generated much interest until recently. At the present time many different scholars are working in this area, and there is little unanimity among them on issues of method and purpose. Many develop their own techniques and terminology. In this brief account, it will be best simply to summarize some of the questions and results that can be expected from this approach and to provide students with a helpful bibliography of important works.

The interpretation of Old Testament *poetry* is one area in which the use of literary analysis has a long history. Some of the work is crucial, but some of it is has not been fruitful. The device usually identified as the distinguishing mark of Hebrew poetry is *parallelism*. The basic structure contains one line that makes a statement followed by another line making a balancing statement either similar to the first, contrasting with the first, or carrying the idea forward in some fashion. These three possibilities are labeled synonymous parallelism, antithetic parallelism, and synthetic parallelism.

Isaiah 1:3 contains the first two types.

> An ox knows its owner,
> And a donkey its master's manger,
> But Israel does not know,
> My people do not understand.

The first two lines are synonymous, as are the third and fourth. But the first pair of lines is in antithetic parallelism with the second pair. The balance of the lines suggests what it is that Israel does not know—its owner, its master's manger, or both. Israel does not know the Lord. Yet the lack of a direct object in the second pair of lines also suggests that Israel does not know anything at all. The verse is poetry, and poetry plays with overtones of meaning.

Another common element of poetry is the use of *figurative language*. Psalm 18:2 contains several metaphors for God.

> The LORD is my rock and my fortress and my deliverer,
> My God, my rock, in whom I take refuge;
> My shield and the horn of my salvation, my stronghold.

Psalm 1 uses similes to contrast the destinies of the righteous and the wicked. The one who lives by the law of the Lord "will be like a tree firmly planted by streams of water . . ." (v. 3a). But the wicked "are like chaff which the wind drives away" (v. 4b). Such usage of symbolism is one element shared between biblical poetry and poetry from many other places and times and shows how the modes of reading used in other literature may also apply to the Bible. The text itself must guide the reader here. Old Testament poetry rarely uses rhyme. Many Old Testament scholars have tried to define its metrical schemes, but others deny that biblical poetry has meter. The attempt to find it is apparently an example of trying to impose a foreign criterion on material it does not fit.

Narrative literature calls for an analysis of its three universal elements: plot, setting, and character. For example, plots may be broadly classified as either comedy or tragedy. Comedy moves from misfortune or distress to fortune, "from rags to riches." In tragedy, the hero is destroyed because of a character flaw. There are few tragic narratives in the Old Testament. The story of Saul is the outstanding exception. The Deuteronomistic history has elements of tragedy in it, recounting as it does the reasons why Israel and Judah were destroyed. They did not obey the covenant. Yet the text leaves open the question of the future of the people. In the introduction to this history, Deut. 30:1-10 promises that if the people in exile return to God, he will restore them to the land. Reading the text as a whole draws the reader into the question of whether the history is comedy or tragedy. The historians during the exile were posing the question to their own generation, and the text raises the question for all succeeding generations.

Evaluation

As with other types of criticism, the method can yield very helpful results, but those results may be distorted by inappropriate assumptions. Since literature has meaning apart from the question of reference to the real world, some literary critics have ignored the historical issues raised by the biblical texts as irrelevant. It is not faithful to the text, however, to disregard something the text itself emphasizes. Consequently many scholars insist both historical and literary methods must be used to read the Old Testament. No one method is sufficient to grasp all of its dimensions. Yet none of the disciplines described thus far answers the question of the present relevance of the Old Testament. It is important to ask *how* it functions as an authoritative book for Christians today.

Hermeneutical Approaches

As noted above, the New Testament frequently cites the Old Testament; and in doing so it provides a wealth of examples of how those texts have continuing significance. Only the most important uses can be treated here.

Prophecy

Peter's claim that Jesus is the Christ (Matt. 16:16) focuses on one of the main Christian assertions about the Old Testament, that Jesus is the fulfillment of messianic prophecy. Strictly speaking, this hope refers to the promise to David that his dynasty would last forever (2 Sam. 7:12-16). This belief gave rise to a series of passages in the Old Testament which look forward to the reign of a descendant of David (e.g., Psalm 2; Isa. 9:6-7; 11:1-10; Jer. 23:5-6; Ezek. 34:23-24). Christians defined Jesus' identity by reference to such passages. Matthew traced the genealogy of Jesus through the Davidic line. Paul referred to him as the seed of David (Rom. 1:3). From this kernel grew the idea that many other verses also referred to Jesus. Martin Luther thought that it was the Old Testament passages that dealt with Christ that continued to have relevance for Christians.

Obviously, this testimony of Scripture is important, but the Christological importance of the Old Testament does not exhaust its significance. Most of the texts do not deal directly with the hope for a Messiah. By appealing to the scheme of prophecy and fulfillment, many other topics and passages can be included, such as the gift of the Spirit at Pentecost (Joel 2:28; Isa. 32:15; 44:3), the resurrection (Dan. 12:2), and the expectation of a new heaven and a new earth (Isa. 65:17; Rev. 21:1). Passages that are not prophetic, however, are still left out.

Typology and Allegory

Sometimes Christians have found Christological significance in texts where it is not obvious by reference to a "fuller sense" (*sensus plenior*). This concept is used in several ways. In *typology*, a person, place, event, or thing in the Old Testament is viewed as a divinely intended prefiguring of a later person, place, event, or thing. For example, atonement in the sacrificial system foreshadowed the final atonement of Jesus on the cross. The Book of Hebrews presents Jesus as the great high priest who intercedes for believers (Heb. 8:1–2). The Old Testament passages about sacrifice and priesthood are not predictive and do not refer to Jesus, but they help interpret his importance.

It is clear that the biblical writers made use of the method of typology in their exegesis. They used the patterns in the earlier scriptural traditions to interpret later realities. This method shares the shortcoming of prophecy and fulfillment, however, in the limitation of its scope. It has little to offer in reading the wisdom literature.

In *allegorical* interpretation, the reader seeks a symbolic understanding of the persons, places, events, or things in a text. Paul made use of the word *allegory* in Gal. 4:21-31. He wrote concerning

Sarah and Hagar, "Now this is an allegory: these women are two covenants" (v. 24a, NRSV). He identified Hagar with the Mosaic covenant and Sarah with the promise, using literal women to represent theological concepts. Some interpreters would identify Paul's technique in this passage as analogy or typology, because the story concerns itself with the question of whether God's promise can be accomplished through human effort (works) or by God's action alone (grace). It resembles allegorical exegesis, however, in identifying historical characters with theological ideas. In the Middle Ages, this method developed into a scheme of finding a fourfold meaning in every passage. The allegorical method fails because of the lack of control on its use. An interpreter would be limited only by his own ingenuity. A biblical writer such as Paul might use it in arguments with his contemporaries, because he had to reason in ways they could accept. Such usage does not justify similar practice by modern Bible readers.

Multiple Fulfillment

Sometimes the idea of a fuller sense is used to claim *multiple fulfillments* of prophecy. From this perspective, a prophecy might have had reference to one set of events in the mind of the author or the original audience; but later readers might find a different significance in it. The prophecy of the Immanuel child in Isa. 7:14 is one example. In the context of Isaiah 7, the verse seems to refer to the birth of a child at the time of the invasion of Judah by Israel and Syria when Ahaz was king in Jerusalem. The wider context of Isaiah 6–11 presents the child as messianic, and the Gospel of Matthew interprets the verse as a prophecy of the virgin birth.

Multiple fulfillment of prophecy is a complex issue, and a full discussion cannot be given here. It involves the whole understanding of prophecy and also the question of meaning in any text. In brief, the Old Testament itself presents the words of the prophets and the other traditions as living testimonies to the God who saves. Since this God continues to guide his people and also history, later events can be expected to share similarities with earlier ones. New developments lead readers to see new significance in old texts. Often the fulfillment of a particular prophecy left certain aspects unrealized. Such a text might take on new life when new acts of God come to pass. Nevertheless, the Old Testament has much broader significance than prophecy and fulfillment.

Salvation History

Since much of the Bible is a narrative of God's saving activity, some interpreters have found the permanent relevance of the Old Testament in the history of salvation (*Heilsgeschichte*). Many have emphasized that the Old Testament records the mighty acts of God in the past. The story of God delivering Israel from Egypt, Babylonia, and other threats in the past reached its climax in the life, death, and resurrection of Jesus in the New Testament. This approach acknowledges the centrality of the biblical witness to God's activity in particular events in this world. Yet believers have had difficulty in agreeing upon how God has been involved in history. Furthermore, events such as creation, resurrection, and spiritual regeneration are difficult or impossible to study by historical methods. Finally, the death and resurrection of Jesus are not events in the political history of Israel. How then can they be connected with that history and placed on the same level of reality?

The Authority of the Old Testament

One can follow the lead of New Testament witness and use the Old Testament as normative for theology and ethics. Paul said it was "profitable for teaching, for reproof, for correction, for training in righteousness; that the man of God may be adequate, equipped for every good work" (2 Tim. 3:16b-17, NASB; cf. 1 Cor. 10:1-11). According to the Gospels, Jesus treated it the same way. In the Sermon on the Mount, he emphasized the importance of the Law and the Prophets and applied the commandments in a stricter fashion than stated in the text. He used Hosea's words as a guide to God's view of ritual: "I desire compassion, and not sacrifice" (Matt. 9:13, NASB; cf. Hos. 6:6). On the question of the resurrection, he faulted the Sadducees in part for not knowing the Scriptures (Matt. 22:29).

Accordingly, the Old Testament is a reliable guide for knowing what to believe and how to live. The cry of the seraphim in Isaiah's call vision (Isa. 6:3) remains a primary statement about the nature of God—he is holy. The doctrine of creation is affirmed in Genesis, the Book of Psalms, and the Prophets. The reality of sin and the offer of salvation figure throughout the books. The legal texts and the wisdom writings teach the values which human conduct should protect, and the narrative texts give examples of what can happen when people either honor or dishonor them. Psalms guides believers in expressing their worship of God.

The limitation of the Old Testament as Christian Scripture, however, derives from the new revelation of God in Jesus Christ. Because this new revelation has been given, the older one can only be judged incomplete. It is authoritative, but its authority must be interpreted in the light of the new word. This is why Jesus can go beyond Moses on questions such as divorce, swearing, or retaliation (Matt. 5:31-42). This is also why the New Testament requirements supercede Old Testament requirements concerning the Sabbath, circumcision, and the food laws.

In conclusion, the interpretation of the Old Testament in the Christian church must use a variety of methods and hermeneutical approaches. The richness of God's revelation calls for a corresponding fullness in reading awareness. The gospel cannot be understood without its Old Testament preparation, but the New Testament provides the final word for the significance of the Old Testament today.

▼

For Further Study

Alter, Robert. *The Art of Biblical Narrative*. New York: Basic Books, 1981.

Alter, Robert, and Frank Kermode, eds. *The Literary Guide to the Bible*. Cambridge: Harvard University Press, 1987.

Brueggemann, Walter, and Hans Walter Wolff. *The Vitality of Old Testament Traditions*. 2d ed. Atlanta: John Knox, 1982.

Campbell, Anthony F., and Mark A. O'Brien. *Sources of the Pentateuch: Texts, Introductions, Annotations*. Minneapolis: Fortress, 1993.

Goldingay, John. *Approaches to Old Testament Interpretation, rev. ed.* Downers Grove, Ill.: InterVarsity, 1990.

————. *Theological Diversity and the Authority of the Old Testament.* Grand Rapids: Eerdmans, 1987.

Gunkel, Hermann. *The Psalms: A Form-Critical Introduction.* Translated by Thomas M. Horner. Philadelphia: Fortress, 1967.

Gunneweg, A. H. J. *Understanding the Old Testament.* Old Testament Library. Philadelphia: Westminster, 1978.

Habel, Norman C. *Literary Criticism of the Old Testament.* Guides to Biblical Scholarship. Philadelphia: Fortress, 1971.

Hayes, John H., ed. *Old Testament Form Criticism.* San Antonio: Trinity University Press, 1974.

McKenzie, Steven L., and Stephen R. Haynes, eds. *To Each Its Own Meaning: An Introduction to Biblical Criticisms and Their Application.* Louisville: Westminster/John Knox, 1993.

Morgan, Robert, with John Barton. *Biblical Interpretation.* Oxford: Oxford University Press, 1988.

Noth, Martin. *A History of Pentateuchal Traditions.* Translated with an introduction by Bernhard W. Anderson. Englewood Cliffs, N.J.: Prentice-Hall, 1972.

Rast, Walter E. *Tradition History and the Old Testament.* Guides to Biblical Scholarship. Philadelphia: Fortress, 1972.

Ryken, Leland. *How to Read the Bible as Literature.* Grand Rapids: Zondervan, 1984.

Steck, Odil Hannes. *Old Testament Exegesis: A Guide to the Methodology.* Translated by James D. Nogalski. Atlanta: Scholars Press, 1995.

Tucker, Gene M. *Form Criticism of the Old Testament.* Guides to Biblical Scholarship. Philadelphia: Fortress, 1971.

Chapter Seven

Modern New Testament Interpretation

Lorin L. Cranford

How is the student of the Bible supposed to interpret the text of the New Testament? This central issue has occupied the attention of New Testament scholars increasingly in our century. With the rise of the modern era came a new interest in the biblical text. The growing number of translations into various languages vis-a-vis the large number of Bible societies has sought to make the NT text more understandable to the untrained Bible reader. Protestantism has centered itself on the authority of the biblical text, thus making correct interpretation of the text more crucial. The adoption of a method of interpretation—the "reading" of the text—has increasingly been scrutinized. Our interpretive conclusions will be largely determined in advance by the method of reading adopted, consciously or unconsciously.

Describing the method(s) to be used unavoidably creates an artificial arrangement. Written description moves from point to point somewhat in a linear progression, but the actual reading of the text will never take place this way. The dynamics of reading are more like a spiral than an arrow. Interaction with various methods will occur repeatedly in the process, hopefully with forward movement leading to solid interpretive conclusions.

Interpreting the New Testament in the last half of the twentieth century has become more challenging with the increasingly diverse ways of reading a text. European approaches remain largely centered in probing the historical background and meaning of a given passage in the New Testament. Alternative American approaches, however, have mushroomed in our pluralistic culture with increasing focus on the literary aspects of the text. The goal of interpretation has also been a topic of vigorous discussion. Is it exclusively to determine the historical meaning of the text? Or, to move from that perceived meaning to modern application? Or, is the division between what it *meant* and what it *means* an artifical and false separation? Many argue that the two are so interrelated that they cannot be separated.

The discussion below attempts to underscore both the historical and literary dimensions as well as the emergence of the methods, but not necessarily in chronological order. Rather, a more logical basis is adopted with the intent of moving from historical to literary aspects.

With the Renaissance came renewed interest in ancient history, and subsequently the development of the historical method, as opposed to the dominant "dogmatic" method that had been the justification of horrible abuse in the name of Christ. For the last two centuries some form of historically oriented approach to NT interpretation has dominated Protestant NT scholarship in the Western world.

Canon Criticism

A logical starting point in exegesis is with the determination of what constitutes sacred Scripture as an authority base for faith and practice. In the 1960s and 1970s the Old Testament scholar Brevard Childs began advocating an approach that has come to be termed canon criticism (or, canonical criticism). James A. Sanders, who coined the term canonical criticism, likewise has promoted this approach. The core aspect of canonical criticism is to stress the context of the biblical canon as a foundational clue to interpretation. Childs advocates the canon as "final product" as adopted by the early Christian community of faith, whereas Sanders insists on the "canon as process" as his canonical context. Both, however, want to interpret a given NT passage in the context of the canon in both its literary and historical aspects. How early Christianity came to regard certain documents as authoritative, while rejecting many other documents, is important background understanding. Literarily, the existence of *four* Gospels in a *specific sequence* is based on the hammering out of theological issues in early Christianity and provides helpful clues to the interpretation of each document.

Christianity has four diverse intepretations of Christ that have a fundamental unity but likewise present different portraits. We are the beneficiaries of this rich perspective. On the one hand, this powerfully reminds us not to harmonize the life of Christ in only one dimension. The early church rejected such efforts as simplistic. On the other hand, the existence of four Gospels with fundamental unity stresses the solidarity of the church's understanding of its Founder. In this unity-amidst-diversity perspective of canon criticism we have interpretive clues for contemporary understanding of Christ. This approach is not without its weaknesses, as James Barr has ably pointed out (*Holy Scripture*, 1983), but it does emphasize that exegesis is but *one* stage of the process *leading to* theological understanding.

Textual Criticism

Once certain documents come to be regarded as sacred Scripture, the next task is to determine as far as possible the exact wording of the original writing. Since no original text of any NT document is now available, the Bible student needs to "establish the text" before any exegesis of this text can be attempted. Ultimately, this is accomplished by the careful comparison of all existing Greek manuscripts and early translations containing the NT passage under consideration. Evaluating the over five thousand Greek manuscript portions now available requires the implementation of highly technical procedures with the intent of determining the "original reading of the text." In contrast to the classical scholar who has to work with few and very late manuscripts, the NT scholar is faced with a huge amount of material to evaluate. Currently, two significant methods of text criticism dominate: (1) rigorous eclecticism, advocated by G. D. Kilpatrick and his student J. K. Elliott, and (2) rational eclecticism, whose chief advocates include Kurt Aland, Bruce Metzger, Gordon Fee, and E. J. Epp.

The basic difference between these is the weight given to internal evidence over external evidence. The internal factors have to do with discernable tendencies within the content of the Greek manuscripts themselves. Included are *transcriptional* probabilities, that is, tendencies of those who made copies of the NT text. Four guidelines (sometimes called "canons") are followed: (1) a shorter reading is to be preferred to a longer reading; (2) the reading different from its parallel is to be preferred; (3) a difficult reading is to be preferred to an easy one; (4) the reading that best explains the origin of the others is most likely the original. The other internal aspect is *intrinsic* probability. This category analyzes the text from the perspective of authorial intent by examining the NT author's grammar, style, vocabulary, theology, rhetorical purpose, and so forth. The reading in a specific text most in line with these factors of an author is preferred. Rigorous eclecticism, favored by Kilpatrick and Elliott, gives overwhelming weight to these internal factors.

Rational eclecticism seeks to give adequate consideration to both internal and external factors. These include the dating, geographical origin of Greek manuscripts, and especially the family relationships, or text types. Three text types—Alexandrian, Western, and Byzantine—arose in the process of copying the NT. The greatest external weight of evidence is given to the reading with the earliest date, widest geographical distribution, and concurrence among text types, especially the Alexandrian and Western text types. These are then considered along with the above mentioned internal factors in coming to a conclusion about the most likely original reading. This more balanced approach is reflected in the two most popular printed editions of the Greek New Testament, the United Bible Societies 3d edition text (UBS[3]) and the Nestle-Aland 26th edition text (NA[26]). The Greek text in these two is virtually the same; the major difference is in the organization of the critical apparatus of each that enables quick assessment of the various readings found in the manuscripts. While years of training and experience in analyzing manuscripts is required to become an expert, the serious Bible student can become sufficiently familiar with the procedures so as to understand better the reasons for the adopted reading in a printed Greek NT. Additionally, the *Textual Commentary on the Greek New Testament* by Bruce Metzger (1975) provides notes explaining the reasoning behind the adoption of the readings in the UBS[3] Greek text. The results of careful evaluation lead to confidence in the accuracy of the adopted reading, which then provides a solid basis for exegeting the wording of the passage. Working through the procedure also creates humility and appreciation for those who so laboriously copied the NT text by hand in order to preserve the message of the gospel.

Historical Criticism

At this stage the Bible student is ready to begin analyzing the statements found in the NT passage being studied. Arising as a distinct exegetical method in the early nineteenth century, historical criticism presupposes the view that Christianity is a history-based religion. The evolution of historical criticism in the last two hundred years has taken different turns, some of which have been destructive, but biblical scholars of all theological persuasions today use some form of this method to interpret Scripture. The "history" implied here is of two varieties: the history *in* the NT text and the history *of* the NT text. The latter, which one usually finds discussed in the introduction of commentaries and in NT introductions, has to do especially with how the text came into being, as well as with its transmission and interpretation in Christian history. The former has to do with the history implicit within the NT text itself. The NT interpreter has to take the bits of historical reference within the text, add to them the data available from other contemporary sources, and then attempt to reconstruct a history as a background to facilitate better understanding of the text itself. With gaps in the available data such reconstruction often deals in historical probabilities rather than certainties, but this is important even if absolute certainty is impossible. Paul's confrontation with Peter in Gal. 2:11-14 is an example. If this took place after the Jerusalem council meeting in Acts 15 (cf. Gal. 2:1-10), then Peter's hypocrisy is all the more culpable and Paul's stinging condemnation of it all the more understandable. However, if it took place before the Jerusalem council then Peter's actions are easier to understand and Paul's harsh words less comprehensible. The chronological conclusions drawn here impact the details of the passage. Thus historical criticism, positively applied, can aid the interpretative process as well as call attention to important questions arising from the text.

Social Scientific Exegesis

In recent times the application of sociological principles to interpreting ancient texts is proving its value. Western individualistic culture increasingly recognizes the community aspect of the ancient world in which Christianity was born. Awareness of this has prompted the attempt to apply modern social science insights to the interpretation of the NT. Key individuals leading this effort include Gerd Theissen, E. A. Judge, Howard Clark Kee, Richard A. Horsley, and Wayne A. Meeks. Sociological approaches range all the way from simple social description to sociological analysis. In Gal. 2:11-14 social science insights would probe conflict resolution between individuals and groups in the ancient Jewish and Hellenistic worlds. Ancient strategies and models of leadership could also provide understanding. Implicit in this method is extensive comparative studies of ancient texts with relevant NT passages. The most questionable aspect here is the application of modern social paradigms to NT texts, both as to whether such can be done and then, if so, which model is more appropriate to apply. The social history reconstruction phase of the method is proving to be quite helpful; only time can tell whether the sociological analysis aspect will be helpful. Liberation theology's use of the latter often raises questions here.

Grammatical Criticism

"If textual criticism is concerned with establishing the wording of the text, and historical criticism with investigating the history *in* and *of* the text, grammatical criticism is concerned with analyzing a text through its language" (Hayes/Holladay, *Biblical Exegesis*, 59). Several aspects of such analysis emerge. First, the grammar of the text must be studied. This includes the parsing of Greek words, and study of phrase and clause patterns. In this activity legitimate parameters of possible meaning can be determined. Once conclusions are drawn, then a provisional translation of the text should be made; this will serve as the basis for subsequent revision and further understanding. Second, sentence structure should be analyzed both internally as well as how sentences "fit together" to establish progression of thought within a paragraph. This can be set forth schematically in a block diagram, as illustrated in Gal. 2:11–14 below. Third, key words and phrases need to be examined more closely after being isolated by the diagram. In statement (1) below, this especially has to do with the words "opposed" and "self-condemned." This necessitates consulting Greek dictionaries and concordances. (The following is my translation.)

2:11   But

       when Cephas came

          to Antioch,

       to his face

(1)   *I opposed him*

       because he stood self-condemned.

2:12   For

           before certain ones came from James

(2)   *he was in the habit of eating with the Gentiles;*

           but

           when they came

(3)   *he began to withdraw*

           and

(4)   *separated himself from them,*

           because he feared those of the circumcism.

2:13   And

(5)   *the rest of the Jews played the hypocrite with him,*

                so that even Barnabas was carried away

                        by their hypocrisy.

2:14   But

         when I saw

               that they did not follow the true path

                       of the gospel,

(6)   *I said to Cephas*

         before them all,

                  although a Jew,

             Since you live like a Gentile

                    and

                not like a Jew,

        how can you compel the Gentiles to live like Jews?

In statement (1), Paul's opposition to Peter is qualified in three ways: time, "when Cephas came to Antioch"; manner, "to his face"; reason, "because he stood self-condemned." The historicial identification of "when . . ." has been alluded to in the discussion of historical criticism. The manner and reason for Paul's opposition are important aspects. Thus analysis of individual words and phrases is crucial. But how do these six statements fit together to establish a progression of thought? Careful study reveals a pattern. The "for" between statements (1) and (2) suggest that statements (2) and following give a reason for statement (1), primarily as an elaboration of the "because . . ." expression. Statements (2)–(4) relate to Peter's contradictory actions before the delegation from James arrived (statement [2]) and afterward (statements [3] and [4]). The impact of Peter's action is set forth in statement (5).

Statement (6) essentially repeats statement (1) by recapping Paul's words of opposition to Peter as a response to statements (2)–(5). One can detect Paul's concern to recount his opposition to Peter by stating it and then defending it.

Tradition Criticism

One of the first areas of examination, once basic grammatical analysis is completed, is to probe whether the author has used pieces of tradition in the creation of the NT text under consideration. In the Gospels careful comparative study of double or triple tradition materials reveals that much of the material in the synoptic Gospels was passed along in a relatively fixed form, most likely in both oral and written form, from the time of Jesus' ministry (A.D. 27–30) until the Gospels were written in the 60s and 70s. How much was passed down orally and how much in written form is considerably discussed among NT scholars, but probably a combination of both forms best accounts for this so-called "oral period" of the synoptic Gospels. Regarding the remainder of the NT, the concern of tradition criticism is to trace out the use of early Christian tradition in the NT texts and how the author incorporated them into his writing. The most obvious type of material used was OT texts, but early Christian hymns (Phil. 2:5-11), confessions of faith (1 Tim. 3:16), words of Christ (*verba Christi*) not contained in the Gospels (Acts 20:35) among others were used by NT writers. As far as possible the history of each detected piece of tradition should be probed. How the NT author applied it to his subject can then be better understood.

Source Criticism

Source criticism and form criticism are very closely linked to tradition criticism. As applied to the synoptic Gospels, source criticism attempts to understand the literary relationship among the first three Gospels. They have basically the same structural outline, in contrast to the fourth Gospel. The vast majority of the text of Mark is reproduced almost word-for-word in either Matthew or Luke or both. Yet both Matthew and Luke differ in sequential arrangement of *pericopes*, sometimes in agreement with one another against Mark. Occasionally they contain together episodes in Jesus' ministry not found in Mark while at other times they go their own separate ways. Two perspectives dominate modern scholarship today. First, the two-document hypothesis sets forth the view that

Mark was written first, then Matthew and Luke independently used Mark as well as a common second source (called Q after the German word *Quelle,* meaning "source"). On the other hand, the two-Gospel view reverses this sequence of literary dependency. Mark was written last and was something of a condensation of Matthew and Luke. Both viewpoints assume a literary dependency, that is, that the later writer(s) had access to a written form of the earlier Gospel(s). In all likelihood, a dependency on both written and oral sources can best account for the similarities and the differences among these three Gospels.

Elsewhere in the NT, source criticism is concerned with the author's use of sources to write. For example, the so-called "we" section in the latter chapters of Acts may indicate that the author was drawing from a personal diary in recounting his story.

Form Criticism

As pioneered in NT studies by Martin Dibelius and Rudolf Bultmann in the early part of the twentieth century, form criticism was concerned with two areas: to trace out the existence of discernable fixed forms of material, and then to analyze how those forms functioned in early church life. Some forms are easily detectable, such as parables, miracle stories, sayings of Jesus. Commonality of literary structure is one important aspect. For example, miracle stories begin with some need, describe the miraculous action of Jesus, then detail the results of the miracle. In comparative studies one learns that this pattern characterized the telling of miracle stories in ancient life generally. Comparisons of those miracle stories in the Gospels with those in the surrounding literature can provide helpful insight into the approach of the NT writers.

However, detecting the literary form of NT material was for Dibelius and Bultmann but the preparatory step to probing the *Sitz im Leben* (setting in life) of a particular form. This had to do with the so-called "oral period" between Jesus' earthly ministry and the writing of the Gospels some thirty or so years later. Because the stories were told widely in early Christian circles and applied to different situations and needs, this had a shaping effect on the stories that eventually were incorporated into the written Gospels. Thus one can understand something of why the differences in narrative details show up in the particular Gospel writers. This way of accounting for these differences has proven to be the most problematic part of Dibelius's and Bultmann's use of form criticism. The detection of literary forms and comparative studies with similar forms outside the NT has proven to be the most enduring aspect for Gospel studies.

For Acts and the NT letters, form criticism has focused on the detection of different forms used by the author. In Acts, insight is to be gained by studying the way Luke used different types of speech material (defense speeches, missionary speeches, etc.) and types of narrative material, ranging from episodic narrative describing a single event to narrative summaries (e.g., Acts 2:43-47) describing long periods of time by characterization of tendencies. For the epistles, the recent comparative work in ancient letter writing is proving quite fruitful, as the work of William Doty illustrates.

Redaction Criticism

Whereas tradition, source, and form approaches concentrate on the "microscopic" view (the small picture) of texts, redaction criticism focuses on the "macroscopic" view (the big picture). In fact, this tendency of earlier approaches to slice up the text into small pieces prompted NT scholars like Gunther Bornkamm, Hans Conzelmann, and Willi Marxsen in the 1950s and 1960s to advocate looking at the Gospel in its entirety in order to assess its theological message. Increasingly, recognition has been made that the Gospel writers were more than historians describing the life of Jesus. They were theologians espousing an interpretation of the significance of Jesus to their targeted readership. This author-perspective can be traced in the differences of narrative where two or more writers describe the same event in Jesus' ministry and in how each writer incorporates his sources and weaves together his story of Jesus. Mark is more action oriented, containing very little speech material, whereas Matthew builds much of his gospel story around long speeches given by Jesus. Another distinctive is Matthew's more extensive use of OT reference to support Jesus' ministry. In redaction criticism the attempt is made to allow each Gospel writer to "tell his story" and not harmonize the separate accounts into a flat modern biography of Jesus.

Literary Criticism

In the middle of this century NT scholars increasingly began questioning whether the historical approach to the NT was adequate for gleaning the needed insights from the texts. This has led to attempts to apply modern literary analysis techniques to the NT texts. The term "literary criticism" has been around for a long time, but its meaning has shifted repeatedly. Thus one has to ask what is intended by this label. Earlier it tended to refer to pursuit of authorship, time, place and date of composition—the things normally treated in NT introductions, or else it referred to the literary aspects of tradition, source, and form criticism. In American circles the rise of the movement to study the Bible as literature, mostly due to the separation-of-church-and-state heritage forcing state universities to literary approaches, has given impetus to a new understanding of literary criticism. Dissatisfied with the inability of historical approaches to provide a consensus reconstruction of NT history, scholarly interests shifted to the literary aspects of the NT. Pivotal in this shift has been the work of Amos N. Wilder, a literary critic and NT scholar. Additionally, the dry rationalism often controlling historial methods has prompted many to investigate the text's aesthetic and imaginative qualities, as well as its formal literary dimensions.

The emergence of the "New Criticism" movement in literary circles beginning in the 1940s helped provide the tools needed for NT application. Areas such as the relationship of content to form, the significance of structure for meaning, the capacity of language to direct thought and to mold existence itself have become points of concern in these newer methods. As a method distinct from those listed under the label "literary criticism," several investigative procedures will be followed. Included in them should be (1) classification of genre, (2) identification of major themes, (3) determination of structure, and (4) concern for distinctive features of the narrative. In Gal. 2:11-14, one would recognize this as an episodic narrative, falling as the last narrative proof (1:13–17, 18–24, 2:1–10; 11–14) of the independency of Paul's gospel preaching from human authorization (1:11–12). The structure and distinctives have been alluded to above in the block diagram discussion.

Structuralist Criticism

Structuralism attempts to probe the structures of thought that lie below the surface-level language of the text, especially in narrative texts. NT structuralist scholars like Daniel Patte, John Dominic Crossan, and Dan Via build on the work of Ferdinand de Saussure, Algirdas Julien Greimas, Vladimir Propp, and other French and Russian literary critics. The key presupposition of structuralism is that certain "deep structures" of thought are embedded in the human brain for all time. Language then functions at two levels: the surface level and the deep structural level. The surface level structure has to do with easily perceivable rules of grammar and style. But as we understand English, there are several ways of "saying the same thing." That "same thing" points to the deep structure, without which only one way to express an idea would exist. These structures shape the formation of human existence and expression, both consciously and unconsciously. The goal of the structuralist is to read the text in a way to perceive these structures, thereby providing a richer understanding of the text. The structures especially include constructs of binary oppositions (good/bad, light/darkness, left/right, etc.). The difficulty of this approach lies in the very technical means used to uncover these deep structures. For this reason not many NT scholars have become adept at utilizing the procedures, although limited application does provide insight otherwise missed.

Discourse Analysis

Much less technical is the probing of the language of the text at its surface level. Utilizing the same presuppositional basis of Saussure and Greimas, Eugene Nida has spearheaded the application of these principles to Bible translation, the most notable product being the "Good News for Modern Man" translations in various languages of the world. Scholars including John Beekman, John Callow, and Robert Longacre have extended this approach of text analysis for exegetical purposes. The best example of this procedure is the handbook series "Helps for the Translator" published by the United Bible Societies. The above analysis of the block diagram of Gal. 2:11-14 represents my own application of these principles to exegesis. This procedure is easier than structural analysis to comprehend and apply, and proves to be a rich source of exegetical understanding of the text.

Rhetorical Criticism

Probing the language of the text is also the emphasis of George Kennedy, who attempts to analyze the rhetorical strategy of an author against ancient principles and patterns of rhetoric. This approach extends beyond earlier efforts which were content to detect devices such as figures of speech in the text. The most influential application of this is found in the epoch-making commentary on Galatians by Hans Dieter Betz in the *Hermeneia* series. Betz applied ancient principles of Greek rhetoric to the exegesis of Galatians and has demonstrated how effectively Paul utilized those principles in making his case for the gospel message in the letter. To be sure, Betz's view has been modified and refined, but it stands as the most important English language commentary on Galatians in the second half of the twentieth century. The Gal. 2:11-14 passage in this analysis stands as a pivotal narrative proof demonstrating the independency of Paul's gospel message.

Narrative Criticism and Reader Response Criticism

Structural criticism, discourse analysis, and rhetorical criticism concentrate on the language of the text, while reader response criticism and narrative criticism focus on the narrative flow of ideas in the text. Both approaches employ the modern literary paradigm of the movement of thought: (1) *real author* ==> (2) *implicit author* ==> [2a] *narrator* ==> *TEXT* ==> [3a] *narratee* ==> (3) *implicit reader* ==> (4) *real reader*. Each category has significance, but [2]–[3] are especially important, for they pertain to the "fictional" world of the text. Categories [1] and [4] have historical concerns and more properly relate to historical exegetical interests, especially category [1]. For these two literary approaches the world of the text is the center of attention, because from it comes the necessary dynamic to generate meaning.

These two literary approaches are concerned with the text as it stands in its entirety, on the modern literary assumption that a text once composed gains an independent existence from whoever first wrote it. Meaning in the text is not found by attempting to reconstruct authorial intention, the impossibility of which has been demonstrated by the failure of historical methods to reach consensus at this point. Therefore, to these literary critics, the text is not a means to the mind of the author, and thus the goal of exegesis; rather, the text is a worthy goal of study in itself, for it has its own existence and can generate meaning(s).

Another distinctive of these approaches is the concept of meaning. Traditionally, both historical and earlier literary approaches assume that meaning lies inherently in the text itself and this meaning (possibly equal to the mind of the author) is to be uncovered by careful analysis of historical and/or literary dimensions in the text. By contrast, these two modern approaches presuppose that meaning is generated in the interaction of the reader with the text in the moment of reading. Thus, meaning is dynamic rather than static. To be sure, the text contains inbuilt signals of meaning, but these are catalysts for generating meaning, not meaningful in themselves. Two horizons come together in the act of reading: the horizon of the text and the horizon of the reader. Both horizons shape the perception of meaning gained from the act of reading. The *dichotomous* view of historical methods that sought first "what the text meant" and then "what the text means" is rejected as a false separation of meaning. The dichotomous view assumes that meaning becomes static (to these literary critics: imprisoned) in the moment of writing and serves as the basis of modern application when correctly recovered from the text. But if meaning is dynamic and generated in the act of reading, the "then" and "now" aspects collapse into a unified sense of meaning readily applicable to the situation of the reader, for his/her situation has helped shape that sense of meaning.

Thus to some literary critics every reading of the text is valid; no right or wrong interpretations exist because the traditional view assumes static meaning locked up in the text and levels of correctness in uncovering it. For others, the control factor that produces "better informed" readings has to do with the reader's developing self-consciousness of his/her own existence. Sensitivity to personality traits, cultural and ethnic heritage, and so forth, helps produce more influential and life-molding readings of the text. Additionally, growing skills in "reading" the text (such as awareness of literary technique) serve as controlling factors to produce better readings. The distinctives between narrative and reader response criticisms surface in the varied application of these literary techniques. Narrative criticism, the earlier of the two to be applied to biblical narratives, gives more room for historical concerns. The pursuit of the real author, while not as crucial as that of the implicit author and narrator, nonetheless provides helpful clues to developing a profile of the implicit author. The link between real author and implicit author is the difference between a movie and a portrait. The real author is constantly moving and changing through time and space. The implicit author is the real author captured at a specific moment in time, the moment of composition of the narrative. The writing process freezes this author forever as to what he thought, who he was at that given moment. He was not the same person before this composition moment, neither will he ever be the same person subsequent to this moment. Thus, narrative criticism endeavors to thaw out this "fictional" author as a major source of generating meaning in the reading of the text. The process is achieved through analysis of the narrative schema. Although differing methods have been adopted, they involve analysis of the narrative act and narrative strategy. The narrative act identifies the implicit author as to his assumption of knowledge and narrational vantage point. Does the implicit author project himself into the narrative to become the narrator? For example, a shift from third person to first person frame of reference signals such a move. Or, does the implicit author create a character who speaks, and is this character serving mainly as the voice of the implicit author? The narrative strategy pertains to the detection of setting, plot, and characters, the elements that together comprise the story line.

Reader response criticism, in contrast to narrative criticism, focuses major attention on the implicit reader in the text. This construct refers to the image of intended readership in mind at the time of composition: what would these people become upon correct reading of the text? Thus these individuals were "fictional" as well, for they existed in their idealized state only in the mind of the author. To be sure, there was some connection between the implicit reader and the initial real reader(s) of the text. But reader response criticism is first concerned to develop a profile of the implicit reader, using many of the same analysis techniques as narrative criticism. The linkage of the implicit reader to the initial real reader is of little concern; far more important is the linkage of the implicit reader to the modern reader at the moment of his/her reading of the text. How the profile of the implicit reader in the text challenges, and molds the modern reader is "the bottom line" issue for reader response criticism. Reading texts, especially sacred texts, should change the reader. The more clearly the implicit reader profile is grasped, the more likely the reading will effect change in the reader. Alan Culpepper's pivotal commentary on the fourth Gospel represents one of the best and most influential efforts at reading a NT text this way.

One encouraging trend in the last decade of NT scholarship in American circles is the effort of segments of literary critical approaches to reach out to those oriented to the more traditional historical methods in an effort to find ways to merge the two perspectives into a more wholistic way of interpreting NT texts. Currently in Society of Biblical Literature circles those in social science criticism and in narrative/reader response criticism are working more closely to find a more wholistic approach. In the final analysis, only an integrated approach to exegesis will prove most helpful. The nature of the NT text seems to demand such, for it contains both historical and literary elements. An adequate interpetative approach must seek to give appropriate attention to both aspects.

Of course, this does not relieve the tension between certain approaches that utilize contradictory and mutually exclusive presuppositions, for example., the differing ways that meaning is defined between historical and literary methods. The presuppositional base of any resulting integrated method must be carefully thought out; its relevance to specific procedures within the various approaches should be carefully scrutinized. Additionally, the compatibility of aspects of the various approaches has to be worked through. The settings of both the composition of the text and the modern reading(s) of the text must be given due consideration. Acknowledgement must be made that individual interpreters will inevitably highlight one or two methods over others simply out of personal preference and/or training. But this does not necessarily skew the method followed by the interpreter. In fact, this may provide some distinctives that ultimately add to the richness of the community of faith's interpretation of a given passage. Certainly, the belief in the priesthood of the believer supports the diversity of interpretative viewpoint.

▼

For Further Study

Aland, Kurt, and Barbara Aland. *The Text of the New Testament.* Translated by E. R. Rhodes. Grand Rapids: Eerdmans, 1987.

Aune, David E. *The New Testament in Its Literary Environment.* Library of Early Christianity, vol. 8. Philadelphia: Westminster, 1987.

Barr, James. *Holy Scripture: Canon, Authority, Criticism.* Philadelphia: Westminster, 1983.

Beardslee, William A., and David J. Lull, eds. "New Testament Interpretation from a Process Perspective." *Journal of the American Academy of Religion* 47 (March 1979): 3–128.

Beekman, John, and John Callow. *Translating the Word of God, with Scripture and Topical Indexes.* Grand Rapids: Zondervan, 1974.

Betz, Hans Dieter. *Galatians: A Commentary on Paul's Letter to the Galatians.* Hermeneia—A Critical and Historical Commentary on the Bible. Philadelphia: Fortress, 1979.

Childs, Brevard S. *The New Testament as Canon: An Introduction.* Minneapolis: Fortress, 1985.

Conzelmann, Hans. *The Theology of St. Luke*. Translated by Geoffrey Buswell. Minneapolis: Fortress, 1982.

Cranford, Lorin L. *Study Manual of the Epistle to the Galatians: Greek Text*. Fort Worth: AlphaGraphics, 1988.

Culpepper, R. Alan. *The Anatomy of the Fourth Gospel: A Study in Literary Design*. Edited by Robert W. Funk. New Testament Foundations and Facets. Philadelphia: Fortress, 1983.

Dibelius, Martin. *From Tradition to History*. Translated by B. L. Woolf. New York: Scribner, 1934.

Doty, William G. *Letters in Primitive Christianity*. Guides to Biblical Scholarship. Philadelphia: Fortress, 1973.

Elliott, J. K. "In Defense of Thoroughgoing Eclecticism." *Restoration Quarterly* 21 (1978): 95–115.

Epp, Eldon Jay. "Textual Criticism." In *The New Testament and Its Modern Interpreters*, edited by E. J. Epp and G. W. MacRae, 75–126. *The Bible and Its Modern Interpreters*, edited by Douglas A. Knight. Philadelphia: Fortress, 1989.

Fee, Gordon D. *New Testament Exegesis: A Handbook for Students and Pastors*. 2d ed. Louisville: Westminster/John Knox, 1993.

Hayes, John H., and Carl R. Holladay. *Biblical Exegesis: A Beginner's Handbook*. 2d ed. Atlanta: John Knox, 1987.

Horsley, Richard A. *Sociology and the Jesus Movement*. New York: Crossroad, 1989.

Judge, E. A. *Social Pattern of Christian Groups in the First Century*. London: Tyndale, 1960.

Kee, Howard Clark. *Christian Origins in Sociological Perspective*. Philadelphia: Westminster, 1980.

Kennedy, George. *New Testament Interpretation Through Rhetorical Translation*. Chapel Hill: University of North Carolina Press, 1984.

Kilpatrick, G. D. "Collected Essays of G. D. Kilpatrick." In *The Principles and Practice of New Testament Textual Criticism*, edited by J. K. Elliott. Leuven: Leuven University Press, 1990.

Meeks, Wayne A. *The First Urban Christians: The Social World of the Apostle Paul*. New Haven: Yale University Press, 1983.

Metzger, Bruce M. *The Text of the New Testament*. 3d ed. Oxford: Oxford University Press, 1991.

Patte, Daniel. *What Is Structural Exegesis?* Guides to Biblical Scholarship. Philadelphia: Fortress, 1976.

Sanders, James A. "Text and Canon: Concepts and Method." *Journal of Biblical Literature* 98 (March 1979): 5–29.

Theissen, Gerd. *Sociology of Early Palestinian Christianity*. Translated by John Bowden. Philadelphia: Fortress, 1978.

Via, Dan O. Jr. *Kerygma and Comedy in the New Testament: A Structuralist Approach to Hermeneutics*. Philadelphia: Fortress, 1975.

Wilder, Amos N. "Rhetoric of Ancient and Modern Apocalyptic." *Interpretation* 25 (1971): 436–53.

Chapter Eight

Contemporary Philosophical, Literary, and Sociological Hermeneutics

John P. Newport

Pre-Modern and Modern Hermeneutics

The interpretation of the Bible, both historically and in contemporary life, cannot be understood in depth without reference to philosophical, literary, and sociological considerations. From a historical perspective, biblical interpretation is closely related to an understanding of the philosophical and cultural climate of both ancient and modern times.

Philosophical Influences in the Hermeneutics of the Early Church

For the first several centuries of its existence in the Western world, the Christian church lived in an intellectual world which employed the categories of Platonism and Neoplatonism. Thus the church thought that it was advantageous to expound its faith by utilizing the categories of this philosophical system.

The insight that influenced biblical interpretation was the Platonic theory that the material world, the world of day-to-day experience, was not the real world but merely a shadow of reality. The real world was the world of forms or ideas. The literal or surface meaning of a text thus was seen as too crude or vulgar to represent the true or ultimate meaning. It was assumed that at least a second or third meaning lay universally beneath the letter and

could be found by allegorical interpretation. Jerusalem could refer to the literal city in Palestine or, allegorically, to the church.
Morally, it could refer to the human soul. The word *sea* could
mean a gathering of water, the Bible, the present age, the human
heart, the active life, the heathen, or baptism.

The allegorical method was used by Origen and others to help
meet the criticism of Celsus and other pagans that the Christians
were obscurantists and irrationalists. In their own way and in their
own historical situation these allegorists were attempting to con-
textualize the Christian message for their particular audience in a
new missionary environment. Unfortunately, the negative results
outweigh the positive attempt at contextualization.

Philosophical Influences in the High Middle Ages

The allegorical method continued as the dominant methodology for biblical interpretation until the thirteenth century. At that
time scholastic theologians looked to another secular philosophical system, that of Aristotle, for insights that shaped their methodologies. Aristotelian epistemology, with its emphasis on the
physical senses as the primary avenue of knowledge of the eternal
spiritual forms, pushed biblical interpretation back toward a greater respect for the this-worldly and historical dimensions of Scripture. For a Platonist, the soul (spirit) was seen as hidden or
imprisoned in the body (letter). The Aristotelian sees the spirit expressed in the letter of the text, authored by God. The truth and
meaning of the text are expressed by the letters.

This concern for the primacy of the literal sense is reflected in
the work of Thomas Aquinas, the greatest of the medieval theologians. The insistence of Thomas on the literal sense excluded allegorical interpretation but did not exclude recognizing that the
Bible often employs metaphorical or figurative language. When the
language used is figurative, then the literal sense is the figurative
sense. As a result, the literal sense was much richer than a sense
that could be derived simply from a literal reading of the text without regard to the nature of the language.

Synchronic Exegesis

In the mid-twentieth century scholars saw the limitations of
the historical-critical methods. While these diachronic methods
can help to uncover a great deal about the development preceding

a text, they do not yield a great deal of insight about the text itself. Thus, there has developed what is called *synchronic analysis,* which involves viewing things in and of themselves apart from the historical progression of which they are a part. The synchronic exegete concentrates on the literary presence of the text as a whole, on the narrative world that the author has constructed. This narrative world is what is signified and should be the focus of attention. The authors of each of the Gospels have, in a sense, painted pictures and created narrative worlds. By creating these narrative worlds they are doing something to or for their readers.

Narrative Criticism

Since the late 1960s literary aspects of *narrative* have increasingly become the center of interest. The Gospels as they stand in their story form, rather than their sources, historical background, or theological themes, are the subject of study. The narrator of the biblical stories plays a pivotal role in shaping the reaction of the reader to the passage he or she is reading. The narrator achieves this response in a variety of ways, ranging from presenting and withholding information from the reader to explicit commentary.

Just as there is a narrator in each of the Gospels, so also each Gospel has its narratee. Usually the *narratee* is unmentioned, unnamed, and almost invisible except in Luke 1:1-4. Theophilus is the narratee in the Gospel of Luke. He is named at the beginning and is the person to whom the book is addressed. The characterization of Theophilus as "lover of God" should influence how one responds to the style and story which the narrator unfolds.

For example, for real readers to be able to assume the role of the implied reader of Matthew's Gospel, they must regard themselves as a member of the believing community presupposed by Matthew's Gospel. Matthew was obviously relating Christ to the Jews in light of the Old Testament. Why does Matt. 5:1 choose to report the sermon as taking place on a mountain? The answer comes as we recognize that Matthew repeatedly draws analogies between the life of Jesus and the Old Testament exodus, wilderness wanderings, and conquest. In Matthew's account, after Jesus returns from forty days in the wilderness, he "ascends the mountain" where he presents his interpretation of the law of God. Jesus' preaching on the law on the mount is therefore deliberately compared to Moses receiving the law on Mount Sinai.

Structuralism

Structuralism was one of the first synchronic exegetical methods to have an impact on modern biblical scholarship. At a meeting in France in September of 1969, a group of biblical scholars began for the first time to apply the insights and methods of structuralism to the biblical texts. Structuralism, as the name implies, concerns itself with structures of language to which the particular linguistic expressions in Scripture belong. Related to the discipline of linguistics, it tries to explain how language functions at a deep structural level. It does not probe behind the text historically, as historical-critical scholars do; but it concentrates on the text itself as a literary phenomenon. It is interested in the mental structures of human thinking that express themselves in these texts and symbols. Interpretation depends upon the unconscious meaning in the deep structure underlying a text.

According to structuralists, the human mind structures thought by way of a closed system of signs or codes that are organized according to universal patterns in the brain. These patterns bridge from one culture to another and basically determine the writer's view of reality or worldview. Therefore, this system operates at the subconscious level. For the structuralists, there is a wide variety of languages, but beneath the surface the same basic narrative structure governs all languages. It is for this reason that structuralists find in narrative units in the Bible, such as the parable of the good Samaritan (Luke 10:29-37), the same fundamental structure as is found in Russian folktales.

The author of a text may have only consciously intended the meaning that historical critics discover as the intention of the author. However, the author as a human being and a member of a given social culture would passively have assimilated a variety of structures capable of bearing messages. These structures would have been utilized in the composition of the text. The meanings they bear would be just as much a part of the total meaning effect as the meaning consciously intended by the author. In fact, the meanings that flow from deep structures, according to the structuralists, can be analyzed with even greater certainty than the meaning intended by the author. This is true because the identical deep structures are found in all humans and all literary works.

Russian folktales, for example, begin with an initial correlated sequence where the social order is somehow disrupted. The rest of the narrative consists in attempts to reestablish the social order.

The final correlated sequence shows the social order eventually being reestablished, and then life continuing as normal.

The structure found in the Russian folktale, according to structuralists, is basically the same structure that is found in any narrative. In the parable of the good Samaritan, for example, the order that is set up at the beginning—a man going from Jerusalem to Jericho—is disrupted by the activity of the robbers. Various heroes are mandated to reestablish order: the priest, the Levite, and finally the good Samaritan, who actually accepts his mandate to reestablish the order. The story ends at this point, but one can infer that the final correlated sequence will follow. This means that the man will get to Jericho. The overall structure is, then, the same as that found in the Russian folktale.

The good Samaritan, the wounded man, the ideal religious persons, the robbers, the kingdom of heaven, and the kingdom of Satan all fit together to constitute a deep mythological structure beneath the surface of the parable. This parable is not just an example story that was given primarily to encourage the helping of sick people by the roadside. Rather, it is a very fundamental parable of the kingdom that challenges traditional religious persons and values.

Grant Osborne notes weaknesses of structuralism. One is the loss of human freedom. If individuality is replaced by a closed system of codes, determinism results. Most scholars now reject rigid views of a closed or universal system of laws. They recognize that while the human mind does at time imply semantic opposition (such as good-bad, light-darkness), thought-structures cannot be forced into so limited a category. A second weakness is the reductionistic tendency. Structuralism forces the ideas and plots of a text into artificial theoretical constructs and ignores the complexities of individual surface expressions.

The Reader-Response Approach

Beginning in the late 1960s and becoming more prominent in the early 1970s, the reader-response approach stresses the reciprocal relation between the text and the reader. This is opposed to an earlier emphasis on the autonomy of the text.

Wolfgang Iser is one of the foremost scholars studying literature with this methodology. According to Iser, the historical-critical method can do a great deal about uncovering the history behind the text and the intention of the author. Structuralism can do a great deal about digging down beneath the text and uncovering the cultural codes and the narrative and mythical structures that are there. Ultimately, however, the full meaning of the text is supplied by the reader.

The philosophical background for reader-response criticism is found in the writings of the German philosopher Hans-Georg Gadamer, author of *Truth and Method*. According to Gadamer, the act of interpretation does not so much unlock the past meaning of the text as establish a dialogue with the text in the present. Understanding the text involves a "fusion of horizons" between past and present. In other words, when studying those passages where Paul reflects on his past life—such as Romans 7 and Philippians 3—we do not study Paul but the texts he wrote, and the texts speak to us in our present situation rather than recreate the original author's past situation. This means that in Gadamer's hermeneutics the intent of the author is not decisive for determining the meaning of the text for a given reader. In contrast to the Enlightenment's negative appraisal of pre-understanding as a barrier to interpretation, Gadamer makes it a positive factor, indeed the key to true understanding.

Working with such assumptions Gadamer developed his now familiar idea of the "fusion of horizons." The "life-worlds" or horizons of the author and interpreter find themselves fused in a concentration upon the object, the thing said or pointed to in the text. The reader expands the horizon of the text by appropriating it in a particular historical situation. The text, in turn, questions its readers by challenging and enlarging the structures they have brought to it. As they encounter alien elements questioning them through the text, the readers are forced to revise their assumptions; out of this process comes the fusion of horizons. In short, Gadamer's hermeneutic moves from the author and the text to a union of text and reader, with roots in the present rather than in the past.

It should be noted that this approach has no clear criteria for avoiding subjectivism. In fact, each moment of reading can produce a new and innovative understanding. Gadamer does not develop a methodology for distinguishing true from false interpretation. It is overly simplistic to say that the reader alone rather than the author or text produces meaning.

The Liberation Approach

The most frequent appeal for a reader-response theory in biblical studies comes from those who might be called "ideological readers." This term refers to those who read the Scriptures with a definite, usually political or ethical, agenda. The most prominent types of ideological readers are liberation theologians, feminist scholars, and African-American theologians.

Liberation theologians read the text, attending primarily to what they perceive are the needs of the contemporary society. Many base their interpretations from the perspective of the modern political philosophy of Marxism. Such a reading will bring certain elements of the text into prominence, in particular those texts concerning the liberation of the oppressed. The exodus, which is certainly a major biblical theme, takes on even larger proportions in the writings of theologians of liberation such as Norman Gottwald.

Evangelical interpreters should remember that the Bible has been used to oppose freedom for slaves. Appeals to divine authority to justify slavery amount to using the Bible, however unwittingly, though perhaps sincerely, as an instrument of power and domination for social or religious control. For some, it is a very short step to move from calling the Bible the Word of God to calling the interpreter's personal gloss on the text the Word of God.

Because of this possibility, certain interpretations of the Bible are described by some as an ideological smokescreen for the power interests of a group of aging, middle-class, white, Anglo-Saxon, North Atlantic/North American males. Here is a postmodern challenge for evangelical interpreters of major proportions.

The Feminist Approach

There are many differences among biblical scholars who are classified as feminists. Some seek simply to explore the biblical characters, books, and themes that are relevant to the situation of the modern woman. Other feminist scholars want to read the whole text from a female perspective to see what differences it makes if the reader is a woman rather than a man. Still others seek to read the Bible as women in order to "explode the myth of patriarchy." They seek to show the innate prejudice of the Scriptures against women and to expose the Bible as a potential and possible tool of oppression. All three types of feminists are united in the sense that they approach the text with a definite social objective in view. Some appear to utilize reader-response theory in order to give a methodological justification for allowing a reader's personal convictions to play a greater role in interpretation.

Some feminists accept the Bible as only one among four sources of authority which include experience, tradition, biblical witness, and intellectual research. In principle, for these feminists,

tradition, historical research, and experience have equal authority
to Scripture. In practice, they do not give tradition this parity. From
their perspective, patriarchy has tended to dominate the history of
theology. This means that feminists believe they they can use only
selective and radical reinterpretations of their heritage. Experience,
therefore, refers not to human experience in general, but to the experience of oppressed women struggling for liberation in concert
with others of marginal race, class, or status.

A number of evangelical scholars note the value of what might
be called ideological readers, even when they tend to be unbal-
anced. Some feminists, for example, read the Bible with colored
glasses, which often leads to distortion. However, such readers do
bring out important issues and themes that other, less interested,
readers miss. In fact, in many respects the church down through its
history has fallen behind the beginnings of the equality of the sex-
es that we find with Jesus and earliest Christianity. Thus a high
view of the role of women has indisputable elements of truth. But
these sensitive evangelical scholars are critical of those more radical
feminist and liberation writers who tend to give experience or a
preconceived perspective authority equal to that of the Scriptures.
It is easy to allow the context to control the text. If the sociological
approach is uncritically embraced, a view shaped by culture with
its own intellectual and social history becomes the guide for interpreting Scripture and gospel. The sociology of knowledge determines the theology of knowledge. Evangelical Christians firmly
resist this reversal.

Even Gadamer anticipates the charge that the reader-response
model is a reversion to pure subjectivity. He insists that, though the
understanding may be described in part as understanding oneself
in the text, the proper stance is one of subordination. We open ourselves to the superior claims the text makes and respond to what it
has to tell us. We do not take control of the meaning which the text
affirms. Rather, we seek to serve the text, letting its claims dominate our minds so that a valid interpretation and application
issue forth.

In this connection, evangelical scholars call for an openness to
new and more intensive studies of the context of texts used by rigid
patriarchal interpreters. An example of this type of work is found
in the writings of Sharon Gritz on 1 Tim. 2:8-15 in her book, *Paul,
Women Teachers, and the Mother Goddess at Ephesus.*

The Approach of Deconstruction

An area of literary studies which became prominent in the 1980s is deconstruction. It came as the "new wave" from France. Like the previous imports (existentialism, structuralism), deconstruction has brought strong reactions, both positive and negative, from English and American scholars.

Deconstruction is most closely associated with Jacques Derrida. His first major writings appeared in 1967, but his major influence came in the 1970s and continues in the 1980s and 1990s. Derrida is part philosopher and part literary critic. Derrida's extreme language skepticism calls into question the act of literary communication. A clear-cut meaning can never be established.

The New Testament scholar John Dominic Crossan has been active in bringing Derrida's thought to bear on issues of biblical interpretation. This influence is most readily seen in his book, *Cliffs of Fall: Paradox and Polyvalence in the Parables of Jesus* (1980), in which he analyzes the parables from the Derridean perspective. He finds that the metaphorical nature of the parable has a "void of meaning at its core . . . it can mean so many things and generate so many differing interpretations because it has no fixed, univocal or absolute meaning to begin with." Instead of searching for the meaning of the parable, Crossan plays (a favorite metaphor of deconstructive method) with the word of the text. For Crossan, the Bible, like other works of literature, always deconstructs itself.

Perhaps the most explicitly deconstructive study of Old Testament texts is found in Peter Miscall's *The Workings of Old Testament Narrative*. Miscall concludes that to attempt to pin down a single meaning to the text is misguided. Most exegetical issues are undecidable.

It is not surprising that a deconstruction approach should turn first to Jesus' parables, given their imaginative power. As extended metaphors, the parables cannot be reduced to a single "point." The parables renew our religious imagination, force us to view the world in a new manner, and compel us to make a choice between the old and the new way. The trouble comes when the parables are taken to be paradigmatic for all biblical literature.

The Return to an Emphasis on Authorial Intent

As we have noted, Gadamer has been one of the most important influences on reader-response criticism. Gadamer's views have been sharply criticized by E. D. Hirsch. Hirsch argues that Gadamer's rejection of the intent of the author as a norm of textual meaning is harmful. Gadamer's view means that the text really has no one meaning that can be determined. Rather we should accept an endless stream of meanings as perceived by successive interpreters. The result is that there is no practical way of deciding between conflicting interpretations. In contrast, for Hirsch, actual texts and speech-acts are the expressions of real individual persons. Consequently, meaning cannot be separated from the intentions of actual persons, whether of humans or of God.

Hirsch also argues that Gadamer overstates the influence of the interpreter's context on the perception of meaning. Gadamer exaggerates a difficulty into an impossibility. It is difficult to bracket out a person's cultural categories in interpreting an ancient text. However, the work of biblical and literary scholars, Bible translators, anthropologists, and archaeologists demonstrate that it is possible to transcend imaginatively one's own categories with some degree of success and identify sympathetically with the categories of a different culture. The text can be seen as having a meaning (the original author's) irrespective of the various perspectives from which the interpreters may be viewing it.

Hirsch further points out that Gadamer has confused meaning and significance. The meaning of the text is that intended by the author, and is thus a determinative entity. Significance, on the other hand, which involves the value or impact of a text in relation to the interpreter, will vary from context to context. Paul's concept of justification by faith meant exactly what Paul intended for it to mean, no more and no less. The contemporary significance of the concept for psychology or the health professions, for example, may well transcend what Paul consciously intended. New contexts lead to new significance for an original meaning. The same point could be made by saying that an original determinate meaning may have various applications in different cultural contexts.

Significance for Evangelical Hermeneutics

In summary, we need to keep in mind both the objective and the subjective poles of revelation and of Scripture. The objective pole gives us an anchor of stability and an authority for all seasons, preventing us from wandering into free-floating subjectivism. The subjective pole, on the other hand, gives us vitality and flexibility and rules out legalistic and insensitive pseudo-orthodoxy.

Interpretation of the Bible is central for evangelical Christians. They have always made a high view of biblical authority a basic tenet of their faith. In spite of the widespread debate over the exact formulation of such issues as inerrancy, evangelicals consistently stress that Scripture alone must dictate our faith. Scholarly evangelicals recognize the complex nature of that interpretation. However, with Hirsch, they would generally agree that the intention of the author is both a possible goal and a necessary first step in leading to the determination of the significance of the Bible in our day.

There have been strong disagreements over the use of the philosophical, literary, and sociological methods of interpretation. Those who unqualifiedly accept and employ them may consider those conservative scholars who do not to be naive. The latter, however, often see the critics as destructive and in some cases as not accepting the normativity of the Bible.

However, the study of contemporary literary, philosophical, and sociological approaches reminds interpreters that we must have a self-critical stance toward our tendencies to impose our own agenda upon our exposition of the Scriptures. We need to practice what Paul Ricoeur and others have called "a hermeneutics of suspicion." We may mistake purely human concerns about the ordering of human lives for "religous" ones, or for divine commands. Long before Freud, the biblical writers called attention to this capacity for very deep self-deception through their language about the deceitfulness and wickedness of the human heart. Hence, there is also the need for suspicion about the possibility of fallibility in one's own interpretation of Scripture. Our own interpretations should remain the object of suspicion and critical evaluation. How to give substance to this goal is one aspect of the study of hermeneutics.

Evangelicals thus should agree with Heidegger and Gadamer to the extent that interpreters often impose conceptual grids on a text like the Bible without due reflection. A person's particular context tends to shape the understanding and interpretation of the message of the Bible. However, the horizon of the hearer is not the decisive, let alone the only, maker of meaning. In this respect reader-response theory in its more radical forms claims too much. But neither is meaning a mere "item" to be handed over as if it were a physical object. Every Christian interpreter understands something of what Heidegger meant when he spoke of language bearing meaning within the horizon of time. However, most evangelical interpreters would support the priority of seeking to determine the divinely inspired author's intended meaning as the basic or primary beginning for biblical interpretation.

FOR FURTHER STUDY

Barton, John. *Reading the Old Testament: Method in Biblical Study.* London: Darton Longman and Todd, 1984.

Crossan, John Dominic. *Cliffs of Falls: Paradox and Polyvalence in the Parables of Jesus.* New York: Seabury, 1980.

Culler, Jonathan. *Structuralist Poetics: Structuralism, Linguistics, and the Study of Literature.* Ithaca, N.Y.: Cornell University Press, 1975.

Derrida, Jacques. *Writing and Difference.* Chicago: University of Chicago Press, 1978.

Dockery, David. *Biblical Interpretation: Then and Now.* Grand Rapids: Baker, 1992.

Fackre, Gabriel. *The Christian Story: A Pastoral Systematics.* Vol. 2. Grand Rapids: Eerdmans, 1987.

Gadamer, Hans-Georg. *Truth and Method.* Translated and edited by Garrett Barden and John Cumming. New York: Crossroad, 1982.

Gottwald, Norman K. *The Bible and Liberation: Political and Social Hermeneutics.* Maryknoll, N.Y.: Orbis, 1983.

Hirsch, E. D. Jr. *The Aims of Interpretation.* Chicago: University Press, 1976.

———. *Validity in Interpretation.* New Haven: Yale University Press, 1967.

Iser, Wolfgang. *The Act of Reading.* Baltimore: John Hopkins University Press, 1978.

Keegan, Terence J. *Interpreting the Bible.* New York: Paulist Press, 1985.

Longman, Tremper III. *Literary Approaches to Biblical Interpretation.* Foundations of Contemporary Interpretation. Grand Rapids: Zondervan, 1987.

Miranda, Jose Porfirio. *Marx and the Bible: A Critique of the Philosophy of Oppression.* Translated by John Eagleson. Maryknoll, N.Y.: Orbis, 1974.

Miscall, Peter D. *The Workings of Old Testament Narrative.* Philadelphia: Fortress, 1983.

Osborne, Grant R. *The Hermeneutical Spiral: A Comprehensive Introduction to Biblical Interpretation.* Downers Grove, Ill.: InterVarsity, 1991.

Ricoeur, Paul. *The Conflict of Interpretations.* Edited by Don Hide. Evanston, Ill.: Northwestern University Press, 1974.

Thiselton, Anthony C. *New Horizons in Hermeneutics.* Grand Rapids: Zondervan, 1992.

PART TWO

Implications of
Authority, Inspiration,
and Language

▼

Chapter Nine

The Inspiration and Truthfulness of Scripture

Steve W. Lemke

The issue of the inspiration and authority of Scripture has generated intense discussion and debate in evangelical circles, especially in the last few decades. The importance placed on these issues is not unfounded. Our view of the inspiration and authority of Scripture plays a primary role in shaping our hermeneutic method and our theology. Indeed, a high view of the inspiration and authority of Scripture is a defining characteristic of evangelical Christianity.

This article will attempt to provide an even-handed description of the various models proposed by scholars on these issues, identifying the strengths the advocates of each model would enunciate and the weaknesses its critics would allege. A concluding section will suggest the hermeneutical implications flowing from a constructive evangelical view of biblical inspiration.

Revelation, Inspiration, and Illumination

It is important that the student of the Bible understand the proper distinction between the revelation, inspiration, and illumination of Scripture. *Revelation* means unveiling that which was hidden. God has chosen to reveal himself (his character and purpose) in history through his deeds, in words through Scripture, and in an ultimate and personal way through Christ.

Inspiration is the process God used to communicate his message through his written Word. Millard Erickson has defined inspiration as "that supernatural influence of the Holy Spirit upon the Scripture writers which rendered their writings an accurate record of the revelation or which resulted in what they actually wrote being the Word of God" (Erickson, 199). Although in popular discourse we speak of a sermon or book as being "inspirational," the inspiration of the biblical canon is of a higher, qualitatively different level of authority than mere human inspiration. The very word *canon* suggests a measuring stick by which all other things are evaluated. The biblical canon is the measuring stick of Christian orthodoxy. No later claim to revelation can equal or supersede the canon of Scripture. Since the biblical revelation is the inspired Word of God, it is the definitive, authoritative, normative guide for the Christian faith. One may distinguish the *process* of inspiration (the method by which God interacted with the human author to produce the Scripture) from the *product* of inspiration (the divine authority with which the completed canonical Scripture speaks). The process of inspiration has significant implications for the product of inspiration, but these elements of inspiration should be considered separately.

Illumination is the experience in which spiritual discernment of Scripture is provided by the Holy Spirit. God's Spirit opens human minds to perceive and understand the truth already made known through revelation and recorded in Scripture through inspiration. Illumination provides discernment of God's inspired canon, but never supersedes or supplements it.

Leading Theories About the Nature of Inspiration

There are five broad perspectives regarding the inspiration of the Bible, although each of these perspectives could be subdivided in a variety of ways. The first two perspectives, illumination and mechanical dictation views of inspiration, have virtually no advocates among evangelicals. The next two perspectives, dynamic and plenary verbal views of inspiration, have been the subject of intense discussion and debate in evangelical denominations over the last three decades. While these first four perspectives see the process of inspiration as being uniform throughout Scripture, a relatively recent proposal, the multi-methodological view, allows for a variety of processes of inspiration. The following discussion identifies the strengths of each view that its advocates would assert, and the weaknesses which its critics would identify.

Illumination Views of Inspiration

Illumination views of inspiration claim that Scripture contains the noble insights of great people of faith. Their thoughts may be inspirational to the reader, but the authors are not viewed as being divinely inspired. Scripture is on a par with other great works of literature. There is diversity among those who hold illumination views on inspiration. Some maintain that Bible writers are merely inspired as are all great writers, secular or sacred. Others assert that all Christians bear the Spirit's inspiration. They tend to equate inspiration with illumination. Still others claim divine inspiration for only certain portions of the Bible that the writers could not have known naturally.

The *strength* claimed for this view is that its emphasis on the human element accounts for the diversity and apparent contradictions of Scripture. Apparent contradictions, inconsistencies, and pre-scientific worldviews are accounted for by human fallibility. The diversity of Scripture is understood as different human perspectives which arose from different individuals or cultures at different times. Illumination views of inspiration tend to be more palatable for naturalistically minded thinkers who view supernatural inspiration as an offense to their reason.

The *weaknesses* of the illumination views of inspiration lie in their depiction of Scripture as internally inconsistent and lacking any real authority. The Bible would be internally inconsistent if it claimed to be inspired by God but were not. Rather than being a great work of literature, such a book would be fraudulent. The illumination view of inspiration undermines biblical authority in that one person's opinion is no better than another's if there is no word from God. The Scriptures of all the world religions are on the same par, according to this view, along with other religious and non-religious literature. None of these illumination views adequately account for the supernatural, authoritative nature of the biblical revelation.

The Mechanical Dictation View of Inspiration

The mechanical dictation perspective views Scripture as the divine Word of God, with humans being only instruments or stenographers through whom God spoke his message (Exod. 31:18; 32:16; 34:1; 34:27–28; Ezek. 2:9–3:4). There is little or no human element in the inspiration of Scripture. It is perfect and without any errors.

The *strengths* of the mechanical dictation view are its consistent authority and simplified hermeneutics. The adherents of this view have no doubt about divine authorship. If God is the author of every word, then the historical, cultural, and literary background of the human authors make no real difference in interpretation. Each verse is a proposition that may be believed without qualification apart from an understanding of biblical culture and language.

The *weaknesses* of the mechanical dictation view are many. Its impersonal process of inspiration seems at odds with the fact that God ordinarily works through people, not propositions. Why did different biblical authors write with such different styles and vocabularies? Some opponents would describe the mechanical dictation view as a gnostic-like bibliolatry because it de-emphasizes the human element in inspiration. Advocates of mechanical dictation in a sense claim a higher divinity for the Bible than for Jesus, because while Jesus was both fully human and fully divine, they depict the Bible as having no real human element. The mechanical dictation view also faces the challenge of harmonization and repetition. Not only must apparent contradictions be harmonized, but explanations must be offered as to why it would be necessary for God to reveal a perfect record with so much repetition, that is, why are there four Gospels, and why are there duplicative accounts in the Books of Samuel, Chronicles, and Kings?

The Dynamic View of Inspiration

In the dynamic perspective, Scripture is described as containing the Word of God. The "kernel" of the Word of God is in the "husk" of human perspectives. The dynamic inspiration model emphasizes the inspiration of the authors more than the inspiration of the words they recorded. This process of inspiration is suggested in 2 Pet. 1:20-21, (NIV): "Above all, you must understand that no prophecy of Scripture came about by the prophet's own interpretation. For prophecy never had its origin in the will of man, but men spoke from God as they were carried along by the Holy Spirit." God inspired great people of faith with a message to communicate. God inspired thought by thought rather than word by word. The biblical authors then wrote down this inspired message in their own language and worldview. Indeed, this seems to be precisely the process Luke describes in explaining how he came to write Luke (and presumably Acts also):

Inasmuch as many have undertaken to compile an account of the things accomplished among us, just as those who from the beginning were eyewitnesses and servants of the word have handed them down to us, it seemed fitting for me as well, having investigated everything carefully from the beginning, to write it out for you in consecutive order, most excellent Theophilus; so that you might know the exact truth about the things you have been taught (Luke 1:1-4, NASB).

In this perspective, the Bible provides a trustworthy account of the means for salvation, but its cosmology, grammar, and history may reflect the spirit of the times of the human author. Ancient cosmology and apparent contradictions are explained as a result of the human element in inspiration. While the biblical writers' personalities and vocabularies are reflected in their writings, God ensured that what was written was what he intended.

Two primary *strengths* claimed by advocates of the dynamic view are that it parallels the pattern of the incarnation and that it adequately accounts for apparent contradictions. First, just as Jesus was both divine and human, so is Scripture. Just as Jesus emptied himself of some of his divine prerogatives in his *kenosis* (Phil. 2:5–8), so likewise biblical language cannot contain the fullness of divine glory. The human role in the dynamic process retains the personal character of the incarnation, rather than merely becoming propositions to be affirmed. Second, while affirming the inspiration of the religious and ethical teaching in the Bible, apparent contradictions in historical or scientific material are easily explained as having a human origin.

Two *weaknesses* for which the dynamic view of inspiration has been criticized are that it leads to inconsistent biblical authority and the "slippery slope" argument. The threat of inconsistent authority has concerned some critics because if only certain portions of the Bible are inspired, unusual hermeneutical prowess is required to distinguish the timeless truth from the timebound teachings. The "slippery slope" argument asserts that if we cannot have confidence in all sections of Scripture, how can we have confidence in any area of Scripture?

The Plenary Verbal View of Inspiration

The plenary verbal perspective describes Scripture as being the Word of God. "Plenary" means "fully," and "verbal" emphasizes that inspiration extends to the very words themselves, so that every word of the Bible is inspired. God so supervised the process of inspiration such that every word is as God would have it. The plenary verbal inspiration model emphasizes the inspiration of the words of Scripture: "All Scripture is God-breathed and is useful for teaching, rebuking, correcting and training in righteousness, so that the man of God may be thoroughly equipped for every good work" (2 Tim. 3:16–17, NIV).

From this perspective each biblical statement can be read as a true proposition to be affirmed. Because they believe God inspired each word, plenary verbal advocates believe that all apparent contradictions may be harmonized in some fashion. Jesus and Paul apparently took this approach to the inspiration of the Old Testament, because they based arguments on a single word in the Old Testament text (John 10:34–35; cf. Ps. 82:6); the tense of a verb (Matt. 22:32; cf. Exod. 3:6), and the distinction between a singular or plural noun (Gal. 3:16; cf. Gen. 12:7). Jesus even stated that not a single letter of Scripture would be taken away (Matt. 5:18).

God's intervention does not override the human element completely, however. The human authors still had a role in word choice (hence the difference in vocabulary between Paul and John, etc.). Just how the precise process of inspiration took place, how God superintended the writing of Scripture without violating the human author's word choice, plenary verbal interpreters often describe a mystery.

One primary *strength* of the plenary verbal view of inspiration is that it maintains a high view of biblical authority while allowing for the human element in inspiration. It offers a consistent base of biblical authority because every verse of Scripture speaks with equal authority. The interpreter can have confidence in every word in the Bible. Yet this view does not remove the human element, as does the mechanical dictation view. Some role for the style of the human authors is reflected in the various books without compromising their divine inspiration.

Two *weaknesses* often alleged against the plenary verbal view of inspiration involve the challenge of harmonization and the dilemma of the human element. Because each word is the Word of God, the plenary verbal advocate must explain all "Bible difficulties," cosmology, differences in parallel accounts, and so forth. Attempts at harmonization often appear forced or unrealistic to the critics of this view. The mysterious role of the human element in the process of plenary verbal inspiration also concerns its critics.

The propositional truths of plenary verbal inspiration seem more mechanical than personal.

Some who contest the plenary verbal position believe its advocates have a dilemma. If the plenary verbal view emphasizes the human element in word choice, the door seems open to human error. If the plenary verbalist emphasizes God overriding human word choice, then the position is reduced to mechanical dictation. So the "slippery slope" argument can be raised against the plenary verbal view as well, sliding into either the mechanical dictation or the dynamic view.

A Multi-Methodological Approach to Inspiration

Other scholars have proposed that Scripture can be viewed as equally inspired (the product of inspiration) even if God chose to reveal his Word by a variety of means (processes). The *method* of inspiration does not limit the *level* of inspiration and authority. Old Testament scholar John Goldingay in his *Models for Scripture* has proposed four methods of inspiration, each appropriate to a particular type of text: the witnessing tradition (narrative or historical materials gathered in the usual manner of a historian), the authoritative canon (the torah, given word-by-word by mechanical dictation), inspired Word (in prophecy a very specific plenary verbal message of which the prophet could say "Thus saith the Lord"), and experienced revelation (apocalyptic spiritual truths revealed to the author in a dynamic pattern of inspiration). One might add to Goldingay's schema other methodologies appropriate for other biblical genres, such as "wise counsel" (wisdom literature in which God inspired the wisdom of the ages to communicate his truth), and "worshipping response" (the psalms in which the authors lift their voices to praise the Lord or to express their prayers in their own framework of theological understanding). From the multi-methodological perspective, different *processes* of inspiration do not entail different *products* with reference to authority. All Scripture is inspired, but it should be read according to its genre. As I. H. Marshall ably expresses it:

> On a human level we can describe its composition in terms of the various oral and literary processes that lay behind it—the collection of information from witnesses, the use of written sources, the writing up and editing of such information, the composition of spontaneous letters, the committing to writing of prophetic messages, the collecting of the various documents together, and

so on. At the same time, however, on the divine level we can assert that the Spirit, who moved on the face of the waters at Creation (Gen. 1:2), was active in the whole process so that the Bible can be regarded as both the words of men and the Word of God. This activity of the Spirit can be described as "concursive" with the human activities through which the Bible was written. This hypothesis does full justice to the claim in 2 Timothy 3:16 that all Scripture is God-breathed; it is the product of the inspiration of the Spirit of God. What is being asserted is the activity of God throughout the whole of the process so that the whole of the product ultimately comes from him (Marshall, 42).

The *strengths* of the multi-methodological approach are that it is true to the biblical authors' own self-descriptions of the process of inspiration, that it is sensitive to the significant differences between various biblical genres, and that it still maintains a high view of biblical authority. It combines the best strengths of each of the four standard views of inspiration, with various parts of the Bible being inspired through a variety of processes of inspiration.

The *weaknesses* identified by critics of this approach include concerns about its diversity of processes of inspiration and the relation of process to product of inspiration. Advocates of single-process views of inspiration attack the multi-methodological proposal from both sides—those from the illumination and dynamic perspectives are uncomfortable with any of Scripture being produced by a mechanical dictation or plenary verbal process, while mechanical dictation and plenary verbal advocates have difficulty with some Scripture being revealed by an illumination or dynamic process. Further, one might question how a variety of processes of inspiration would not affect the product of inspiration as to its biblical authority.

The debate over the inspiration of the Bible has centered between the dynamic view and the plenary verbal view. Within this debate, the authority and inerrancy of Scripture have been significant issues. One's view of biblical inspiration has significant implications for one's view of the authority and inerrancy of Scripture.

The Inerrancy of Scripture

The Definition of Inerrancy

Since the term *inerrancy* has been the subject of intense and heated discussion over the past few decades, it is important to define precisely what that word means. Some diversity exists between various definitions of inerrancy. The Chicago Statement on Biblical Inerrancy defines inerrancy as "being free from all falsehood, fraud, or deceit" (Geisler, 496). David S. Dockery has defined inerrancy as "the idea that when all the facts are known, the Bible (in its autographs, that is, the original documents), properly interpreted in the light of the culture and the means of communication that had developed by the time of its composition, is completely true in all that it affirms, to the degree of precision intended by the author's purpose, in all matters relating to God and His creation" (Dockery, 80, cf. 89–91).

Many inerrantists qualify their definition of inerrancy with a number of significant limitations or exceptions. Properly speaking, most scholarly definitions of inerrancy refer only to the original manuscripts, not to our present Bible translations. Definitions of inerrancy such as the Chicago Statement on Biblical Inerrancy exclude the following from their definition of error: errors not in the original autographs; meanings not deliberately intended by the author, errors in grammatical form or misspellings, lack of precision by using round numbers or free (inexact) citations, observational descriptions of nature which do not meet modern scientific criteria, topical rather than chronological arrangement of materials, variant selections of material in parallel accounts, and apparent errors and contradictory accounts in the Bible which might ultimately be harmonized.

Views of Inerrancy

There is diversity rather than uniformity among those who call themselves inerrantists. The following are representative of a number of perspectives on inerrancy. *Propositional Inerrancy* (called variously Blunt Inerrancy, Strict Inerrancy, or Absolute Inerrancy) affirms that every sentence in the Bible is viewed as a true proposition, including those relating to science and history. Any compromise from this standard is seen as a threat to the integrity of the entire Bible. Propositional inerrancy affirms plenary verbal inspiration while trying to distance itself from a mechanical dictation view of inspiration.

Pietistic Inerrancy (also known as Fideistic, Naive, or Spontaneous Inerrancy; or Simple Biblicism) is a non-critical approach that simply assumes that all statements in the Bible are true. This is the approach of most laypersons in evangelical churches. It simply overlooks apparent contradictions, assuming by faith that there is some explanation. Pietistic inerrancy is an expression of simple trust in the Bible rather than an interest in more technical scholarly discussions about the doctrine of inerrancy.

Nuanced Inerrancy affirms that how one understands inerrancy depends on the type of biblical literature under consideration. Some portions, such as the Ten Commandments, seem to have been given through a mechanical dictation form of inspiration. Epistles and historical materials might be described as given in a plenary verbal form of inspiration. Material such as the proverbs seems to require a freer view of inspiration, such as the dynamic view. Because of the close link between inspiration and inerrancy, this approach argues, it is essential to articulate one's view of inerrancy carefully in light of the various literary genres in Scripture. Inerrancy is word by word in some passages (such as in law), but in other passages (such as in narrative) a long passage taken together is inerrant.

Critical Inerrancy (also known as Full or Complete Inerrancy), while holding that each word in Scripture is as God would have it, allows for a number of qualifications (round numbers, inexact quotations, etc.) such as those in the Chicago Statement on Biblical Inerrancy. Critical inerrancy makes cautious use of critical methodologies such as form and redaction criticism. It affirms the truth of everything in the Bible to the degree of precision intended by the author. Biblical references to scientific matters are often understood as phenomenological descriptions (how they appeared to the writer). This view understands that the biblical authors often did not intend to be exhaustive in every detail.

Functional Inerrancy (also known as Limited Inerrancy or Infallibility) views the Bible as inerrant when it speaks concerning matters of faith or ethics, but not necessarily in areas like science and history. Functional inerrancy affirms that the purpose of the Bible is to bring people to salvation and growth in grace. The Bible accomplishes its purpose without fail (infallibly). This view affirms that the Bible is sufficiently accurate in factual matters to accomplish its redemptive purpose but seeks to avoid describing the inerrancy of Scripture exclusively in terms of facticity in all areas. Instead, it speaks of the Bible in terms of truthfulness and faithfulness. Limited inerrancy affirms that the Bible is inerrant in all matters of faith and practice as well as matters which can be empirically verified. Inspiration did not grant modern understanding. The Bible may thus contain errors of science or history, but it secures fully truthful teaching about belief and behavior.

Arguments Against the Doctrine of Inerrancy

Challenges raised by critics of the doctrine of inerrancy often include the original autograph problem, the apparent discrepancy problem, the epistemological problem, and the semantic problem. The *original autograph problem* arises because no original autographs are available today. Critics thus suggest that appealing to the inerrancy of the autographs is a smoke screen because it implies that the Greek and Hebrew texts we have available to us, as well as modern English translations, are not inerrant. The acknowledgement that we have trustworthy but not inerrant versions of the Bible undercuts the argument that inerrancy is essential for an authoritative Bible and trustworthy knowledge about God.

The *apparent discrepancy problem* argues that the phenomena of Scripture do not support the doctrine of inerrancy. Prominent inerrantists themselves admit that the Bible contains "inadvertences," "problem passages," "apparent discrepancies," "verbal differences," "seeming contradictions," "Bible difficulties," and the like. But they insist that these must not be called "errors." Some examples of these difficulties include differences between parallel accounts, such as 2 Sam. 10:18 recording that seven hundred charioteers were killed, while the parallel account in 1 Chr. 19:18 states that seven thousand charioteers are killed. Or, while in 2 Sam. 24:1 it is God who commanded that the census be taken, in 1 Chron. 21:1 Satan is credited with telling David to take a census. In some New Testament verses there seem to be inexact or erroneous citations made of the Old Testament. For example, Eph. 4:8 quotes Ps. 68:18 as saying, "He gave gifts to men," (NASB) when in fact the psalmist wrote, "Thou hast received gifts among men" (NASB). At other times, the wrong book appears to be cited. Matt. 27:9–10 cites the prophet Jeremiah, when in fact the quotation seems to come from Zech. 11:12–13. Nor does the appeal to the author's intent resolve all difficulties. For example, in Matt. 13:31–32, Jesus based his parable of the mustard seed on the fact that it is "smaller than all other seeds" (NASB). Botanists claim some orchids have seeds smaller than the mustard seed. Is Jesus' analogy in this passage not based upon the factual size of the mustard seed?

The *epistemological problem* concerns whether the truths of the Christian faith are best described as propositional or as personal. Some object to the word "inerrancy" because they feel it suggests a mechanical rather than a personal process. They worry that overly relying on Aristotelian logic causes problems with other doctrines which appear to transcend logic. For example, strict use of the law of non-contradiction would insist that Christ must be either divine or human, but he could not be both. But of course the church affirms Christ as both fully divine and fully human. Likewise, they argue, there may be a middle ground between a purely divine and a purely human Bible.

Some evangelicals who prefer not to use the term *inerrancy* raise the *semantic problem*—they believe the word *inerrant* allows for no exceptions. The critics argue that using the word *inerrancy* with numerous exceptions as many inerrantists do makes it "die the death of a thousand qualifications." Those who dislike the term *inerrancy* suggest that it is difficult to understand how a sophisticated, qualified doctrine of inerrancy with numerous exceptions differs substantially from the high view of biblical inspiration put forth by some non-inerrantists. They assert that inerrancy emphasizes the wrong tasks, defending the minutiae of the Bible instead of proclaiming its saving message. They agree that Scripture is absolutely trustworthy regarding spiritual, redemptive, and ethical themes, but see no need to debate discrepancies of number and grammar. They prefer to use terms such as the *infallibility* or *trustworthiness* of Scripture.

Non-inerrantists are concerned that using the term "inerrancy" may commit the error of claiming more for the Bible than can be defended convincingly. The opposite error is just as dangerous—the error of so emphasizing minute inconsistencies in Scripture that the divine authority of the Bible is diminished.

Arguments for the Doctrine of Inerrancy

Advocates of inerrancy use at least five lines of argument in defense of inerrancy: the argument from God's character, arguments from logic, evidence of scriptural affirmations, the historical argument, and the authority argument. The *argument from God's character* affirms that since God is trustworthy, his Word must also be trustworthy. Scripture repeatedly affirms that God is truthful (Num. 23:19; 1 Sam. 15:29; John 7:18; Rom. 3:4; Titus 1:2; Heb. 6:18). A truth-speaking God can be taken at his Word. Since Scripture is God-breathed (2 Tim. 3:16), it is the truth.

Logical arguments for inerrancy often use the law of non-contradiction, which asserts that statements are either true or false; hence the Bible is either errant or inerrant. Some would utilize the correspondence theory of truth, arguing that the Bible corresponds to reality in every detail. Others would utilize logical syllogisms such as the following:

- Major premise: God does not err
- Minor premise: The Bible is God's Word
- Conclusion: The Bible does not err

Scriptural affirmations also support the inerrancy of Scripture. Jesus affirmed that Scripture cannot be broken (John 10:35), and not even a single letter would change of God's Word (Matt. 5:18). Not only did the New Testament writers recognize the inspiration of the Old Testament, but Paul was conscious that his message was from God (1 Thess. 2:13); and Peter recognized Paul's writing as being on a par with the Old Testament Scripture (2 Pet. 3:15). Scripture is thus self-authenticating in that it affirms its own truthfulness.

Patterns in church history have been cited as evidence of the need for a doctrine of inerrancy. Those who have not affirmed the inerrancy of the Bible have frequently later deviated from basic Christian doctrines and have lost their spiritual vitality. Although the word *inerrancy* is a relatively recent phenomenon, overwhelming evidence exists that very high views of biblical inspiration and authority have been held throughout church history.

The authority problem arises as a practical dilemma if some Scripture were not accepted as true. Who decides which Scriptures are inspired? Can only those with unusual hermeneutical skill decide such issues, leaving the typical Christian in confusion about what is authoritative in the Bible? How can people trust their eternal salvation based on a document riddled with errors?

Many arguments and counterarguments are offered between errantists and irerrantists. Each biblical exeget must weight these issues and determine one's own personal convictions. It is essential that one's stance affirm a high view of biblical authority.

The Authority of the Bible

The authority of the Bible is evidenced both by internal and external evidence. The *internal evidence* includes the Bible's self-attestation of its own authority as delegated by God (2 Tim. 3:16; 2 Pet. 1:21). Christ recognized the Old Testament writings as authoritative (Matt. 5:17; John 10:35). The unity of the Bible requires that all Scripture speak with divine authority. The *external evidence* for the authority of the Bible includes its practical effects in the lives of people, its cumulative influence, its remarkable survival, its confirmation in the findings of archaelogy, and the inner witness of the Holy Spirit.

The Bible thus has both intrinsic and extrinsic authority. It has *intrinsic authority* because it is the Word of God, an authority delegated by virtue of its status as *God's* Word (John 5:39–40). The Bible has *extrinsic authority* as Christians acknowledge the Bible as God's Word and apply its principles to their lives. Only those who accept the Scripture as extrinsic authority for their lives can appropriate its spiritual resources for Christian life and maturity (John 20:31; Heb. 4:12). Acknowledging biblical authority entails being willing to submit our presuppositions and worldview to the authority of Scripture, rather than imposing our own agenda and interests on the Bible. It is important that we acknowledge both the intrinsic and extrinsic authority of the Bible; one without the other is incomplete and one-sided. Scripture is our authoritative and normative guide for the church, the Christian life, and the Christian interpretation of reality.

Contours of a Constructive Evangelical View of Biblical Authority and Inspiration

High views of Scripture such as those enunciated by David S. Dockery (above) and Millard Erickson (following) frame a mainstream evangelical view of biblical inspiration and authority: "The Bible, when correctly interpreted in light of the level to which culture and the means of communication had developed at the time it was written, and in view of the purposes for which it was given, is fully faithful in all that it affirms" (Erickson, 233–34). Note several significant elements of these affirmations.

1. A high view of biblical inspiration affirms that all Scripture is true. All Scripture is given by inspiration of God (2 Tim. 3:16). The Bible infallibly and faithfully assures the truth of all that it affirms. When properly interpreted, Scripture never leads into error, but is wholly trustworthy in all matters.

2. A high view of biblical inspiration presupposes a confessional stance. Since they presuppose the truth of Scripture, those with a high view of inspiration are predisposed to approach Scripture with a *hermeneutic of consent* rather than a *hermeneutic of suspicion*. Belief in the divine inspiration of Scripture and reliance on the illumination of the Holy Spirit are necessary prerequisites to understand Scripture at its deepest levels (John 14:26; 15:26; 16:13-15; 1 Cor. 2:13). While evangelical scholars may find limited use of critical methods fruitful, they are mindful of the danger of any method with an antisupernatural bias which would undermine the divine authorship of Scripture. The insights discovered by use of modern and postmodern critical methodologies is tempered by the awareness that a complete understanding of Scripture requires spiritual discernment. Julius Wellhausen, whose name is most often associated with Old Testament source criticism, later came to regret some of the practical effects in the church of his earlier work: "I became a theologian because I was interested in the scientific treatment of the Bible; it has only gradually dawned upon me that a professor of theology likewise has the practical task of preparing students for service in the Evangelical Church, and that I was not fulfilling this practical task, but rather . . . was incapacitating my hearers for their office" (Wellhausen, quoted in Jepsen, 247). Confessional presuppositions greatly color one's approach to the Bible and the interpretations one derives from it.

3. A high view of biblical inspiration takes authorial intent seriously. The divine Author stands behind all the human authors of Scripture. Discovering what the message meant to the people of that day is essential in discovering what it means now. Subjective opinions should not be imposed on the text; not all interpretations of Scripture are correct. The purpose and intent of the human authors and the divine Author of Scripture are of the utmost significance for adequate biblical interpretation.

4. A high view of biblical inspiration makes good hermeneutics imperative. Careful research of the language, customs, history, and geography of the biblical era are essential to understanding the message God was communicating to the people in that generation, in order that we might undertand its message for our own generation. This use of the grammatical-historical method assumes that the plain sense of Scripture is the correct understanding unless there are clear signals in Scripture that the passage should be interpreted differently. Christian scholars will want to utilize any interpretive device which enriches our understanding of Scripture. Paige Patterson, while warning against undiscerning use of historical criticism, has stated that "the reverential use of historical-critical method should not be rejected" (Patterson, 57).

5. A high view of biblical inspiration is careful not to impose modern standards of truth or accuracy which were unknown in that era and alien to the author's purpose. Modern scientific standards ought not be applied anachronistically as the only criteria of truth. Scripture was written in the premodern world, not the modern or postmodern world. As Carl F. H. Henry expresses it, "To uniformly impose the same formula of verbal precision upon the entire content of Scripture raises unnecessary difficulties in defining inspiration" (Henry, 4:206). Responsible hermeneutics demands that we strive to understand what Scripture meant in its own era so we can discover its timeless truths and apply them to our lives. We must thus investigate the purpose intended by the author, the language and literary forms available to him, and the culture surrounding him. Evangelicals do not impose a wooden literalism on biblical interpretation, but are sensitive and flexible to genre and diverse cultural expressions.

6. *A high view of biblical inspiration, while acknowledging that there are phenomena in Scripture which appear inconsistent or inaccurate, affirms that these difficulties can be resolved.* In most cases, a logical explanation can be made to affirm the truth of these diverse accounts. In a few cases, an evangelical exegete must simply affirm by faith the truth of accounts for which adequate explanation is not yet available. As evidenced in the Chicago Statement of Biblical Inerrancy, most evangelicals would not count as errors such phenomena in Scripture as a lack of modern technical precision, irregularities of grammar or spelling, observational descriptions of nature, the use of hyperbole and round numbers, the topical arrangement of material, variant descriptions in parallel accounts, or the use of free citations.

7. *A high view of biblical inspiration views the Bible as a divine/human book.* Scripture was produced through what J. I. Packer in *Fundamentalism and the Word of God* calls the "concursive" action of God and persons (Packer, 80). A high view of biblical inspiration does not require a mechanical dictation view of inspiration which undermines the human element in inspiration. Although the analogy is inexact, there are similarities between Jesus Christ's being fully divine and fully human with the divine and human authorship of the Bible. God worked through and with humans to produce our biblical canon.

A high view of biblical inspiration is essential for a healthy evangelical faith. Those who deny the truth of the Bible or approach it with suspicion and antisupernatural presuppositions will never fully understand the significance of Scripture. God's Word, illuminated by the Holy Spirit, is foundational for a meaningful knowledge of God and His creation.

▼

For Further Study

Beegle, Dewey M. *Scripture, Tradition and Infallibility.* Grand Rapids: Eerdmans, 1973.

Bush, L. Russ, and Tom J. Nettles. *Baptists and the Bible.* Chicago: Moody, 1981.

Carson, D. A., and John D. Woodbridge, eds. *Scripture and Truth.* Grand Rapids: Baker, 1992.

"The Chicago Statement of Biblical Hermeneutics." *Journal of the Evangelical Theological Society* 25 (1982): 397-401.

Davis, Stephen. *The Debate About the Bible: Inerrancy versus Infallibility.* Philadelphia: Westminster, 1977.

Dilday, Russell. *The Doctrine of Biblical Authority.* Nashville: Convention Press, 1982.

Dockery, David S. *The Doctrine of the Bible.* Nashville: Convention Press, 1991.

———, and Robison B. James, eds. *Beyond the Impasse? Scripture, Interpretation, and Theology in Baptist Life.*

Draper, Jimmy. *Authority: The Critical Issue for Southern Baptists.* Old Tappan, N. J.: Revell, 1984.

Erickson, Millard. *Christian Theology,* one vol. ed. Grand Rapids: Baker, 1985.

Farmer, H. H. "The Bible: Its Significance and Authority." In *The Interpreter's Bible,* 1:3–31. Nashville: Abingdon, 1951.

Geisler, Norman L., ed. *Inerrancy.* Grand Rapids: Zondervan, 1979.

Goldingay, John. *Models for Scripture.* Grand Rapids: Eerdmans, 1994.

Henry, Carl F. H. *God, Revelation, and Authority,* 6 vols. Waco: Word, 1979.

James, Robison, ed. *The Unfettered Word,* Waco: Word, 1987.

Jepson, Alfred. "The Scientific Study of the Old Testament." In *Essays on Old Testament Hermeneutics.* Edited by Claus Westermann. Richmond: John Knox, 1963: 246–84.

Marshall, I. H. *Biblical Inspiration.* Grand Rapids: Eerdmans, 1982.

Newport, John P. "Southern Baptists and the Bible: Seeking a Balanced Perspective," *Southwestern Journal of Theology* 34 (1992): 31–42.

Nicole, Roger R., and J. Ramsey Michaels, eds. *Inerrancy and Common Sense.* Grand Rapids: Baker, 1980.

Packer, J. I. *"Fundamentalism" and the Word of God.* Grand Rapids: Eerdmans, 1958.

Patterson, Paige. "The Historical-Critical Study of the Bible: Dangerous or Helpful?" *The Theological Educator* 37 (1988): 57.

Pinnock, Clark H. *The Scripture Principle.* San Francisco: Harper & Row, 1984.

The Proceedings of the Conference on Biblical Inerrancy. Nashville: Broadman, 1987.

Radmacher, Earl D., and Robert D. Preus, eds. *Hermeneutics, Inerrancy, and the Bible*. Grand Rapids: Zondervan, 1984.

Rogers, Jack B., and Donald McKim. *The Authority and Interpretation of the Bible: An Historical Approach*. San Francisco: Harper and Row, 1979.

Warfield, B. B. *The Inspiration and Authority of the Bible*. Reprint ed. Philadelphia: Presbyterian and Reformed, 1948.

Chapter Ten

The Authority of the Bible

R. L. Hatchett

Many social commentators have observed that our era has lost a clear sense of authority. Our commitment to biblical authority is challenged by the absence of authority or encounters with conflicting authorities (pluralism). Yet the promise of evangelical and spiritual renewal rests in the conviction that each local church must trust the entire Scripture as its rule. This article addresses the authority of Scripture in three parts. The first studies the power of Jesus' prophetic deed and word. Then several models will show how historical circumstance influences the exercise of authority. Finally, a constructive proposal will emphasize the Spirit's mediation of the authority of the Bible in and by the church.

Jesus' Authority and Scripture

Jesus' authority is one of the key themes of the Gospels. The principal Greek word used in the New Testament for authority, *exousia*, may simply suggest power, though it can be contrasted to the intrinsic power of *dynamis*. *Exousia* bears the idea of control or rule and is used of the right to rule, domain of rule, or even the ruler. Two lengthy sections of the Gospel of Matthew portray the conflict arising from Jesus' exercise of authority. In the first of these sections, the Sermon on the Mount concludes by noting the crowd's astonishment that Jesus "taught them as one having authority, and not as the scribes" (Matt. 7:28–29). Jesus presumed to speak for himself without need to cite authoritative interpreters. Three trios of miracle stories (Matt. 8:1–9:38) each followed by a teaching passage, display Jesus' authority in deed as well as word. In the first three miracles, a leper bowed and acknowledged Jesus' power to heal (Matt. 8:2), a centurion who knew about "authority" also recognized Jesus' spiritual authority (Matt. 8:9), and Jesus vividly displayed his power over sickness and demonization (Matt. 8:15–16). In the discussion following the miracles (Matt. 8:18–22), Jesus asserted radical authority, discouraging and seemingly disqualifying would-be followers. In a second trio of miracle stories, Jesus calmed the storm (Matt. 8:23–26). Seeing nature conform to his spoken word (echoing God's creation via word), the disciples asked in wonder "what sort of man" Jesus was that even wind and sea were obliged to obey (Matt. 8:27). Jesus exercised authority over nature (Matt. 8:23–27), the demonic (Matt. 8:28–34), and disease and sin (Matt. 9:1–8). In the teaching passage that follows (Matt. 9:9–17), Jesus again demonstrates his authority over sin by calling a tax collector as his disciple—a person who was considered religiously disqualified. Finally, in the third trio of miracles, he revealed his power over death and disease (Matt. 9:18–26), healed two blind men who believed that he was able to heal (9:27–31), and cast out demons to the amazement of the crowd (Matt. 9:32–34). In the final teaching passage (Matt. 9:35–10:1) Jesus, moved with compassion for the multitudes, calls and commissions his disciples to the work of the harvest. Jesus' missionary sermon follows.

Another long section later in Matthew shows Jesus' authority. The Pharisees challenged Jesus' authority and interpretation of grace and forgiveness in Matt. 18:1–35. "Some Pharisees" thought they had Jesus, thinking his "no divorce" policy was in contradiction to Scripture which allowed divorce with certificate (Matt. 19:7). Jesus appealed to the biblical account of creation, noting God's purpose for lasting marriage covenants. He believed that proper interpretation of Scripture rested upon discernment of God's will. Otherwise we may come to Scripture minimalistically, just to get its permission for something we want to do. We may confuse God's concession to human hard-heartedness with his ideal. The rich young ruler (Matt. 19:16) was challenged to discern that even outward obedience to the law did not win participation in the kingdom. Kingdom living is possible only with submission to God's will.

Jesus' opponents protested the vineyard worker parable. They resisted its teaching that God exercises power and authority in his kingdom by offering mercy and a hope for eschatological reversal (Matt. 20:16; 19:23–28). In prophesying his crucifixion (Matt. 20:17–19), Jesus acknowledged the suffering obedience to come and redefined authority as self-giving service or ministry. Two disciples lusting for political authority sought places of rulership (Matt. 20:20–24), but Jesus forbade his followers to rule as those who love to show power. The triumphant entry and cleansing of the temple provoked another challenge to Jesus' authority (Matt. 21:23). Jesus answered a question about his authority with a question of his own: he demanded that his disputants evaluate John's ministry—whether it was from heaven or from men (Matt. 19:25). Fearing crowd reaction, they surrendered their authority to rule on this decisive issue. Jesus, like John, exhibited a prophetic authority and unity with God's will that was rejected by his critics. The irony of these power politics could hardly be greater. The power brokers held all ostensible authority yet their power came "from men" and they were ruled by the fear of the crowd. Jesus did not depend upon his popular support or power. He exercised fearless freedom in the face of power, thereby showing his authority was "from God." The faith of Christ finally led to his death when both crowd and power turned against him. The parable of two sons (Matt. 21:28–32) exhibits the Pharisees' hypocrisy. They say "yes" to God by their religiosity but deny John's prophetic commission; but kingdom mercy permits those who have said "no" to God (tax collectors and prostitutes) to submit to the kingdom ingathering.

The early church encountered questions about authority when Jewish leaders demanded to know the authority for the apostles' ministry (Acts 4:7). The apostles simply and boldly reported that their word and deed proclaimed the resurrection of Jesus. The power people, however, seemed weak and double-minded; those with power over the people were controlled by public opinion. Again genuine authority is seen in witness: with such boldness the church began its mission.

Historical Models

Texts are read and applied in historical contexts. Communities, as in the early church and Reformation eras, lay claim to texts by means of an interpretation. The Enlightenment provides the conceptual framework for post-reformational theology and the historical-critical method.

Origen: Allegory as Authority

Origen, the greatest biblical scholar of the early Greek-speaking church, practiced allegorical interpretation. After skillfully ascertaining the literal meaning, he sought to disclose deeper, spiritual meanings that lay behind the text. Allegory was socially potent: the Alexandrian Jew Philo used allegory to show the compatibility of the apparently alien Hebrew and Greek worlds. He influenced both cultures with his argument that the Old Testament's spiritual sense incorporated the best of Greek thought.

Similarly, Origen read Scripture allegorically to demonstrate its place in the Christian community, to disclose its mystery, and to prevent misunderstanding. He struggled on several fronts. First, Jewish readers challenged the Christian claim on the Old Testament, noting the everlasting nature of the Hebrew covenant and the spiritual reading practiced by Christians. Second, others followed the heretic Marcion's insistence upon strict literalism. Marcion rejected the view of God literally portrayed in the Old Testament as mean and immoral. Third, Gnostic groups depreciated God's involvement in creation and history. The Gnostics used allegory to uncover Scripture's secret knowledge and claim it as their own.

For Origen, allegory was the answer. The deeper spiritual sense exhibited the Christian character of the Old Testament and allowed for the creating work of the Father. Allegory delivered Christians from envisioning God in immoral or physical terms (having an arm or tongue). Origen believed the Scripture writers never intended these images literally though they may help the simpleminded. He argued against the Gnostics that allegorical interpretations must conform to the authoritative doctrinal affirmations of the apostles ("rule of faith"). While Irenaeus had been cautious not to go beyond the "rule of faith," Origen exercised less restraint. He defended the rule of faith but he did not feel bound by it. He spoke boldly where the rule was silent.

Origen believed authority rested not in church office but in the special gift of the Spirit that aided the hearing of the mystical word. The priest and apostles of Scripture represented teachers (not church officials) who are morally and intellectually qualified for the ministry of removing the skin or veil of the literal sense which blinded Christians opposing allegory.

A brief word may distinguish Origen and the Alexandrian school from the Antiochene school of interpretation. Origen's background is philosophical or symbolic allegory (Stoics and Philo). The Antiochenes were trained in the ancient rhetorical schools ultimately seeking moral principles from texts. One of the steps of rhetorical interpretation was *exegesis* which consisted of *methodikē*, an analysis of usage and style, and *historikē*, an explanation of the story by commenting on the allusions to provide the necessary background. The Antiochenes, such as the great preacher Chrysostom, were drawn to *historikē*, not as historical critics but because preaching required moral examples. Similarly, typology noted correspondence between two occasions of God's working. While typology was generally more restrained than allegory, both schools were trained to go beyond the literal sense because they held the Scriptures as authoritative.

Roman Catholicism: Church as Authority

Protestant polemicists have claimed traditionally that the Roman Catholic Church recognized two equal sources of authority: the church and Scripture itself. Contemporary interpreters suggest that Scripture alone was understood as the earliest and normative tradition of the church. Yet the Council of Trent (1545–63) declared that the church was guardian over unwritten tradition and the interpretation of Scripture.

Subsequent to the Council of Trent, Catholic theologians reacted to the Protestant claim of "sola scriptura." Some, called "minimalists," thought Scriptures were authoritative solely because the church had approved them after they were written; others suggested that Bible writers were only protected from making errors. Vatican I (1869–70) rejected the notions of "subsequent approval" and "negative assistance from errors" as dishonoring Scripture and ignoring the positive impact of inspiration.

It was primarily the Jesuits who argued for "content inspiration," claiming that only portions of Scripture were inspired and authoritative. With the church to guide them, readers could conclude without fear that other portions may reflect the limitations of the writer. One such thinker, J. B. Franzelin, influenced the Vatican I proceedings. He held that God as author gave the thought-content of scriptural books to human authors (who may have held these ideas naturally). He distinguished the inspiration of the formal thought-content from the mere assistance given to the human author's expression in material words.

The Dominicans more conservatively affirmed the verbal text as authoritative but noted two authors: God was seen as the primary author and the human writer as the secondary or instrumental author. M. J. Lagrange, who championed the church's adoption of critical methods, emphasized the role of the human authors, speaking in Thomistic fashion of their "intellectual enlightenment." Thomas's analogy of an artist (God) and knife (human author) communicated the complete and mutual responsibility of each. Nothing was uncaused by knife or artist. Generally the dogmatic theologians preferred the content and/or word inspiration while exegetes preferred instrumentality.

The Vatican II (1962–65) documents attempted to place Scripture at the center of the theological enterprise and to encourage (perhaps empower) the laity and scholars to study Scripture. They affirmed inspiration within the scope of God's effort to save: ". . . we must profess of the books of Scripture that they teach with certainty, with fidelity and without error the truth which God wanted recorded in the sacred writings for the sake of our salvation."

Since the time of the Counter-Reformation, a hierarchical system of authority with ascending levels of power has existed: priests with authority over laity, bishops with authority over priests, and finally the pope. The belief that Christ's authority is mediated by the faith of one man entrusted to provide guidance to God's will and normative judgment for the entire church is called *monarchialism*.

The Reformation: Spiritual Witness as Authority

Martin Luther personified the Reformation's dependence on Scripture alone (*sola scriptura*) as the authoritative source in theology. He followed the late-medieval call for the return to the literal meaning in doctrinal disputes. He began as a "primitivist," preferring a return to an early vision of theology as an effort to engage Scripture with guidance from the early church fathers, rather than the Scholastic's logical analysis and ordering of theological systems. These Schoolmen practiced a rigorous application of a newly available logic ending in an overly tedious and unnatural treatment of both Scripture and the church fathers. But Luther believed that theology's return to the Bible and the church's desperately needed moral reform would converge.

Luther's personal struggle informs his attitude and approach to both theology and text. He came to hate God whom he viewed as a demanding judge eager to condemn inevitable spiritual failures. He agonized over his sins and his works of penance, knowing that even his best efforts were tainted and unworthy as recompense to God. He rejected the theology of glory which saw in humanity's noble efforts signs of God's grace inspiring mankind to ascend to the divine. For Luther every human contemplation and deliberation of God was mercilessly judged in God's revealing himself in the suffering of the cross. The theology of the cross shattered all vain imagination about what God must be like. Thus one must depend upon the good news message of God and not on human words concerning God. Luther encountered Christ, gospel, and salvation in the Scripture; his confidence in the Bible and brave trust in Scripture over tradition are rooted in this encounter. This gospel provided the framework with which Luther read the Scripture; sadly, while never omitting them, he spoke disparagingly of the Books of Esther, James, and Revelation as unfit for Scripture because they fail to show Christ.

Calvin brought humanist hermeneutics to the service of the Reformation. Rather than searching for transcendent truths to be placed in one's theological system, he sought to read the Bible for the author's intention or the natural meaning of the text. He was sure that the Holy Spirit was behind all Scripture, at times even envisioning the authors as secretaries; but he also noted the human authors' distinctive styles.

Calvin treated the Bible as rhetoric. The commentator must identify general concepts (*loci*) of the text. Particular passages could then be examined and related to the main thrust of the author. Calvin believed that Scripture's rhetoric, though less refined than the classics, was rich in persuasive figures and narration. This lower rhetoric corresponded to his notion of accommodation; Calvin thought God had lowered himself to use human language. Calvin concentrated not on the form of the words, which may be crucial for prooftexting or allegorizing, but rather on argument in its own context.

Calvin argued that the authority of Scripture was self-authenticating. Against Catholicism, he argued that neither the church nor human wisdom can validate God and his message. Instead, God vouches for himself in the inner testimony of the Holy Spirit. Against the spiritualists he insisted that Scripture is the authoritative locus of God's word to humanity.

Protestant Scholasticism: Doctrine as Authority

The face of the Lutheran and Reformed movements changed dramatically in the century after Calvin and Luther. Their followers, teaching in state-sponsored schools, earned the name "Protestant Scholastics," even though their work was more concerned with the emerging rationalism of the Enlightenment than with Catholic Scholasticism. The Reformers' vision of theology as a primer for reading Scripture (Calvin's purpose for the *Institutes*) and the Spirit's validation of Scripture were eclipsed by attempting to justify rationally and reformulate logically their mentor's teaching. Like the Reformers, they were confident of Scripture and its clarity. But the Bible was so immersed in history and culture that supratemporal doctrinal presuppositions and teachings had to be extracted and arranged systematically. The Bible's authority was thought to be centered not merely on its apostolic authorship or witness, but on its role as a source of data for systematic theology. In such a scenario God's absolute guardianship over the composition, selection, and preservation of Scripture was essential to insure the purity and logical cohesiveness of the materials to be extracted for theology. Ironically, they effectively created Scripture's replacement—a system of theology. In these mainstream Reformation traditions, power was entrusted to those who mastered theological systems—*presbyterianism*.

The Enlightenment: The Autonomous Reason as Authority

Enlightenment thinkers praised self-authority or autonomy above all, wrongly assuming that submitting to God's authority necessitated the loss of human freedom. With the emergence of modern science, nature appeared more self-sufficient. God seemed less important—he was relegated to merely religious matters. Even the faithful saw him as supranatural, standing apart from as well as above Nature. A more philosophical notion of God emerged which focused on central attributes of God common to many religions.

René Descartes inaugurated the modern or critical era of philosophy. His method for achieving knowledge illustrates his insight and influence. First, he argued that a knower must subject every truth claim to rigorous doubt. The thinker must dismiss any claim which is capable of being doubted by a reasonable person. Only "clear and distinct" ideas could be used in subsequent deliberations. Second, he called for the division of the phenomena under investigation into as many parts as possible or necessary. Third, the parts of the problem should be put in order and enumerated, from the easiest to the most difficult.

Descartes' method was influential in shaping how modern interpreters approach their task. Modern theorists tended to dismiss all tradition, accepting only those elements which the independent, objective individual understood as rationally acceptable. Truth was reduced to that which is certain. This lust for certainty motivated an unrelenting search for the indubitable starting point (axiom or foundation). Descartes' methodology also assumes that reality can be examined in atomistic (piece by piece) fashion. Further, many modern theorists held that strict logical inference from certain premises was essential to genuine investigation. Descartes' method expressed the mindset of an entire era.

At the end of the Enlightenment a German philosopher in this critical tradition would picture reality as belonging to two great realms. Humans were geared to work and know in one realm, but a second realm including religion and ethics permitted merely practical value judgments. Immanuel Kant effectively reduced Christianity to ethical instruction. He believed that local and concrete expressions of religion were by their nature corrupt. Pure religion was capable of rational confirmation and accessible to all, not the privileged few who had heard from God (Moses or Jesus). Curiously the Bible was still of interest to many rationalists and deists; but reason was the source of authority standing as judge over tradition and Scripture. The reader discovered convictions in Scripture which met the standard of reason. Such a mindset yielded Jefferson's Bible, retaining rational principles but rejecting most revelation.

Another tradition including Hegel and Marx held that knowledge was not objective but was dependent upon one's context. Hegel thought he remembered what most philosophers had omitted—time-temporality. Thus he did not rush to premature judgment that a branch was a different thing from a bud and a flower. The dynamic of history showed these things to be one organic whole, not three separate entities. The dynamic drama of history involved struggle between opposing viewpoints (thesis and antithesis) bringing forth a superior synthesis. This drama was composed of discernable epochs with remarkable, even catastrophic, transitions between each epoch (i.e., Marxism in economic theory or Dispensationalism in conservative Protestant theology).

The historical-critical method emerged from the Enlightenment. "Critical" suggested an evaluative posture, not an attitude of ridicule. The independent, knowing subject must assess the text according to some standard (Descartes' legacy). The principle, or test, of analogy was often employed, that is, to accept a historical report the historian would ask if anything analogous had occurred in his/her own experience. This interpretation assumed that the historical writing of the text could be reconstructed, and that the reader's experience was the standard for evaluating the plausibility of the text. The historical reconstruction often worked within a developmental scheme (one of Hegel's legacies). For example, in F. C. Bauer's interpretation, the general unity of the early church pictured in the New Testament gave way to a reconstruction: a confrontation between Jewish Christianity (thesis) and a pro-missionary gentile Christianity (antithesis) culminating in early Catholicism (synthesis).

Conservative scholars took up these methods with the conviction that the textual and the historical coincided. Perhaps because of Christianity's historical nature, cultural and linguistic insights proved useful in the hands of a B. F. Wescott and F. F. Bruce.

G. Ernest Wright: Revelation in History as Authority

Some theologians place the focus of authority on God's acting in history, especially in great acts of deliverance such as exodus and resurrection. Such acts display patterns for understanding God's working in other saving events. The Bible is the record of God's continual intervention in general human history. The cumulative record of God's saving acts is called holy history, or salvation history. In the mid-1960s, G. Ernest Wright was the most prominent American claiming that God is known by his revelatory historical events and subsequent interpretive words or inferences. A strong apologetic motive existed: God seemed more believable, more concrete, in history without relying upon a person hearing a word from God. Israel was also seen as holding a distinctive view of history which provided the foundation for most of what is good in Western cultures. Israel's linear view of history was superior to the cynical, pessimistic view of its polytheistic neighbors. It offered one God who revealed himself in history, rather than many gods to be placated by ritual. Critics such as James Barr offered humbling objections. In Scripture, word often preceded deed, and much in Scripture such as Wisdom literature seemed an unfruitful laboratory for such a theory. Advocates often doubted whether the events actually happened. Others charged that Wright retreated from "real" history into a sacred history which cannot be verified. However, Wright's emphasis on salvation history rightly maintained Christianity's historical character, God's persistent activity in the world, and the illuminating character of archetypal events (types for things to come). But word and deed are difficult to separate; an overemphasis on deed challenges the inherent authority of the text by reducing it to only a witness of historical, revelatory events.

Scripture as Rule: Prospectus for Obedience

Ironically there is a sense of Scripture's deficiency in the preceding models of authority. Each theorist or theory sought an authoritative locus in some feature of the text: its true doctrine (Protestant Scholasticism), its history or distinctively Hebrew outlook (Wright), its universal and timeless ethical principles (Enlightenment), or its witness to hidden mystery (Origen). Also, no one of these approaches account sufficiently for the wide variety of biblical literature: God speaking (prophecy), speaking to God (psalms), speaking about God (didactic and narrative), and so forth. Each affirmation of biblical authority is shaped by its cultural and philosophical context and its vision of God. While humility demands we be mindful of history's shaping our approach to Scripture, readers need not resign to mere historicism when they believe that God's word can shape and establish reality (Genesis 1).

Authority rests finally upon the trinitarian God: a Creator Father who has revealed himself supremely in Jesus' life, death, and resurrection; and whose Spirit continues to work in his church(es) and world. Authority is mediated by his Spirit's direction: the canon is the final rule and source; the church is locus and guide to faithful reading of the canon; and the world is the context for mission.

Canon and Spirit

Scripture's authority is best understood in light of the incarnational language about Jesus. The church confessed Jesus was not only chosen by God (adoptionism), but he was both "fully God and fully man" (Chalcedon). The heresy of doceticism (that Jesus only seemed human) should not be duplicated concerning Scripture. The Bible is a truly human document with history, context, and style. The Bible is truly and fully the Word of God with his sponsorship of what is reported (his act and speech) and its reporting. Only depending upon Scripture as canon (rule) can protect the church from misguided interpretations. Without a sense that Scripture is our guiding rule, readers may seek only a reconstruction of historical events and ignore the Bible's own narration of these events. Without a sense that Scripture is our rule and standard, our philosophical notions of God (i.e., Platonic and Enlightenment) will obstruct our reading the concrete, historical reports that God took on human form and spoke to particular human situations (e.g., women's dress in worship).

Without the Spirit the canon cannot function as rule. The church's conviction about and interpretation of Scripture rests upon the Spirit's witness (as with Calvin). God has not given some simple proof of the Scriptures or single method of interpretation above limitation or bias; he has given the Spirit to guide the church and his canon as source and rule.

Theological and historical interpretation must begin with the text of the canon with what is typically called the *literal sense*. Overly ambitious definitions of the literal meaning, as the author's absolutely precise intention or the author's psychological state, invite numerous theoretical objections. Authors can seek to say just enough and not too much (providing a flexible range of meaning). Some genres of Scripture invite the reader to explore various applications or insights. For instance, readers may ask if they are rocky ground (Mark 4) or innocent sufferers (Job). Modern readers typically assume that the author's primary purpose is description, but authors use their language and intend for it to achieve numerous purposes beyond mere description. For example, a teacher shouting "Indianapolis is the capital" may seem to scold as well as inform. Inferring the author's intention from a text, therefore, is executed with great risk. Yet while philological and historical investigation has difficulty arriving at the single precise meaning, it can identify inappropriate renderings. The literal sense is theoretically troublesome yet unavoidable. The literal reading is necessary, but does not exhaust the meaning of the text. Some interpreters equate literal meaning with God's intended meaning, divorcing the text from the human author's "intended meaning." The literal sense can also be linked to the dramatic or narrative sense with which the reader can identify.

A doctrinal or *Christological* reading, promoting the virtue of faith, locates the story of Christ at the center of biblical narrative. All of the canon is to be compared to and appropriated in view of Christ. An *ethical* reading, promoting the virtue of love, illumines all behavior in light of Christ's suffering love. An *eschatological* reading, promoting the virtue of hope, observes the promissory nature of God's Word as manifest in the resurrection. Such reading calls the church to embody God's future now and anticipate its coming in fullness. These various readings, central for theology and proclamation (Acts 2:16), are rooted in the experience of God in Christ; but the experience is rooted in the text. The hermeneutical mystery remains: the canon is our final standard for our speaking of Christ, yet our confession of Christ guides our reading of the canon.

Church and Spirit

The Bible's authority cannot be understood without the church. The Spirit brings about conviction leading to confession of Christ, and leads the church, which is comprised only of believers. The corporate confession and practice of the church is called tradition. While Baptists are guided by tradition (e.g., the Chalcedon model) the Scripture is the supreme authority. At the heart of the Baptist experience is the tradition of missions established when William Carey broke with centuries of tradition seeking to be directly obedient to Christ. He followed the Bible and not the antimissionary tradition, but a Baptist tradition of the church assisted Carey's faithful reading. Baptists seeking to restore the New Testament church called for a believing and obedient people, and they were baptized and freely submitted to the discipline of the church (Matthew 18). Baptists depended on corporate interpretation benefiting from all the members' gifts. Thus Carey, sensing that the church was addressed by Jesus' commission, submitted his individual reading; the community discerned God's will through prayer, prophetic reading of Scripture, and testimony. This scandalous inefficiency is nullified by the frequency of God's working through patience and suffering and the pattern of corporate decisions in the narratives of the New Testament (Acts 1:16–26; 4:23–31; 6:1–6; 9:26–30; 11:1–18; 14:26–15:35).

The local church is needed to discern contextual obedience when application across cultural lines is unclear (cf. 1 Tim. 2:9). Some entrust decisions to one (monarch or pope) or to ministerially and theologically confirmed leaders (Presbyterian and Reformed tradition). Baptists have entrusted the whole congregation to discern God's will. To this day most Baptists vote—one person, one vote. The scholar's knowledge and leader's vision must be submitted to a believing, Spirit-possessing body. Some other reforming groups were too tied to culture, state, and the regional notion of a church to enact this New Testament practice.

World and Spirit

Biblical authority demands that we look to the world because the Creator convicts the world through his Spirit and calls his church to mission in proclaiming Jesus. This article has called the church to a transforming focus upon the God of Jesus Christ, his canon, and his church. But the world can rebuke our aversion to suffering (hypocrisy) and correct our misinterpretation (as with Galileo). We listen to the world not to shape God's Word in its image but because God desires to restore his image in the world.

▼

For Further Study

Dilday, Russell H. Jr. *The Doctrine of Biblical Authority.* Nashville: Convention Press, 1982.

Dodd, C. H. *The Authority of the Bible.* New York: Harper & Row, 1958.

Fackre, Gabriel. *The Christian Story: A Pastoral Systematics.* Vol. 2. Grand Rapids: Eerdmans, 1987.

Farmer, Herbert H. "The Bible: Its Significance and Authority." *The Interpreter's Bible.* Vol. 1. Nashville: Abingdon, 1952.

Foul, Stephen E., and Gregory Jones. *Reading in Communion: Scripture and Ethics in Christian Life.* Grand Rapids: Eerdmans, 1991.

Garrett, Duane A., and Richard R. Melick, Jr., eds. *Authority and Interpretation: A Baptist Perspective.* Grand Rapids: Baker, 1987.

Gnuse, Robert. *The Authority of the Bible: Theories of Inspiration, Revelation and the Canon of Scripture.* New York: Paulist, 1985.

Green, Garrett. *Imagining God: Theology and the Religious Imagination.* San Francisco: Harper and Row, 1989.

Green, Garret, ed. *Scriptural Authority and Narrative Interpretation.* Philadelphia: Fortress, 1987.

James, Robinson B., ed. *The Unfettered Word: Southern Baptists Confront the Authority-Inerrancy Question.* Waco: Word, 1987.

Johnson, Luke T. *Decision Making in the Church: A Biblical Model.* Philadelphia: Fortress, 1983.

Johnson, Robert K., ed. *The Use of the Bible in Recent Theology: Evangelical Options.* Atlanta: John Knox, 1985.

Kelsey, David H. *The Use of Scripture in Recent Theology.* Philadelphia: Fortress, 1975.

Ramm, Bernard. *The Pattern of Religious Authority.* Grand Rapids: Eerdmans, 1959.

Reventlow, Henning Graf. *The Authority of the Bible and the Rise of the Modern World.* Translated by John Bowden. Philadelphia: Fortress, 1985.

Rogers, Jack B., and Donald K. McKim, *The Authority and Interpretation of the Bible: An Historical Approach.* San Francisco: Harper & Row, 1979.

Woodbridge, John H., ed. *Biblical Authority.* Grand Rapids: Zondervan, 1983.

Yoder, John H. "The Hermeneutics of the Anabaptists." *Essays on Biblical Interpretation: Anabaptist-Mennonite Perspectives.* Edited by William M. Swartley. Elkhart: Institute for Mennonite Studies, 1984.

Young, Frances. "The Rhetorical Schools and Their Influence on Patristic Exegesis." *Making of Orthodoxy: Essays in Honor of Henry Chadwick.* Edited by Rowan Williams. New York: Cambridge University Press, 1989.

Chapter Eleven

Language: Human Vehicle for Divine Truth

Millard Erickson

The issue of religious language occurs because of the need to objectify and preserve the revelation God has given. Until the relatively very recent invention of photography and of audio and video recording, the only way for a revelation to be preserved from perishing with its original recipient has been through the use of language. Even in the case of nonverbal communication, such as gestures, facial expressions, or body language, these forms of communication can be translated into verbal form, where they are less ambiguous, and can be preserved indefinitely. Thus, a raised thumb can be translated into, "Could I have a ride?" "You're out!" or "Good! I approve!" depending upon whether given by a hitchhiker, an umpire, or a spectator. By requiring interpretation, the act of recording helps remove the ambiguity in acts of revelation.

Language and Objectivity

This translation into language also introduces objectivity. While one is merely seeing or hearing something, there is no way of getting inside another's consciousness to ascertain what the other person is experiencing. Only when this experience is transformed into language, when the person says, "I see . . . ," using terminology familiar to the other person, is it possible to understand what the first person is experiencing, and even (if the experience is also available to the hearer) to confirm or verify it. This is particularly important when the revelation has come in a subjective form, such as a dream, a vision, or an inward hearing of the divine message. The process by which the revelation of God is transformed into objective language, whether spoken or written, under the supernatural influence of the Holy Spirit, is known as *inspiration*, and when the product is written it is known as the inspiration of *Scripture*. That process renders the product a faithful record or reproduction of the revelation, or, in other words, renders it actually the Word of God.

This does not completely solve the problem of communication of the message, however, for sometimes the content of the message goes beyond the effective capacity of the available language. Then the meaning may be only partially apprehended by the hearer or reader. While the causes of the lapse may be severe, including the recipient's imperceptiveness, insensitivity, inattention, or unfamiliarity, it may result partly from the fact that language, being an immanent human possession, cannot fully capture the truth about a transcendent God. A prime example of this difficulty is found in Jesus' conversation with Nicodemus in John 3, and is especially helpful because the difficulty occurred even when the communicator was the master teacher, Jesus Christ, who was himself the living Word of God. When Jesus tried to explain to Nicodemus what was necessary for him or any person to enter the kingdom of God, he used the expression, "No one can see the kingdom of God unless he is born again," (John 3:3, NIV). Nicodemus responded to this with a literal interpretation, based upon his experience and knowledge of birth: "How can a man be born when he is old?. . . Surely he cannot enter a second time into his mother's womb to be born" (John 3:4, NIV). The ensuing discussion gives us insight into the nature and function of biblical language, and how we may more fully and more effectively gain correct understanding of its meaning and purpose.

The Challenge of Analytic Philosophy

There has always been considerable interest in biblical language. Frequently, however, this was largely linguistic and *philological* in nature. It was aimed at getting at the precise meanings of terms (lexicography) and of the relationships among these verbal signs (grammar and syntax). More intensive inquiry regarding the relationship of these verbal signs to one another, their objects or referents, and the knower of the signs arose in the twentieth century, focusing upon religious language in the 1960s and 1970s.

Much of this attention came as the result of the rise of a particular variety of philosophy, or a whole shift of direction or purpose of philosophy, known as linguistic or analytic philosophy. Whereas much earlier philosophy had been synthetic in nature, attempting to put together comprehensive explanations of the nature of things (metaphysics) or of the process by which knowledge is acquired (epistemology), the aims of this school of philosophy were restricted to attempting to elucidate the meaning of propositions and seeking to understand the larger categories of the nature of meaning.

In its earlier form, usually referred to as *logical positivism*, analytical philosophy attempted to specify the categories of meaning and to stipulate the criteria of meaningfulness. It classified cognitively meaningful propositions into two types: *a priori* (analytic), or mathematical type statements, such as "a triangle has three sides" and *a posteriori* (synthetic) scientific type statements, such as, "the specific gravity of lead is greater than that of water." Basically, logical positivism contended that the meaning of the former type of statement was contained implicitly within the subject. The meaning of the latter type of statement was the set of sense data which would verify or falsify it. All other statements, particularly those that grammatically appeared to be *a posteriori* synthetic but could not satisfy the latter criterion of meaningfulness (referred to as the "verification principle") were deemed literally "non-sense" and therefore meaningless.

It soon became apparent that this approach to meaning was too narrow to be useful. The verification principle, in particular, was seen to be meaningless on its own grounds. Thus, instead of prescribing ideal criteria of meaningfulness to which language must conform, it sought to describe the various types of language usage under the concept of *language games*. Just as one does not impose the rules and the operating procedures of one game or sport (such as chess) upon another (checkers), so each type of language usage must be understood in terms of its own characteristics or rules.

When applied to the study of biblical language, this yields two important and helpful guidelines. The first is that the Bible must be seen to be composed of several different "genres" of materials, such as narrative, didactic or discursive materials, parables, and so forth. The second is that different understandings of the nature of meaning must be seen in declaratives or assertions (which are correctly referred to as "propositions"), interrogatives (questions), and imperatives (commands).

Analogical Language

With respect to declarative statements, there is a traditional classification of the ways in which symbols (words) involved in the propositions relate to the objects they ostensibly represent (their referents). *Univocal* statements are those in which there is an exact correspondence between two or more uses of a term. An example would be the term *animal*, when applied to a cat and to a dog. *Equivocal* statements are those in which the term relates to its reference in a fashion totally different from the usual usage with experience from which it is drawn, such as "dog" when applied to an animal and a certain constellation. In *analogical* use of language, some elements in the symbol apply to two or more referents and others do not, such as the word *foot* applied to the end of a bed, and to an appendage to the human body.

The concern of religious language with respect to this dimension of meaning does not apply so much to propositions dealing with observable facts or historical occurrences. With respect to these, it is possible to examine the referent directly (or through the usual methods of historical research) to determine the degree of univocity within it ("the leg of the chair," "the head of the table," etc.). The greater difficulty comes with respect to theological propositions, in which the referent may lie outside sense experience. Take the statement of Jesus in Luke 11:13 (NIV), "If you [fathers] then, though you are evil, know how to give good gifts to your children, how much more will your Father in heaven give the Holy Spirit to those who ask him!" Here we have a metaphor, not a simile. Jesus did not say, "God is like a father." He said (at least by implication), "God is a father." The question, however, is how much God (as heavenly Father) is like a human father, or perhaps in this context, the extent to which human fathers are like the heavenly Father. What is involved, then, in such forms of representational meaning is to determine the relative amount of univocal and equivocal elements, or, to put it differently, the degree of analogy between the symbol and its referent.

Inductive Methods

Another way of putting this issue is to examine the methods of inductive logic. Here there are two major methods, the method of agreement and that of difference. In the *method of agreement,* the more instances in which two factors occur together, the higher the probability of a positive correlation. In the *method of difference,* when one factor is found without the other, the presumption of positive correlation is overthrown.

As applied to the issue at hand, the analogy is examined and those points which are different are identified and eliminated. To take the case of Jesus' conversation with Nicodemus, what Jesus did was to distinguish his conception of the new birth from Nicodemus's idea of a second natural birth: "Flesh gives birth to flesh, but the Spirit gives birth to spirit" (John 3:6, NIV). A similar action is found in Jesus' discussion of the resurrection. A group of Sadducees, who rejected the idea of the resurrection, posed a hypothetical case for Jesus, of a woman who had been married successively to seven brothers under the law of levirate marriage, being widowed each time. Assuming a literal or univocal relationship between life here and life following the resurrection, Jesus said, "You are in error, because you do not know the Scriptures or the power of God. At the resurrection, people will neither marry nor be given in marriage; they will be like the angels in heaven" (Matt. 22:29–30, NIV). Similarly, Paul responds to those who ask, "How are the dead raised? With what kind of body will they come?" by saying, "How foolish! What you sow does not come to life unless it dies. When you sow, you do not plant the body that will be, but just a seed, perhaps of wheat or of something else" (1 Cor. 15:35–37, NIV).

Both Paul and Jesus are differentiating the idea of the resurrection body and resurrection life from the natural body and natural life. Some, on the basis of belief in a numerical identity (that the same body which is buried is the body which will be raised) also hold to a qualitative identity (that the body will be the same as before death). Even holding that we will eat physical food in heaven, they overlook the *differentia,* the equivocal elements. The body is not merely raised, now never to die again, but it is *changed.* Both Paul ("foolish") and Jesus ("you are in error, because you do not know the Scriptures") are calling attention to this oversight of indications of such change. That more is involved than simply this earthly body becoming incapable of dying is seen from the fact that Paul distinguishes between "raised imperishable" and "be changed" (1 Cor. 15:52), and says "we will all be changed—in a flash, in the twinkling of an eye, at the last trumpet" (1 Cor. 15:51, NIV). Notice that this process of differentiation may require consultation of other biblical material, where contrasting images may indicate that some facet of the image under examination is not to be applied literally to the referent.

The Analogy of Faith

We must be careful, of course, to avoid eisegesis, that is, reading ideas into a Scripture passage, even if taken from other portions of Scripture. We are suggesting, however, that the content supplied by Scripture elsewhere be utilized as a guard against improperly making univocal that which is not intended to be such. This is sometimes referred to as the *analogia fidei*, or analogy of faith. It is also sometimes called the perspicuity of Scripture, or the idea that Scripture interprets or illuminates Scripture. This method rests upon the assumption of the inspiration and authority of all of Scripture, as well as the unity of Scripture, stemming from the fact that although the Bible was written by many different human authors, all of them wrote under the inspiration of the same Holy Spirit. Thus, there is an organic character to their variegated expressions and applications of the truth to the particular situations and problems to which they were relating. Many of these are contextualized forms of an aspect of the universal or eternal truth. The danger is that we will take out of its context this aspect and universalize it, that is, treat it as if it were the whole of the truth. An example is found in James's teaching that faith without works is dead (James 2:17). This could be construed in such a way as to argue that salvation is by faith plus works, although even the context seems to guard against this (James 2:18, 22–23). When, however, the passage is compared with other passages dealing with the same subject, it becomes apparent that this is only one aspect being emphasized in a given situation (Gal. 3:1–14 and Heb. 11:17). Yet it does prevent us from universalizing the contradictory statement as well.

Deductive Methods

An examination of deductive logic will also be helpful. Contraries are universal opposite statements, such as "All A is B" and "No A is B." Contradictories, on the other hand, negate one another, without both being opposite extremes. Only one need be a universal statement. Thus, "All A is B" and "Some A is not B" are contradictories, as are "No A is B" and "Some A is B." What we are dealing with here, however, are subcontraries, such as "Some A is B" and "Some A is not B." These do not contradict one another. They rather are complementary. The images with which we are working are of this type. Only when one extends one of these, to universalize it, such as, "All A is B," is difficulty encountered. The use of several images can thus help isolate the truly univocal factors by eliminating the equivocal matters.

Discernment and Illumination

The meaning being conveyed by language is objectively present in the symbols used. It is not always, however, present in the surface meaning of those symbols in such a way that it can be fully explicated by pointing directly to features of those symbols. Rather, the role of the language used in the Bible to refer to transcendent or trans-empirical referents is to evoke *discernment*. In this regard, the meaning relates to the symbols in much the same way that meaning relates to mathematical symbols or rather abstract and complex formulas in fields such as physics. The meaning is objectively present. It is not simply brought to the encounter by the would-be perceiver or knower. Yet it may not be obvious to all, or initially, to any. The meaning may not be explainable using other language in such a way as to make it discernible. It is necessary for insight or discernment to occur. Once this happens, it is apparent that it is present and was present all along.

In Scripture, numerous images are often used for the same truth in an effort to elicit this insight or discernment, or to disclose truth which is not immediately and directly recognizable. Jesus used numerous parables to try to reveal a difficult or elusive truth. For example, he utilized several parables about the kingdom of God in his attempt to bring understanding to his hearers. These parables, seen especially in Matthew 13, each highlight different dimensions of the truth of the kingdom. He is, in effect, saying, "The kingdom is like this . . . and like this . . . and like this . . . , and also like this . . . Do you see what I mean?" Similarly, Jesus used numerous figures of speech or images to attempt to arouse understanding in his hearers of the nature of the relationship between him and his believers and followers. So, for example, he used such imagery as the way (the road), the vine and the branches, the sheep and the shepherd, and the friends. All of these were attempts to lead persons to grasp the much larger whole.

It is in this way that language functions in representing the more difficult truths of the transcendent. There is, however, a special dimension to the process of discernment/insight, that deserves special attention, namely, the *illumination* by the Holy Spirit.

In his discourse in John 14–16, Jesus indicated that the Holy Spirit would serve the ministry of guiding the disciples into all truth (16:13). He would do this by taking the teachings Jesus had given and bringing them to their remembrance (14:26). He would glorify Jesus (16:14). He would do all of this by giving the sort of *disclosure* of meaning that we have been discussing above. This is similar to the disclosure referred to by Jesus in a statement to Peter and through him to the disciples. Jesus had just asked the disciples who people said that he was. He had then asked them who they said that he was, and Peter replied, "You are the Christ, the Son of the living God" (Matt. 16:16, NIV). Jesus then commented, "Blessed are you, Simon son of Jonah, for this was not revealed to you by man, but by my Father in heaven" (v. 17, NIV). Another example, of a negative type, is found in the "blasphemy against the Holy Spirit" passages (Matt. 12:25–29; Mark 3:23–27; Luke 11:17–22), where persons who had heard the words of Jesus and seen his mighty works nonetheless attributed these to Beelzebub, the prince of demons.

Analyzing Language

Particular care is needed in recognizing those expressions which are indicative in nature, but which employ less literal usage of language. Among these forms are humor, riddles, satire, and rhetorical questions. In ordinary use of language we can usually recognize these and interpret them accordingly. Sensitivity to nuances of meaning may be necessary to interpret these expressions in written discourse, however. For example, satire should be seen in Paul's reference to human wisdom being foolishness to God (1 Cor. 3:19–20), rather than an exact parallel, which would suggest that God does not understand human wisdom.

A familiarity with the unique characteristics of the particular language involved is also helpful in discerning meaning. Among the more obvious of these characteristics is the parallelism of Hebrew poetry, recognizing which enables one to understand that we are here dealing with reiterated rather than complementary meanings. Similarly, familiarity with various idioms found in the language being used will spare us unconsciously introducing unnecessary distortion.

We have concentrated primarily upon the substantive or declarative type of sentence. Other forms of language are also to be found, however: interrogatives, imperatives, wishes, doxologies, benedictions, and so forth. While the detailed examination of each of these types of material exceeds the scope of this essay, what our current understanding of the nature of biblical language does for us is to remind us to examine carefully the different types of discrete uses and to treat each appropriately. One of the failures of logical positivism was to make one type of language the paradigm, and to dismiss all other uses as "emotive."

Guidelines for Biblical Interpretation

Several practical guidelines for biblical interpretation emerge from this study of the nature of biblical language:

1. Compare with Other Contexts. The expressions of biblical truth were in many cases written to specific situations, and thus were already contextualized. To avoid universalizing one application of the truth, we will want to compare a biblical passage on a given subject with others dealing with the same topic.

2. Pray for Illumination. The meaning of the biblical language is related to empirical experience, but goes beyond anything that can be fully and literally explicated by direct reference to the content of the symbols. The additional understanding comes as insight into those symbols, and is granted by the Holy Spirit in what we term "illumination." The biblical interpreter will therefore pray that the Spirit of God will lead him or her into that discernment.

3. Be Conscious of Your Presuppositions. Because the Bible is inspired in such a way that it is just what God wanted to convey, it is important to examine carefully the meaning in the original setting before attempting to relate it to our present time and situation. This requires that we carefully endeavor to understand our own perspectives and understandings which we bring to the biblical text, and seek to filter them out so that the Word of God is truly heard.

▼

For Further Study

Campbell, James Ian. *The Language of Religion.* New York: Bruce, 1971.

Charlesworth, Maxwell John. *The Problem of Religious Language.* Englewood Cliffs, N.J.: Prentice-Hall, 1974.

Clark, Gordon Haddon. *Language and Theology.* Phillipsburg, N.J.: Presbyterian and Reformed, 1979.

Ferré, Frederick. *Language, Logic and God.* New York: Harper & Row, 1961.

Gilkey, Langdon. *Naming the Whirlwind: The Renewal of God-Language.* Indianapolis: Bobbs-Merrill, 1969.

Hamilton, Kenneth. *Words and the Word.* Grand Rapids: Eerdmans, 1971.

High, Dallas. *New Essays on Religious Language.* New York: Oxford University Press, 1969.

Hordern, William. *Speaking of God: The Nature and Purpose of Theological Language.* New York: Macmillan, 1964.

Macquarrie, John. *God-Talk: An Examination of the Language and Logic of Theology.* New York: Harper & Row, 1967.

Metz, Johann Baptist, and Jean-Pierre Jossua, eds. *The Crisis of Religious Language.* New York: Herder and Herder, 1973.

Tilley, Terrence. *Talking of God: An Introduction to Philosophical Analysis of Religious Language.* New York: Paulist, 1972.

Chapter Twelve

Translations and Hermeneutics

Thomas V. Brisco

The task of translating lies at the heart of hermeneutics. On the one hand, most people read the Bible in translation rather than in the biblical languages—Hebrew, Aramaic, and Koine Greek. The history of the Bible is a history of translations made necessary as the gospel penetrated new lands. As familiarity with the biblical languages declined, the Bible was translated into new languages. Today the Bible is perhaps the most translated book in history. On the other hand, the act of translating itself involves important hermeneutical issues. How do you convey meaning from one language to another? What is the task of the translator? These questions are crucial to understanding, and understanding lies at the heart of hermeneutics.

The array of English translations available offers the interpreter valuable tools for the hermeneutical task. Each translation reflects the different method and goal of the translators. Translating teams make innumerable grammatical, syntactical, textual, and even interpretive choices that reflect their best judgments. By comparing various translations an interpreter often uncovers hermeneutical questions or discovers nuances that require further investigation. Systematic consultation of several standard translations embodying a variety of approaches is basic to good hermeneutics. This is especially true of interpreters with little or no knowledge of the biblical languages, but even experienced exegetes can benefit by such comparison.

To maximize the use of translations as hermeneutical tools, a student needs some basic knowledge of translation theory and the criteria used to evaluate translations. Moreover, an appreciation of the history of the English Bible gives perspective.

The Bible in English

Early English Translations

The numerous English translations available today betray the humble beginnings of the Bible in English. Although Christianity reached the British Isles quite early, a complete translation of the Bible in English did not appear until the fourteenth century. Latin dominated the western church; Jerome's *Vulgate* (completed in 405) was the principal Bible used in the English church. However, sporadic attempts to translate portions of the Bible into Old English (before 1100) provided limited access to the Bible to those unskilled in Latin. Bishop Aldelm of Sherborne (ca. 700) translated the Psalms into English. Especially noteworthy was the Venerable Bede, the scholarly monk of Jarrow. He encouraged translating parts of the Bible so that the less-educated clergy could be more adequately equipped for service. Although no copies survived, Bede was working on a translation of John's Gospel at his death in 735.

Some Latin manuscripts from the ninth and tenth centuries have an English translation "glossed" or written between the lines of the Latin text. Perhaps the most famous is the *Lindisfarne Gospels* now in the British Museum. These early attempts, though laudable in their intent, failed to provide a complete English translation; neither were they intended primarily for common people (although some metrical paraphrases of biblical stories circulated more widely). The Norman Conquest in 1066 changed both the English culture and language. The Middle English period (ca. 1100–1550) witnessed the first complete Bible in English. John Wycliffe (1330–1384), Master of Balliol College at Oxford, and two close associates—John Purvey and Nicholas of Hereford—collaborated to produce the translation. Wycliffe's ecclesiastical views precipitated the work. He challenged the hierarchial structure of the church and insisted that each person had a responsibility before God to obey God's law—the Bible. Consequently, the Bible must be accessible in common language.

The *Wycliffe Bible* appeared in two editions, both translations of the Latin text. The first edition was a slavishly literal rendition of Latin into English. Most scholars believe Nicholas of Hereford and, perhaps, John Purvey contributed significantly to this earlier edition. A second edition was completed about 1396, the work principally of John Purvey. Written in a more common idiom than its predecessor, the second edition circulated more widely. A prologue to this edition describes how Purvey sought to establish the best Latin text possible for his work. Purvey insisted that the translator focus upon "sentences" (i.e., "meaning") not mere words. Unfortunately the church condemned Wycliffe's views as heretical. His followers, dubbed "Lollards," suffered persecution. Both Nicholas of Hereford and John Purvey were forced to recant their work. In 1408 a synod meeting at Oxford passed thirteen articles—the Constitutions of Oxford—one of which prohibited Bible translation without approval of church authorities.

Sixteenth Century Translations

By the sixteenth century many factors paved the way for a period of intense activity in English Bible translation. The Renaissance, with its recovery of classical learning, the fall of Constantinople to the Turks (1453) forcing Greek scholars westward, the Hebrew Renaissance (printed editions of the Hebrew Bible by 1488), and Gutenberg's invention of the printing press (ca. 1450) all played a part. The Protestant Reformation (1517) with its emphasis on vernacular versions, provided a catalyst for new translations. In England the political and religious ferment of the Tudor dynasty associated with the break with Rome profoundly influenced the course of the English Bible.

William Tyndale (1484–1536) towers above English translation in the sixteenth century. A Greek scholar educated at Oxford, Tyndale desired to provide the English plowboy a Bible he could read. Despite strong ecclesiastical opposition which forced him to flee England for the continent, Tyndale produced an English New Testament by 1525, printed at Worms in 1526. Tyndale based his translation on the Greek text established by Erasmus in 1516; thus his English New Testament was translated from the Greek. A revision of the New Testament appeared in 1534.

Tyndale never finished a complete English Bible. He translated the Pentateuch, Jonah, the historical books from Joshua to 2 Chronicles, and excerpts from other Old Testament book; but betrayal and imprisonment prevented the completion of his task. In

October 1536 Tyndale was executed by strangulation and burned because of his work. Yet his death marked the beginning of a sequence of English translations in which the style and phraseology of Tyndale's hand is unmistakable.

Even before Tyndale's death Myles Coverdale produced the first complete English Bible of the sixteenth century in 1535. The *Coverdale Bible* utilized Tyndale's New Testament, completing the Old Testament translation in consultation with German and Latin versions. By now Henry VIII was moving toward a break with Rome; Coverdale benefited by the emergence of Archbishop Thomas Cranmer and Thomas Cromwell in Henry's court, both of whom favored a Bible in English. Coverdale's Bible was the first to remove the apocryphal books from the Old Testament and place them in an appendix between the testaments. John Rogers, a close associate of Tyndale, used the pseudonym Thomas Matthew to produce the *Matthew Bible* in 1537. Ironically the Matthew Bible was the first English Bible to bear a royal license even though it largely reflected the work of William Tyndale.

Coverdale oversaw a revision of the Matthew Bible known as the *Great Bible* (1539), so called because of its large size. Copies of this Bible were ordered placed in every English church. But soon after Henry VIII grew wary of the pace of change and the increasing dissent; as Cromwell fell out of royal favor more stringent laws were passed to control access to the Bible. The short reign of Edward VI saw several minor translations (e.g., *Cheke's Bible*, 1550), but the Book of Common Prayer was the more significant legacy of Edward's reign. Under the reactionary Catholic monarch Mary Tudor ("Bloody Mary"), many reformers fled to the continent to escape persecution and death. Bible translation in England ceased. But in the early years of the reign of Elizabeth I, the Genevan exiles led by William Whittingham produced the *Geneva Bible* (1560). Known as "Shakespeare's Bible," this translation proved immensely popular, particularly among those with Puritan leanings and in Scotland. The Geneva Bible was superior to previous English versions, especially in its translation of the Old Testament. But the Calvinistic bent of the work and the appended notes, though less inflammatory than Tyndale's, made the Geneva Bible unsuitable in the Elizabethan Settlement. Consequently, Archbishop Matthew Parker oversaw a revision of the Great Bible known as the *Bishops' Bible* (1568). But the Bishops' Bible was no match for the scholarship found in the Geneva Bible. Despite its ecclesiastical backing, it could not displace previous versions. English Catholics, too, prepared an English translation based on the Vulgate during Elizabeth's reign. The *Rheims-Douai Bible* (NT, 1582; OT, 1609–10) was translated by English Catholic scholars who chose exile in France.

When Elizabeth I died and James I of Scotland came to the throne in 1603, many translations were widely available. At Hampton Court Conference (1604), James took the suggestion of Oxford Puritan leader John Reynolds that a new translation be made. Seven years later the *Authorized Version* or *King James Bible* (1611) capped the series of translations begun by Tyndale. Fifty-four scholars worked on the translation in three teams: one each for the Old and New Testaments and one for the Apocrypha. Their charge was to revise the Bishops' Bible while avoiding sectarian notes and controversies. The work of previous translators, especially Tyndale, is clearly evident in the new version. But the level of biblical scholarship and literary acumen brought to the task by the translators assured that the King James Version was the best of its day. Not all received it as such; vociferous objections arose in several quarters. But the innate superiority of the version eventually overcame opposition. The King James Version became *the* Bible of English-speaking peoples for generations and a monument of the English language.

However, several factors necessitated fresh translation attempts; no translation, no matter how adequate for its time, is immune from these factors. First, advancements in textual criticism, coupled with the discovery of earlier biblical manuscripts, make possible the reconstruction of a better critical text. The King James translators had available to them a text based on a few relatively late manuscripts. Today that situation has changed dramatically by the discovery of the great uncial manuscripts (e.g., Codex Sinaiticus) and early Greek papyri of New Testament documents. Earlier Hebrew texts, including the Dead Sea Scrolls, have provided more ancient manuscripts for textual critics. Secondly, our knowledge of the biblical languages has increased significantly during the last one hundred years. Koine Greek papyri from Egypt, for example, have shed much light on New Testament words while Ugaritic has enriched our knowledge of Hebrew. Third, the English language has changed. Updating translations to reflect contemporary usage of any language makes it easier to understand the Bible's timeless message. By the late nineteenth century these factors prompted the first major revision of the King James Version, the *Revised Version* (RV) of 1881–1885 and triggered an unparalleled explosion of English Bibles—over two hundred in the twentieth century.

Modern Translations

Modern English versions can be characterized as *revisions* or *new translations*. A revision is based on a previous version, although the revisors work from the original languages and are free to make any textual or language changes deemed preferable. Revisions preserve the best of an earlier version while improving the work in light of new insight. In addition to the King James Version (Authorized Version), the Revised Version (RV, 1881–1885), the American Standard Version (ASV, 1901), the New American Standard Bible (NASB, 1971), the Revised Standard Version (RSV, 1963–1971), the New Revised Standard Version (NRSV, 1989), and the New King James Version (NKJV, 1982) obviously are revisions as well. New translations represent an attempt to translate the original languages anew. The New English Bible (NEB, 1961–1970), the New International Version (NIV, 1973–1978), and the Jerusalem Bible (JB, 1966) are fresh translations prepared by a committee of scholars.

Many twentieth century English translations are the work of a single person. *The New Testament: An American Translation* (1923–1927) by Edgar Goodspeed, J. B. Phillips' *New Testament in Modern English* (1958), and William Barclay's *The New Testament: A New Translation* (1968–69) are representative of this rather large class. Single author versions often contain creative, even striking, translations of passages, but also suffer from the inherent limitations of the author. Though not to be neglected for the freshness they may cast on a text, for purposes of serious study single author versions are no substitute for major translations prepared by a committee of scholars.

Evaluating Translations

That translations differ is obvious. The questions to be faced are why do they differ and how can the differences be utilized by interpreters? To raise these questions does not imply that there is a "best" translation; indeed there are many good translations available, all offering competent, dependable versions of the Bible. Determining the best translation in any given setting depends upon for whom the translation is intended and for what purpose it will be used. Still, certain key criteria for evaluating translations should be used by students to appreciate and utilize the distinctions of each version. The following remarks explore these criteria emphasizing issues relevant to interpretation. The student is encouraged to conduct his/her own evaluation of the major translations. A good starting place is the preface of each translation which often contains pertinent information. Additional resources are listed in the "For Further Study" section.

Translations differ in two broad ways: the underlying text upon which the translation is based and the goal of the translators or "translation theory" embraced by the authors. The former is a matter of textual criticism while the latter is a linguistic concern. Appropriate criteria for both areas must be employed.

Criteria for Evaluation of a Translation

1. The identity and qualification of the translators. A knowledge of the background and capabilities of the translators can be useful. In general, larger, theologically diverse committees are preferable to single translators or smaller, homogeneous committees. Translation is a complex task requiring skills in wide-ranging areas: textual criticism, three biblical languages, a host of cognate languages and ancient versions, and English literature, among others. Committees offer a higher concentration of skills than any one person possibly can. Further, a mixture of theological backgrounds inhibits theological bias which might invade a translation. The *New World Translation* produced by the Jehovah's Witnesses exemplifies this unfortunate trait in its translations of key Christological passages.

2. The underlying textual basis of the translation. Textual criticism is dealt with fully in another article in this volume and need not be repeated here. Yet the underlying text is a crucial factor in evaluating translations. Textual criticism has moved far beyond the knowledge of the Greek and Hebrew texts used by early English Bible translators, including the KJV. Modern translations, with the exception of the NKJV, opt for a critical Greek text reflecting an eclectic approach to textual questions. The traditional Masoretic Text of the Old Testament can now be compared with Dead Sea Scroll materials, Targums, the Samaritan Pentateuch, and other early versions. This means that translations differ occasionally in choice of variants; that is, they actually translate a different text. Compare the following translations of Hos. 4:7b.

NASB "I will change their glory into shame."

NIV "They exchanged their Glory for something disgraceful."

The different pronouns—"I" and "they"—give a decidedly different meaning to the verse; the difference represents the choice of variant readings of the verse by the two translating teams. Most translations guide the reader where such significant variants occur by italicizing or bracketing disputed words or verses, or by marginal notations giving alternative readings. Students with little or no textual critical background can benefit by comparing translations and noting textual variations. By consulting critical commentaries, the interpreter can gain insight on the nature and possible hermeneutical significance of any variant reading.

3. The theory of translation used by the translators. Perhaps the most obvious way translations differ is in the theory of translation employed by the translators. Here an appreciation of the translator's task is important; there is a "hermeneutic" to translation. To translate from one language to another requires an incisive understanding of both languages and the cultures each represents. No two languages are alike; they differ grammatically and structurally. Languages also reflect a specific culture and historical era. The greater the historical, cultural, and structural differences between languages, the more difficult is the task of translation. These factors are acute for English Bible translators since the biblical documents are historically, culturally, and linguistically quite different from twentieth-century English. Translators must overcome these barriers while remaining faithful to the message of the original text. This goal has been pursued along two broad lines.

Formal equivalency or "word correspondence" theory maintains a close grammatical relationship between the original language and the receptor language (the language into which the text is translated). The translator seeks the most literal rendering of a text permitted in the receptor language. Translating Hebrew or Greek word-for-word results in impossible English, as a quick check of an interlinear Bible reveals. Formal equivalency insists, however, that remaining faithful to the words and structure of the original language lies at the heart of the translator's task. Those who adopt this theory are willing to exchange literary quality in the receptor language for the sake of verbal accuracy when necessary. The result is an English translation that often appears wooden, stilted, and non-idiomatic. For example, the NASB paid special attention to Greek tenses, trying to capture nuances of meaning found in the Greek but difficult to convey in English. Compare Luke 15:32 in the NASB "this brother of yours was dead and has begun to live" with the NIV "this brother of yours was dead and is alive again." The ASV and the NASB best represent this theory of translation.

Dynamic equivalency places the emphasis upon the content of the message of a text rather than the form. Eugene Nida, a leading translation theorist, wrote: "Translating consists in reproducing in the receptor language the closest natural equivalent of the source language message, first in terms of meaning and secondly in terms of style" (Nida and Tabor, 12). Meaning thus takes precedence over matters of structure and style. This is not to suggest that practitioners of dynamic equivalency ignore the structure and idioms of the biblical languages. However, according to this theory the ultimate goal is not to replicate the linguistic patterns of one language into another, but to render the equivalent message of the text into English so as to produce in the modern reader an equivalent effect. This raises the issue of how far the translator can go to achieve equivalent effect yet still remain faithful to the text. Some translations such as the *Revised English Bible* (REB) or the *Good News Bible* (GNB) give much freer translations which stand at a greater grammatical distance from the original text than others. The aim is to communicate ideas in contemporary English. To illustrate compare the following translations of 2 Cor. 1:12.

NASB	NIV	GNB
"For our proud confidence is this, the testimony of our conscience, that in holiness and godly sincerity, not in fleshly wisdom but in the grace of God, we have conducted ourselves in the world, and especially toward you."	"Now this is our boast: our conscience testifies that we have conducted ourselves in the world, and especially in our relations with you, in the holiness and sincerity that are from God."	"We are proud that our conscience assures us that our lives in this world, and especially our relations with you, have been ruled by God-given frankness and sincerity by the power of God."

The NASB preserves more of the word order and idiom of the Greek. Its word correspondence basis makes it more literal, but it does not sound like contemporary English. The GNB recasts considerably the structure and idiom in the attempt to contemporize the message. The NIV strikes the middle ground. Comparison of longer passages in these versions illustrates the differences more clearly (cf. Gal. 4:12–20; Jude 19; Judg. 19 or Jer. 7:1–15).

The question of accuracy or faithfulness must be measured according to the goals of the translators. Most modern translations fall somewhere between the extremely literal ASV and the very free (even paraphrastic) translation by Phillips. The NASB, RSV, and NRSV tend more toward the word correspondence approach, approximating the maxim found in the NRSV preface: "As literal as possible, as free as necessary." Others like the NIV, JB, and NAB offer a moderate dynamic equivalency while the NEB, GNB, and Phillips are decidedly much freer.

4. The question of paraphrases. The distinction between a paraphrase and translation is important. Paraphrases are not translations and should not be treated as such. A paraphraser restates the ancient written thought in contemporary idiom. Paraphrasing permits the expansion of a text to achieve clarity where such expansion is neither required by grammatical conventions nor supported by the text. Compare *The Living Bible*'s paraphrase of Amos 1:1–2 with any standard translation and discover an entire sentence having no textual basis in the Hebrew. The addition represents what the paraphraser (Kenneth Taylor) thought a shepherd would be doing in the Tekoa of Amos's day. At times the paraphraser injects his/her theology as commentary into the work. A comparison of LB's paraphrase of Gen. 6:1–3 with standard translations shows how Taylor dissolved difficult interpretive problems by recasting the text to suit his theology. To be fair, Taylor informs the reader of the difference between a paraphrase and translation in an informative preface to the LB and his work, like that of any paraphraser, must be judged accordingly. Yet the point remains: a paraphrase permits expansion, alteration, or commentary upon the text not permitted by the strict standards of translation. A paraphrase should not be used for study purposes—except perhaps as a commentary—and should not be a person's only Bible routinely read.

The distinction between translation and paraphrase can become blurred, especially in the more free translations like the Phillip's translation or even the GNB. At times the translator(s) exceeds the strict limits of translations either by excessive interpretation or commentary. The student, while not avoiding the freer translations, should exercise care. In any case, the more paraphrastic translations should not be used as one's primary study Bible.

5. *The nature of the English language.* Translations should be judged also on the clarity and quality of the English used. Most recent major translations strive for a literary quality dignified enough for public worship yet appealing for personal devotion. Extremely literal word-correspondence-based translations (ASV, NASB) sacrifice literary quality for grammatical fidelity. This leaves them vulnerable at this point compared to the RSV or NIV. On the other hand, the more highly idiomatic English translations often lack the literary beauty and stately sound of a major translation and are, therefore, less suited to public worship. In many respects this criterion is more a matter of function and audience than hermeneutics. But a student would be well advised to consider how different translations deal with, for example, the distinction between prose and poetry or how or if the translators have sought to capture the style of the biblical writer.

Choosing a Translation

Which translations should a student use and how can the differences be exploited hermeneutically? First, students should use major translations produced by committees of recognized scholars. The KJV, ASV, RSV, NIV, JB, NRSV, NASB, NKJV, and the NEB all qualify as major translations. Second, use a selection of translations reflecting a variety of translating theory. Capitalize on the distinctives. Formal equivalent ("literal") translations are language transparent. They allow the student to "see" more easily the underlying structure of the biblical languages. They give a better feel for biblical idiom. Some translations like the NASB attempt to convey the sense of Greek tenses, perhaps a boon for those untrained in Greek. The translators of the RSV and ASV attempted to translate each occurrence of a Hebrew or Greek word by the same English word, so far as was practical. This practice has been abandoned in more recent translations given the semantic range of words, but it does alert the reader to the underlying biblical words. Dynamic equivalent-based translations are more receptor-language sensitive and allow the interpreter the opportunity to explore how best to express the biblical concept in contemporary terms. At times these translations offer insight on syntactical relationships not found in literal versions. For example, compare the NIV's handling of 1 Thess. 1:3 with the NASB: the more literal "work of faith and labor of love" in the NASB is translated in the NIV "your work produced by faith, your labor prompted by love."

Third, comparison of a wide range of translations can reveal significant interpretive differences which require careful exegetical attention. Consider the following translations of 1 Thess. 4:4 where Paul commends certain activities in light of God's will:

NASB: "that each of you know how to possess his own vessel in sanctification and honor"

NIV: "that each of you should learn to control his own body in a way that is holy and honorable"

GNB: "Each of you men should know how to live with his wife in a holy and honorable way."

The NASB prefers a literal rendering that is ambiguous. Both the NIV and GNB remove the ambiguity by supplying an interpretation of the word translated "vessel." The proper interpretation of the verse is much debated. Here the point is that the translations themselves point the student toward a significant interpretive issue which must be pursued. Additional illustrations may be found by comparing 1 Cor. 4:9; 7:36; and 2 Cor. 5:18–19 in various translations.

Fourth, start with your favorite major translation, reading the text in context many times. Then broaden the scope by reading the text from four or five other translations. Note any textual differences and be prepared to examine them thoroughly. Compare the vocabulary choices, the ways syntactical relationships are expressed, and the manner in which the translators have chosen to convey the biblical idea. Note distinctives and differences and be prepared to investigate. Good interpretation starts with a thorough reading of the text. Very often important insight can be gained which paves the hermeneutical road ahead.

▼

For Further Study

Brooks, James A. "The Text of the New Testament and Biblical Authority." *Southwestern Journal of Theology* 34 (1992): 13–21.

Bruce, F. F. *History of the Bible in English.* 3d ed. New York: Oxford University Press, 1978.

The Cambridge History of the Bible. 3 vols. Cambridge University Press, 1963–70. Vol. 1: *From the Beginnings to Jerome,* edited by P. R. Ackroyd, and

C. F. Evans (1970); Vol. 2: *The West from the Fathers to the Reformation*, edited by G. W. H. Lampe, (1969); Vol. 3: *The West from the Reformation to the Present*, edited by S. L. Greenslade, (1953).

Crim, Keith R. "Versions, English." *Interpreter's Dictionary of the Bible*, Supplementary Volume, 933–38.

Kubo, Sakae, and Walter F. Specht. *So Many Versions? 20th Century English Versions of the Bible*. Rev. ed. Grand Rapids: Zondervan, 1983.

Lewis, Jack P. *The English Bible from KJV to NIV: A History and Evaluation*. Grand Rapids: Baker, 1981.

MacGregor, Geddes. *The Bible in the Making*. New York: Lippincott, 1959.

Nida, Eugene A., and Charles R. Taber. *The Theory and Practice of Translation*. Helps for Translators, 8. Leiden: E. J. Brill, 1969.

In addition, the following issues of journals offer several articles germane to the subject of Bible translations.

The Duke Divinity School Review, vol. 44 (spring 1979). The entire edition consists of major articles reviewing the following translations: RSV, JB, NEB, NAB, LB, GNB, NIV, and the New Jewish Version.

Interpretation, vol. 32 (April 1978). "One Bible in Many Translations," by Robert G. Bratcher; "Translation as Interpretation," by Charles R. Taber; "Old Testament Translations and Interpretation," by Keith R. Crim; "Translations and Interpretation: New Testament," by Lamar Williamson Jr.

Chapter Thirteen

Preunderstanding and the Hermeneutical Spiral

B. Keith Putt

What is the first question in hermeneutical theory? The first question is the question of the "first," of what comes first, that is, the question of beginning. The question concerns the point of origin, the original position from which the hermeneutical process originates. This question inculcates both a spatial and a temporal aspect, since "starting" may refer to a place and/or a time: *Where* does hermeneutics start? *When* does hermeneutics start? Does interpretation begin from a space that is non-hermeneutical? In other words, does hermeneutics rest upon an "objective" foundation that does not itself depend upon hermeneutics? Is there any time during which one encounters a text without there being some hermeneutical antecedents? That is, does there not have to be a "before" to every act of interpretation, or does every "before" already depend upon some prior hermeneutical moment?

If there is no place or time that is not hermeneutical, then is hermeneutics itself consigned to nothing more than a never-ending play of conflicting textual readings? If there are no alpha and omega to hermeneutics, is meaning destroyed in the bottomless pit of indeterminacy? If I am always interpreting here and always interpreting now, can there be any possible situation in which various interpretations may be adjudicated and decisions made concerning true or false explanations? Does the question of truth demand that the question of beginning lead to a nonhermeneutical, objective, and verifiably certain ground for all knowledge? That is to say, can hermeneutics ever avoid the Scylla of subjective eisegesis and relative pluralism or the Charybdis of objective exegesis and absolute monism?

Cartesian Anxiety and the Hermeneutical Circle

The problem of identifying an epistemological source is certainly not a new one. One can discover as far back as in Plato's philosophy a significant attempt to unearth the seed out of which human knowing germinates. Plato develops a theory of *anamnesis* (remembrance), the notion that human learning is not actually the discovery of knowledge—the gaining of what one does not initially have—but merely the remembering of what one already knows but has simply forgotten (Plato, 81–86). Plato's anamnestic epistemology expresses one of the primary tenets of Western rationalism. Operating on the principle that *ex nihilo nihil fit*—out of nothing comes nothing—the rationalist assumes *a priori* knowledge; that is, to begin to know anything depends upon a prior knowing of something. Consequently, knowledge begets knowledge; truth begets truth; meaning begets meaning. At this point, the traditional theory complements the notion of hermeneutical preunderstanding quite well. Unfortunately, however, the legislating model for understanding how one moves from the *a priori* to subsequent knowledge is understood in linear terms. If one accepts such linearity, then not only can one search forward toward new information, but one can research backward to the foundations for knowledge. One can undertake an epistemological archaeology, and "dig" back through the layers until one can discover a bedrock of first principles (*archai*) upon which the edifice of learning rests. Only if such a beginning can be located can there be any hope for establishing objective and certain truth.

This understanding of the necessity for a protological investigation into the validity of knowledge finds its way into modern philosophy and theology through the thought of Rene Descartes. In the contemporary nomenclature, Descartes' philosophy manifests another version of "classical foundationalism," the notion that some ahistorical, immutable, objective, and verifiable substructure for knowledge is the only guarantee of rationality and truth. By utilizing doubt as his *modus operandi*, Descartes established what he took to be the one indubitable certainty upon which he could erect his epistemological superstructure. That certainty is the existence of his own mind, the "self" (Descartes, 63). Descartes seeks such a ground because he assumes that truth is equal to certainty, that the two always come in tandem (Descartes, 51). If such an objective assurance is not found, then one is doomed to the turmoil of a relativism that never leads to truth. If, indeed, there are no first principles (*archai*) establishing knowledge, then only epistemological an-*archy* reigns.

Such anarchy, however, does not merely affect human sciences, the various attempts to understand reality, but cuts to the very heart of human existence. One cannot live without some definite reference point that can give stability and purpose to life. Consequently, Descartes' search for certainty is not only epistemological but also religious and ethical. The fear that no such immutable, absolute foundation can be found results in what Richard Bernstein calls "Cartesian Anxiety" (Bernstein, 16). He argues that this anxiety ensues from just the type of reasoning that one finds in Plato or Descartes. Specifically, it is a type of reasoning that operates disjunctively: *either* knowledge can be instituted on objectively certain grounds, *or* knowledge lies always in ruins, destroyed by the chaos of skepticism. Bernstein suggests that calming that anxiety requires a metamorphosis in thinking; that is, one should no longer reason according to the polarity of objectivism/relativism. Instead of comprehending human knowing as a linear process beginning at a value-free, disinterested atomistic point, one should acknowledge the historicity and contextuality of human existence and recognize that no thinking takes place in a vacuum. Human beings live *in media res*—in the middle of things. Consequently, "[o]vercoming the Cartesian Anxiety is learning to live without the idea of the 'infinite intellect,' finality, and absolute knowledge" (Bernstein, 166).

In contemporary interpretation theory, Cartesian Anxiety has been eased through the idea of the hermeneutical circle, the notion that all understanding depends upon prior knowledge. Since human beings are born into cultures, with histories, and speaking specific languages, understanding always takes place within contexts that have already been structured by previous generations. All new knowledge, therefore, must develop within the crucible of traditions that supply each new generation with the preunderstanding necessary to begin the interpretive process again. Primarily, this preunderstanding comes mediated through various texts that function authoritatively in the community, giving it perspectives from which to encounter reality. As these texts are interpreted and reinterpreted, the circular movement of preunderstanding hopefully progresses toward clearer understanding. As a result, the hermeneutical circle actually moves as a spiral, inculcating both circularity and linearity into the epistemological process. One never starts with some nonhermeneutical objectivity and then proceeds from that foundation to knowledge; instead, one always starts wherever and whenever one is, with whatever perspectives one has been given by history and language.

Biblical Hermeneutics and the Spiritual Spiral

Cartesian Anxiety can certainly move readers of God's written Word to exempt the Bible from the dynamics of the hermeneutical spiral, since those dynamics result in the disenfranchising of any claim to there being *the* absolute meaning of a biblical passage. Christian readers of Scripture can easily become uncomfortable with the idea that no absolute knowledge can be had even with reference to the Bible. When one investigates the nature of biblical revelation, however, one discovers that God has indeed chosen to reveal through history and language and that revelation depends upon various cultural media for its identity. Consequently, that the texts of Scripture are the product of divine inspiration does not void their also (1) being historical texts developing within certain contexts, (2) being transmitted through a tradition, and (3) having to be read and interpreted by each new generation. As a matter of fact, one could argue that the biblical texts demand a recognition of the relational forces inherent within human being-in-the-world. To treat biblical texts as if they were cold "objective" documents communicating information that is ahistorical and unrelated to existence would be to diminish their impact and possibly even to distort the gospel. To accept that biblical hermeneutics shares with all other textual hermeneutics the importance of preunderstanding does not lead to biblical relativism but, instead, to an adventure of faith in which knowledge and truth result from the power of God's Spirit working in history, through language, and out of cultural traditions. If one accepts the validity of the hermeneutical spiral as applicable to biblical interpretation, then a number of implications arise.

1. The first implication is that one can no more approach the Bible without presuppositions than one can approach any written text without certain expectations. The New Testament theologian Rudolf Bultmann has recognized that the Bible is not exempt from

the creative tensions inherent within the hermeneutical spiral. He argues that exegesis without presuppositions cannot be attained precisely because no exegete is a *tabula rasa*, a blank slate upon which the biblical text can simply inscribe its meaning. Instead, as the exegete encounters the Bible, history affects the process in two vital ways. First, the exegete as a historical individual bears the marks of tradition and culture. Second, the Bible is itself a collection of texts that purport to communicate history and that have developed out of history. Consequently, Bultmann argues that at least one presupposition must be accepted, the presupposition of the historical method of investigation (Bultmann, 291). This methodolological preunderstanding colors the perspectives that exegetes take *vis-a-vis* the texts as well as the questions that they ask of the texts.

One can even discover preunderstanding operating within the very texts of Scripture themselves. For example, one of the more obvious principles of biblical hermeneutics concerns the interrelationship between the testaments; that is, the New Testament is actually an interpretation of the Old. New Testament authors often assume a certain amount of Old Testament foreknowledge on the part of their readers. A text such as Hebrews more obviously demands that its readers have prior knowledge of Hebrew history and of the Hebraic religious cult. In Luke, Jesus actually inaugurates his ministry by reading a prophetic passage from Isaiah and identifying himself with its fulfillment. In doing so, Jesus contextualizes himself into the broader hermeneutical milieu of his hearers, precisely the Messianic foreconceptions mediated through rabbinic tradition. Such contextualization allows Jesus to use presuppositions critically. Consider his evaluation in the Sermon on the Mount of the first-century Jewish hermeneutical legacy. Jesus takes the basic preunderstanding operating among his listeners ("you have heard it said . . .") and moves it in a new direction ("but I say to you . . .").

Preunderstanding not only affects biblical interpretation from within the texts themselves but from without as well. Individuals who open God's Word and read it bring with them the forestructures of their lives formed by the history, language, and culture within which they live. Geoffrey Turner suggests that the pertinent presuppositions brought to Scripture include prior interpretations of such concepts as "history," "revelation," "miracle," "God," and "humanity" (Turner, 233–34). Whenever readers encounter these concepts in the biblical texts, they initially interpret them according to the horizons of their own prior knowledge. Not only individual concepts, however, indicate a reader's preunderstanding; this preunderstanding may also be revealed in the motivations that direct specific encounters with the texts. In other words, why is the Bible being read? Is it for historical information, existential consolation, aesthetic appreciation, homiletical creation, or ethical admonition? Such "interests" in the texts influence how a reader interprets the texts, if for no other reason than because interests instigate the types of questions that direct interpretation (cf. Morgan and Barton, 249; Habermas, 196).

2. Duncan Ferguson suggests that the prime presupposition that ought to regulate biblical interpretation is faith. He calls faith *"the preunderstanding which is able to rightly grasp God's self-disclosure"* (Ferguson, 18). Only if readers approach the biblical texts believing that they will encounter God's revelation can adequate interpretation be accomplished. Interestingly enough, Ferguson's identification of faith as the legislating preunderstanding illustrates that the open-ended character of the hermeneutical spiral applies also to biblical interpretation. The Apostle Paul informs his readers in Rom. 10:17 that "faith *comes* by hearing, and hearing by the word of God" (NKJV). Consequently, faith itself is a product of hermeneutics, the result of hearing and, therefore, of interpreting, God's Word. In other words, faith does not function in a Cartesian sense as some nonhermeneutical foundation for proper exegesis. On the contrary, faith can only develop within the dynamics of biblical hermeneutics.

Such a circularity indicates that the process of hermeneutics does not lead to some objective end to the understanding of Scripture. There can be no closure to the disclosure of meaning in God's written revelation; there can be no absolute knowledge within the techniques of biblical hermeneutics. The concept "absolute" derives from two Latin words, *"ab"* meaning "from" and *"solvere"* meaning "to loosen." If something is "absolute," therefore, it is "loosened from" everything else. In the case of hermeneutics, "absolute" meaning would be detached meaning, meaning detached from history, language, culture, texts, presuppositions, and communities. This essay has attempted to present the thesis that meaning never floats freely outside of the contexts of all of the above. God's written Word is and has history; it is written in language; it comes out of cultures; it has been preserved and transmitted through communities; and it is encountered by real human beings within the parameters of their lived experience. Interpreting God's Word always takes place in relationship to a vast architecture of preunderstanding. This architecture does not prohibit the construction of meaningful and true interpretations; however, it does prohibit the exegetical arrogance that claims to have built *the* one, complete interpretive structure. Biblical exegetes should respect the "glass darkly" through which they always view the texts on this side of the eschaton. Their interpretations may be meaningful and true; however, they are never totalized.

3. The creative indeterminacy inherent within the hermeneutical spiral enables interpretation to effect both a critical distanciation and a legitimating appropriation. The endless play of preunderstanding, explanation, and understanding eventuates in both a hermeneutics of suspicion and a hermeneutics of trust. The hermeneutics of suspicion ensues from the recognition that preunderstanding does indeed influence every interpretive conclusion drawn with reference to a biblical text. Because the baggage brought by an exegete to the reading of Scripture can potentially hinder the hermeneutical process, one must always question every exegetical perspective. On the other hand, appropriate presuppositions can aid the interpreter in asking the "right" questions, adopting the "right" perspective, and allowing the text to reveal itself through the framework of a particular preunderstanding. Recognizing one's own, as well as another's, presuppositions enables one to maintain a discriminating skepticism while concurrently effecting a believing acceptance that meaning and truth may be discovered within the biblical language (cf. Ricoeur, *Hermeneutics*, 131–44).

The critical significance of the hermeneutics of suspicion should not be underemphasized. Turner contends that interpretive "disagreements can be explained and possibly even overcome in a hermeneutical critique of preunderstanding" (Turner, 242). The conflict of interpretations primarily comes out of the differences among various hermeneutical forestructures. Preunderstanding supplies the lenses through which an interpreter views a text, and it may supply lenses that are more opaque than translucent. It may also supply lenses that are actually mirrors, reflecting the theological expectations of the exegete instead of mediating the meaning of the text. Exegesis can easily metamorphose into eisegesis whenever presuppositions work surreptitiously to lead interpreters to "find" in the text what they actually "put" there, to "look" into the texts and see their own image.

One of the more troubling hermeneutical approaches, that of allegorism, flourishes primarily because of the disparity between what a text seems to "say" and what an exegete assumes it "means." Philo of Alexandria's allegorizing methodology illustrates well the way in which biblical interpretation can be dominated by theological expectations. Philo presupposes that the Old Testament is God's Word. As a matter of fact, he comes quite close to accepting a dictation theory of inspiration. Torah is not just God's Word; it is God's words. Some of those words, however, do not fit the theological framework around which Philo builds the superstructure of his hermeneutics. For example, he finds Gen. 6:5–7 particularly troubling, primarily because if taken literally, the passage would indicate that God both changes (regrets) and has emotions (grief). To believe that God changes, however, is a great impiety, according to Philo (Philo, 22). Furthermore, to accept that God has passions, such as grief, is to ascribe to the eternal and holy deity characteristics that pertain to weak and unholy humanity (Philo, 52). If, however, this passage cannot be literally revealing attributes of God, what could possibly be the reason for God's inspiring the use of such language? Philo answers that the language of the text is designed to help the feeble-minded, those who are poorly equipped intellectually to think the true nature of God (Philo, 63–64). As good physicians often do not tell patients the truth about their conditions so as not to dishearten them and slow their recovery, so, too, God as the physician of human souls chooses to speak a language that accommodates individuals in their intellectual weakness (Philo, 67–69). When, therefore, this passage "speaks" of God's wrath, it actually refers to the difference between acting out of passion or out of reason. Human actions are only worthy if done out of reason and not out of fear or anger (Philo, 71–72). Consequently, Philo has allegorized the passage into revealing not something about God but something about ethical motivations.

Whether one agrees with Philo's theological presuppositions and, therefore, with his interpretation of Gen. 6:5–7 is not important. What is important for this essay is that Philo's hermeneutics illustrates quite well that the meaning of a biblical passage is in some way influenced by what the exegete brings to the text. In Philo's case, he brings a particular Hellenistic philosophical theology and reads the Bible through the lenses supplied by that preconceived theory. In doing so, he shows the inherent danger in allowing presuppositions to operate uncritically.

4. A fourth implication of the hermeneutical spiral concerns the role of the text and the relevance of the fundamental context within which biblical interpretation should take place. In the midst of all of the conflicting interpretations that arise from various networks of preunderstanding, one thing remains relatively constant—the text. Of course, the constancy of the biblical text is *not* an absolutely fixed point for a number of reasons. First, since the original documents are not extant, all the contemporary interpreter has access to are a plurality of manuscripts with a multiplicity of variant readings, for example, the endings of Mark. Second, if one relies on translated texts, one must realize that different teams of scholars choose different translations, for example, the different readings of Gen. 2:4 in the NASB and in the NIV. If two or more interpreters, however, agree on a specific textual manuscript or translation, then notwithstanding the different interpretive frameworks that each brings to the text, they all must test their interpretations according to the text itself. Biblical texts set restrictions to how they can be interpreted. Consequently, they may have more than one possible meaning, but they do not have an infinite number of meanings. Critical hermeneutics, therefore, cannot escape giving priority to the texts themselves and allowing them to question whatever preunderstanding is brought to bear on them.

The critical dynamics at work between text and interpreter always work within the confines of specific communities. Interpretive communities are the fundamental context within which all interpretation takes place, and they certainly play a significant role with reference to biblical interpretation. On the one hand, the Bible came into being through individuals living in communities; it was canonized and preserved through communities; and it has been interpreted for millennia by various communities. On the other hand, all exegetes who open the biblical texts have done so under the influence of some community of faith; their identities have been formed by that community; they have depended upon the authoritative interpretations of that community as a hermeneutical guide; they have listened to pastors, friends, and, maybe, seminary professors; they have read theologies, sermons, and Sunday school literature; and they have even sung hymns and gospel songs. In these and countless other ways, the preunderstanding of everyone who opens a biblical text has been formed within the matrix of some community or communities of faith. Consequently, one should expect that only within communities can dissimilar interpretations be adjudicated.

The hermeneutical spiral can proceed critically only as interpretations are expressed publicly and opened for communal scrutiny. Exegetes can avoid relativism and subjectivism, not by denying the efficacy of preunderstanding or by inventing some absolute criteria for meaning and truth, but by submitting their interpretations to other members of the community. By keeping the hermeneutical dialogue going, by listening to the different voices, individuals can allow the spiral to progress toward clearer understanding. The dialogue may result in either the validation of one's preunderstanding or in its rejection. Either way, one discovers in community the critical awareness that leads to a better comprehension of God's written Word and a genuine encounter with God's self-revelation.

5. The apostle Peter addresses the above-mentioned issue of interpretive communities and in doing so introduces a fifth implication of the hermeneutical spiral for biblical hermeneutics. In 2 Peter 1:20, he states that "no prophecy of the scripture is of any private interpretation" (KJV). One may well read this verse as indicating Petrine agreement with the thesis that hermeneutics should never take place outside the milieu of specific communities. Individuals should not be so arrogant as to think that they can approach Scripture alone, outside of the parameters of ecclesiastical tradition and authority. As Anthony Thiselton states it, one certainly may read the Bible in the privacy of one's own room; however, one always brings to that reading the history, tradition, language, and authority that have been mediated through some community (Thiselton, 65). One cannot read the Bible as a solipsist but must submit one's interpretations to be judged in the marketplace of alternative explanations.

In verse 21, Peter gives his reason for claiming the need for communal validation. He argues that no Scripture came as the result of some individual's deciding to write it. Instead, Scripture came into being only because "holy men of God spake as they were moved by the Holy Spirit." The Bible has a history, a tradition mediated through various individuals in the Hebrew community who allowed themselves to be directed by God's Spirit. The Spirit, working in history and using human language, directed human beings to speak (write) God's revelation. What Peter has introduced into the discussion of the hermeneutical spiral is the significance of the

Spirit for biblical interpretation. One might say that Peter has revealed that the Spirit is the source of life for Christ's spiritual body—the church—and gives it the hermeneutical energy it needs to seek more intimate knowledge of God through the written Word. The life-giving dynamic of the Spirit actually expresses another type of spiral, a spiral that begins with the Spirit and ends with the Spirit. The Spirit initiates Scripture by inspiring individuals-in-community to write God's Word. The Spirit then preserves that Word throughout history and continues to work through the language of the texts to accomplish God's purposes. The same Spirit also guides interpreters in every generation so that they might understand God's Word. Throughout the entire process, it is the Spirit who exercises authority over history, tradition, culture, and language—as a result, exercising authority over the very process that shapes preunderstanding—always leading exegetes to understanding and to truth. Ultimately, the goal of the process is for individuals to know better the Spirit of God operating through the process.

Understood pneumatologically, biblical interpretation depends upon hermeneutical inspir(al)ation. It is the Spirit that breathes life into the process and that is revealed through it. Hermeneutical inspir(al)ation "starts" with the Spirit and "ends" with the Spirit; however, the "starting" and "ending" are not absolute points on some Cartesian linear scale. As Jesus admits in John 3:8, the Spirit is like the wind that blows from somewhere to somewhere; yet, no one knows exactly where those "somewheres" are. Perhaps the indeterminacy of the hermeneutical spiral as it moves from (pre)understanding through interpretation to understanding is another example of the creative uncertainty of the Spirit's working through the procedure, always inspir(al)ing new meaning, new truth, and new life.

▼

For Further Study

Bernstein, Richard J. *Beyond Objectivism and Relativism: Science, Hermeneutics, and Praxis.* Philadelphia: University of Pennsylvania Press, 1983.

Bleicher, Josef. *The Hermeneutic Imagination: Outline of a Positive Critique of Scientism and Sociology.* Boston: Routledge & Kegan Paul, 1982.

Bultmann, Rudolf. "Is Exegesis Without Presuppositions Possible?" In *Existence and Faith: Shorter Writings of Rudolf Bultmann,* 289–96. Cleveland: World, 1960.

Descartes, René. *Discourse on Method.* In *The Rationalists.* Translated by George Montgomery, 39–96. Garden City, N. Y.: Dolphin, 1960.

Duncan S. Ferguson, *Biblical Hermeneutics: An Introduction.* Atlanta: John Knox, 1986.

Fish, Stanley. *Is There a Text in This Class?: The Authority of Interpretive Communities.* Cambridge: Harvard University Press, 1980.

Gadamer, Hans-Georg. *Philosophical Hermeneutics.* Translated and edited by David E. Linge. Berkeley: University of California Press, 1977.

———, *Truth and Method.* New York: Crossroads, 1982.

Habermas, Jürgen. *Knowledge and Human Interests.* Translated by Jeremy J. Shapiro. Boston: Beacon, 1971.

Hartman, Geoffrey, "Criticism, Indeterminacy, Irony," in *What Is Criticism,* edited by Paul Hernadi. Bloomington: Indiana University Press, 1981.

Heidegger, Martin. *Being and Time.* Translated by John Macquarrie and Edward Robinson. New York: Harper and Row, 1962.

Klein, William W., Craig L. Blomberg, and Robert L. Hubbard Jr. *Introduction to Biblical Hermeneutics.* Dallas: Word, 1993.

Morgan, Robert, and John Barton. *Biblical Interpretation.* Oxford: Oxford University Press, 1988.

Ommen, Thomas, "The Pre-Understanding of the Theologian." In *Theology and Discovery: Essays in Honor of Karl Rahner, S.J.,* 231–61. Milwaukee: Marquette University Press, 1980.

Plato, *Meno.* In *The Dialogues of Plato.* Translated by B. Jowett, 1:349–80. 2 vols. New York: Random House, 1937,. [Classical citations instead of page numbers have been used as documentation in the text.]

Philo. *On the Unchangeableness of God.* In *Philo.* Translated by F. H. Colson and G. H. Whitaker, 10–101. New York: G. P. Putnam's Sons, 1930. [Classical citations instead of page numbers have been used as documentation in the text.]

Ricoeur, Paul. *Hermeneutics and the Human Sciences: Essays on Language, Action and Interpretation.* Edited and translated by John B. Thompson. New York: Cambridge University Press, 1981.

———. *The Philosophy of Paul Ricoeur: An Anthology of His Work.* Edited by Charles E. Reagan and David Stewart. Boston: Beacon, 1978.

Searle, John. *Intentionality: An Essay in the Philosophy of Mind.* Cambridge: Cambridge University Press, 1983.

Thiselton, Anthony C. *New Horizons in Hermeneutics.* Grand Rapids: Zondervan, 1992.

Turner, Geoffrey. "Pre-Understanding and New Testament Interpretation." *Scottish Journal of Theology* 28 (1975): 227–42.

PART THREE

Applying the
Grammatical-Historical
Method
▼

Chapter Fourteen

The Grammatical-Historical Method

William B. Tolar

No element of interpretation is more important to an accurate understanding of the Bible than is the grammatical-historical method. It is the *sine qua non* for any valid understanding of God's Word. Without an honest, careful, intelligent use of grammatical and historical knowledge, there is little or no hope for a correct interpretation of documents written in foreign languages within several different ancient historical contexts. To fail to use proper grammatical rules or to ignore those historical contexts is most certainly to guarantee failure in understanding the writers' intended meanings.

It is a moral imperative for the interpreter to do his or her best to understand the text correctly so as to discover the meaning placed there by the original author. Anything less is intellectually dishonest and spiritually immoral and unworthy of a person of integrity.

No one comes to biblical interpretation without his or her own contemporary cultural preunderstandings. No reader is totally objective and free of presuppositions which profoundly influence one's interpretation. We need all the help we can get in order to move from our language and culture into the different languages (whether Hebrew, Aramaic, or Greek) and cultures of the writers without changing or distorting their meaning. The grammatical-historical method is an absolutely essential procedure in meeting that need.

The Grammatical Principle

Years ago this writer heard one of his college professors tell about the King of England's visit to St. Paul's Cathedral in London upon its completion. Having been designed by the brilliant Sir Christopher Wren, it was expected to be a masterpiece. Upon seeing it, the king declared that it was "awful" and "artificial." In today's vernacular those words would have been devastating and insulting to the architect, but in that day they were extremely complimentary. "Awful" meant "full of awe" and "artificial" meant "artistic in the superlative degree." Words have meanings, but these can change with time and context. To understand any language, whether spoken or written, one must begin with the meanings, of words as they were intended by the original author.

The Bible was written under divine inspiration in human languages and thus must be interpreted grammatically first of all. The "ideal" way would be to study it in its original languages. This is not possible for most students of Scripture, but we do have skilled linguists who have made excellent translations into English. Lifetimes of study have enabled them to express accurately in our language the many nuances of meaning in those original languages. A good translation, one more clearly or literally based on the original text rather than a free paraphrase, is a "must" for the sincere interpreter.

Words and Sentences

Words are the building blocks of language, but they are joined together in sentences within contexts which may alter their original individual meaning. Thus we must concern ourselves not only with knowing the meaning of individual words but also with understanding their relationships in sentences, in paragraphs, and in their genre. Basic ideas can be communicated by single words, but complexities of thought are expressed in sentences, and sentences are grouped into larger units such as paragraphs and genre. We will begin by considering words and then move to words in relationship.

English translations are based upon Hebrew, Aramaic, and Greek words preserved in a canon of carefully-evaluated texts. What did those words mean when used by their author? Those original languages had grammatical rules which governed both the use of individual words and their relationships. We must take those rules seriously! Because their words had linguistic as well as historical contexts, we must know both. Just as words must be understood in light of words which precede and follow them within a sentence, so must a verse of Scripture. An old adage is still valid: "A text without a context is usually only a pretext."

But the "contextual" principle extends beyond the immediate word context to the book (or genre) of which it is a part to all the texts on the same subject in all the writings by that author to the context of the Testament (Old or New) of which it is a part and finally, to the outer context of the entire Bible.

People who study Hebrew, Aramaic and/or Greek learn to recognize the "forms" of those words because the case, tense, mood, voice, person, and number all influence the form used and, thus, affect the meaning. This study is called "morphology." If a student is studying in the original languages, it is extremely important to know both the meaning of the word and its form. If either is unknown and/or incorrectly identified, then correct understanding is impossible. Good English translations seek to express these factors clearly so that the average reader can understand them and arrive at the correct meaning.

1. *The meaning of individual words.* The study of the meaning of words is called lexicology or lexicography. There are tools, called lexicons, to help students of Hebrew and Greek. Standard lexicons give the meanings of words and also include clues to help the student find the more difficult forms. Analytical lexicons are kinds of language dictionaries which tell the reader the main root from which the form comes. The English-only reader can find help in this area by using a Bible dictionary, a good Bible "word study" type of book, a commentary and even a standard English dictionary.

Words can be studied with an eye to their etymology, their history, their meaning for the author, and their meaning when compared with synonyms.

- Etymological word study analyzes the original or "root" word from which another word is derived. A good example of this would be to study the Greek *baptizo*, from which our English word *baptize* comes. By studying root words we sometimes gain helpful insights.

- Historical word study analyzes the word's use in time (before the author's day and up to and including the author's day).

- Cognate word study investigates the meaning of equivalent words in similar (cognate) languages. Modern lexicons provide help in studying these matters. An exhaustive concordance helps Bible students by alphabetizing Bible words and listing every place they appear by book, chapter, and verse.

• Comparative word study investigates the word's contemporary usage in the literature of the biblical author's era, especially usage by the author in his own literary and historical context. The author's current usage is probably the single most important factor in properly interpreting a word.

2. *Words in relationship: sentences.* Individual words do have basic meanings, but they can be changed by the words which surround them. Words contribute to a larger idea when they relate in usage within a sentence. This relationship is called "syntax" and is a study of thought relations.

Hebrew, Aramaic, and Greek grammars analyze forms and syntax for students of those languages. English-only readers should use an "as-literal-as-possible" translation. Syntax, whether studied in the original languages or in English, is absolutely essential for a correct understanding of the ideas in the text. Interpreters should remember as they study syntax that the meaning of sentences is also governed by literary genre (e.g., poetic, apocalyptic, etc.)

Because they express either "kind" or "time" of action, *verbs* must be studied carefully. The "tense" of a verb is crucial in knowing what the author meant. Did he mean past, present, or future? Did he mean continuing or completed action? The "mood" relates a verbal idea to reality. For example, the indicative mood says a thing is an actuality while the subjective, optative, and imperative moods indicate contingency and possibility (including a command). Active, middle and passive "voices" denote action by or upon the subject. "Person" and "number" of verbs must be understood for clear meaning to be ascertained.

Infinitives, participles, adverbs, conjunctions, and particles all play an important role in both Hebrew and Greek. English readers can benefit from good translations, word study books, and scholarly commentaries which draw from linguistic expertise. But there is *no* excuse for anyone's careless, negligent reading of a biblical text whereby these syntactical elements are ignored in the English.

Nouns are also important for biblical interpretation. While Hebrew and Greek differ at many points on nouns, such elements as case, prepositions, adjectives, pronouns, and articles can also be discussed for our purposes under the general study of nouns. Scholarly translators render these into English expressions in such a way that a person can readily understand if a noun is the subject or object in a sentence.

Grammatical knowledge of the original languages obviously gives an advantage to an interpreter. An idea may well be determined by one's understanding of a preposition or an article, but caution should be taken and a thorough study made before one builds a theological doctrine on too narrow a base. A good example is the Greek word *eis* which is translated "for" in Acts 2:38— "be baptized . . . for the forgiveness of your sins" but rendered "at" in Matt. 12:41—"because they repented at the preaching of Jonah. . . ." Translate it "at" in Acts 2:38 and notice the possible impact it could have for the understanding of baptism's relationship to salvation.

Clauses are also crucial. Both Hebrew and Greek use clauses as significant elements in their language systems. While the structural relations of Greek clauses are either coordinate or subordinate, the Hebrew has distinctive features whereby sentences or clauses serve as noun clauses or verbal clauses. Both languages have various kinds of clauses: relative, causal, comparative, temporal, conditional, and so forth. Serious study of the Bible includes learning the implications of these various kinds of clauses.

In Hebrew, conjunctions can introduce several kinds of clauses. Greek clauses are more precise but they need to be studied carefully in their context. The reader should respect the syntactical structure and word connections as used by the biblical author.

Figurative Language

One of the inescapable responsibilities of the Bible interpreter is to decide whether the author intended his word (or words) to be taken "literally" or "figuratively." Both kinds of language are found in the Bible.

In thinking about such issues we are faced with a greater semantical or philosophical question as to the nature of language itself. Some people think that all language is figurative. How can the average reader of the Bible know if the author intends his words to be understood literally or figuratively? Are there guidelines? If so, what are they? The grammatical method is crucial to the answer. The student of Scripture must not equate "literal" or "historical" with what is true and "figurative" or "allegorical" with what is false. Both kinds of language serve as vehicles for truth.

Most figurative language finds its origin in the life and culture of the writer who uses it. Middle Eastern prose was far more figurative than western people realize. Poetry, poetic expressions, symbolism, mysticism, and emotional feelings were far more a part of the biblical cultures and literature than the typical American may understand since our culture is so much the heir of Greece and Rome—with our critical, analytical approach to life and our scientific, technological mindset.

In order to communicate some ideas, the biblical speaker or writer found it advantageous to start with the familiar and move to the unfamiliar by using comparisons. Those comparisons might be clear or unclear to the listener or reader. Another way was to move from the concrete or particular to the abstract or general. The more acquainted one is with the cultural and historical context of the biblical author's era, the better one will understand the meaning of that particular author's figurative language.

The serious student of Scripture will need to study much more about the Bible's use of figurative language than this writer can give to the subject here. For purposes of brevity and clarity, we will organize our ideas under "brief" and "long" figures of speech.

1. Brief figures of speech. Many years ago the writer cut out an article from the daily paper which told of a college student in another state who was rushed to the emergency room of the school's clinic suffering from a severed hand and a gouged-out eye. When asked what had happened, he replied that he had simply done what the Bible had commanded him to do! He obviously was referring to Jesus' teaching in Matt. 5:29–30. He had interpreted a figure of speech, a hyperbole, in an unbelievably literal way!

Some passages appear to be obviously literal and others clearly figurative, but some are not so clear. They seem to be between those polarities as if capable of being interpreted either way. Although space will not allow us to examine all kinds used in the Bible, we will look at a few and then list others for the reader to study on his or her own.

Two of the most familiar figures of speech are the *simile* and the *metaphor.* They both communicate by making comparisons; but whereas the simile uses the word "like" or "as," the metaphor does not. The metaphor is more direct and forceful, but more likely to be taken literally than the simile. When God is described as having human body parts (e.g., a hand or an arm), we should recognize that as a special kind of metaphor called an "anthropomorphism."

Less well known is the *metonymy* which uses the name of one thing for another because of the close association of the two. A good example is in Luke 16:29 where the word *Moses* means the "Torah" (or Law) and the words *Moses and the Prophets* mean the whole Jewish canon (which Christians now call the Old Testament).

Hyperbole (the deliberate exaggeration or over-statement to make a point) is obviously used in John's Gospel where he writes about the world not being large enough to contain all the books if everything Jesus did and said were written down (John 21:25).

A *euphemism* is an intentional understatement in order to soften the effect of an otherwise shocking, offensive, or harsh way of stating the same thing. Instead of bluntly saying a person "died," one says "fell asleep" or "passed away." Both the Old and the New Testaments (especially their English translations) often use euphemisms for human bodily functions such as sexual or toilet activity.

2. *Long figures of speech.* The word "long" as used here is relative because these may be as "brief" as the above mentioned figures of speech, but as a general rule they tend to be longer.

The *parable*, which is usually defined as an extended simile, is one of the best known long figures of speech in the Bible. Jesus was a master at using parables, but he was not the first nor the last Jewish teacher to employ them. His parables were not simply illustrations for his sermons nor interesting stories to teach universal moral lessons. They constitute a special genre of literature and need thorough study.

The *allegory* is usually defined as an extended metaphor. Whereas a parable usually teaches one central truth without the inner details being interpreted as signifying additional ideas, the allegory has a plurality of points of comparison and the inner details are important as signifying additional information.

There is a difference between legitimately interpreting biblical figures of speech as having "other" intended meanings and in "allegorizing" Scripture. The latter is an invalid method which approaches a passage with the *a priori* conviction that beneath the surface meaning there is a deeper, higher, or "other" meaning. This can obscure the true meaning put there by the author if he only intended the "at-face-value" meaning. "Spiritualizing" is a form of allegorizing.

A *riddle* is a concise expression which intentionally seeks to challenge the ability of the listener or reader to understand and explain it. Samson used a riddle in Judg. 14:12–20 and John in Revelation 13.

A *fable* is a fictitious story intended to teach a moral lesson. It characteristically uses animals or plants to depict human virtues and vices. Jotham, the son of Gideon, used a fable in Judg. 9:7–20 to proclaim judgment against the men of Shechem. Jehoash, king of Israel, used one in 2 Kings 14:9 in trying to persuade Amaziah, king of Judah, not to invade the Northern Kingdom. Ezekiel the prophet began with a riddle and developed it into an allegory (Ezek. 17:1ff.).

"Dark" or *"hard" sayings* are found in both Testaments. They are usually brief but will be mentioned here. These are statements which cause perplexity or puzzlement on the part of the listener because of an innate complexity of meaning or lack of obvious clarity (Ps. 78:2; John 16:25).

Special Issues

A *proverb* is a brief wise saying intended to help people live responsible, fulfilled lives. While the Book of Proverbs contains the largest collection, others are scattered throughout the Bible. They are a part of "Wisdom" literature and need to be studied under that genre. A proverb usually seeks to convey a single idea or comparison. It may be the exception to the rule that a verse needs the one before and after it in order to be interpreted.

Poetry and *drama* are special kinds of literature and can be studied under "Wisdom" literature also. The interpretation of Job, Jonah and the Book of Psalms (along with many shorter passages) are all vitally affected by one's understanding of this genre.

Symbols pose a unique challenge to the interpreter. They are often discussed along with typology in books on hermeneutics. A symbol is usually defined as a sign which suggests meaning rather than stating it. The symbol itself is usually a literal object which is used to teach some lesson. It is essential that the interpreter know the cultural setting of the symbol. The literary context is also important. Biblical writers used different things as symbols: numbers, colors, metals, jewels, names, animals, water, oil, clay, book, flesh, among others. Sound hermeneutics need to guide the wise interpreter in this area.

Typology is a special kind of biblical interpretation. Preachers and scholars of an earlier era gave more attention to it than do contemporary ones. It is based upon the belief that there is some kind of prefiguring or foreshadowing between certain persons, events, and things in the Old Testament with later persons, events, and things in the New Testament. This is true because God controls history and used these things or persons to point the way to and help prepare for his greater, later revelation in Christ. Unlike allegory, typology affirms historical reality; but it is figurative in its methodology even while affirming the literalness of its subjects and objects.

Apocalyptic literature presents a hermeneutical challenge to the modern interpreter. Associated primarily with the Books of Daniel and Revelation, it is a unique literary form. It was a popular means of communication among Jewish people just before and after the birth of Jesus. Many commentaries and study guides on Daniel and Revelation will give introductory information on the apocalyptic style. Highly figurative, with extensive use of symbols, it needs special care and study. Readers in that era had a context which enabled them to understand the intended meaning of the author, but centuries of time changed that for us. We need to use all the hermeneutical tools at our command but still interpret with humility and love because others will differ with us on it.

The Historical Principle

Louis Berkhof rightly declares that "The Word of God originated in a historical way, and therefore, can be understood only in the light of history" (Berkhof, 13). He goes on to say it is "impossible to understand an author and to interpret his words correctly unless he is seen against the proper historical background."

History is about people—and people live at places (geography) and in association with other people (society). They have things (material culture) and ideas (intellectual and religious culture). Some of their culture (including written records) often survives them and is studied by other people (anthropologists and archaeologists). All of these factors are true of the Hebrews and the Christians of the biblical era. This information greatly enhances our understanding of the biblical authors' historical background and thus better equips us to interpret their documents.

Key People

1. The author. Good hermeneutics demands that we learn all we can about the biblical author himself. What does his book tell us? Is there information about the author in other biblical passages? Are there non-biblical references which add information? Are these reliable? Are they fair and objective or biased? What about his family? What are we told by reliable sources about his character, temperament, education, religious beliefs (including ethical values), and the external circumstances of his life? How much do we know about his culture? What was his native language and what did he do for a living? Did he study with recognized scholars? Who were they and what did they believe? How influential were they on his life?

Does the author tell us his motives and objectives in writing? Can we infer them from what *he* says? Is he answering specific questions asked by his readers? Does he include historical, cultural, geographical, and literary data in his writings which clue us to his knowledge, ability and interests?

2. The original listeners or readers. Does the author identify and describe his original audiences? Valid interpretation demands that before we try to understand what a writer is saying to us, we must do our very best to understand what he *said and meant* to that original group. God spoke through that human author *first to them.*

Without this guideline, our imaginations can run wild! It is unthinkable that God would say one thing to them and say something totally different to us in the same identical words. We may be able to apply the meaning to a different situation, but that must not change the original meaning. The best axiom is that there was *one meaning* but it may have *many applications.*

Again, what about those original audiences? Do we know their culture, values, circumstances, character, needs, and so forth? Were they living in circumstances which throw light upon what and why the biblical writers wrote or spoke to them? Was Jesus speaking *only* to believers in the Sermon on the Mount? Or was he speaking primarily to non-believers so as to convert them? Or was he aiming the "sermon" at both followers and non-followers? Answers to these questions will make a profound difference in how one interprets certain verses in those passages! This is especially true of the words "destruction" and "life" in Matt. 7:13–14.

Is the author answering questions asked by readers as in 1 Corinthians? Do answers to their specific questions constitute universal norms for all times and ages? Or, are we simply to draw "spiritual principles" from them and apply them to our lives today? Does individualized advice given to a particular person(s) imply eternally valid commands for God's people of all cultures? Instead of greeting our fellow Christians with a "holy kiss" as Paul admonishes the early Christians, can we simply shake their hands? Did Paul's admonition for a woman not to teach a man (1 Tim. 2:12) apply only to the particular situation where Timothy was living in Ephesus at that time or does it apply to all women in all ages, regardless of changed circumstances and different cultures? Is his earlier prohibition (2:9) of wearing gold and pearls to be interpreted the same way? If not, why not? What hermeneutical basis can one give for a different interpretation or application?

3. *Other speakers (or written sources).* Occasionally a biblical author will allude to, quote, or introduce other speakers or written sources. The interpreter needs to study these passages carefully. The Bible does not endorse everything it records. We need to note whether it simply uses or actually affirms the extra source. It may be very important to distinguish between the biblical author's words and those of the speaker. The Bible does not endorse everything spoken by Job's friends! Paul quotes, but rejects, three negatives in Col. 2:21. Psalms 14:1 and 53:1 quote but do not agree with the fool's statement that "there is no God."

Society—People in Relationships

Humans are not only individual beings; they are social persons who live in a variety of relationships with other people in families, clans, tribes, cities, provinces, nations, and foreign countries. All of these profoundly influence them and their culture.

This was true of the biblical authors. The societies of that era had both material and immaterial elements in their cultures. How and what people thought and believed, cherished and valued, lived and died for, how they reared their children, treated their aged parents, governed themselves, transmitted their values and memories—all influenced their lives and were reflected in their oral and written records. Both political and religious conditions affected those nations so profoundly that they left a deep impression upon their literature.

Archaeological discoveries in the last two centuries have revolutionized our knowledge of biblical cultures. The finding and translating of hundreds of thousands of inscriptions from Mesopotamia (modern Iraq) and from Egypt enable the current Bible student to understand those ancient societies better than any generation of interpreters since Bible times!

While God certainly inspired the biblical authors, he did not lead them to write in a historical vacuum. To be understood by their contemporaries required that they communicate in known cultural norms. Language itself is a cultural phenomenon. Extant written documents—whether on clay, rock, papyrus, or parchment—are all part of a people's material culture but include information about their immaterial culture such as religious beliefs. These archaeological artifacts and their data are vital components of the historical principle of hermeneutics. They enable us to understand those early people as real persons in a real world. The literature of non-biblical religions were mostly mythological, discussing people and places which never existed in time and space. Books on archaeology, Bible atlases, and Bible handbooks aid the student with excellent geographical understanding of the biblical text.

1. Mesopotamia. Through archaeological discoveries such as the Nuzi (or Nuzu) Tablets, and the Mari Tablets, we have contemporary records from Abraham's era which reveal important insights about the society of his day. These tablets throw light upon various parts of the patriarchal narratives in Genesis such as a son's birthright (cf. Jacob and Esau); marriage and property rights (cf. Abraham and Eliezer); household gods or "teraphim" which served as deeds for property (cf. Jacob and Laban); and levirate marriage (cf. Ruth and Boaz), among others. The Ebla Tablets (from ca. 2300 B.C.) tell us that Sodom and Gomorrah were in existence earlier than Abraham and Lot's time and corroborate the reality of cities thought by some people to be only fictitious places in ancient Israelite imaginations!

When Abraham lived in the area of Ur about 2000 BC, the Chaldees had a banking and a postal system, libraries with dictionaries and encyclopedias, and "ziggurats" or temple-towers for religious purposes (apparently like the "tower" of Babel in Gen. 11). There is no evidence of monotheism; all archeaological data thus far shows only polytheism. Sun, moon, and star worship were prominent—especially moon worship—and human sacrifices appear to have been made.

2. Egypt. Knowledge of the brilliant Eyptian civilization has exploded since the deciphering of the Rosetta Stone in the early nineteenth century. Archaeological discoveries such as the fabulous gold treasures of "King Tut" have put new light on passages like Exod. 11:2, 35–36; and 32:2–4. The more we have learned about ancient Egypt through extrabiblical records, the more we can see the incredible integrity of the Egyptian data in the Book of Exodus.

3. Canaan. The Bible has extensive textual material on Canaan. The land and its peoples are a major focus from Abraham's era until the time of Malachi, except for the lengthy Hebrew experience in Egypt. Biblical records tell us much about religious life in this era.

Canaanite deities were mythological personifications of nature phenomena, with fertility cults, ritually sponsored immorality, and often even including human sacrifice.

The modern student needs to know that the Canaanites did not think human sacrifice was brutal and barbaric. It was the supreme proof of one's devotion to the deity. Was Abraham as devoted to his God as the pagans were to theirs? Would he sacrifice his dearest son, his hope for the future, his visible sign of the covenant? Did he believe that his God could and would carry out the covenant promises (specifically stated as being through Isaac) if this son died?

When the Hebrew people later prepared to enter Canaan under Joshua, Moses condemned and solemnly forbade certain religious practices of the inhabitants (cf. Deut. 18:9–14). One such practice involved making children "pass through the fire." This appears to be a covert reference to Molech (or Moloch) worship which promoted the burning to death of newborn children as an act of supreme devotion. This helps to explain why the Mosaic code levied the death penalty for worshipping Molech (Lev. 20:1–5).

Clay tablets found at ancient Ugarit (Ras Shamra in modern Syria) have provided extra-biblical information about the Canaanite society and religion, giving us an enlarged picture of this important culture. How can a person properly interpret the Books of Joshua and Judges or understand the critical issues involved in Elijah's struggle with the pagan religion of Jezebel in 1 Kings or the theological implications of Gomer's involvement with Baal in Hosea without using the insights of the historical principle of hermeneutics?

4. *Assyria.* Biblical and non-biblical information about Assyria are keys to interpret adequately the Books of Jonah, Amos, Hosea, Isaiah, and Micah. Passages like 2 Kings 15:19 and 16:7 (and Isa. 20:1) are explained by knowing the rising power of the Assyrians and the extension of their empire as recorded in their inscriptions. The words of Rabshakeh (2 Kings 18:21; Isa. 36:6) become clear when we know there was a rather influential Egyptian party in Judah during the reign of Hezekiah (Isa. 30:1–7).

Isaiah 36–39 (and parallel passages in 2 Kings 18:13–20:2 and 2 Chron. 32) are illuminated by the Assyrian king Sennacherib's contemporary inscription, found by archaeologists at the site of ancient Ninevah, which mentions Hezekiah by name as being shut up in Jerusalem like "a bird in a cage." But the great king did not claim that he ever got the bird out of the cage! We know that he did not!

5. *Babylonia*. There is abundant historical and archaeological information in extra-biblical sources from Babylonia which help with the study of Jeremiah, Lamentations, Ezekiel, and Daniel. Many passages (Isa. 13:1–22; 14:1–23; 21:1–10; 39:1–8; 43:1–2; and 47:1–15) are better understood when one knows historical data about Babylonia. Without a knowledge of the nature of pagan religion and some historical geography, a reader might not understand Jeremiah's reference to the valley of Hinnom as the "valley of slaughter" in 7:31–33 (and 19:6), and the valley's later use as a garbage dump for Jerusalem, and the New Testament's use of the word and concept of "Gehenna" as a fitting image of hell. The Babylonian captivity made such a powerful impact upon the Hebrew people politically, culturally, and religiously that Old Testament scholars classify it and the Egyptian exile/exodus as the two most important historical events in the history of ancient Israel!

6. *Persia*. Records from and about ancient Persia (modern Iran) help us understand biblical accounts in the post-exilic Books of Haggai, Zechariah, Esther, Ezra, Nehemiah, and Malachi. The marked change in the political position and constitution of Israel during Persian rule must be kept in mind when interpreting many passages (Zech. 7:1–5; 8:19; Ezra 4:4–6; Neh. 5:14–15; Mal. 1:8).

It was the discovery and deciphering of the Behistun inscription which made possible the translation of hundreds of thousands of clay tablets from Babylonia and Persia. It did for the cuneiform texts what the Rosetta Stone did for Egyptian hieroglyphics. It was like finding a key to several ancient civilizations! The writings of the Greek historian Herodotus are valuable for the study of the Persian period even though he is not always reliable.

7. *Greece and Rome*. These two awesome intellectual and political powers of the intertestamental period are quite well known from their own prolific writers. Their documents enhance the student's knowledge of the biblical world just before, during, and after the time of Christ's birth. While these pagan authors help us understand the history, philosophy, and religion of this era from their viewpoint, contemporary Jewish writers also assist us by their literature preserved in the Apocrypha and Pseudepigrapha.

A Bible student must not naively move from Malachi to Matthew and assume the historical context is the same! Radical changes both within and without Jewish life occurred during this time. When the Old Testament records closed, Greece was just coming on the world scene and Rome was yet to come.

But at the beginning of the New Testament era, Roman political and military power are dominant even though Greek philosophy and culture are pervasive throughout the Mediterranean world. Some knowledge of first century pagan culture is essential to the interpreter of every book in the entire New Testament!

Greek historians such as Polybius, Diodorus of Sicily, Strabo, Plutarch, and Dio Cassius help us understand this period, as do the Roman historians Cicero, Livy, Tacitus, and Suetonius. Extensive and impressive archaeological ruins verify the extent, might, and brilliance of these pagan societies. But major changes were going on *inside* the Jewish culture as well and we need to know about them because they are crucial to New Testament interpretation. Some Jews became more "liberal" and appreciative of non-Jewish philosophies and life styles, while others totally rejected all such foreign influences.

The powerful, more conservative Pharisees and the more liberal Sadducees who opposed both Jesus and Paul were non-existent in the Old Testament but came to prominent religious leadership during the two centuries before Christ. Their rise to power and their theological differences were both related in some measure to their different responses to the threat of Greek culture, called Hellenism.

The Sanhedrin gained great power during this same time and a scholarly class called "scribes" came virtually to replace the priests as teachers of the Jewish people. Without the help of extra-biblical Jewish sources such as the writings of Josephus, we would be at a tremendous disadvantage in understanding the historical context of Jewish life at the time of Christ. Jewish thinkers developed more fully the doctrines of life-after-death, the messianic hope, and the existence of angels and demons than had been done in the Old Testament era. The synagogue, so basic to Jewish life in the New Testament records, came from its obscure origin in the Babylonian exile to incredible religious influence during this time.

Both Jews and Christians were faced with subtle, sophisticated seduction by these intellectually intriguing and aesthically appealing non-biblical cultures. Paul's classical Jewish training under Gamaliel, his life and education in Graeco-Roman Tarsus, the benefits of his Roman citizenship, and his knowledge of the multinational cultures of his day are all reflected in his writings. To know something about them is to interpret Paul better! Knowing the history, culture, geography, and religious practices of the cities in biblical Asia (the western coast of modern Turkey) and Rome's willingness to persecute its perceived enemies will help tremendously in the interpretation of the Book of Revelation.

Geography

1. Garden of Eden. The average American reader thinks of a "garden" as a small plot of ground in back of one's home for planting a few vegetables and flowers. Yet careful reading of Gen. 2:8–15 reveals four rivers:

- The Pishon "flows around the whole land of Havilah, where there is gold" (NASB). A good Bible dictionary and a good Bible atlas show Havilah as being on the southern coast of the Saudi Arabian peninsula! The Hebrew word translated in the NASB as "flows around" is literally "surrounds."

- The Gihon "flows around the whole land of Cush." "Cush" is translated by some scholars as "Ethiopia" and so identified in scholarly writings—and Ethiopia is on the east coast of the continent of Africa!

- The Tigris (assuming it is the same as the one by that name today) flows out of the mountains of eastern Turkey through modern Iraq for more than a thousand miles before reaching the Persian Gulf.

- The Euphrates (on the same above assumption) flows out of central Turkey through part of modern Syria and on through Iraq for more than fifteen hundred miles into the Persian Gulf.

In light of the above geographical information and if one has a serious regard for the contents of the biblical text, a person has to have a different understanding of the word "garden" than a small plot of ground! Early Jewish and Christian scholars understood the Pishon and the Gihon rivers as the Blue and White Nile of east central Africa and thought of the Garden of Eden as stretching from those rivers up through the great Nile delta in Egypt all the way across modern Sinai, Saudi Arabia, Kuwait, Israel, Lebanon, Syria, Jordan, Iraq and southeastern Turkey! What a difference a knowledge of geography can make in understanding the biblical text!

2. Paul. In Acts 13–28, numerous references are made to cities, provinces, and so forth. Knowledge of geography is essential to understand Paul's incredible energy and zeal to spread the gospel. Luke uses place names extensively. A good Bible dictionary and a good Bible atlas will make Acts take on a new dimension of reality. A personal journey to those places will increase that sense of reality a thousandfold! To stand today in the actual theatre ruins of Ephesus or to see the remaining stones from the great temple of Diana (Artemis), both mentioned in Acts 19, brings the biblical account into living reality. Following Paul's journeys through the mountainous terrain of modern Turkey today even in an automobile will make one have a new understanding of Paul's words in 2 Cor. 11:26 where he says he experienced "dangers from rivers, dangers from robbers . . . dangers in the city, dangers in the wilderness . . . " (NASB).

3. John. John's exile to Patmos (Rev. 1:9) is better understood if one knows that Roman historians tell us that emperors used the small, rocky, volcanic island in the first century as a prison for criminals to quarry rock. And the letters in Revelation 2–3 take on far greater meaning when a person studies the history, culture, and religion of the seven cities where the churches were located. Background studies would enormously enrich a minister's preaching from those passages.

Topography

Knowing the topography of biblical lands can provide information and more accurate understanding of some passages of Scripture. The following are examples.

1. David and Saul. In 1 Samuel 24 and 26 David had a chance to kill Saul but did not do so. After each close encounter, David stood on a ridge across a narrow gorge and told Saul how he had spared the king's life. David had the evidence: a piece of Saul's robe and the king's spear and water jug taken from his bedside. But how could David be so close as to talk with Saul and yet Saul's soldiers could not kill him with an arrow or catch him by quick pursuit? One only has to be in the rugged terrain (or see pictures of it) where these events took place to understand that topography made it possible.

2. Jesus. Luke 10:30–37 tells us the parable of the good Samaritan. When Jesus says a man was "going down from Jerusalem to Jericho; and he fell among robbers" (NASB), one only has to drive that route to understand how literally and graphically Jesus was speaking. Jerusalem is about 2,600 feet above sea level and Jericho is about 1,000 below it. Within the distance of eighteen miles the elevation drops about 3,600 feet. But the modern road does not follow the ancient route. In Jesus' day he would have had in mind the way through the Wadi Qilt. A narrow road today follows that torturous path around hair-pin curves. In the deep shadows and sharp turns of that deep gorge one can clearly understand how travelers could be beset by robbers easily and quickly.

Conclusion

To be better interpreters we must know and practice good hermeneutics! *The grammatical-historical method* helps us fulfill Paul's admonition to Timothy: "Be diligent to present yourself approved to
God . . . handling accurately the word of truth" (2 Tim. 2:15, NASB).

For Further Study

Aharoni, Yohanan. *The Land of the Bible.* 2d ed. Translated and edited by
A. F. Rainey. Philadelphia: Westminster, 1979.

Aharoni, Yohanan, Michael Avi-Yonah, Anson F. Rainey, and Ze'ev Safrai.
The Macmillian Bible Atlas. 3d ed. New York: Macmillan, 1993.

Albright, W. F. *Archaeology and the Religion of Israel.* Baltimore: The John
Hopkins Press, 1968.

Berkhof, L. *Principles of Biblical Hermeneutics.* Grand Rapids: Baker, 1950.

Blaiklock, E. M. and R. K. Harrison, eds. *The New International Dictionary of
Biblical Archaeology.* Grand Rapids: Zondervan, 1983.

Bright, John. *A History of Israel.* 3d ed. Philadelphia: Westminster, 1981.

Bruce, F. F. *New Testament History.* New York: Doubleday, 1971.

Cate, Robert L. *A History of the Bible Lands in the Interbiblical Period.* Nashville: Broadman, 1989.

Ferguson, Everett. *Backgrounds of Early Christianity.* Rev. ed. Grand Rapids:
Eerdmans, 1993.

Finegan, Jack. *The Archaeology of the New Testament: The Life of Jesus and the
Beginnings of the Early Church.* Rev. ed. Princeton: University Press, 1992.

————. *The Archaeology of the New Testament: The Mediterranean World of the
Early Christian Apostles.* Boulder, Colo.: Westview Press, 1981.

Hallo, William W. and W. K. Simpson. *The Ancient Near East: A History.*
New York: Harcourt Brace Javanovich, 1971.

Mazar, Amihai. *Archaeology of the Land of the Bible: 10,000–586 B.C.E.*
New York: Doubleday, 1990.

McCray, John. *The Archaeology of the New Testament.* Grand Rapids: Baker,
1991.

Mickelsen, A. Berkeley. *Interpreting the Bible.* Grand Rapids: Eerdmans, 1963.

Ramm, Bernard. *Protestant Biblical Interpretation.* Grand Rapids: Baker, 1970.

Schoville, Keith. *Biblical Archaeology in Focus.* Grand Rapids: Baker, 1978.

Snaith, Norman H. *The Jews from Cyrus to Herod.* New York: Abingdon, n.d.

Stern, Ephraim, Ayelet Gilboa, and Joseph Aviram, eds. *The New Encyclopedia
of Archaeological Excavations in the Holy Land.* 4 vols. New York: Simon &
Schuster, 1993.

Woude, A. S. Van Der, ed. *The World of the Bible.* Grand Rapids: Eerdmans,
1986

Chapter Fifteen

Inductive Bible Study
Methods

Thomas D. Lea

Are you a systematic shopper whenever you purchase an expensive item such as a car? A systematic shopper will examine a prospective car for gasoline ratings, safety features, appearance, size, and resale value. A systematic shopper will analyze the total cost of the car and, if necessary, the cost of financing the car. A systematic shopper will check consumer reports, the opinions of friends, and the advice of a skilled mechanic. After checking the desirability of a car from all of these angles, the systematic shopper will then decide which car to purchase. An inexpensive car may not have a good safety record. An attractive car may be too expensive to maintain. A car with excellent gasoline ratings may be too small. Systematic shoppers will examine and analyze all of these features before deciding on which car they want.

Systematic Bible students must study the Bible in this way. There is no single method of Bible study which will guarantee that a reader or a student will obtain all the information needed from the Bible. Effective Bible study demands the use of many complementary methods which reinforce one another. Using these methods adds strength to the understanding of the learner. To understand the Bible, we must look at the Bible from many perspectives.

Inductive Bible Study

To get an overview of an entire book, the student must read through the book at a single sitting. Students who follow this approach will grasp the broad sweep of the book and can develop a personal outline of the book. This approach to Bible study is called *synthetic* Bible study.

Those who want to handle smaller portions of Scripture will focus on the paragraphs and verses of a book or a chapter of the Bible. Here they will observe the tense, voice, mood, person, and number of verbs. They will look at such words as "therefore," "so that," "for," or "because" to provide information about the intent of the author. In analyzing smaller portions of the Bible, students are practicing *analytical* study. Another approach to Bible study emphasizes the application of the Bible to personal behavior. This method, known as *devotional* study, seeks to evaluate, correlate, and apply Scripture in the lives of individuals and local churches. In a sense, devotional study is the culmination of all Bible investigation because it emphasizes the new life and congregational transformation which the study of Scripture should cause.

All of the previously mentioned methods of Bible study fall into the category known as inductive Bible study. In practicing inductive Bible study, we will examine the facts or features of a book of the Bible or a passage of Scripture. After making the observations of what is in the passage we will attempt to interpret and apply what we have read. These three steps of observing, interpreting, and applying form the foundation of inductive Bible study. We call the process inductive because we first bring together the facts, then from these we draw conclusions about meaning and application. The inductive process moves from the general to the particular. We will use inductive Bible study to carry out six different types of Bible investigation:

1. In synthetic Bible study we will gather information about the general content or message of an entire book of the Bible.

2. In analytical Bible study we will gather information about the content, meaning, and application of a verse or paragraph of Scripture.

3. In devotional Bible study we will emphasize the relevance of Scripture to our behavior and that of others.

In addition to these three methods we will also briefly note the biographical, theological, and topical method of study.

Synthetic Bible Study

Flying over the Western United States from San Francisco to the Dallas-Ft. Worth area, one sees below a panorama of beautiful mountains, arid deserts, majestic forests, and wavy grasslands. Driving over much of the same territory in an automobile makes one experience the rugged landscape bump by bump. When we travel in an automobile, we lose the sense of the succession of mountains, plains, and forests. However, we receive a detailed introduction to the terrain.

In an air journey we receive an overview of the topography of the territory. In an automobile journey we see a maze of detail about the terrain, but we do not get an overview. The air journey is comparable to the view of the Bible which a person receives in synthetic Bible study. The journey by automobile is comparable to the view of the Bible which a person receives in analytical Bible study.

How to Synthesize

The synthetic approach to Bible study consists of reading a book of the Bible continuously, repeatedly, and independently. In reading continuously we emphasize reading without reference to the chapter and verse divisions. These divisions were added by early Bible editors and may not reflect the thought divisions of the writers. We should read the book at a single sitting. Reading the book in bits and pieces rarely helps us to visualize the complete relationship between the parts.

We should also read the book repeatedly. Each reading should grapple with a different aspect of the organization of the book. A first reading should determine the main theme of the book. What idea is primary with the author as he writes? Paul, for example, stated the main theme of Galatians in an opening passionate appeal in Gal. 1:6–10. He was concerned to oppose the false idea of the gospel which was troubling some of his readers.

A second reading should observe how the author develops the theme. In 1 Cor. 7:1; 8:1; 12:1; and 16:1 Paul used the phrase "Now concerning" (or "Now") to introduce a topic which was of deep interest to him and the Corinthians. This phrase became a device which Paul used in order to develop the emphases of his correspondence with the troubled Corinthian church.

A third or a fourth reading should help the student to develop the author's outline. The repeated reading of Hebrews will help a Bible student to realize that the author has developed his theme of "the superiority of Christ" by contrasting Christ with the

Old Testament prophets (Heb. 1:1–4); angels (Heb. 1:5–2:18); Moses (Heb. 3:1–19); Joshua (Heb. 4:1–13); and Aaron (Heb. 4:14–10:18). The personal discovery of this information will come as the student examines the book both continuously and repeatedly. The joy and stimulus obtained from this personal discovery will make additional study a delight.

In reading a book of the Bible continuously and repeatedly, individuals must also read the book independently. They must not begin their study and research merely by consulting such helps as commentaries or Bible study aids. Read with the desire to discover personally the outline or overview of the book. The extensive use of a commentary in an early stage of investigation can hinder a student from developing personal creativity in Bible study.

The use of a paragraphed version of the Bible provides assistance in obtaining an outline of Scripture. The paragraphs represent the opinion of an editor, but they can be useful in grouping together the thoughts of the biblical writer.

As each paragraph is read, its contents can be summarized in a sentence or a statement. Those statements which develop the same topic can be grouped together as developments of major points of an outline. A complete outline might make each paragraph of the biblical text a subpoint of an outline. A less complete outline would combine those paragraphs which amplify the same point into a single point of an outline.

A Synthetic Study of 1 Corinthians

An initial reading of 1 Corinthians will require between thirty and forty-five minutes. In this first reading a student can observe that the Corinthian church faced many internal problems. Pride, contention, immorality, and heretical beliefs troubled the fellowship. Immaturity by the members prompted them to favor the more spectacular spiritual gifts such as speaking in tongues over the less visible gifts such as showing mercy. Greed prompted a stinginess in giving.

In a second reading we can observe two additional features. In 1 Cor. 1:11 Paul referred to some information which he had received from the household of Chloe. This "household" may have consisted of Chloe's servants, or it may have consisted of a group of Christians who met at her home in Corinth. These people gave Paul an oral referral about the problems in Corinth. In 7:1 Paul mentioned that the Corinthians had written him. He probably received a letter from the Corinthian Christians asking his opinion about certain questions. Perhaps Stephanas, Fortunatus, and Achaicus had carried the letter to him (16:17).

It is possible that chapters 1–6 contain information about problems which Paul learned from Chloe's household. Chapters 7–16 may contain information about problems mentioned in a letter which Paul received from Corinth. We may make a general division of 1 Corinthians into two sections. After we read the salutation in 1:1–9, we can learn about the problems which Paul learned by a report from Chloe's household (1:10–6:20). We can also see the problems discussed by the church in a letter to Paul (7:1–16:4). The phrase "Now concerning" (or "Now") appearing in 7:1; 8:1; 12:1; and 16:1 may introduce some of those problems, referring respectively to a misunderstanding of marriage (7:1–40); the eating of food offered to idols (8:1–13); the misuse of spiritual gifts (12:1–14:40); and the collection of money for Jerusalem Christians (16:1–4).

Repeated reading and reflection on the content of 1 Corinthians can uncover further information about the outline of the book. Our brief overview provides insight into the dynamic forces which led Paul to write the book. Some people from Chloe's household had told Paul about problems in the church. Others in Corinth had written with a request for help in confronting problems. Paul was responding to oral and written information about the church in Corinth. He was confronting deep problems which demanded his attention. He was not merely writing a few interesting ideas for the Corinthians to consider. His readers desperately needed his advice.

Analytical Bible Study

When chefs skillfully blend ingredients to make delightful entrees, they are practicing synthesis. They are putting the ingredients of the entree together. When customers later inquire of the chef the name of the ingredient which provided the unusual taste, they are practicing analysis. They are trying to separate the ingredients of the entree into basic parts.

Complete Bible study demands both synthesis and analysis. In synthesis the student can grasp the sweeping picture of the content of the book. In analysis the student can divide the book into its parts for detailed study. Viewing the Bible synthetically provides added insight into meaning and a basis for more accurate interpretation. Viewing the Bible analytically allows the student to notice small details which provide a careful, complete, and precise grasp of its teaching.

How to Study Analytically

To analyze a passage of Scripture, copy on a sheet of blank or ruled paper the words from a biblical passage. Arrange the segments of the passage in a pictorial way so as to indicate how the components relate to each other. For example, place the main statements of the paragraph such as declarations, questions, or commands at the left margin of the paper. Clauses linked by "and," "but," "either," "or," "neither," and "nor" make main statements. They should be written from the left margin. Clauses introduced by "so that," "in order that," "because," or "when" present subordinate statements and modify the main statement. If a clause or a group of words modifies a main statement, indent it beneath the line of the main statement. Sometimes the groups of words may be sufficiently brief that they may remain in the original order of the text. Larger groups of words, phrases, clauses, or parallel thoughts should be placed under one another on the sheet.

Skill in developing this pictorial outline will develop through practice. The outline does not demand grammatical precision. It is to be used to show the relationships between the statements of a passage.

After the student has developed the pictorial outline, two additional types of study can be undertaken. First, the student can make a more detailed verbal outline of the paragraph under study. Second, the student can record personal observations on the outlined text to note both explicit and implicit truths related to it.

To develop the more detailed outline, the student should use the declarative, interrogative, or imperative verbs as major points. The modifiers of the main verbs will then become the smaller subheads beneath the major points.

To record observations, the student will note key words, warnings, commands, promises, reasons, or questions. Contrasts, comparisons, and illustrations will also appear in the text. Students can produce observations by asking such questions as: Who is speaking? What is being said? When was the statement given? Where did the event occur? Why was it spoken or done? How did it affect the hearers?

An Analytical Study of Phil. 4:6–8 (NASB)

Even though this section is not usually designated as a paragraph, we will use it as a basis for our analytical study. When we develop a pictorial outline of this passage, we will write the words as follows:

Be anxious for nothing,
but in everything let your requests be made known to God
  by prayer and supplication with thanksgiving
And the peace of God shall guard your hearts and your minds in Christ Jesus
  which surpasses all comprehension
Finally, brethren, let your mind dwell on these things
  whatever is true
  whatever is honorable
  whatever is right
  whatever is lovely
  whatever is pure
  whatever is of good repute
  if there is any excellence and if anything worthy of praise

A glance at this pictorial outline shows that the words contain three commands together with a promise. The phrase, "by prayer and supplication with thanksgiving," shows how the requests are to be made known to God. The clause, "which surpasses all comprehension," describes the peace of God. The clauses beginning with "whatever is true" describe the kinds of things on which Christians are to think. We can construct a more detailed outline of the passage such as:

God's Prescription for Anxiety

  I. God gives commands concerning anxiety (4:6)
    1. Do not be anxious
    2. Let God know your requests
  II. God promises to guard the personality with his peace (4:7)
  III. God commands believers to reflect on right things (4:8)

We can use this outline in teaching the passage. For the preacher it becomes a help in developing the sermon. We can use both the pictorial outline and the detailed outline to record observations on the passage. Among observations which we can make by reading, reflecting, and researching through the passage are:

1. Paul is not content merely to tell the Philippians not to worry. He gives them a practical activity to perform instead of worry. They are to tell God about their requests.

2. Paul uses four words in describing types of prayer. A study of commentaries or a knowledge of the original language could assist

in determining the difference, if any, between "prayer," "supplication," "thanksgiving," and "requests."

3. We do not make these requests known to God, to inform him. He already knows about them. We want to transfer the responsibility for the anxieties to God instead of retaining them for ourselves.

4. The peace of God is an experience given to the Christian by faith in Christ. Parallel passages such as Rom. 5:1 and Col. 1:20 show the method and means of grace.

5. Some versions use the word "guard" instead of the word "keep" of the KJV. The term is a military word used of a Roman sentry who is keeping guard.

6. The thinking of verse 8 is undertaken to promote righteous behavior. It is not an end in itself. It is meditation with moral transformation as a goal.

Each of the above observations can be used for further application of the passage in teaching, preaching, or Christian living. For example, much emphasis is given today to the practice of meditation. Religious groups reflecting an Eastern influence often emphasize meditation as an end in itself. They claim that meditation leads to greater self-understanding and to relaxation. While this may be true, the type of meditation used by Christians is aimed at moral ends. It is not an end in itself. Christians are to meditate on righteous and uplifting themes. As they do this, they will fill their minds with that which will please God. This will promote righteous living.

Devotional Bible Study

Raymond Davis (in his book, *Fire on the Mountains*, 1966) tells the story of a group of Christians from the Wallamo tribe in Ethiopia, who were visiting in the home of a missionary. During their visit one of the children of the missionary bounded into the living room, followed by the family dog. The small terrier approached the visitors in a friendly fashion, but the Wallamos drew back in apparent fear.

Laughingly the missionary assured his guests, "You don't need to be afraid of this little thing. He won't hurt you." One of the Wallamos replied that it was not a question of fear. They had felt that Christians should not have dogs in their homes, and they responded with Paul's words to "beware of dogs" (Phil. 3:2) as support for their beliefs. The missionary took advantage of the opportunity to explain the meaning of the Pauline command in order to prevent a serious mistake by these committed believers who took biblical statements at literal face value. Paul did not reflect a bias against canines, but he compared the actions of some heretical teachers to snarling, barking curs.

The potential for practical, moral, and theological error is great among those Christians who have little knowledge of applying the Bible personally. Awareness of these problems must guide Christians as they practice devotional study of the Scripture.

Devotional study aims at changing personal behavior. Those who practice devotional study must approach the Bible with a desire to listen readily to God's voice. Several procedures can be used to assure wisdom and accuracy in making application of Scripture.

Guidelines in Practicing Devotional Study

Some who use the Bible to promote moral and spiritual growth can abuse Scripture. Some Christians will feel that any means for obtaining a blessing is justified in Bible study. The following principles are intended to provide a wise use of the Bible in moral and spiritual growth.

First, those who practice devotional study of the Bible must understand the true grammatical-historical sense of the verse or section of the Bible. Some well-intentioned Christians, eager to find a practical use of Scripture, will utilize an application which violates Scripture's meaning. The result can be either trifling or confusing. At a time when few medicines were available to treat illnesses, Paul advised Timothy to use a little wine for his stomach problems and for his numerous weaknesses (1 Tim. 5:23). A Christian with a nervous stomach today should not take this suggestion as a guideline for personal physical problems.

Second, we must view the Bible more as a book of general principles than as a collection of detailed directions. If the Bible were too specific, it would be linked to a time and a culture. If the Bible were a collection of rules, then a Christian might obey the letter of the rules and miss the spirit of genuine godliness. The words of James in 2:1–7 are not relevant in providing instructions for seating in most Christian churches. Most churches have seats which are available on a first-come, first-served basis. Normally the poor are not placed in uncomfortable seating in comparison to the wealthy. The words of James, however, do provide guidance for Christians in dealing with the problem of bias against the poor and toward the rich. The principle of the passage is thus useful in our time and culture to stimulate us to show compassion for the poor.

Third, some commands of Scripture are to be obeyed according to their spirit rather than in a literal fashion. Literal obedience would sometimes entail drastic consequences. Jesus' suggestion in Matt. 5:29–30 to pluck out offending eyes and cut off offending hands is not to be taken literally. Jesus is eager that Christians confront personal sin with relentless firmness rather than pamper and nurture it in any form.

Fourth, the student should correlate the passage with other sections of Scripture. This principle represents an effort to compare the topic or the passage being investigated with other passages which teach the same truth. Jesus' teaching about prayer in Matt. 7:7 seems to be an unqualified promise of an answer for those who continue asking. We should modify our understanding of this Scripture in the light of such passages as James 4:3 and 1 John 5:14–15 which show that the motives of the petitioner and the will of God are also factors in answered prayer. Our correlation of the passage which we are studying will help us to realize that sometimes the Bible writers do not provide discussion about the possible applications of a passage when they initially discuss it. Our comparison of one passage with another which deals with a similar topic can assist us in making a wise application.

Practicing Devotional Study

In practicing devotional study of Scripture we can list the specific areas in which the truth from a writing can be applied. We can apply the truth personally and to others. We can apply truths in the political, economic, and social arenas as well as in the spiritual arena. In probing areas of application it is helpful to use key questions. Among questions which we can address to a passage are:

1. What am I to believe as a result of this passage?

2. What am I to do as a result of this passage? Are there actions which I must begin or change? Are there attitudes which I must confront such as fear, worry, hate, resentment, or jealousy?

3. What have I learned about relationships? Does this passage teach me a new truth about my relationship with God? Do I see new insights into my relationship with others in my family, community, congregation, or world?

4. Is there a promise which I need to claim? Are there conditions for claiming this promise? Is there some word of encouragement or hope for me?

We must not use these questions in a mechanical way. They serve as an aid in probing possibilities for application. To assure that all application moves from theory to practice, it is helpful to state a devotional application in the form of a principle. This principle will provide a goal toward which we can direct our own energies in devotional application.

In the analytical study of Phil. 4:6–8 we examined the passage for its meaning and interpretation. We can find additional devotional help in applying the passage in our lives as we reflect on it again. This passage forbids the attitude of worry. As an antidote to worry it prescribes sharing the need or problem with God. As we obey God by sharing the need with him, we accept that his peace will protect our total personality. In maintaining a triumph over a fretful spirit, we must deliberately foster thought patterns which are true, righteous, and pure. We can state our application in the form of a principle which we can apply to an imagined situation of medical need: Instead of worrying about the results of my recent medical physical, I will share my concern with God and trust his peace to guard my health.

Note that prayer in this instance must not take the place of doing all that is possible in caring for one's own body. A prayer affirming trust in God should supplement the finest type of physical care and medical treatment which can be obtained.

When we study the Bible in the devotional manner, we overcome the temptation to allow our Bible study to degenerate into spiritual sterility. This method of approach also allows Scripture to become living and relevant in daily experience.

Other Inductive Approaches

The three methods of synthetic, analytical, and devotional study provide insight into the personal assistance which inductive Bible study provides. Additional varieties of inductive Bible study include biographical, theological, and topical study. We will survey these additional varieties of inductive Bible study.

Biographical Study

Biographical study examines the actions and attitudes of biblical characters. The study will uncover virtues which we should imitate and faults which we should avoid. A complete concordance is an indispensable tool for carrying out biographical study. A Bible encyclopedia or dictionary will also prove useful.

As a first step a student should collect all biographical facts about the person being considered. A complete concordance will list each biblical appearance of the name of the individual. Some characters will be known by more than one name. The author of the Second Gospel is known as John (Acts 13:13), Mark (Col. 4:10), or John Mark (Acts 12:12, 25). A glance at the individual's name in a Bible dictionary or encyclopedia can often provide a list of the names used for the individual in the Bible.

Some insights about a biblical character will come from material outside the Bible. For example, many standard Bible dictionaries or encyclopedias will indicate that John Mark was "stump-fingered." The normal understanding of this term is that John Mark had a deformed or injured hand which prevented his doing manual work and may have inclined him to a clerical career. Such information enriches the biblical portrait of John Mark.

When you have collected all the information about a biblical character, organize it either chronologically, geographically, or topically. The life of John Mark provides a helpful illustration of the value of biographical study of the Scriptures. The Bible makes reference to John Mark using his three possible names in Acts 12:12, 25; 13:5, 13; 15:37, 39; Col. 4:10; 2 Tim. 4:11; Philem. 24; and 1 Pet. 5:13. The study of these verses shows that Mark was a man who failed spiritually and then made a comeback in usefulness. His return to service after a dismal performance provides encouragement for stumbling, wavering Christians today. An organization of the Scriptures dealing with John Mark in a generally chronological pattern appears below:

Mark, the Man Who Made a Comeback

I. Mark's Home Background and Early Life—Acts 12:12

II. Mark's Opportunity—Acts 13:5

III. His Failure—Acts 13:13; 15:36–41

IV. His Comeback—Col. 4:10; Philem. 24; 2 Tim. 4:11; 1 Pet. 5:13

The study of Mark's life provides a positive illustration of someone who made a return to usefulness in God's service by continuing to use the spiritual gifts which God had given him. Mark refused to quit in the face of failure.

Theological Study

Theological biblical study examines doctrines or topics of spiritual interest which appear in a given text or book of the Bible. The

Letter to the Ephesians treats the topic of the church. Paul discussed the resurrection of both Christ and believers in 1 Corinthians 15. The author of Hebrews frequently discussed the value of faith in Hebrews 11.

Christians will expect the Scriptures to provide information about God, Jesus Christ, and the Holy Spirit. They will anticipate insights concerning the effects of sin, the nature of human beings, and the method of salvation. They will desire truths concerning the spiritual life, the mission of the church, and hope for the future. All of these points deal with theology, and many more subjects such as these appear in Scripture.

Theological study of the Bible uses several different steps in accomplishing its task. Repeated reading of a book of the Bible will uncover the theological emphases which the writer is advocating. Careful thought and reflection on a passage in addition to the reading can uncover the beliefs of the writer. In 1 Cor. 15:1–28 Paul assumed that the resurrection of Jesus provided evidence that the Christian had life after death. This is a logical deduction, particularly from Paul's words in 1 Cor. 15:20–22.

Some sections of Scripture are devoted to statements about specific theological issues or ideas. James 2:14–26 discusses the relationship between faith and works. Isaiah 6:1–8 shows both the holiness of God and the urgency of missions. Romans 3:21–31 shows the importance of the death of Christ. To uncover the doctrines which these sections present, the student should carry out a careful analytical study of the passage. Theological insights will emerge from the analytical study.

One source for learning the sections of the Bible in which a specific doctrine or idea is discussed is to read an article on the topic in a Bible dictionary. Students may also use a topical dictionary to biblical passages such as *Nave's Topical Bible.*

The Letter to the Hebrews provides the most complete discussion in the New Testament of the humanity of Christ. Among passages discussing the humanity of Christ are Heb. 2:17–18; 4:14–16; 5:1–10; and 7:23–26. A study of these passages will show that the author made the following emphases:

1. Christ's experience resembled that of human beings in that he shared their trials, temptations, sorrows, and pain (2:17; 4:15).

2. His similar experiences have made him merciful and have proven his faithfulness (2:17).

3. His participation in the human condition allows him to remove the sin which separates us from God (2:17).

4. Christ's demonstration of obedience allows him to present an example for believers to follow (2:18; 4:15–16).

5. Christ's sinlessness despite constant temptation allows him to offer believers grace and power as they face temptation (2:18; 4:15–16).

6. Christ learned the full meaning of obedience by his loyal commitment to the Father while he suffered (5:8).

7. The intercession of Christ secured a full salvation of divine protection and blessing (7:25).

Topical Study

A study of the topical teachings of the Bible can yield a treasury of spiritual information. We can investigate such personal topics as prayer, learning the will of God, and forgiving others. Husbands and wives can grasp biblical principles for parenting and relating to one another. Churches can learn the roles and requirements for church leaders.

Most topical study will focus on personal or group spiritual needs rather than merely seeking to learn theology or study biblical personalities. Topical study treats such themes as the tongue, the conscience, or practicing forgiveness. It is primarily practical in its aim.

In beginning topical study we may use a single book of Scripture or the study of a theme appearing throughout Scripture. If a book is used, the subject chosen should be relevant to the main emphasis of the book. For example, we would not use the Book of Revelation for information about church giving, for this topic is not an issue in Revelation.

Two approaches are useful in carrying out topical study. We may use a more direct method and isolate a word or a phrase by listing its appearances in the Bible. For example, we could study the subject of "fasting" by using a concordance to find the listings in Scripture of words such as "fast" or "fasting."

We could also use an indirect method by studying a general idea instead of a specific term. This method of topical study may use several words. To study a general topic such as prayer, we might look for words describing prayer such as supplication, intercession, thanksgiving, and confession. We would also want to investigate such topics such as hindrances to prayer, encouragements to prayer, and factors in answered prayer.

After we have collected all the materials needed for each topic, we could summarize each topic with brief practical conclusions which a group could easily understand and apply. In studying a large topic such as prayer it may be best to break it into smaller segments such as "prayer in Paul" or "prayer in the Psalms." The study of the topic of prayer throughout the entire Bible would involve a lengthy investigation, and we could not easily share the results of this study with an audience.

Conclusion

An emphasis on inductive Bible study will encourage an individual Christian to undertake personal study of the Scriptures for the purpose of spiritual growth. It is important to realize that the Holy Spirit will help to make clear the spiritual application of Scripture (1 Cor. 2:12). The thrill of making personal discoveries about the meaning and application of Scripture provides a challenge to practice inductive Bible study.

▼

For Further Study

Adler, Mortimer. *How to Read a Book*. New York: Simon and Schuster, 1940.

Balchin, John F. *Understanding Scripture*. Downers Grove, Ill.: InterVarsity, 1981.

Braga, James. *How to Study the Bible*. Portland: Multnomah, 1982.

Finzel, Hans. *Opening the Book*. Wheaton, Ill.: Victor, 1987.

Gettys, Joseph. *Teaching Pupils How to Study the Bible*. Richmond: John Knox, 1950.

Green, Joel B. *How to Read the Gospels & Acts*. Downers Grove, Ill.: InterVarsity, 1987.

Henrichsen, Walter A. *A Layman's Guide to Interpreting the Bible*, Rev. ed. Colorado Springs: Navpress, 1978.

Jensen, Irving L. *Independent Bible Study*. Chicago: Moody Press, 1963.

Lea, Thomas D. *Survival Kit 3: A Guide for the Journey*. Nashville: Convention Press, 1986.

Osborne, Grant R., and Stephen B. Woodward. *Handbook for Bible Study*. Grand Rapids: Baker, 1979.

Tenney, Merrill C. *Galatians: The Charter of Christian Liberty*. Rev. ed. Grand Rapids: Eerdmans, 1957.

Traina, Robert A. *Methodical Bible Study*. Privately published, 1952.

Chapter Sixteen

An Introduction to Textual Criticism

James A. Brooks

Before the invention of printing about 1450, all books, including the Bible, could be reproduced only by manual copying. This laborious process inevitably resulted in errors called variant readings. Sometimes scribes also deliberately changed a text, occasionally to promote either orthodoxy or heresy, but usually in an honest attempt to correct what they thought was an error. Textual criticism is the scholarly discipline which attempts to restore the original text of an ancient document. In the case of the Bible, it is necessary because no original manuscript (MS, plural MSS) has survived and because all of the surviving copies differ at many places. It must precede translation, exegesis, and biblical and systematic theology.

The Old Testament Text

The Old Testament (OT) text, or at least the Hebrew text, has been transmitted with a large degree of uniformity in comparison with the New Testament (NT) text. Nevertheless no one Hebrew MS or printed edition can be accepted as representing the original in every instance.

Sources of Textual Information

1. Medieval Hebrew Manuscripts. The medieval Hebrew text, whether in MS or printed form, is called the Masoretic Text (MT) because it is the work of a group of Jewish scholars known as the Masoretes. These scholars, who flourished between about A.D. 500 and 1000 in Babylonia and Tiberias in Palestine, carefully preserved what probably had already become the standard consonantal text by providing it with vowel points, marginal readings, and marginal notes.

There is no complete catalogue of medieval Hebrew MSS, and the exact number is not known. Certainly there are several thousand. Some contain the entire OT, some a major division such as the Pentateuch or the Prophets, some a single book, and some only a small fragment. Only a few have been used in an attempt to establish the original text. One of the most important is the Leningrad (now again St. Petersburg) Codex B–19A, which is usually referred to as L. It is the earliest copy of the entire OT and is dated in 1008. The earliest dated MS of any portion of the OT is the Cairo MS containing the Former and Latter Prophets. It is referred to as C and was copied in 895. The Aleppo Codex (A) was produced about 930 and originally contained the whole OT. It was badly damaged in anti-Jewish rioting in 1947. The surviving portions were obtained by the Israeli government in 1958.

One could also include here the thousands of small fragments discovered in the Cairo geniza (a synagogue storeroom) about 1890. These date from the fifth to the seventh Christian centuries and show the state of the text at the beginning of the Masoretic period. Still further one could include here Origen's *Hexapla* of the third Christian century. The first column contained the Hebrew text and the second a transliteration of it in Greek characters. Only small fragments have survived, mostly of the Book of Psalms. It also gives insight into the state of the text at the beginning of the Masoretic era.

2. *Manuscripts from the Judean Desert.* By far the most important of these were discovered at Qumran in 1947 and following. There is a complete scroll of Isaiah, and it is the only one containing an entire book. Other scrolls contain substantial portions of Samuel, Isaiah, Jeremiah, Habakkuk, and Psalms. Although some portion of every book except Esther has been found, the remaining scrolls, about two hundred in number, are quite fragmentary.

The Qumran community existed from about 150 B.C. until A.D. 68 when it hid its library in anticipation of Roman reoccupation. Therefore all the biblical MSS are earlier than A.D. 68, but some appear to have been brought to Qumran rather than made there and to be as early as 250–200 B.C. Therefore these MSS are about a thousand years earlier than the Masoretic MSS described above.

Other highly fragmentary biblical MSS have been found at
Masada (pre A.D. 73), the Wadi Murabba'at (pre A.D. 135), and Nahal
Hever (pre A.D. 135).

3. *The Samaritan Pentateuch.* The earliest surviving MS is from the
tenth Christian century, but the text which it and other MSS appear
to preserve goes back to at least the second century B.C. and possibly even the fifth century. Certainly the Samaritans were a distinctive Jewish sect by the late fourth century B.C. when they built their
own temple on Mt. Gerizim. The fact that they accepted only the
Pentateuch confirms that they had their origin before about 250
B.C. when the Prophets were accepted as Scripture by most Jews. On
the one hand, the Samaritan Pentateuch contains a host of sectarian, harmonizing, and expansionist changes (there are about 6,000
differences from the MT); on the other, it appears to preserve a
nonsectarian type of Hebrew text which was in use in the last several centuries before the Christian era and which was not subjected
to later standardization.

4. *Versions.* Certainly the most important of these is the Septuagint, which is abbreviated LXX because of the tradition that it was
translated by seventy Jewish scholars. It was in fact produced between about 250 and 150 B.C. by Alexandrian Jews for use by the
Greek-speaking Jewish community there. It was adopted by the early
Gentile church as its Bible. Thereupon it was rejected by most Jews,
who then produced new translations—those of Aquila, Theodotion,
and Symmachus. It was preserved by Christians, and the earliest MSS
are fourth century. The LXX differs from the MT in thousands of
places. Many of its variants no doubt are due to the involved mechanics of translation and to editing, adaptation, and interpretation
by the translators themselves, but most scholars believe that it was
based upon a variant form of Hebrew text which was in general use
in the third and second centuries before Christ. Where it can be retranslated into Hebrew, it can be used to determine an early form of
the Hebrew text—much earlier than the MT and a little earlier than
that of the Dead Sea Scrolls. Other versions, such as the Latin and
Syriac; the Aramaic Targums; and quotations in rabbinic and patristic writings are also consulted but are of minimal value.

Printed Editions

The first edition of the complete Hebrew Bible was printed in
1488. The Second Rabbinic Bible of 1524–25, however, became the
"received text" for the following four centuries. In addition to

several minor ones, two major critical editions have been produced in the twentieth century: *Biblia Hebraica*, edited by Rudolf Kittel, Paul Kahle, and others, third edition 1937 (BHK); and *Biblia Hebraica Stuttgartensia*, 1967–77 (BHS). Both are based on the Leningrad MS L which was mentioned above but have differing apparatuses containing readings from other Hebrew MSS and from versions. A new edition based on the Aleppo MS A (above) is being prepared by the Hebrew University of Jerusalem.

History of the Text

Little is known about the history of the OT text. It is reasonably certain that between the third century B.C. and the first Christian century there was much variety in the textual tradition. The Qumran MSS are characterized by variety of textual tradition. Sometimes they agree with the MT, sometimes with the LXX, and sometimes with the Samaritan Pentateuch; and sometimes they have a unique reading. Therefore they provide evidence of the existence of at least three different recensions: one which later became the basis of the MT, one which earlier was the basis of the LXX, and one which earlier was the basis of the Samaritan Pentateuch. Even some quotations in the NT which differ from both the MT and LXX suggest the existence of other types of text. Beginning in the first Christian century, however, the type which became the basis of the MT began to displace the others, and during the Masoretic period it was the only type in use. For example the MSS from Masada, the Wadi Murabba'at, and Nahal Hever are virtually identical with the MT.

Principles of Textual Criticism

Most OT textual criticism begins with the assumption that the best edition of the MT (at present BHK and/or BHS) is nearest to the original. Then most textual critics correct it by comparing it to the Qumran MSS and other Hebrew MSS (including the Samaritan Pentateuch) and to the versions (especially the LXX). Occasionally when none of the textual witnesses provides a satisfactory reading, resort is made to conjecture. One may observe such corrections in the margin of the RSV, NRSV, NEB, REB, NIV, and other English versions—even including (rarely) the NKJV and NASB. Corrections are usually made on the basis of weighty internal considerations (see these below in the section on principles of NT textual criticism).

The New Testament Text

Sources of Textual Information

New Testament textual critics are blessed with more and earlier textual evidence than any other branch of textual criticism. This fact inspires confidence that the original text can be recovered from the mass of textual witnesses without resort to conjecture.

1. *Greek Manuscripts*. The NT was written in Greek, the universal language of the day, and certainly the most important source of textual information is the Greek MSS themselves. These are usually divided into four subdivisions. First, the papyri were written in uncial script on papyrus. (Papyrus was the most common writing material in antiquity and was manufactured from a reed which grew in the Nile Delta. Uncial script is comparable to printing in all capital letters.) These date between the second and seventh centuries. All are fragmentary, but five papyri dating from the third century contain substantial portions of Luke, John, the Pauline Epistles, 1 and 2 Peter, Jude, and Revelation. They are designated in a critical apparatus with a gothic "P" and a super numeral, thus $\mathfrak{P}^{46}$. There are ninety-nine (latest count, 1994) on the official list.

Second, the uncials are written in uncial script on parchment. (Parchment was a writing material manufactured from animal skins.) There are about three hundred uncials, and their dates are third to eleventh centuries. The two most important (B and א, below) are fourth century. Only one (א) now contains the entire NT, but at least three others originally did so. They are designated in a critical apparatus with capital letters and/or numerals preceded by a zero, thus א (Codex Sinaiticus), B (Codex Vaticanus), Θ (Codex Koridethi), and 049.

Third, the minuscules are written in minuscule or cursive script, most of them on parchment but some of the latest on paper. The earliest is ninth century. Because of their late date the minuscules are not as valuable as the papyri and the uncials. There are more than 2,800, and they are designated by numerals not preceded by a zero, thus 33 (probably the most important minuscule).

Fourth, the approximately 2,300 lectionaries are sixth century and later. Because of their late date and because they contain only a selection of passages intended to be read in public worship, they are even less valuable than the minuscules. They are designated by a numeral preceded by an italic "l," thus *l*[69].

2. NT Versions. As early as the second century the NT began to be translated into Latin and Syriac. A Coptic translation followed in the third century and still others later. The earliest versions are earlier than most surviving Greek MSS, and where they can be retranslated into Greek they provide valuable information for the restoration of the original text of the NT.

3. NT Patristic Quotations. Late in the second century the NT began to be quoted extensively by Christian writers, namely by Irenaeus of Lyons in Gaul or southern France about 180, Clement of Alexandria in Egypt about 190–200, and Tertullian of Carthage in North Africa about 200–220. These writers are also earlier than most Greek MSS and provide evidence for the early text. Of course later writers also quote frequently and are of varying degrees of value.

History of the Text

1. The Handwritten Text. The history of the handwritten text is difficult to reconstruct, but an attempt must be made because decisions about variant readings depend in part upon it. It would appear that during the second and third centuries variant readings multiplied rapidly because of such things as the use of amateur scribes and the shattering effects of persecution. On the one hand what is known today as the Western type of text may reflect this tendency toward diversion. On the other it would appear that an effort was begun in Alexandria to edit and restore the text, and this led to the Alexandrian type of text. (A text-type is a group of MSS which have much in common.) Also the MSS circulating in one locality probably began to have more in common with each other than with those circulating in other localities. This also may have limited diversity.

In the fourth century the trend toward diversion of MSS was reversed, in large part because of the cessation of persecution. During the latter half of the fourth century another text-type emerged in the large area between Constantinople and Antioch. It was the Byzantine type of text. By the eighth century it had become the dominant text in the Byzantine Empire. During the Renaissance it was introduced in Western Europe by Byzantine scholars who had migrated there at the invitation of European universities and kings or to escape the Turks. It was the only type in use at the time of the invention of printing.

Most contemporary scholars consider the Alexandrian type to be the nearest to the original and the Byzantine type the furthest removed from the original with the Western text in the middle. (Some scholars also identify a fourth type, the Caesarean, but it is probably an early form of the Byzantine. Nobody has claimed originality for it.) Date is one consideration in preference of the Alexandrian; internal evidence (below) is another.

Those who embrace the above position must explain how what is certainly the latest type of text and probably the least authentic was able to displace the earlier and better types. The answer is very simple. It won by default. Beginning in the third century, a knowledge of Greek began to die out in the western portion of the Roman Empire. This of course resulted in reduced use of the Greek NT in that area. In the fourth century the barbarians invaded the western Empire and destroyed education and learning and weakened Christianity. In the seventh century the followers of Mohammed poured out of the Arabian peninsula and swept across Egypt, North Africa, and Spain in the West and Palestine, Syria, and Mesopotamia in the East—enfeebling Christianity and the use of the Greek NT as they conquered. The Alexandrian and Western types of text simply ceased to be used, but the Byzantine type flourished in the Byzantine Empire until it fell in 1453.

2. The Printed Text. The first Greek NT to be printed was that of the Complutensian Polyglot in 1514. It was not actually published until 1521 and had little influence on the later history of the text. The first to be published was that of Erasmus in 1516, the year before the beginning of the Protestant Reformation. Erasmus had access to no more than six or eight late MSS, and with one possible exception all contained the Byzantine type of text. For this reason, and because textual criticism was virtually unknown at the time, he could not have produced anything except a Byzantine NT. As a matter of fact, he did a poor job with the materials he had, and his Greek NT is one of the less creditable of his works. Nevertheless, with only minor corrections, his Greek text was reprinted so often during the next century that it came to be known as the *textus receptus* or "received text" (TR). With one possible exception it was the only type of text to be printed until 1831.

Although the TR dominated during the seventeenth and eighteenth centuries, manuscript evidence was collected and sound principles of textual criticism were formulated which led to its overthrow in the nineteenth century. In 1831 Karl Lachmann completely abandoned the TR and produced a critical text. He modestly claimed only to restore the fourth century text, but even so he was widely attacked for daring to question the TR. Between 1841 and 1872 Constantine von Tischendorf published eight critical editions of the Greek NT. Between 1857 and 1872 S. P. Tregelles produced one edition. The ones who did more than any others to dethrone the TR were B. F. Westcott and F. J. A. Hort in their *New Testament in the Original Greek* (2 vols., 1881–2). Their first volume set forth a critical text (without an apparatus, however) which had much in common with the great fourth century codices B and א. In the second volume they explained their textual theory, and it was the second volume which convinced most scholars of the superiority of the Alexandrian text-type and the inferiority of the Byzantine. Although they did not attempt to construct a family tree of MSS— probably an impossibility—they used the principle of genealogy to show that the numerical preponderance of Byzantine MSS is of no significance. They showed that Byzantine variants are often conflate in nature, that is, they have combined two or more earlier readings. They pointed out that no Christian writer before 325 cites a Byzantine reading. And they showed that internal evidence (see below) usually supports the Alexandrian text.

Westcott and Hort did not convince everybody in their own day, and there are still a few holdouts today. Their claim that the Alexandrian type, which they called the Neutral text, is an unedited survival of the original is no longer widely held; instead it is thought that the Alexandrian type is an early, good quality attempt to restore the original text. Not all of their arguments have stood the test of time. Nevertheless, the vast majority of NT textual critics today accept their basic conclusion that the Alexandrian text is nearest to the original and the Byzantine furthest removed from it.

Between 1902 and 1913 H. F. von Soden edited another major critical edition. It is no longer used very much because his odd textual theory yielded a somewhat inferior text and because the apparatus, although the most extensive ever produced for the entire NT, employs a system of MS designations which is quite different from any other and very difficult to decipher.

Major critical editions have also been produced for several books of the NT: *Concerning the Text of the Apocalypse* (2 vols., 1929) by H. C. Hoskier; *Novum Testamentum Graece: Evangelium secundum Marcum* (1935) and *Evangelium secundum Matthaeum* (1940) by S. C. E. Legg; and *The New Testament in Greek: The Gospel According to St. Luke* (2 vols., 1984–87) by the American and British Committees of the International Greek New Testament Project.

During the last century various handbook type of editions have been published, but by far the most important are the United Bible Societies' *Greek New Testament* (4th ed., 1993) and the Nestle-Aland *Novum Testamentum Graece* (27th ed., 1993). Both of these contain the same text, which is often called the Bible Societies' Text and which is the most widely used Greek text today, but they have different apparatuses. The former treats about 1,450 places of variation and gives more evidence than any other handbook type of edition and more than some major editions. The latter treats about 11,500 places of variation and gives less evidence than the UBS edition but more than many handbooks.

Principles of Textual Criticism

In the past various theories of textual criticism have been employed, but today only three or four are followed. The one which dominates is called Rational or Moderate Eclecticism. (The term "eclecticism" implies that the critic is free to choose the MSS or text-type and the principle[s] of textual criticism which are most appropriate in each textual decision.) The essence of rational eclecticism is that equal weight should be given to external and internal evidence.

External evidence is the evidence of the textual witnesses themselves. Preference is usually given to the variant reading having the earliest attestation, the most geographically diverse attestation, and the most Alexandrian attestation, especially when the reading is also supported by some Western witnesses. It should be noted that the theory of rational eclecticism depends in part—but only in part—upon the assumption that the Alexandrian type of text is nearest to the original. (No one would claim today that it is the original.)

Internal evidence involves, first, extrinsic probabilities, that is, what scribes did while copying MSS. Unless there appears to be an accidental omission due to skipping between words with similar beginnings or endings, preference is usually given to the shortest reading on the assumption that scribes had a greater tendency to add to the text than to subtract from it. Preference is usually given to the reading which is different from a parallel passage because scribes had a tendency to harmonize such passages. This principle is especially important in the synoptic Gospels and where OT quotations are involved. Then preference is usually given to the most difficult reading, that is, difficult for ancient and medieval scribes who tried to clear up such difficulties. A difficulty may be theological, moral, liturgical, historical, or grammatical. Finally, preference is given to the reading which, if assumed to be the original, best explains the origin of the other(s). The origin of other readings is explained by using the other principles of internal evidence. Internal evidence also involves intrinsic probabilities, that is, what the author probably wrote. Consideration must be given to his grammar, vocabulary, style, and theology.

It is not often that all of the above items will point to the same reading. When they do not, the textual scholar must weigh the evidence and decide which principle or principles is or are the most relevant. He or she must provide a rational explanation for the choice. This is the essence of rational eclecticism. Bruce Metzger's comments on the variant readings "let us have [echōmen] peace with God" and "we have [echomen] peace with God" in Rom. 5:1 provide a clear example. Although the former reading has far better support in the manuscript evidence, Metzger opts for the latter: "Since in this passage it appears that Paul is not exhorting but stating facts ('peace' is the possession of those who have been justified), only the indicative is consonant with the apostle's argument" (A Textual Commentary on the Greek New Testament, 2nd ed., 1994, 452). Textual choices are not arbitrary or subjective if a rational explanation is provided, one which will commend itself to most capable and open-minded scholars.

The dominance of rational eclecticism can be seen from the fact that it lies behind the text which is found in the United Bible Societies' and Nestle-Aland Greek texts and behind most recent translations of the NT: RSV, NRSV, NEB, REB, NASB, NIV, JB, NAB, and GNB. It is the only theory which considers all the evidence—every principle of textual criticism which has commended itself to most reputable scholars.

Attention must now be turned to alternative theories. One is called the Majority Text method. It accepts as original the variant reading which is attested by the majority of extant Greek MSS. Therefore it contains a Byzantine type of text, but it is not identical with the TR. According to one count, it differs from the TR in over 1,800 places, although most of them are trivial. Two editions are based on this theory: The Greek New Testament According to the Majority Text (2d ed., 1985) edited by Z. C. Hodges and A. L. Farstad; and The New Testament in the Original Greek According to the Byzantine/Majority Textform (1991), edited by M. A. Robinson and W. G. Pierpont. An English translation is in preparation.

The best argument in favor of the Majority Text is mathematical probability: unless a reading were the original, it is statistically improbable that it could be in 80–90% of surviving MSS. The claim rests upon the assumption that the transmission of the text has not been greatly disrupted. Such has not been the case. Mention has already been made of the use of amateur scribes in the early centuries, the devastating effect of persecution, the making of translations and then "correcting" Greek MSS by the translations after the latter had become more authoritative, and the disruptions caused by the barbarian and Islamic invasions. It needs to be recognized that in many instances the MSS are evenly split and that there is no majority text. The Byzantine MSS did not constitute a majority until about the eighth century. Prior to that time the theory would have supported another text-type. The theory is valid only if consideration is limited to Greek MSS. There are far more Latin MSS than Greek, and none of these is Byzantine. The principle of genealogy invalidates the claim because it is obvious that more MSS were produced during the middle ages than in antiquity and that a larger percentage of the former survived. The theory completely ignores internal evidence. In no other branch of textual criticism are MSS merely counted.

As was noted above, the TR is not significantly different from the Majority Text. The only way it can be defended is dogmatically with such arguments as: God gave the Greek Orthodox Church the task of preserving the original text; God guided Erasmus in printing the original text; the Greek text of the Reformation must be the original text; the Greek text lying behind the KJV must be the original; and modern textual criticism which prefers the Alexandrian text is naturalistic, theologically liberal, and unbelieving. There is simply no evidence to support any of these assertions. It is just a fact that many—probably most—conservative, Bible-believing, reverent scholars recognize the secondary nature of the TR and the Majority Text.

The remaining theory of NT textual criticism is usually referred to as rigorous eclecticism. It has been advocated by only a few scholars, but they have been very vocal. As yet, however, they have not produced a Greek text of the entire NT or a translation. Rigorous eclecticism makes all of its textual decisions on the basis of internal evidence alone, and even there it tends to consider only intrinsic probabilities. Intrinsic probabilities, however, are most difficult to determine. Most decisions must be tentative because all good writers often express themselves in unexpected ways.

Rigorous eclectics justify their disregard of external evidence because they believe that during the second and third centuries the textual tradition was disrupted beyond all hope of recovery. They think that the main culprit was not persecution but a widespread attempt to correct the common Greek of the NT by classical, Attic standards. It is most unlikely, however, that during the early centuries there were very many Christian copyists who had a knowledge of classical Greek. Most of the early Christians were from the lower, uneducated classes. Even if Attic standards had been imposed on NT MSS, the main effect would have been upon style rather than substance. In fact the method is most applicable to a kind of variant which is relatively infrequent and unimportant. If Attic vocabulary and grammar had been injected by some scribes, it is likely that they would have been removed by others who found them to be unfamiliar and difficult. Rigorous eclecticism is correct that no MS and no text-type contains the original text in every instance, but some MSS and text-types are certainly nearer to the original than others. Especially in instances where internal evidence is indecisive, the testimony of the best MSS is weighty.

Conclusion

Textual criticism is not a mathematical, exact science. It always deals in probability, never in certainty. Therefore all textual scholars and all those who evaluate their work—including the writer and readers of this chapter—should maintain an attitude of humility and open-mindedness and should respect the positions of others. It needs to be realized that no Christian doctrine depends upon the choice of a particular variant reading or even a complex of variants. One's theology should not be an issue in textual criticism. No MS or text-type is heretical. It must also be admitted that it has not been part of the providence of God to transmit the original text exactly. This is seen in the fact that no two surviving MSS are exactly alike and no printed edition corresponds exactly to any Hebrew or Greek MS.

Nevertheless, it is a part of Christian stewardship to attempt to produce and then to use the best possible Hebrew and Greek texts—the ones closest to the original. This is the task of textual criticism.

▼

For Further Study

Aland, Kurt, and Barbara Aland. *The Text of the New Testament.* Translated by E. F. Rhodes. 2d ed., rev. and enl. Grand Rapids: Eerdmans, 1989.

Elliot, Keith, and Ian Moir. *Manuscripts and the Text of the New Testament: An Introduction for English Readers.* Edinburgh: T&T Clark, 1995.

Greenlee, J. Harold. *Introduction to New Testament Textual Criticism,* rev. ed. Peabody, Mass.: Hendrickson, 1995.

Klein, Ralph W. *Textual Criticism of the Old Testament: From the Septuagint to Qumran.* Philadelphia: Fortress, 1974.

Metzger, Bruce M. *The Early Versions of the New Testament: Their Origin, Transmission, and Limitations.* Oxford: Clarendon, 1977.

————. *The Text of the New Testament: Its Transmission, Corruption, and Restoration.* 3d ed., enl. New York: Oxford University Press, 1992.

————. *A Textual Commentary on the Greek New Testament.* 2d ed.: United Bible Societies, 1994.

Vaganay, Léon, and Christian-Bernard Amphoux. *Introduction to New Testament Textual Criticism.* Translated by Jenny Heimerdinger. Cambridge: Cambridge University Press, 1991.

Weingreen, Jacob. *Introduction to the Critical Study of the Text of the Hebrew Bible.* Oxford: Clarendon, 1982.

Würthwein, Ernst. *The Text of the Old Testament: An Introduction to the Biblia Hebraica.* Translated by E. F. Rhodes. Grand Rapids: Eerdmans, 1979.

Chapter Seventeen

Reading the Genres of Scripture

Rodney Reeves

The apostle John faced an ecclesiastical crisis. There were members of his community of faith who did not recognize the full humanity and deity of Jesus. Obviously, distance required the apostle to address the church in writing. How could he correct his "children," bringing them back to his opinion, without provoking them to secede from the community? He could send an essay, explicating the virtues of a theologically correct view of Christ. Perhaps a more subtle approach—presenting a balanced Christology in Gospel form—would be more effective. Maybe a straightforward, personal appeal—a letter—would persuade the church not to join the rebellion. More than likely John was not as pensive in sorting out his literary options as the foregoing scenario would suggest. In fact, John used all three literary conventions when he warned the church about heretical Christology: the Gospel, an essay (1 John), and a personal letter (2 John). Johannine literature (Gospel, letter and apocalypse) provides an excellent example of the literary conventions available to first-century authors. Indeed, biblical writers produced an unparalleled repository of literature which preserves the wide variety of literary genre extant from the days of Moses to the time of Christ. It is not surprising, then, that a study of the literary quality of the Bible is required in world literature courses in many colleges and universities.

To Jews and Christians, however, the Bible is more than a great book of world literature. It is the Word of God. One would expect sacred Scripture to preserve the revelation of God's will for humanity only in propositional form—a series of requirements for righteous living. Instead, we also find proverbs and parables, letters and lyrics, stories and similes. Why does the Bible contain such a diverse collection of literary genres? Biblical authors used different literary conventions in order to accomplish different purposes. The psalmist used poetry to encourage reflection and worship; the prophet anticipated judgment and called for repentance through divine speech, "thus saith the Lord." Each literary form, therefore, reveals literary function. Determining what the author is trying to say involves our recognition of the genre employed—a literary decision which facilitates authorial intent as well as a reader's comprehension. Hence, before we can discover the meaning of what was written, we need to understand how it was written.

Narrative

Primarily, the Bible is a book of stories. Aptly entitled "Genesis," the first book of the Torah contains stories of how it all began: the origin of the world, humanity, sin, destruction, covenant, and Israel. Then, from Moses to Ezra, the story of Israel is chronicled. A people of humble beginnings, Israel emerges briefly as an international power, only to become "a byword among the nations, a laughingstock among the peoples" (Ps. 44:14, NASB, as are all quotes in this chapter). The Old Testament story ends with the inspiring example of a people struggling to rebuild their lives in the hope of God's restoration of Israel. Then, moving from the Old to the New Testament, the story of Jesus is presented as "good news" (Gospel). The familiar account of a righteous, barren, elderly couple is eclipsed by the new story of a young virgin who gives birth to a covenant child who is called "the Son of God." The New Testament chronicles the life of Christ and the progress of the Jesus movement. From the shores of the Galilean sea to a Roman prison the followers of Christ spread the good news of God's salvation for all people. Even the letters of Paul provide a "narrative world" by which the reader can track the development of the Christian mission. Like the Hebrew Scriptures, the New Testament story ends with the affirmation of the ultimate triumph of God and his people in the Apocalypse.

Children have always enjoyed hearing the stories of the Bible. Adults need to recover the splendor of reading the narrative portions of Scripture as delightful stories that together tell the main story. The careful reader not only pays attention to every detail of every story but is also able to keep the "big picture" in focus. That is to say, the biblical narratives must be read at microscopic and macroscopic levels.

The narrative portions of the Old and New Testaments are episodic: each story has its own plot, major and minor (sometimes called "round" and "flat") characters, carefully established settings, narrators, story time, ironies, conflicts, heroes, villains, and so on. Recognizing these vital details enhances the reader's understanding of each story. For example, in the story of Jesus and the Samaritan woman, a reader may miss the irony of the narrator's comment, "so the woman left her waterpot" at the well (John 4:28). Having become "a well of water springing up to eternal life" (John 4:14), just as Jesus predicted, she would never thirst again (John 4:13). There are no wasted words in biblical stories. Every characterization, narration, transition in setting, plot twist, editorial comment, and discourse contributes important details to the story.

Consider the episode of Jesus and the man born blind (John 9:1–41). Notice how the author uses tension to keep the conflict between Jesus and the Pharisees constantly before the reader. First, the disciples ask the leading question (v. 2); then, the neighbors force the issue when they bring the sighted man to the Pharisees (v. 13). The narrator adds that Jesus healed the blind man on the Sabbath (v. 14). "The Jews" question the sighted man's parents who are afraid of being "put out of the synagogue" (vv. 18–22); the sighted man sarcastically (or innocuously?) invites the Pharisees to follow Jesus (v. 27); the man born blind puzzles the Pharisees with a riddle (vv. 31–33); the Pharisees finally explode with the patronizing retort, "You were born entirely in sins, and are you teaching us?", and the narrator adds: "And they put him out" (v. 34). As the tension builds, the reader is able to track parallel subplots: the sinner who was born blind becomes sighted (physically and spiritually), the sighted become blind because of their sin. The subplots intersect when the sinner becomes the teacher of the Pharisees who cannot see the Light of the World (vv. 5, 33). Ironically, the Pharisees admit: "We are not blind too, are we?" (v. 40). Thus, Jesus offers in discourse that which in the story has become axiomatic:

"If you were blind, you would have no sin; but since you say, 'We see,' your sin remains" (v. 41).

At times, however, such a microscopic investigation may cause the interpreter to miss the "whole story." Concentrating on the intricate detail of every literary brush stroke, the reader may never see the entire picture. In the Gospels, for example, there is literary design in the way each writer tells the whole story of Jesus—especially in the arrangement of individual episodes. For example, the story of Jesus healing the man born blind is yet another contribution to the overall theme of John's Gospel, "seeing is believing." Consequently, each episode should not be read outside of its literary context. Consider the parable of the Pharisee and the publican found only in Luke's Gospel (18:9–14). The narrator prefaces the parable by explaining that Jesus told this parable for the benefit of "certain ones" who were self-righteous and judgmental. The tight, compact characterization of the stereotypical publican and Pharisee set up the powerful punch line: "Everyone who exalts himself shall be humbled, but he who humbles himself shall be exalted" (18:14). But as if the point of the parables were lost to some of his readers, notice how Luke fleshes out the two characters of the parable in his Gospel. First, we meet the self-righteous Pharisee, a "certain ruler" who has kept all of the commandments all of his life (18:18–25). Then we encounter the publican, a social outcast by the name of Zaccheus, known by his vocation and stature (19:1–10). Again, the aphorism of Jesus rings true: "This man went down to his house justified rather than the other" (18:14). Every story makes up part of the picture and every picture tells a story.

As the foregoing example suggests, the Bible contains historical accounts as well as fictional stories, such as the parables of Jesus. The same literary qualities of historical narratives appear in biblical parables. Jesus was fond of telling stories. These parables, as well as those found in the Hebrew Scriptures, also contain the basic elements of a story: plot, characterization, irony, setting, narrative time. Consider, for example, the shocking twist in the plot of the story of the rich man and Lazarus (Luke 16:19–31). Or again, Nathan's characterization of the poor man's affection for his little ewe lamb that evokes deep emotion (2 Sam. 12:1–4). Further, it is ironic when the prodigal son hits bottom and is forced to dine on the dirty food of unclean swine (Luke 15:11–32). The fact that the good Samaritan helps the man in distress on the Jericho road provides an ingenious setting for the parable which explicates true neighborliness (Luke 10:30–37). The only difference between these stories and the historical accounts of the Bible, of course, is that these parables were stories crafted by Nathan and Jesus to prove a point. But before the interpreter rushes to find the meaning of each parable, we must utilize the same tools for reading the parables as literary critics use in reading other biblical narratives.

The accounts of Jacob and Esau are episodic narratives which have all the classic elements of a great story. *Setting*: God answers the prayer of the righteous barren couple, rewarding them with twins. *Characterizations*: Esau, the man's man, is described by the narrator as a "hairy man" and a "skillful hunter, a man of the field," who "had a taste for game" (Gen. 25:27–28; 27:11); Jacob, his mother's favorite, was "a smooth man," a "peaceful man," who lives "in the tents" (Gen. 25:27; 27:11). Note the subplots of the main story: Esau sells his birthright; Jacob deceives Isaac; Esau is cursed by Isaac; Jacob's retreat from Esau; Jacob dreams of heaven; Laban deceives Jacob; Jacob deceives Laban; Jacob wrestles with the mysterious man; Jacob and Esau reconcile; Jacob settles in Shechem (Gen. 25:19–33:20). What is the main plot? It is the story of a man who has "striven with man and God" and discovers the meaning of covenant. (Perhaps it could be subtitled: "what goes around comes around!") *Irony*: Rebekah uses deceitful practices against Isaac (the covenant keeper) in order to fulfill God's covenant choice of Jacob; the hard-headed Jacob, who dares to wrestle with "God," rests his head on a rock as he dreams of heaven; Esau, the red-haired man who gave up his inheritance for "red stuff," proclaims to Jacob at their reunion: "I have plenty, my brother; let what you have be your own" (Gen. 33:9). The biblical writers were literary craftsmen who used stories—lessons from the past—to preserve history. The creative genius of these divinely inspired storytellers deserves skilled readers who appreciate their craft and seek to understand the meaning of God's Word.

Poetry

In addition to its timeless stories, the Bible is known for its poetry. How many people, relatively unfamiliar with Scripture, can quote Psalm 23? In addition to the Psalms, Job, and Song of Solomon, much of the prophetic material and some of the Torah appear in poetic form (see, for example, Isaiah 40–66, Genesis 49, and Exodus 15). Although the poetic quality of the Bible seems universally recognized, scholars have puzzled over the essential characteristics of biblical poetry. What distinguishes poetry from other genres? Most students would identify the use of rhyme as the major distinctive feature of poetry. However, most poems in the Bible do not rhyme. Instead, scholars have determined that the most common feature of biblical poetry is rhythm. Poetry set to music (i.e., lyrics) obviously requires some rhythmic pattern. The Psalms represent a collection of the songs of Israel's worship—songs of praise and thanksgiving, songs of lamentation and confession. Some scholars maintain that these poetic forms even betray metrical patterns in the arrangement of syllables, words, lines, and strophes. Those who have heard the recitation of the Psalms in the Hebrew language recognize the rhythmic tones of a song as much as the quotation of the Scriptures.

A feature of biblical poetry which contributes more to its meaning than rhythm is *parallelism*. The most frequent form of parallel lines in biblical poetry is *synonymous parallelism*. This can be found when two lines of a verse are similar in form and content, appearing as parallel statements, synonymous in meaning. Consider, for example, Ps. 38:1:

> O LORD, rebuke me not in Thy wrath;
> And chasten me not in Thy burning anger.

The second line intensifies the first in order to clarify and emphasize the penitent's prayer for absolution.

Antithetical parallelism is another distinctive form of biblical poetry. This occurs when the second of the two lines contrasts the meaning of the first. For example, the psalmist exclaims:

> Some boast in chariots, and some in horses;
> But we will boast in the name of the LORD, our God (Ps. 20:7).

Sometimes the antithesis is clearly seen in parallel statements which assert both the affirmative and negative side of reality. In his response to Eliphaz, Job affirms:

> I have not departed from the command of His lips;
> I have treasured the words of His mouth more than my necessary food (Job 23:12).

Another common form of poetic symmetry in the Bible is *climactic parallelism*. With this configuration, several lines build to express an idea which reaches resolution in the final expression:

> For the enemy has persecuted my soul;
> He has crushed my life to the ground;

He has made me dwell in dark places, like those who have
long been dead.
Therefore my spirit is overwhelmed within me;
My heart is appalled within me. (Ps. 143:3–4).

The standard use of figurative language in biblical poetry has led
some scholars to believe that the metrical and symmetrical patterns
that may appear in biblical poetry are incidental (or, as even some
maintain, nonexistent). They believe that the metaphorical imagery
common in biblical poetry is the singular distinctive feature of this
genre. Metaphors and similes, ubiquitous in biblical poetry, are analogical expressions which offer a comparison of the similarities between two realities. A *simile* correlates two ideas using "like" or "as."
For example, the psalmist writes: "Surely I have composed and qui-
eted my soul; Like a weaned child rests against his mother" (Ps.
131:2); and "As the deer pants for the water brooks, So my soul pants
for Thee, O God" (Ps. 42:1). A *metaphor* is a more blunt, direct comparison between two objects, ideas, or experiences. For example,
"God is King" (Ps. 47:7), "The LORD is my shepherd" (Ps. 23:1), and
"The LORD is my rock" (Ps. 18:2) are all metaphors comparing Yahweh to the majesty of a king, the loving care of a shepherd, and the
security of a rock foundation.

Figurative language causes the reader to draw upon life's experiences in order to interpret poetic imagery. Since poetry is a reflective medium, it invites the reader to share in the experience of
discovering reality through comparison, not by proposition. Poetic
language seeks not to break new doctrinal ground or blaze theologically innovative trails. By its standard use of metaphorical expressions, poetic form enables the reader to see the familiar truths of
the Bible in new ways. These provocative images lack the precision
of literal language. Instead, poetry invites speculation, imagination, and a great sense of discovery. How limited our description of
God would be without poetic form. It should come as no surprise,
then, that the worship book of the Hebrew people, the Psalms, enables the believer to express the inexplicable through imaginative
metaphors and similes. Indeed, the reality of God is more expan-
sive than mere words can convey—but poetry tries.

Letters

Recipients

Although some letters have been preserved in Old Testament
narratives (2 Kings 19:10–14), a more resourceful study of the

epistolary genre in the Bible is found in the New Testament. Over one-third of the content of the New Testament, twenty-one of the twenty-seven book canon, exists in epistolary form. The New Testament contains both personal and corporate letters. Paul and John wrote letters to individuals, such as Philemon, Timothy, Titus, and Gaius (3 John), as well as to specific churches in Rome, Ephesus, Corinth, Philippi, Thessalonica, and Colossae. Sometimes single letters were addressed to several groups and enjoyed a wider circulation, such as "the churches of Galatia" (Gal. 1:2), "the twelve tribes who are dispersed abroad" (James 1:1), and the "aliens, scattered throughout Pontus, Galatia, Cappadocia, Asia, and Bithynia" (1 Pet. 1:1). Many scholars have asserted that Ephesians was a circular letter intended for several Pauline churches. Some have even argued that the Revelation of John qualifies as an epistle, written to the seven churches named in the book. The original recipients of certain "general epistles," however, remain completely anonymous. For example, we do not know the identity of the "Hebrews," the "elect lady" (2 John 1), or the addressees of 1 John, 2 Peter, and Jude.

Purpose of Writing

For the most part, the letters of the New Testament were written to specific congregations for particular reasons. For example, almost all Pauline correspondence was *responsive*; Romans may have been the only letter sent by Paul to establish initial contact with a church. Paul's letters, therefore, represent only one part of a larger dialogue. The Pauline epistles were not the result of some impetuous desire to "touch base" with the churches; Paul had his reasons for writing. In fact, in most of his letters, Paul was arguing for something. Sorting out Paul's argument enables the modern reader to uncover the occasion for the letter. To understand *why* Paul wrote his letter enables us to understand *what* Paul meant in his letter. Of course, background information about the recipients of the letter provides an important historical context for interpretation. Furthermore, the modern reader should ascertain as much information about the author as possible since letter-writing reveals as much about the sender as the receiver. By reconstructing the "life situation" which prompted the author to communicate by letter to a particular community, modern interpreters make the quantum leap of reading a first-century text as if they were the original recipients. In our attempt to understand what Paul wrote to the

Galatians, we want to know why *this* man sent *this* letter to *this* particular church.

Literary Form

Letter writing was a popular means of communication in the first-century Mediterranean world. The Pauline epistles, as well as other letters in the New Testament, exhibit a generic form common in the first century: introduction, main body, and conclusion. Some scholars maintain, however, that the letters of the New Testament possess distinctive features which exemplify a unique epistolary form and therefore reveal a particular literary function. For example, Paul's letters are lengthier than the common private letter and contain additional epistolary features not found in common Hellenistic letters. Most Pauline epistles follow a particular format: salutation, thanksgiving, body, *paraenesis,* and closing.

The hellenized *salutation* ("grace to you") has been replaced by the Pauline greeting, "grace to you and peace from God" (Rom. 1:7; 1 Cor. 1:3; 2 Cor. 1:2; Gal. 1:3), which included the Jewish salutation, "*shalom.*" Paul used the standard X to Y (writer to addressee) greeting. Yet, in some of his letters, Paul listed his partners as co-authors; for example, "Paul and Silvanus and Timothy to the church of the Thessalonians" (1 Thess. 1:1; see 2:18, "for we wanted to come to you—I, Paul, more than once"). Then again, Paul may have included the names of his co-workers in the address, identifying them as letter carriers, in order to acknowledge their authority to transmit apostolic messages. Paul would often end his letters with a doxology (2 Cor. 13:14) or a prayer (Gal. 6:18). Sometimes Paul would even sign off with his own pen (2 Thess. 3:17; Gal. 6:11; Col. 4:18). Except for Galatians, Paul also included in his letters a lengthy thanksgiving, sometimes as a prayer to God, for the faithfulness of the community. Although offering a word of thanksgiving was not unique, most hellenistic letters included only a brief acknowledgement of the goodness of "the gods."

Paul's epistolary creativity reaches full expression in the main body and *paraenetic* sections of his letters. In the body of the letter, Paul used a variety of arguments to persuade his readers to adopt his perspective. Most of his arguments were based on theological convictions derived from the Hebrew Scriptures and his own religious experience. Occasionally, Paul relied upon the authority of the Jesus tradition (1 Cor. 7:10). Whatever the basis of his defense, Paul operated under the conviction that his apostolic authority was sufficient for all his churches—that he spoke on Christ's behalf (1 Cor. 7:12; Gal. 1:1, 11–12, 16; 2 Cor. 13:3). Every contingency, every circumstance, every problem caused Paul to relate his gospel message to the needs of his churches. As a result, one should not read the letters of Paul as an exhaustive compendium of Pauline theology. The Pauline epistles, as well as the rest of the New Testament letters, demonstrate how the gospel of Jesus Christ addressed the needs of different people, under different circumstances, of a different time and place. Therefore, it is imperative for modern readers to read the timely arguments of Paul as contingent expressions of the timeless truth of the Gospel. Before we can know what it means to "walk in the Spirit," we must know what Paul meant to convey to the Galatians when he argued against fulfilling the "desire of the flesh" (Gal. 5:16).

Prophecy and Apocalypse

When the wicked were prospering and the righteous were suffering, divine seers received visions and prophets pronounced warnings of the approaching justice of God. Old Testament prophets delivered oracles of judgment to the political and religious leadership of Israel, warning them of imminent divine retribution. The perennial interpreters of current events, the prophets would see the corrupt monarchy and profane temple operating under the shadow of an emerging international power as a sure sign of divine judgment. When Judah looked to Egypt to stave off the Assyrian aggression, Isaiah pointed out the inevitable: "Woe to those who go down to Egypt for help, and rely on horses, and trust in chariots . . . and in horsemen . . . the Egyptians are men, and not God, and their horses are flesh and not spirit. . . . And all of them will come to an end together" (Isa. 31:1–3). The prophets believed that God would work within history, using even Israel's adversaries, to effect his will.

In order to substantiate the surety of God's judgment, the prophets exposed the current social injustices and religious crimes of Israel. Picturing Yahweh as the judge and jury, the prophet delivered God's indictment of Israel, charging that the people had broken their covenant (Hos. 4:1–19). Sometimes the prophet would recreate a funeral dirge, offering cries of woe, mourning over the imminent death of Israel (Amos 5:1–3). Despite the apparent gloom and approaching doom of Israel, the prophets did not despair in total resignation. They persisted in including the "even now" message of repentance and hope of restoration (Jer. 15:5–7, 19–21). Yahweh wanted Israel back; ultimately, the goal of the prophet's message was the renewal of the covenant between Israel and God. Therefore, modern readers of the prophets should first seek to determine how the prophetic message related to Israel's circumstances and how the covenant promises were fulfilled in Israel's day before claiming contemporary applications.

Apocalyptic Literature

With the fall of the monarchy, exilic prophets began to see the actuality of the Kingdom of God as a suprahistorical phenomenon, that is, in apocalyptic terms. Divine seers used apocalyptic imagery as their prophetic medium to reveal the future reign of God. Instead of propping up broken dreams of the Israelite nation effecting God's justice on earth, the apocalypticists believed that Yahweh himself would bring an end to history (Dan. 7:9–10; Zech. 9:14–17). The final conflict between evil and good signaled the end of the world. In the aftermath, God would create a new heaven, new earth, new temple, new Jerusalem (Zech. 14:3–9; Rev. 21:1–4). These visions, similar to some dreams, contain surrealistic images which defy a literal interpretation, such as a beast with ten horns (Dan. 7:7; Rev. 17:3). Apocalyptic literature relies upon common symbols to reveal the shadowy world of the eschaton. Hence, biblical apocalypses were not intended to be read as literary constellations whereby one can predict the future. Apocalyptic symbols are analogical images which affirm the certain future of God's victorious reign over evil. Becoming familiar with stock symbolism of other apocalyptic works enables the modern reader to make sense of the strange images found in the symbolic world of the Apocalypse. Indeed, the more we understand the literary devices of any particular genre in the Bible, the better we understand the meaning of Scripture.

▼

For Further Study

Alter, Robert. *The Art of Biblical Narrative.* New York: Basic Books, 1981.

———. *The Art of Biblical Poetry.* New York: Basic Books, 1985.

Caird, G. B. *The Language and Imagery of the Bible.* Philadelphia: Westminster, 1980.

Culpepper, R. Alan. *Anatomy of the Fourth Gospel: A Study in Literary Design.* Philadelphia: Fortress, 1983.

Doty, William G. *Letters in Primitive Christianity*. Guides to Biblical Scholarship. Philadelphia: Fortress, 1973.

Fee, Gordon D., and Douglas Stuart. *How to Read the Bible for All Its Worth*. 2d ed. Grand Rapids: Zondervan, 1993.

Osborne, Grant R. *The Hermeneutical Spiral: A Comprehensive Introduction to Biblical Interpretation*. Downers Grove, Ill.: InterVarsity, 1991.

Petersen, David L., and Kent Harold Richards. *Interpreting Hebrew Poetry*. Guides to Biblical Scholarship. Minneapolis: Fortress, 1992.

Roetzel, Calvin J. *The Letters of Paul: Conversations in Context*. 3d ed. Atlanta: John Knox, 1990.

Russell, D. S. *Divine Disclosure: An Introduction to Jewish Apocalyptic*. Minneapolis: Fortress, 1992.

Ryken, Leland. *How to Read the Bible as Literature*. Grand Rapids: Zondervan, 1984.

Ryken, Leland, and Tremper Longman III, eds. *A Complete Literary Guide to the Bible*. Grand Rapids: Zondervan, 1993.

Sawyer, John F. A. *Prophecy and the Prophets of the Old Testament*. The Oxford Bible Series. Edited by P. R. Ackroyd and G. N. Stanton. Oxford: Oxford University Press, 1987.

Chapter Eighteen

From Biblical Text to Theological Formulation

David Kirkpatrick

Hermeneutics and the Character of Theology

Christian theology is a most unusual discipline! Not only does its long history house normative and evocative theological statements, but its interpretation processes seek to make these statements as relevant and as fresh as next Sunday's sermon. Throughout its impressive and extensive history, the discipline of theology has struggled with its own identity. It has had to contend with political interests, as well as with other academic disciplines, in order to maintain its own credibility. It has generated conflict, questioned its own enterprise, especially from the perspective of various philosophical options; and, yet, on other occasions, it has challenged and redirected these very same options. Historically, the discipline has expressed a wide variety of purposes and intentions, but its consistent work has been that of pushing back the intellectual horizons of faith in search of the meaning and the truth that it believes to be revealed in the Christian gospel. Because its primary objective is to make the Christian faith pertinent to each new generation, the task of reappropriating, restating, even refocusing the past so that it speaks ever again with a contemporary voice is an absolute necessity.

Christian theology is unavoidably a hermeneutical discipline, prizing "the interpretive consciousness of the Christian community,"

275

while upholding Jesus Christ as the "primary *explicandum*" or focus of understanding (McGrath, 1–3). Only interpretation bridges the gap between the realities of the past and those of the present, realities often considered mutually exclusive. The historical and literary analyses that are so instrumental to the work of theology only become germane in interpretation, contemporary dialogue, and, more often than not, reinterpretation. Inasmuch as Christian theology attempts to communicate the truth of God's word so that faith in God is made meaningful and given contemporary relevance, the process of theological thinking is interpretation. In this sense, theology is hermeneutical! Neither the church nor its theologians have ever been able to escape the interpretive process required of the discipline. As a second order discipline, Christian theology is an interpretation of, and a response to, the theological imagination inscribed in the biblical text.

"Faith Seeking Understanding"

Simply put, Christian theology interprets for the present the church's historic faith. It reflects the church's own self-understanding, offering critical insights into what it means to respond in trust to the revelation that Jesus of Nazareth is the Christ of God. In listening to the Christian gospel, Christian theology attempts to take seriously the process of critical reflection made necessary by the reality of faith. Theology is actually born as "faith seeking understanding" (*fides quarens intellectum*), according to Anselm's classical model. As a reflective discipline, theology not only endeavors to understand the cognitive meaning of faith, but also struggles to challenge faith toward its practical implications. Evangelical faith is a search for the understanding rooted in the language of the Christian Scriptures, a narrative language anchored in the past but with the capability of confronting the reader as a fresh, contemporary word of truth. In a hermeneutical initiative given birth in the desire to understand, faith interrogates the biblical text in order to make possible a theological formulation with contemporary relevance (Hart, 47–48).

The hermeneutical task challenges the community of faith to think critically. In this way, the church is strengthened because it is encouraged by this same process of interpretation not only to understand the content of faith, but also to understand the significance of worship and the challenge of a transforming praxis. While meaningful worship is the goal of the gathered community of faith, the individual believer, as well as the entire community, needs to recognize how important it is to be involved in the world of human suffering. For these reasons, and a dozen more, the church needs to begin to think critically about God, about the world as God's creation, and about one's own self-understanding. Faith in God itself causes us to think and to ask incisive questions. While the heart of Christian faith is a relationship of trust, through this trust flows the discernment that identifies the needs of the human condition. Although the hermeneutical process actually begins in faith, it moves toward understanding by asking fundamental questions shaped not only by the biblical text but by life itself. As the critical awareness that characterizes "faith seeking understanding" grows, it needs to be suspicious of glib and naive answers, but it should also learn what it means to trust the Word of God radically rather than the principalities and the powers that demand blind obedience. It is this critical awareness that keeps theology open for dialogue, asking questions not only of the biblical text, but also of the Christian community, so that the church, responding in faith and humility, is strengthened and its evangelistic mission is accomplished.

Theology, therefore, becomes a process of questioning dialogue, a continuing process that spirals with each question toward a better understanding of the salvation that comes through faith and that leads to grace and humility. Theology's reflective process is open to all members of the believing community, meaning that interpretation is the priestly responsibility of all believers. No one in the Christian community "is excused the task of asking [critical] questions or the more difficult [task] of providing and assessing answers" (Karl Barth, *Church Dogmatics*, III/4:498). If faith is a response of the Christian community to the Word of God, then theology is the reflective formulation of what this response means about believing and acting responsibly in the world. The dual task of both understanding faith and pointing believers to responsible action is foundational to theology's rationale.

An evangelical hermeneutic assumes a dynamic relationship between theological formulation and the biblical text. Captured by the imagination of the biblical narrative, the process of thinking (theologically) attaches itself to the narrative of the text and combines this attachment with a quest for understanding. As important and as foundational as the biblical text is for theology, the process of theological formulation necessitates examining an even

wider variety of historical and theological documents. These additional sources are not only prerequisite for understanding the
church's historic faith but are also indispensable in the continual
development of doctrine. Changes in the linguistic and cultural
milieu as well as the development of the hermeneutical process create the need for reinterpretation of earlier formulations and make
a reexamination of the church's classical language a necessity.

Several reasons could be given for the reinterpretation of the
classical "two natures" Christology at the Council of Chalcedon
(A.D. 451). Even though one may be sympathetic with the soteriological concerns of Chalcedon in describing the relationship between the divine and the human natures of the Christ, the
language of "substance" philosophy from Greek seems abstract,
distant, and strangely paradoxical to the modern ear, especially
when compared to the familial language found in the Gospel narratives. Because of Chalcedon's philosophical context and the subsequent interest in interpreting its abstract language, the question
historically has been how can two substances, so paradoxically different, be united? Understood in the light of Chalcedon's historical
setting, however, and the fact that the Christological formulation
was driven by the question of salvation, the issue can be restated as
how to understand the personal involvement of God in the suffering of humanity so that in this solidarity there is redemption. In
other words, a new contemporary question to an old problem.

Asking questions of what it means to believe is at the heart of
the theological enterprise. Because these questions have a history,
theological formulation is most often (if not always) reformulation. The theological reflection of the Christian community works
out of this history, examining the presuppositions and the prior
understandings that have been brought to the hermeneutical task,
often because of the experience of faith, making the critical discernment that leads to theological discourse possible. In other
words, the reflective aspect of faith, that is, faith thinking about
faith, is never accomplished without presuppositions. Because of
the church's need to know and to understand more adequately the
faith-that-is-believed, theological reflection structures the church's
understanding of its faith, challenges the sinful interests of the self-
serving elements of the church, and establishes the identity of the
Christian community as the "people of God."

No single explanatory system or view of reality can account for
all of the phenomena associated with believing in God. Theological

interpretation is, in fact, best served by incorporating competing structures, rather than using a single logic to force theological meaning into some predetermined grid. The question is whether or not a single system, understood here to mean the logical development of a rational enterprise based upon a fundamental concept, is the fitting structure for theological formulation. A system so construed suggests that its originator has the capability of understanding the whole of reality. When the idea of God is added, it must fit into the system without any disruption or confusion. Not only is God confined to a particular rational structure, but the understanding of God is made to conform to the cohesiveness and the presuppositions of the system. As precarious as this has been for theological formulation, the church has often organized its theology along the lines of a formal system. The most comprehensive example of such a system is the great *Summa* of Thomas Aquinas. Most lists would also include the *Fount of Wisdom* of John of Damascus and the *Sentences* of Peter Lombard. Some historians would include Origen's *On First Principles* as an example of incorporating the revelation of God into a preconceived philosophical concept, but most would not construe his impressive work to be a formal system.

A critical question for theology is whether or not it can create systems in the same way that philosophical programs have consistently done. Obviously, it has tried, but formal theological systems have been unable to discount the reality of Jesus Christ, who is not an idea or a universal principle, but the *person* of God's self-disclosure. The fundamental focus of faith seeking understanding, rather than being an attempt to construct a comprehensive system, is an attempt to bear witness to this Christ, to his life, to the relevance of the cross, and to the significance of the resurrection for a contemporary world (Weber, 1:50–55). Theological thinking, because it "thinks after" the event, must never be construed to be an end in itself. The rationale of evangelical theology must not be to design a Christian creed that makes God only part of a comprehensive structure of being. Rather, because Christian theology works within the boundaries of the biblical story, because it cannot get around the person of Jesus Christ, and because faith itself is, at least in part, that which is "hoped for," its understanding can never be comprehensive in a philosophical sense (1 Cor. 13:9, 12). Those who would build comprehensive ontologies usually neglect the "not yet" of faith. The consideration of eschatology alone as a structural limitation for the theological process forces one to ask questions and to seek continually an understanding of the Word of God. The "not yet" of eschatology is, in essence, a final argument against comprehensive systems, because it highlights the limitations of reason and the necessity of faith as trust. Systems may be provocative, dialectical, and often synthetic; but in reality they are only comprehensive arguments providing their own comprehensive answers. Systems have invariably been constructed so that they either conceal the presuppositions that have created them, or they demand that thinking follow the logic presupposed and consistently established in the system's prolegomena. For this reason, theological systems seldom employ a dialogical openness, preferring instead a self-determining logic. On the other hand the acknowledged limitations that stem from faith, the openness and the humility with which one must stand before God, trusting the divine compassion, understand that a definition of Christian faith is difficult if not ill-advised.

How then can faith forge an understanding? A good beginning is to distinguish between the principle "faith seeking understanding" as a hermeneutical method (not a closed system) and "the pluralistic structure of thinking" that is required of theology. The basic distinction is that "understanding" always means understanding something (being), while "faith" always means trusting God. There is a fundamental "identity in this difference that makes it possible for the one to 'seek,' or be open to, the other" (Scharlemann, "Fides," 233–36). This delineation not only creates the hermeneutical identity but makes interpretation possible for the theologian. On the other hand, Christian faith is always faith in Jesus Christ, "a believing, trusting faith." At the same time, it is that "something which is believed." Christian theology functions confessionally as a believing, trusting faith and works at the task of understanding the content of faith. Neither is mutually exclusive; but as Robert P. Scharlemann suggests, one is dependent upon the other. Christian theology adopts Jesus Christ as its criterion because Jesus Christ is the "word of faith" (Rom. 10:8).

Faith in Jesus Christ is a personal response to the divine initiative, a response which becomes the ground for a new and hopeful relationship with God—a relationship of trust! In the light of this faith, and its attending consequences, Christian theology pursues its inquiry. As a discipline requiring intellectual integrity, it becomes the responsibility of both individual and community. Implicit in the process is the demand for rigorous self-discipline. The process of understanding, which is not an end in itself, intends to move faith to transform both church and world. The hermeneutical process, then, functions as an interplay between the text, the reader, the church as faith's contextual community, and the world. This interplay keeps the dialogical interests of theology alive and specific. To make theological formulation the end of the process too easily turns the church's doctrine into dead dogma, making theological reconciliation without capitulation impossible. Theology then becomes needlessly harsh, community is indeed impossible, if not dangerous, while the dialogue so necessary to the hermeneutical process surrenders either to empty compromise or to the raw display of power—both of which bring confusion. The understanding of faith that portends a transforming praxis needs the reflective consciousness of a critically-formulated theology, so that its activity is not blind. Neither thinking nor praxis can be ignored in the dynamic process known as theological hermeneutics.

Like preaching, theology interprets the scriptural language of faith, with the goal of its fresh appraisal and acknowledgement. While the metaphorical language of the text opens the possibility for understanding, as a key unlocks a door, the truth of the gospel invites all who believe to participate in the reflective work of the believing community. Consequently, the hermeneutical reality of faith is evidenced not only in confession and reflection but in its willingness to move to praxis—to the responsibility of action exemplified in the cross of Christ and demonstrated in love of neighbor. As important as confession is to evangelical faith and to its reflective inquiry into the truthfulness of the Christian witness, Christian theology must not become a narrow confessionalism where all that is required is intellectual assent! Because its work is implicit in the process of "faith seeking understanding," theology must always be kept open to the reflective interests of the inquiring mind, that is, if confession of faith is to become mission.

The Importance of Texts

In its broadest sense, Christian theology is a linguistic art form, textually oriented, and hermeneutically sensitive. As a construction of the theological imagination, invariably and necessarily tied to the essential texts of the biblical revelation, theological formulation is grounded in the historical events that gave rise to the text and to the saving message of "God for us" conveyed by these same texts. It is in the sacred text that Christian theology encounters the symbols that constitute the revealing grammar of faith that comes to life only in interpretation. Theological thinking actually starts when it encounters the symbols of the text (Scharlemann, "Concepts," 513–27).

Although the contextual differences between the first century and all subsequent interpretations are increasingly severe, the text itself in its canonical form still manages to catch and stimulate the creative imagination of evangelical theology. The point is well taken that theological hermeneutics "appropriates the resources of the text in response to the Word it conveys, so that one moves increasingly . . . from [the] 'understanding of language' to 'understanding through language,' from a knowledge of the text to the knowledge which the text fosters" (Wood, 40–42). While this epistemological interest actually intensifies the importance of the text in that it does not leave the text behind, it does mean that the text must be used as an instrument of interpretation rather than as the object of one's faith. Implicit within this point of reference is the reason why the biblical text is taken to be the church's fundamental hermeneutical referent. Simply stated, the Bible is the written Word of God! In an attempt to "restore the concept of biblical revelation to its full dignity," Paul Ricoeur underscores the importance of the biblical text for theological formulation: "If the Bible may be said to be revelation this must refer to what it says, to the new being it unfolds before us. Revelation, in short, is a feature of the biblical world proposed by the text" (*Essays*, 104).

The privileged status of the New Testament lies in its being the textual vehicle through which the early church bore witness to Jesus Christ as the incarnate Word. This neither encourages neglect of the Old Testament in any way nor diminishes its importance; rather, the witness of the New complements the testimony of the Old as "both testaments bear witness to the one Lord, in different ways, at different times, to different peoples" (Childs, 85). Often neglected by contemporary hermeneutics, the theological ground of the text; that is, its understanding of God, is not only crucial to the text's identity, but it also has the most profound hermeneutical implication. The revelatory character of the text does not in any way inhibit the hermeneutical process as the interpreter moves its theological and ethical inferences dialogically from text to contemporary context. As revelation, the text expresses the intent of the God whose self-disclosure is "for us," but it also means that the reader must be open to being addressed by the language of the text (Wood, 39). In essence, understanding the text as sacred Scripture establishes for the community of faith the proper theological context for hearing the Word of God, adding focus and purpose to the hermeneutical process through its theological-christological content.

The biblical writers themselves sensed the importance of interpreting texts. Luke describes how Jesus himself drew from the entire Old Testament: "interpreting [for the disciples] in all the scriptures the things concerning himself" (Luke 24:27, RSV). The apostle Paul referred to the significance of interpreting the Old Testament Scriptures when he wrote to Timothy that "all scripture is inspired by God and profitable for teaching, for reproof, for correction, and for training in righteousness" (2 Tim. 3:16, RSV). In a response to the Corinthian congregation the same apostle reminded the church that the Scriptures had been "written down for . . . instruction," implicitly calling for interpretation (1 Cor. 9:10, NASB).

The normative function of Scripture suggests a wide variety of hermeneutical considerations. The basic question, however, is how the interpreter approaches the text itself. One possibility considers the interpreter to be drawn into the world of the text. Another option, and invariably a better one, suggests it is *through* the text that the reader is confronted with its meaning and consequences. The biblical text is not self-referential. Rather, this textual world points beyond itself to the one who has entered into our world to transform it. The text requires interpretation. Consequently, the development of theology cannot avoid theological exegesis. The text, in fact, makes the reader an interpreter. In facing the world of the text, there is always the possibility of understanding its theological intent as relevant, because the text alone speaks to the contemporary context, but only through interpretation. Consequently, systematic theology must not become the kind of discipline that can be plotted on some numerical graph, rewritten as speculative dogma or restated as an encyclopedic history. Rather, as an interpretative discipline, it should seek to integrate the various voices heard within the biblical text in order to discern in the world of the text and its relationship to the church's tradition, and within the multiple contexts of both, the reality and grace of God revealed in Jesus Christ, in his life as well as his cross and resurrection.

The God Question

Theological themes are varied and sometimes problematic, but the overarching question for Christian theology is the question of

God. As the hermeneutical process moves from text to theological understanding and beyond, the methodological question can be put quite precisely: is it possible to understand any part of theology without having previously dealt with the question of God as the primary concern? Theological interpretation in every instance anticipates the mystery of God, not only in reading the biblical text but also in examining all that is prior to the hermeneutical process. Just as the narrative events of Scripture anticipate the disclosure of the reality of God, theology addresses the text as a harbinger of the truth of God's self-disclosure. The biblical text itself is a hermeneutical referent in the process of faith seeking understanding because it bears witness to Jesus Christ, the text's central message. When theology speaks of revelation as self-disclosure, it means the "gift in which God grants to us the possibility of knowing him" (Weber, 1:171). Theology, then, is more of a constructive response than a discovery, more interested in manifestation than verification. In other words, God is not a philosophical problem or a discovered actuality to be spoken about in some general manner. To speak in this way would be to identify God as an object of conceptual certainty, making God an objective reference that could be captured by reason. Instead of projecting the idea of God as a general presupposition, evangelical theology references the activity of God in history, specifically in the events in the history of Israel, and primarily in the incarnation of Jesus Christ. The biblical witness to God's activity, itself a contextualized hermeneutic, is the primary source for theology's construction of its basic format.

The hermeneutical problem for theology is to speak consistently about God in the light of the biblical revelation and with a "logic" that is also consistent with the narrative's own presentation. As the hermeneutical process moves from text to theological formation, the attempt is to interpret the mystery of God's divine compassion revealed in the history of Jesus Christ through the witness of God's Holy Spirit. This trinitarian and historical theology is an attempt to reconstruct the meaning of God in terms of the divine compassion revealed in the cross, thereby deconstructing God as a non-active metaphysical construct. One of the primary reasons for the church's trinitarian theology is to prevent the revelation of God from being cut off from God himself and his *continuous* self-giving through the resurrected Christ and the living witness of the Spirit. A scholastically rigid theology too easily cuts itself off from the living God of the biblical witness. The result is often an institutional theology, an institutionalized hermeneutic, and a theology that is used to justify its own institutional ethic. Rather than presenting the revelation of God as static, evangelical theology is a testimony that the revelation of faith is an experienced reality given and received in a living relationship. T. F. Torrance's summary statement is worth noting: "Any disjunction between God and his self-revelation through Christ and in the Spirit could only mean that in the last analysis the gospel is empty of any divine reality or validity" (Torrance, 14). Trinitarian theology is a move away from the notion of God as an indefinite ontological concept, to an understanding of God as the one who acts out of divine compassion, identifying with humanity's sin and its suffering. The doctrine of the Trinity itself is a recapitulation of theology's reflective interests. Otto Weber calls the doctrine the "classic example of a 'dogma,' in that it interprets the testimony of Scripture" (Weber, 1:350). It has functioned in the history of the church as the hermeneutical response to the uniqueness of God. In Jesus Christ and through the witness of the Spirit, the "unity, life, and revelation [of God] are expressed . . . in reflection and interpretation" (Weber, 1:371). If this one subject, meaning trinity, is not considered essential in the formation of Christian doctrine, the discipline of Christian theology loses its textual ground, and evangelical talk about God becomes irrelevant (Pannenberg, 13). In the light of the divine compassion expressed as Trinity, the cross is radically reinterpreted. From the vantage point of the love of God extended to all of creation, the cross of Calvary not only says that God recognizes the character of human suffering but that the solidarity of God's revelation is to identify with that suffering. Reinterpreted from this vantage point the relationship God has established with his creation through the cross refocuses the question of sin and human suffering as the question of God's redemptive activity. A trinitarian theology of the cross means that the reality of God "exists essentially in relationship" (Weber, 1:379) and that God's true nature, revealed in the suffering and death of Jesus Christ, is one of reconciliation and redemption (2 Cor. 5:19).

Even though the Trinity represents the classical expression of the church's theology, different interpreters of the biblical text have found a variety of theological themes to be significant in the development of Christian theology. The interpreter's primary interest may be the historical recitation of the acts of God, or what it means to understand the world as God's creation; one could seek the meaning of humanity's redemption and how this is accomplished, the reality of human suffering, or even the significance of the cross or the reality of Easter. Without minimizing the significance of these and other issues, for the interpreter of Christian theology, the question of God is still the essential concern. Sometimes the primary question is explicitly stated, often implicitly suggested; however, in most instances, the focus of the problem has been not only the question of the reality of God but whether or not (even how) God can be known. On occasion, some have deliberately avoided the question, suggesting it is an inappropriate, if not an impossible question (Bultmann). For others, the question of the reality of God has been the only question (Barth). On other occasions, the question of God is admittedly a part of the interpreter's own prior understanding. When recognized, this prior understanding brings to the hermeneutical process an open anticipation as well as a preliminary reading of the very symbols which are to be interpreted. When unacknowledged, the hermeneutical process suffers from prejudice and speculation, coloring the doctrine of God with the private agendas of the interpreter, and accomplished usually at the expense of the biblical text.

Even though the question of God has traditionally turned on the question of religious language, the current debate has moved on "from the question of the nature and form of religious language to the more radical question of its possibility as a mode of meaningful discourse" (Winquist, 55). In other words, instead of *how to* make the "language of God" relevant, the current hermeneutical debate focuses on the more radical and critical question of *whether or not* theological language is significant, given our social and scientific context. Because the essential question for every Christian theology is the question of God, the response to this fundamental question should be accomplished within the horizons of Christian theology's textual witness, a history beginning with the plurality of texts found in the Old and New Testaments. There is a sense in which the purpose of the hermeneutical process, from text to theological formulation, is neither more nor less than the process of coming to terms with the intrinsic meaning and significance of the theological language with which it is confronted in the textual history of faith and in dialogue with the contemporary context.

One note of caution should be remembered regarding the theological interpretation of biblical texts. Even though theologians use a wide variety of methods, no hermeneutical process or method has the ability to capture the divine essence. There are, of course, competing methods as well as conflicting interpretations. Instead of being detrimental to faith's understanding, however, competing views have often enhanced the church's search for truth. This is true even of those interpretations that have, on occasion, dissented from the established tradition of the church and have been labeled incompatible with the prevailing opinions of the church's orthodoxy. At this point, one only needs to be reminded of Martin Luther's challenge of papal authority and his critique of the scholastic theology of the medieval church. While massive shifts have occurred in the history of Christian thought, hermeneutical methods and critical commentary have consistently used reason, experience, history, and tradition in their subsequent construction or deconstruction of texts in order to understand more adequately the reality of faith. In other words, no single method or principle completes the task alone. Quite the contrary, even though the texts of sacred Scripture may be understood as the Word of God, the texts' symbols necessitate the mediation of exegesis and interpretation, and the truth claims are most often judged by whether they lead to a faith that works rather than by rational verification.

Whenever Christian doctrine becomes a comprehensive interpretation of the world of the text, so that its meaning is contained within a system or, for that matter, captured by a particular method, it too easily and too quickly becomes esoteric knowledge. In this way, Christian doctrine tends to insulate itself from the counter questions of those outside of faith, making theology a self-contained structure and interfaith dialogue unnecessary, if not impossible. As an esoteric knowledge, Christian theology opens itself up to the charge of being a modern type of Gnosticism. In other words, when the hermeneutical process excludes an interchange with those outside of the faith, it becomes an epistemological system with knowledge accessible only to the initiated. In contrast a hermeneutic of "faith seeking understanding" calls for open dialogue. It actually trusts the word of God and refuses to become party to a process of Theology as indoctrination. As indoctrination theology too easily becomes fixed and rigid because it has been removed from the vital questions that lead to critical self-examination. As a fixed system, theology actually loses its function as a hermeneutical discipline, eventually making a self-serving apologetic the only acceptable form. The end result being that theology is made to serve the political or social agenda of the theologian. We may posit, then, at least for the evangelical theologian, a basic premise for any theological interpretation: given the necessary interpretation of the biblical text, the reality of God transcends not only the hermeneutical process and the theological formulation, but the text itself, its language, and its symbols. Theology has not always made this distinction; to disregard it, however, is to fall into idolatry and to deny the interperative work of the Spirit.

The Hermeneutical Spiral

Asking how it is that one moves from text to theological formulation is a comparatively recent enterprise. To be sure, more than one option exists for answering this question. Theology's more recent history suggests that the hermeneutical options range from Schleiermacher's practical theology, and his practical-experiential approach to the text, to the more recent emphasis of deconstruction, with its explicit hermeneutic of suspicion of all conceptual theologies. Between these two extremes, the theologian can learn from Gadamer's dialogical model, the various options of structuralism, the metaphorical process of Paul Ricoeur, the different types of narrative theology, and reader-response criticism with its emphasis on preunderstanding. The philosophical alternatives supporting these options often create hermeneutical conflict in a rapidly changing environment. Where once common sense rationalism prevailed, other interests have stoked the glowing fires of interpretation. The works of Hegel, Husserl, Wittgenstein, Heidegger, and even Nietzsche have been revisited for resources to meet the growing dissatisfaction with the modern-critical paradigm that has dominated theology since the Enlightenment.

Today, in evangelical circles, theological hermeneutics still requires (1) exegesis, the reading and interpretation of the sacred texts of the Old and New Testaments; (2) historical analysis, because texts not only carry significant historical references but have their own histories; and (3) an awareness of the importance of context for understanding. In addition to these three sources, Christian theology, if it is to be relevant, requires theologians with the ability to recognize the truth of God as it manifests itself in the life of the world (Hall, 20). In the final analysis, theology's hermeneutic is not complete until it has been worked, and often reworked, so that it fosters, in an increasingly "post-Christian" world, a genuine sense of community, inclusivity, and cooperation. Biblical theology need not give up any of its distinctives, but biblical hermeneutics will not be accomplished in a theological, social, cultural, or linguistic vacuum.

The problems of modernity have best been characterized by conflict, often brokenness, and more often than not, divisiveness. In a post-Christian world, an evangelical hermeneutic must work toward the integration of theological disciplines and more specifically, toward the appropriation of the biblical text's meaning within the (con)texts of the interpreter's world. Any emphasis on theological formulation requires wholistic and reconstructive thinking. The idea(l) is not doctrinaire dogmatism, or even biblicism, but the cultivation of an "integrating consciousness" in which the church and the individual believer have the possibility of making a difference in a world that knows already too much about sin and human suffering. Theological hermeneutics, that is, the process of faith seeking understanding, needs to work out of a theological paradigm that focuses the New Testament's emphasis of the cross so that the thinking of faith is made real in its identification with the world (Peters, 221–23). In using the cross as the primary hermeneutical referent, recent theological interpretations have revised the hermeneutical process to include the suffering of God, implicit in the cross, as an essential component in the development of doctrine.

The classical "hermeneutical circle," moving from reader to text then back again, needed expanding in order to include other necessary factors instrumental for development of doctrine. Because the conceptual circle has been the traditional framework for exegesis, theologians have not always considered seriously the hermeneutical significance of conflicting experiences of faith. Using the image of a "hermeneutical spiral" (Osborne, 6) is an attempt to expand and stretch the process of the circle. While continuing to admit to the distance between the reader and the text, as well as the problems of two distinct historical horizons, the spiral broadens the interests of the interpretive spectrum of the circle to include the plurality that is brought to the process of interpretation by contextuality and the interpreter's prior understanding. Without losing the emphasis of the text and by continually returning to the text, the spiraling continuum considers the text's interpretive history, the significance of the text for the history of Christian thought, the metaphorical implications of the text's language, and the social contexts that invariably influence hermeneutical approaches. Considering this plurality carefully qualifies the entire process of moving from text to theological formulation.

Hermeneutics as a spiral indicates simply that there are more than two factors that determine the theological imagination. The theologian does not easily journey from text to theological formulation. This difficulty forces the reader consistently to navigate the prevailing winds of reason and to watch for any confluence of interest that encroaches on the hermeneutical process. If one considered only the philosophical interests historically dominating theology, the sea would still be difficult to sail, due to the complexity of the philosophic issues that have subsequently influenced the formulation of method. Further, the discipline's history suggests that theological thinking has often been as profoundly discursive as it has been formal, since theological method, even when it has been systematically articulated, has been influenced by the personality, training, and interests of the theologian. While the theologian continually utilizes the tools of critical inquiry in the search for the truth of the gospel, the hermeneutical process has been contextualized by the circumstances of history as well as by the theologian's apologetic and/or political concerns. Whether from the perspective of Irenaeus's debate with Gnosticism, Augustine's inquiry into the nature of grace, the synthesis of faith and reason in Aquinas, Luther's polemic against scholasticism, or Barth's "No!" to natural theology, the discipline has been dominated by the search for truth. This means that the hermeneutical spiral becomes part of the dialogical continuum of faith seeking understanding that broadens its focus with each successive reference. The dialogical inquiry of faith activates the hermeneutical process, keeping alive the spiraling interests of textuality, understanding, praxis, and community. In addition, community is not the least of theology's hermeneutical concerns. Only on rare occasions has theology isolated its reconstructive dialogue from the varied and critical interests of the Christian community. When this has happened, both the church and the discipline of theology have been impoverished.

The hermeneutical spiral is dynamic and tensive. As the various components within the interpretive process interact to expand an initial reading of the biblical text, the hermeneutical task is to remember the theological reality (God) to which the text bears witness, while simultaneously realizing that the reality of God is presented in a literary form and that the original meaning of the text is being asked to encounter a context other than its own. Reason's failure to capture the original intent of Scripture through historical critical inquiry alone is actually itself an argument for the dialogical thinking that characterizes the hermeneutical spiral. Even though the dialogical process is filled with tensions and competing arguments, faith's Christological reference becomes the focal point for developing the church's theology. Rather than narrowing or limiting the hermeneutical focus, however, the referent provides both "an opening and a check to continually new figurative applications of (Scripture's) apostolic content," enabling the hermeneutical process to "extend the original meaning [of an ancient text] to the changing circumstances of the community of faith" (Childs, 723–24).

The hermeneutical spiral guides the dialogical process toward the formulation of theology and beyond so that it includes both the worship of God and the practical implications of the Christian ministry. It inquires into the veracity and the meaning of the biblical narrative. It reflects upon its own history as a theological enterprise; and, on occasion, it has had the courage to move well beyond its own textual orientation to speculate concerning the existence, even the non-existence, of God. It has been willing to engage in interfaith dialogue, realizing that this dialogue has consistently shaped essential questions which challenge the church's reconstructive efforts. Dialogical thinking and the reflective character of theology cause the discipline continuously to rework its own interpretive language in order to express and to demonstrate the contemporary relevance of faith. Theology's own internal dialogue, featuring its many competing agendas, holds promise of pushing the spiraling interest toward a greater understanding of faith.

Theological hermeneutics is, therefore, the process of thinking about God, thinking after the event of revelation but in the context of its textual world. The hermeneutical process is an understanding of faith and, because of this faith, a search for the truth of the Christian gospel. But as important as the dialogical process of reflective thinking is in the development of theology, there is yet another instrumental constituent in the understanding sought by faith, namely, the activity of the Spirit (2 Pet. 3:20–21). It is "through the Spirit of God that the reality to which the text points, namely Jesus Christ, is made active in constantly fresh forms of application" and understanding (Childs, 724). In the spirit of faith seeking understanding, theological interpretation applies both trust and suspicion in order to discern the truth: trust because there can be no final interpretation, suspicion because there is no interpretation that is definite. Ultimately, it is the truth of this witness, fully demonstrated in its essential point, the cross of the incarnate one, that calls into question every theological formulation—formulations that are destined always to fall short of the truth. This acknowledgment is both the first and the last essential element in theology's "propriety and precision" (Torrance, 156). Christian theology is from first to last a hermeneutical discipline; interpretation is unavoidable. It is, however, not the process, or the interpreters, or their theological formulations that bear the decisive witness to the truth of God's self-disclosure. It is, in the end, the good news of Jesus Christ alone through the word of the Spirit. The hermeneutical process, then, ultimately spirals back to the theologian who, as interpreter, is not only the subject of interpretation but also the object. If there is an end to the hermeneutical process (and it is easily argued that there is not one), it comes in the faith realization that Christ and the Spirit interpret the theologian.

▼

For Further Study

Barth, Karl. *Church Dogmatics*, 5 vols. Translated by G. T. Thomson. Edinburgh: T. and T. Clark, 1936–1977.

Childs, Brevard S. *Biblical Theology of the Old and New Testaments: Theological Reflection on the Christian Bible*. Minneapolis: Fortress, 1992.

Hall, Douglas John. *Thinking the Faith: Christian Theology in a North American Context*. Minneapolis: Augsburg, 1989.

Hart, Ray L. *Unfinished Man and the Imagination: Toward an Ontology and Rhetoric of Revelation*. Atlanta, Ga.: Scholars, 1985.

Klein, William W., Craig L. Blomberg, and Robert L. Hubbard Jr. *Introduction to Biblical Interpretation*. Dallas: Word, 1993.

McGrath, Alister E. *The Genesis of Doctrine: A Study in the Foundation of Doctrinal Criticism*. Oxford: Basil Blackwell, 1990.

Osborne, Grant R. *The Hermeneutical Spiral: A Comprehensive Introduction*. Downers Grove, Ill.: InterVarsity, 1991.

Pannenberg, Wolfhart. *An Introduction to Systematic Theology*. Volume 1. Grand Rapids: Eerdmans, 1991.

Peters, Ted. "Toward Postmodern Theology, Part 1." *Dialogue* 24 (1985): 221–23.

Ricoeur, Paul. "A Hermeneutic of the Idea of Revelation," in *Essays on Biblical Interpretation*. Edited by Lewis S. Mudge, 73–118. Philadelphia: Fortress, 1980.

Scharlemann, Robert P. "Concepts, Symbols, and Sentences." *Theology Today* 22 (1966): 513–27.

———."*Fides Quaerens Intellectum* as Basis for Pluralistic Method." In *The Whirlwind in Culture: Frontiers in Theology*. Edited by Donald W. Musser and Joseph L. Price, 233–245. Bloomington, Ind.: Meyer-Stone Books, 1988.

Torrance, T. F. *Reality and Evangelical Theology*. Philadelphia: Westminster, 1982.

Weber, Otto. *Foundations of Dogmatics*. Translated by Darrell L. Guder. Grand Rapids: Eerdmans, n.d.

Winquist, Charles E. "The Surface of the Deep: Deconstruction in the Study of Religion." In *The Whirlwind in Culture: Frontiers in Theology*. Edited by Donald W. Musser and Joseph L. Price, 55–66. Bloomington, Ind.: Meyer-Stone Books, 1988.

Wood, Charles M. *The Formation of Christian Understanding: Theological Hermeneutics*. Valley Forge, Pa.: Trinity, 1993.

Chapter Nineteen

Contextualization
in the Hermeneutical Process

Daniel Sanchez

The notion that the gospel needs to be relevant to the sociocultural context of the hearers has been with the church from her inception. As G. Campbell Morgan, in *The Great Physician* (1937), points out, the manner in which Jesus adapted the presentation of the message to different persons (e.g., Nicodemus, the Samaritan woman, Zaccheus) is an example of contextualization. While Jesus preached the same gospel of the kingdom, he adapted its presentation to the needs and backgrounds of the individuals whom he sought to reach.

The writers of the Gospels, as Günther Bornkamm documents in *Jesus of Nazareth*, also contextualized their message to their target audiences. The Jewish orientation of Matthew, for example, is reflected in his emphasis on messianic prophecy, the divine titles of Jesus, and the Aramaisms which he incorporates into his Jewish-Greek language. In *Contextualization*, David J. Hesselgrave adds that John's use of the term "Logos" in his prologue seeks to express the gospel in terms which the Greeks could understand.

The apostle Paul also contextualized the presentation of the message. Aware of the fact that he had a Jewish audience at the synagogue at Antioch of Pisidia (Acts 13), Paul spoke about the patriarchs, the prophets, and the prophecies and presented Christ as the fulfillment of these prophecies. At Athens, however, knowing that his audience was made up of Gentile intelligensia (Acts 17), Paul did not speak about the Jewish patriarchs but instead sought to establish a bridge of communication by speaking to them about the "unknown God" (v. 23), as the creator of all human beings (v. 26), reinforcing his argument with quotations from their own poets (vv. 27, 28). While Paul stressed the importance of retaining the unchangeable *content* of the gospel, he recognized the necessity of adapting its *presentation* so that it could be understood by those who heard it (1 Cor. 9:22). The manner in which the Evangelists and Paul communicated the gospel in the various cultural contexts gives evidence of the fact that a form of contextualization was practiced in the early church.

Historically contextualization has found expression in a number of ways (especially in missionary strategy). Since the 1960s, however, this concept has acquired specialized meanings and has become one of the significant issues in theological, missiological, and hermeneutical circles. A. O. Dyson's article, "Dogmatic or Contextual Theology?" argues that this resulted largely from a paradigm shift among Third World church leaders. They became increasingly aware that the theologies which had been inherited from the older churches of the North Atlantic community often neglected some of the *major concerns* of their sociocultural contexts. An additional motivating factor was articulated by Robert McAfee Brown in "Context Affects Content—The Rootedness of All Theology." Brown pointed out that, to a large extent, all human theologies are influenced by ideological, cultural, and socio-political values.

The Biblical Text and the Modern Cultural Context in Hermeneutical Approaches

While there is general agreement today regarding the need for contextualization, there is disagreement regarding the hermeneutical approaches which are to be employed in this process. In an effort to address this issue, this chapter will focus on the process by which the abiding truth of Scripture can be correctly understood and expressed in a given cultural context. This will begin with an analysis of the manner in which the various hermeneutical approaches deal with the biblical text and the modern cultural context. Some hermeneutical approaches risk failing to do justice to the intrinsic meaning of the biblical text while others risk failing to achieve a fundamental encounter with the modern context.

Approaches That Risk Failing to Do Justice to the Biblical Text

Among the hermeneutical approaches which risk failing to do justice to the biblical text are the allegorical and praxis approaches. The allegorical method is generally not content with the direct sense of the language of the text but searches for symbolic meanings. The allegorical method has been utilized to explore the symbolic meanings of figurative texts such as hymns, poems, metaphors, and parables, but the utilization of this method poses serious problems for the interpretation of the text within its historical context. First, when the allegorical method is employed in the interpretation of biblical texts which are not symbolic, it disregards their inherent meanings. Second, when allegorizers make arbitrary applications, they can mold the meaning of the text to reflect their mode of thinking. When the allegorical method is used in these ways, it risks failing to do justice to the historical dimensions of the biblical text.

A second approach which risks failing to do justice to the biblical text is the praxis method employed by the expressions of liberation theology. As Max L. Stackhouse points out in *Apologia*, the greatest strength of the praxis method is that the hermeneutical task is not viewed as one which is merely cerebral but as one which stresses doing as well as thinking. Reflection, therefore, does not take place in a vacuum but in active participation in a concrete sociocultural context. This emphasis is needed to counteract approaches which perceive the hermeneutical task strictly in "objective" terms. Pastoral concerns often demand that some form of praxis be considered in the hermeneutical process.

While the praxis method has contributed useful concepts to the hermeneutical debate, as William L. Larkin asserts in *Culture and Biblical Hermeneutics*, serious questions have been raised regarding its treatment of the biblical text. This approach generally calls for a dialectical relationship between the modern context and the biblical text. In this relationship the modern context is generally viewed as having preeminence. Viewing the modern context as the "primary source" and the biblical text as "another reference point" raises a hermeneutical question regarding the authoritative nature of Scripture. In this sense, therefore, it can be stated that the praxis approach fails to do justice to the biblical text.

While the allegorical and the praxis approaches make some contributions to the hermeneutical debate, they risk failing to do justice to the biblical text by virtually ignoring its historical dimensions and by allowing the modern context to take preeminence over the biblical text.

Approaches That Risk Failing to Do Justice to the Modern Context

The grammatico-historical approach has several strengths to commend it. It makes a conscious effort to ascertain what the words mean in their historical setting; it seeks to study the text within its broader literary context; and it objectivizes interpretation by preserving the historical and chronological distance between the interpreter and the text. In this sense it can be stated that this approach provides needed safeguards for the hermeneutical task.

While the grammatico-historical method has contributed toward overcoming some of the disadvantages of other approaches, its application often has some inherent weaknesses. First, it can have a tendency to ignore the influence of the modern cultural context upon the interpreter. Second, it can focus on the linguistic history but be reluctant to give due recognition to the cultural or historical conditioning of the perspective of the author of the text. Third, if it assumes that the hermeneutical task can be limited to defining the original meaning of the text, it will be lacking in its present application.

Another hermeneutical approach which risks failing to do justice to the modern context is the historical-critical method. This method has two primary goals: (1) it seeks to ascertain the actual facts about the origin of the document in question; and (2) it seeks to throw light on an obscure narrative by determining the precise nature of the events to which it bears witness.

One of the strengths of the historical-critical method is that it calls attention to the *form* of the narrative. The parabolic form, for instance, does not demand the historicity of the story. A second strength is that it considers the *aims* of the author. An author who is not concerned with certain details (e.g., geography), for instance, is not faulted for what he was not trying to do. A third strength, suggested by Elizabeth Schüssler Fiorenza in *Bread Not Stones*, is that it asserts the meaning of the original witness over later dogmatic and social usurpations, for different purposes.

One of the limitations of the historical-critical method, however, is that by virtue of the fact that it is concerned with the historicity of the biblical text, it risks failing to deal effectively with the modern context. While it strives to help the modern reader to understand the original historical context of the biblical text, it is not within its purpose or scope to attempt to understand the modern context. Some scholars who utilize the historical-critical method even regard as "unscientific" any attempt to address questions of contemporary relevance. While the historical-critical method may "pave the way" for an application of the biblical text by shedding light on its historical context, the focus of this hermeneutical approach is the past and not the present. In this sense, therefore, it can be stated that the historical-critical method risks failing to do justice to the modern context.

While each of the approaches discussed above makes a vital contribution, it often ignores other important aspects of the hermeneutical task. The allegorical and praxis methods stress the importance of giving attention to the modern context, yet they fail to do justice to the biblical text. The grammatico-historical and the historical-critical approaches often fail to do justice to the modern context. The answer in the development of a contextual hermeneutic, however, is not found in discarding these approaches but in utilizing their contributions while supplementing them with key concepts from the social sciences. This ensures that the sociocultural factors which influence the interpreter's understanding of the biblical text are taken into account.

Utilization of Social Science Concepts in the Hermeneutical Task

Some of the conceptual tools provided by the social sciences which facilitate an understanding of a sociocultural context relate to worldviews, cognitive processes, and social structures.

Worldview

Social scientists assert that worldview functions as the basic hermeneutical device of society. It affects the manner in which interpreters perceive the biblical text. The study of worldviews (supernaturalistic, naturalistic, syncretistic) contributes to an understanding of the biblical text as well as the modern context. For example, an understanding of the supernaturalistic worldview which was prevalent among Jewish people during the earthly ministry of Jesus is essential to a comprehension of the manner in which his miracles are perceived. Approaching the New Testament passages describing these miracles with a modern, naturalistic worldview would greatly jeopardize their understanding. The study of worldviews, therefore, is of vital importance to the hermeneutical task.

Cognitive Processes

To understand the biblical text it is often necessary to give attention to the various cognitive processes which are employed in Scripture and in the modern sociocultural context. In *Communicating Christ Cross-Culturally*, David J. Hesselgrave discusses three cognitive approaches: (1) the conceptual approach, which focuses on rational, theoretical thinking; (2) the intuitional or psychological approach, which is instantaneous apprehension without reasoning; and (3) the concrete relational approach, in which life and reality are seen pictorially in terms of the active emotional relationships in a concrete situation.

There are several implications of this for the hermeneutical task. First, interpreters need to be aware of the predominant cognitive process which they are employing as they study the biblical text. There is the danger that the interpreters may be imposing upon the text a cognitive process which is not inherent in it. Second, interpreters need to be aware of the cognitive process which is predominant in a biblical text. A. C. Thiselton asserts in "Semantics and New Testament Interpretation" that there are large areas of the New Testament which are explicitly concerned with rational argument and with elucidation of theological concepts. This seems to be true of Paul's reasoned arguments in Colossians, Ephesians, and Romans. In other portions of Scripture, however, metaphors, similes, symbols, types, parables, allegories, and emblems are employed. The concrete relational approach may be more in harmony with these. Third, it is important for interpreters to know the predominant cognitive process of the contemporary cultural context. In contexts where concrete relational or psychical (intuitive) processes predominate, exclusive reliance on conceptual processes either to gain insights regarding the cultural motifs or to share insights from the biblical text will not suffice. The solution for dealing with different cognitive processes is not to abandon one in favor of another. As Thiselton points out in *The Two Horizons* (441): "Feeling states and the priority of worldhood are important in hermeneutics, and the Cartesian model is too limited as a model for the interpretation of texts. Nevertheless there is room *both* for critical reflection of the text as object and *also* for submission to the text in order that it may speak to man in his 'world'."

Social Structures

An understanding of social structures helps the interpreter in several ways. First, the manner in which a society is structured sheds light on the group's social bonding, communication, and decision-making processes. Second, an understanding of the various types of societies (tribal, peasant, urban) may prevent the interpreter from interpreting the text from a perspective which is alien to its cultural context. For example, the context of the text may be that of a tribal society while the interpreter may be viewing it from the perspective of an urban society. Unless interpreters are aware of this distinction, as Charles Taber correctly observes in "Missiology and the Bible," they may impose an interpretation upon the text which is foreign to it.

It is also important that the interpreter understands relationships between sociocultural groups described in Scripture. To the extent that such factors as sociopolitical relations can be ascertained in the biblical text, a clearer picture will emerge of the interaction which occurred between the various sociocultural groups in Scripture. There are numerous instances in which an adequate understanding of the inherent meaning of the biblical text is dependent to a large extent upon a comprehension of the manner in which cultural groups related to one another (for example, Jews and Samaritans; Hebraic widows and Hellenistic widows; Jerusalem Jews and Galilean Jews). Some of the conceptual instruments from the study of social structures, therefore, can make a contribution to the hermeneutical task. A principle, however, which needs to be kept in mind is that these should always be subordinated to scriptural authority.

Toward the Development of a Contextual Hermeneutic

In the light of the previous discussion the question which we have before us is, how can we develop a contextual hermeneutic which does justice both to the biblical text and the sociocultural context? To address this question we will divide our discussion in two parts: (1) how to deal with biblical texts which have culturally conditioned mandates, and (2) how to treat the questions addressed to Scripture by a sociocultural group.

Dealing with Culturally Conditioned Texts

One of the greatest challenges which the interpreter faces is that of distinguishing between the supracultural and the cultural elements of a biblical text. The complexity of the task demands that it be approached with much prayer, wisdom and integrity. Two concepts that provide assistance in this task are: (1) the distinction between the different foci of the biblical mandates, and (2) the distinction between the inherent *meaning* of the text and its cultural *form*.

How can one distinguish between the different "target groups" to whom the mandates are addressed? In *Christianity in Culture*, Charles Kraft outlines three levels of abstraction at which a command is given in Scripture: (1) culture-specific; (2) general principle; (3) human universal. Culture-specific mandates, such as greeting one another with a holy kiss, relate to a particular cultural context and depend greatly on implicit information imbedded in the context with which the given custom interacts. In general principle commands such as "do not covet another man's cattle," the specific cultural context is less important to an understanding of its meaning. Human universal commands, such as "Love the Lord your God with all your heart," apply to every person in every culture at all times. What is being communicated here is not that one command is more authoritative than the others but that the meaning of some commands, especially the culture-specific, is more dependent on an understanding of the cultural context than the others.

This leads to a discussion of an important distinction which needs to be made between the *form* and the *meaning* of a given command. When Paul said "Greet one another with a holy kiss," his hearers understood what he meant. In that culture it was customary for people (even men) to express their love by kissing one another. That cultural form, however, communicates other meanings in some contemporary cultures. The task of the interpreter, therefore, is to seek to understand the meaning of the mandate and to find appropriate forms in a contemporary culture. In Asian cultures, for instance, it might be bowing respectfully. In the general principle commands the teaching is more obvious, but it may require cultural adaptation. For example, persons could say they have no problem with Exod. 20:17 because they do not own any cattle. The command against covetousness, however, needs to be applied to perhaps another person's car, boat, job, and so forth. Universal commands require even less cultural exegesis, yet they must be carried out within a specific cultural context. Distinguishing between levels of abstraction and form and meaning can help the interpreter to extrapolate the intended message from its cultural forms.

A word of caution, however, needs to be given. Often cultural forms employed in the Bible convey a cluster of meanings which cannot be retained if the form is changed. One example is the metaphor ascribed to Christ: "Lamb of God." Some have suggested that this form needs to be replaced in places where lambs are not known (for example, a seal among the Eskimos). There is such a wealth of meaning connected with the nature of lambs and the sacrificial system of Israel, however, that no substitution could come close to conveying its meaning.

Another precaution which the interpreter needs to keep in mind in dealing with passages which have obvious cultural trappings is that the overall teachings of Scripture must be brought to bear in the exegetical task. As Kraft states in *Christianity and Culture* (1979), "But since nothing in the Bible is 'merely' cultural, we need to look beyond each command to discover how the word and custom symbols were understood by the authors and those to whom they were originally written. That is, we need to look for supracultural meaning in each by getting beyond our own cultural conditioning (with "its plain meanings") to the interpretation of each within its original cultural context."

Seeking a Dynamic Relation Between the Scripture and Culture

How does one deal hermeneutically with vital issues, such as in vitro fertilization, a cultural group's search for a sense of dignity, or the exploitation of the poor, which arise out of a specific sociocultural context?

The concept of the hermeneutical circle (spiral) as expressed by C. René Padilla in "Hermeneutics and Culture," has made a valuable contribution by focusing on the interaction which takes place between the biblical text and the modern sociocultural context in the hermeneutical process. There are differences, however, in the manner in which the relationship between the two is perceived. Some approaches define this as a *dialectical* relationship. The implication of this is that the Bible and the sociocultural context are equally authoritative. Due to the fact that the approach being developed here considers the biblical text to be normative in the hermeneutical process, it favors a *dialogue* which views the biblical text and the modern sociocultural context as being involved in an interactive, dynamic process in which the modern context is willing to be questioned and modified by the biblical text. This dialogue begins as key questions reflecting the interpreter's insider's perspective informed by sociocultural analyses are addressed to the biblical text. It is important that these questions truly reflect the existential concerns of the interpreter's sociocultural context lest the resulting theology focuses on questions no one is asking, while issues which need urgent biblical direction are ignored.

The second step involves listening to answers suggested by the biblical text. In order for the biblical text to speak to these questions, however, it must be allowed to speak in its original sociocultural context. This requires the utilization of the grammatico-historical, historical-critical, and social science tools discussed above.

In addition to asking questions from the text and listening to its answers, the dialogue involves listening to the questions which the text itself poses. The questions posed by the text may call for a reexamination and modification of the insider perspective with which the interpreters have approached the biblical text. This may involve an examination of the broader perspective, such as the worldview of the interpreters' sociocultural group. An analysis of the interpreters' worldview will help them to understand the general frame of reference from which they are approaching the biblical text.

The questions posed by the text may bring to light the inadequacy of the interpreter's questions. This may lead to a reformulation of initial questions which arose from the sociocultural analysis in order that they might reflect the biblical perspective more adequately. The text in due time may suggest appropriate questions. As the dialogue continues, there is a sense in which the text interprets the interpreters and their sociocultural contexts.

After the questions have been reformulated, they are addressed to Scripture once again. It needs to be kept in mind that by the time that this reapproaching takes place, the interpreter should have a clearer understanding of the biblical text. The biblical text approached from a more congenial insider perspective and addressed with deeper and richer questions will be found to speak more plainly and fully.

This dialogue, which is an ongoing (spiraling) process, can lead not only to a reexamination and reformulation of the interpreters' insider perspective (worldview) but also to a consideration of the theological implications of this for their sociocultural context. This reflection may take the form of pointing to themes (that is, problems, aspirations, challenges) which have been reflected in the questions which the interpreter has addressed to Scripture. These themes may also be found in the art forms (poetry, songs, discourses, and writings) of a group in a sociocultural context, giving evidence of the fact that the group has reflected on them, albeit in an informal manner. These intimations of theological reflection may need to be clarified and modified as dialogue with Scripture continues. Some of the biblical themes, for example, may reveal the incompleteness of the range of the themes which the interpreter has brought to Scripture. Theological reflection following the procedure described above can help the group to begin to develop a theology which reflects the application of Scripture to their existential concerns within their sociological context. As Daniel von Allmen suggests, however, this emerging contextual theology will need to remain open for critical evaluation from within the group (insider perspective) as well as from the broader Christian community (outsider perspective).

The model proposed here represents an interdisciplinary approach to the hermeneutical task. It recognizes that each of the approaches discussed above contributes different elements to the hermeneutical task. At the same time it recognizes some of the limitations of these approaches. There is, therefore, in this model not only the tension between the horizons of the biblical text and of the interpreter, but also a tension between the disciplines which are employed. To address the first tension, a dialogue between the culturally conditioned questions of the interpreter and the original culturally rooted biblical text is employed. To address the second, allowance needs to be made for the disciplines to challenge the assumptions of one another as they work to facilitate an understanding of the biblical text. Throughout the process, however, the biblical text is given priority and the disciplines which are employed are viewed as tentative diagnostic tools. This functional control of Scripture over the methodologies which are employed ensures the integrity of the hermeneutical process. This model itself needs to continue to be open to scrutiny and reappraisal to ascertain if in fact it does justice to the biblical text.

The multi-faceted dialogue presented here provides for the type of interaction which can contribute toward an increasing understanding of the interpreters' existential concerns vis-a-vis the biblical text. As the interpreters approach the biblical text utilizing the methodology described above in humility and prayer seeking the leadership of the Holy Spirit, progress can be made toward the goal described by Kwame Bediako (14):

To hear the word of God as coming from our cultures means more than to hear the words (*grammata*) of the Scriptures in our mother-tongues. The message . . . must . . . be "earthed" in our cultures. . . . [This means] to hear Him speaking to [us], address-ing himself to the questionings and longings of [our] minds and hearts in the concrete realities of [our] environments . . . "So shall we all at last attain to the unity inherent in our faith and our knowledge of the Son of God—to mature manhood, measured by nothing less than the full stature of Christ" (Eph. 4:13, NEB).

▼

For Further Study

Barney, G. Linwood. "The Supracultural and the Cultural: Implications for Frontier Missions." In *The Gospel and Frontier Peoples*, edited by R. Pierce Beaver, 48–57. Pasadena, Calif.: William Carey Library, 1973.

Bediako, Kwame. "Comments on: 'Is There More Than One Way To Do Theology?'" *Gospel in Context*, 1 (January 1978):13–14.

Bloesch, Donald G. "A Christological Hermeneutic: Crisis and Conflict in Hermeneutics." In *The Use of the Bible in Theology*. Atlanta: John Knox, 1983.

Bornkamm, Günther. *Jesus of Nazareth*. New York: Harper & Row, 1960.

Brown, Robert McAfee. "Context Affects Content: The Rootedness of All Theology." *Gospel in Context*, 1 (January 1978): 13-14.

———. *Theology in a New Key*. Philadelphia: Westminster, 1978.

Carson, D. A. "A Sketch of the Factors Determining Current Hermeneuti-cal Debate in Cross-Cultural Contexts." In *Biblical Interpretation and the Church: Text and Context*, edited by D. A. Carson, 11-29. Exeter: Paternoster, 1984.

Conn, Harvie M. "Contextualization: A New Dimension for Cross-Cultur-al Hermeneutic," *Evangelical Missions Quarterly* 14 (January 1987): 39–46.

———. *Eternal Word and Changing Worlds: Theology, Anthropology and Mis-sion in Trialogue*. Grand Rapids: Zondervan, 1984.

Dyson, A. O. "Dogmatic or Contextual Theology?" *Study Encounter* 8, no. 3, art. 29 (1972): 1–8.

Engel, James F. *Contemporary Christian Communication, Its Theory and Prac-tice*. New York: Thomas Nelson, 1975.

Fiorenza, Elisabeth Schussler. *Bread Not Stone*. Boston: Beacon, 1984.

Gill, Robin. *The Social Context of Theology*. Oxford: Mowbrays, 1975.

Goldingay, John. "The Man of War and the Suffering Servant: The Old Tes-tament and the Theology of Liberation." *Tyndale Bulletin* 27 (1976): 79–113.

Hesselgrave, David J. *Communicating Christ Cross-Culturally.* Grand Rapids: Zondervan, 1978.

———. *Contextualization.* Grand Rapids: Baker, 1989.

———. "The Role of Culture in Communication." In *Perspectives on the World Christian Movement,* edited by Ralph D. Winter and Steven C. Hawthorne, 390–97. Pasadena, Calif.: William Carey Library, 1981.

Hiebert, Paul G. *Cultural Anthropology.* Philadelphia: Lippincott, 1976.

Ihoe, Don. *Hermeneutic Phenomenology: The Philosophy of Paul Ricoer.* Evanston, Ill.: Northwestern University Press, 1971.

Kato, Byang H. "The Gospel, Cultural Context, and Religious Syncretism." In *Let the Earth Hear His Voice,* edited by J. D. Douglas, 1216–1223. Minneapolis: World Wide Publications, 1975.

Kelsey, David H. *The Use of Scripture in Recent Theology.* Philadelphia: Fortress, 1975.

Kraft, Charles. *Christianity in Culture.* Maryknoll, N.Y.: Orbis, 1979.

Krentz, Edgar. *The Historical-Critical Method.* Philadelphia: Fortress, 1975.

Kuhn, Thomas S. *The Structure of Scientific Revolutions.* Chicago: University of Chicago Press, 1962.

Lang, Bernhard. *Anthropological Approaches to the Old Testament.* London: SPCK, 1985.

Larkin, William J. *Culture and Biblical Hermeneutics.* Grand Rapids: Baker, 1988.

Lonergan, B. J. F. *Between Method and Theology.* London: Darton, Longman and Todd, 1972.

Marshall, I. Howard, ed. *New Testament Interpretation.* Grand Rapids: Eerdmans, 1977.

Morgan, G. Campbell. *The Great Physician.* New York: Revell, 1937.

Ogletree, Thomas W. *The Use of the Bible in Christian Ethics.* Oxford: Basil Blackwell, 1983.

Padilla, C. René. "Hermeneutics and Culture." In *Down to Earth,* edited by John R. W. Stott, 63–78. Grand Rapids: Eerdmans, 1980.

Richardson, A. *The Bible in the Age of Science.* London: SCM, 1961.

Samovar, Larry A., and Richard E. Porter. *Intercultural Communication.* Belmont, Calif.: Wadsworth, 1972.

Shaw, R. Daniel. *Toward a Cultural Hermeneutic.* Pasadena, Calif.: Fuller Theological Seminary, 1986.

Smart, James. *The Interpretation of Scripture.* Philadelphia: Westminster, 1961.

Smart, Ninian. *Worldviews: Crosscultural Exploration of Human Beliefs.* New York: Charles Scribner's Sons, 1983.

Stackhouse, Max L. *Apologia.* Grand Rapids: Eerdmans, 1988.

Taber, Charles. "Missiology and the Bible." *Missiology* 11 (April 1983): 229–45.

Thiselton, Anthony C. "Semantics and New Testament Interpretation." In *New Testament Interpretation,* edited by I. Howard Marshall, 75–104. Grand Rapids: Eerdmans, 1977.

————. *The Two Horizons.* Grand Rapids: Eerdmans, 1980.

van Allmen, Daniel. "The Birth of Theology." *International Review of Missions* 64 (January 1975): 37–52.

van Buren, Paul. *The Secular Meaning of the Gospel.* London: SCM, 1973.

Wink, Walter. *The Bible in Human Transformation.* Philadelphia: Fortress, 1973.

Chapter Twenty

Biblical Criticism and Biblical Preaching

Harold Freeman

The methods of biblical study described in the previous chapters are of varying degrees of interest to different people, but the crucial question is whether they are productive for preaching. That is the criterion by which the value of the method is determined. The intended function of Scripture is that it be "profitable for teaching, for reproof, for correction, for training in righteousness; that the man of God may be adequate, equipped for every good work" (2 Tim. 3:16–17, NASB). Since most lay people do not have access to the critical tools of biblical study, they are dependent upon the preaching they hear to provide an accurately interpreted word of God to them. The entire task of hermeneutics should be seen as a servant of the work of preaching rather than an exercise for a few professionally trained academicians. What practical values for preaching, then, do the various approaches to biblical study offer?

This chapter is written from the perspective that the task of hermeneutics is to determine what the authors meant when they wrote a segment of Scripture and to discern various areas of contemporary significance of that original meaning. E. D. Hirsch calls these two focal points of hermeneutics the *meaning* of the text and the *significance* of the text. With such an approach to hermeneutics, the historically oriented, *diachronic* (meaning that they cut "across time" from our time to the time of the biblical writer) critical methods provide a base for the use of the non-historically oriented, synchronic (meaning that their focus is "with our own time") methods.

Contributions of the Historically Oriented (Diachronic) Critical Methods to Preaching

Textual Criticism

Textual criticism is the discipline that seeks to identify the original wording of an ancient document. Textual criticism of the Bible benefits preaching by preventing non-biblical sermons. By definition, that which was originally contained in the writings by authors inspired by God is Scripture (2 Tim. 3:16a). Any word(s) within the pages of our Bible which is determined to have been absent from those writings is not Scripture. Therefore, it is not possible to preach a truly *biblical* sermon from a passage such as Mark 16:9–20, because it is not in the most reliable MSS. While many of us are glad to give up a passage that speaks of such things as handling snakes and drinking poison, we are more reluctant to give up a compassionate sermon based on John 7:53–8:11. Similarly, we regret giving up a nice doctrinal sermon on the Trinity based on 1 John 5:7b (KJV). Nevertheless, if it is determined that these are additions to the original writings, whether intentional or accidental, biblical preaching based on these texts cannot occur.

Although textual criticism cannot always lead to conclusive answers, an evangelical preacher has a great ally in properly conducted textual criticism. None of the critical approaches to be mentioned subsequently is more important than this. While the other approaches are helpful, textual criticism is foundational. Sermons based on spurious or corrupted texts cannot be genuinely biblical. The determination of exactly what the Scripture said is the starting point for biblical preaching.

Source Criticism

In seeking to identify oral or written materials used by biblical writers in the composition of their works, source criticism offers valuable insights that can shape preaching.

1. A Basis for a Series of Sermons. Instead of preaching through a book of the Bible (particularly one of the Gospels), the preacher could preach through one of the literary sources behind the Gospels. The material that is commonly designated as "Q" material (though some scholars question whether an actual literary source behind this material existed) is generally focused on the "sayings" of Jesus rather than "proto-Mark." Thus, a series of sermons on the teachings of Jesus could follow Q as it surfaces in the Gospels. Proto-Mark typically is more oriented towards the activities and deeds of Jesus. So, a series of sermons on the acts of Jesus could follow the early Markan source as it surfaces through the Gospels.

2. *An Enhancement of the Focus of Redaction Criticism.* A source critic examines the synoptic passages or the historical books of the Old Testament in order to determine the written source(s) a writer used at certain points. A source critic's work is, in one sense, a preliminary matter for redaction criticism, which focuses upon the differing uses of the written sources by the various writers. Source criticism can provide the "base line" by which to notice intentional alterations of the sources, which is a major function of redaction criticism.

Form Criticism

Although form criticism is often laden with speculative conclusions based on debatable assumptions, it can be helpful for preaching if properly used.

1. *Identification of the Parameters of a Text.* One of the surest ways to avoid the plague of proof texting is to recognize the silhouette, or "outer layer," of a literary form. It shows us the boundaries of a section of Scripture which is a complete basic unit within a larger passage. That discovery reminds us that we should treat the entire passage and not a fragment of it out of its context, or at least interpret the smaller segment within its larger context.

2. *Determination of the Purpose of a Sermon.* Originally, one of the basic ideas of form criticism was that the church preserved and orally communicated specific kinds of material in certain forms. The content in these forms was utilized for particular purposes or for particular occasions in the church. More recent form criticism is less sure of the possibility of objectivity in identifying the function of the form in the early church, but seeking to determine a text's purpose is still a valid concept. When we determine the need to preach on an issue, situation, or event in the life of our church, instead of searching randomly through Scripture hoping to find a relevant passage, we can go to a recognized form that was used for that function in the earliest church. In this way, a preaching need originating in a contemporary situation can be addressed by a truly biblical sermon. For example, if a church or community is in a grief situation, we could turn to one of the "lament psalms." The lament psalm accurately reflects the Hebrew community in a similar

situation. Although such passages are structured to give a heavy emphasis to the feelings of grief, there is usually some hope embedded in the lament psalm. Using the lament psalm prevents the preacher from presenting a glib word of optimism in the face of a grim reality and allows the preacher to acknowledge the situation of real grief while offering sure hope.

3. Identification of the Main Idea of a Text. The various forms are structured in such ways that they point to the real focus of the passage. If we recognize the form we are able to distinguish between the peripheral and central components of the text. For example, a miracle story of the nature type should be preached to focus upon the divinity of Christ as exhibited in his power over nature. The focus of the form provides the central idea of the sermon.

4. A Determining Factor for the Sermon Content. Form criticism helps yield the content of the message. For example, the first (Matt. 5:3) and eighth (Matt. 5:4–9) beatitudes take the form of Old Testament wisdom literature. This implies that those described already have the "blessing" which is described. The second through seventh beatitudes (Matt. 5:4–9), in which the blessing is stated in the future tense, are in the form of apocalyptic blessings of the Old Testament and other Jewish literature. This tells us that the focus of these beatitudes is not on the present situation; it is on the eschatalogical teachings of Jesus. Taken together, these two different forms present the "present but not yet" focus of Matthew's eschatalogy.

5. A Series of Sermons Based on One of the Forms. We could preach series of sermons on "The Nature Miracles of Jesus," "The Healing Miracles of Jesus," "The Pronouncement Stories of Jesus," or any of the other forms. Notice that the Gospel writers occasionally follow this pattern themselves. Matt. 8:1–9:34 contains a cycle of ten miracle stories. Mark 2:1–3:6 and 12:13–44 contain twin cycles of "controversy stories."

6. Suggested Form for the Message. One aspect of the philosophy of language tells us that there is an integral relationship between *what* is said and the *way* it is said. In order to preserve the full impact of what is said in the message, the form of the text can suggest a form for the sermon. Ronald Allen (54) suggests that the text of Psalm 116, which is a thanksgiving psalm, can provide the structure for the sermon itself. Allowing the structure of the sermon to be a replica of the structure of the form of the text can provide a welcome alternative to the typically Western, logical, rhetorically structured sermon. It may also provide a more effective structure. Such a structure would begin by announcing the intention to praise God for a great deed done for the person (vv. 1–2), review the crisis and rescue (vv. 3–11), and conclude with a reiteration of gratitude to God (vv. 12–19). Since the text was first preserved and passed along orally, perhaps a repetition of that oral form in the message will more effectively produce the intended result of the text in the life of the congregation; that is, an *expression of praise* to God rather than merely a *knowledge* that God does sometimes intervene in crises.

Redaction Criticism

Redaction criticism emerges out of both source criticism and form criticism. It, too, is fruitful for preaching. This should not be surprising. From redaction criticism we learn that the Gospel writers themselves were preachers, in a way. As they wrote their material they were trying to do for their readers what Christian preachers try to do for their congregations—point out the significance of Christ for the particular group to whom they were communicating. How can redaction criticism help the preacher?

1. Redaction criticism can help identify the point of the passage and the point of the sermon. The benefit of redaction criticism for preaching lies primarily in the area of properly identifying the theological point of a given passage of Scripture. Beginning with the overarching theological thrust of the entire gospel, one can outline carefully the contents of the components of the book. This will be helpful in identifying the real point of any given passage. More helpful yet is studying the variations in the way the same event or saying is recorded in different books. One of the interesting phenomena discovered by biblical study is that the various biblical books, drawing from the same sources, sometimes tell the same story differently or place it in a sequence different from the sequence in another biblical book. Various books will utilize the same sources and narrate the same event but give it a different focus. This is true of the books of the Kings and Chronicles as well as the four Gospels. The editorial work of the writer points the passage to a different purpose or idea than that which it had in another book. The writers work with their sources theologically. The author's selection or arrangement of material drawn from the sources behind the books accomplishes this.

2. Redaction criticism can help preach the text theologically. An analysis of most of our files of sermons previously preached would show that we gravitate toward texts from the New Testament and, usually, the epistles. This is probably due in part to our uncertainty and uneasiness about how to handle narrative texts, which comprise such a large part of the Old Testament. We know enough about the abuses of the allegorical method that we do not want to do that, but we do not know what else to do; consequently, we tend to avoid the narrative texts or we preach them by drawing superficial analogies from them. For example, we will look for the good qualities in the life of Hannah and make those the points of our outlines for a Mother's Day sermon. We make Hannah the focus of the message and emphasize her life more than God's redeeming activity. Old Testament stories, however, were told primarily because they contained a theology about Yahweh and his people. Redaction criticism can help us move beyond allegorical and human-centered messages toward God-centered methods of preaching the biblical narratives.

3. *Redaction criticism can provide more sermon texts and ideas for preachers.* Since the narrative genre comprises a large amount of the biblical literature, we will become comfortable preaching from a much larger reservoir of biblical texts. We can reclaim vast segments of the Old Testament for preaching. An analysis of Christian preaching shows a tendency to use New Testament texts much more frequently than Old Testament texts. Probably this is true because of our sensitivity to the possible misuse of Old Testament narratives and our uncertainty of how to use them. If the redactive process can help us become familiar with identifying the point of a narrative, we shall all probably use the Old Testament more.

The New Testament also will likely provide more sermon ideas. Preachers have tended to think that if they have preached about a given event in the life of our Lord from one Gospel, then that preaching possibility has been "used up." Our tendency to "harmonize the Gospels" prevented our noticing the significant differences that redaction criticism points out in the parallel passages. Redaction criticism tells us that Mark's account of the stilling of the storm is primarily a miracle story; its point is the deity of Christ exhibited by his power over nature. Matthew's account was written for the church that was soon facing persecution. It pictured the church on the stormy sea of life with Jesus coming to calm the storm. It was the assurance that Jesus would see the early church through times of persecution. A sermon based on Matthew's account would point out that Christ will keep his people secure in the storms of life. All of a sudden we have more sermon ideas from the Gospels than we thought we had. Better use can be made of the Synoptics than the old trick of compensating for lack of preparation by going to a parallel account and preaching an old sermon previously preached from another Gospel.

Richard Wells suggests that noticeable differences are significant, for example in the story of the Phoenician woman as told in Matt. 15:21–28 and Mark 7:24–30. Matthew wrote his Gospel for the Jews. He emphasized the contrast between the unbelief of the Jews and the belief of the Gentile woman. Matthew is indignant with the Jews because they will not believe while she, a Gentile, will. A sermon from Matthew's Gospel should stress the *responsibility* of those who have the advantages of exposure to the gospel. Mark wrote his Gospel for the Gentiles. He emphasized the particulars in the passage to point out her faith *in spite of* her ethnic origin. Mark is commending her, a Gentile, for believing in a Jew. A sermon from Mark's Gospel would stress the *universality* of the gospel of Christ.

Another very clear example is the parable of the lost sheep. Luke and Matthew give the parable different interpretations. "Luke uses it as a vehicle to encourage joy over repentance. Matthew puts the parable in a context of a discourse on the nature and responsibility of the Christian community and uses the parable as a picture of the way in which community leaders are to seek after a member who strays" (Allen, 62).

Contributions of the Non-Historically Oriented (Synchronic) Critical Methods to Preaching

Given the assertion at the opening of this chapter concerning the orientation of this writer's hermeneutics toward authorial intentionality, it should be apparent that methods of criticism that do not have the thrust of penetrating the time tunnel back to the time of the author and the production of the text should always be used in conjunction with historically oriented criticism. There is no reason for the historical and literary disciplines to be mutually exclusive. Anchored to the historically oriented critical intent, several of these synchronic methods can offer helpful contributions.

Literary Criticism

Literary criticism takes two directions: one focusing on the language of the text and the other on the reader of the text.

1. Language Oriented Literary Criticism: Discourse Analysis. The primary focus of discourse analysis is not upon the author or the author's intended meaning; the focus is upon the text itself and the relationship of its various components to one another. It does not delve beneath the text but analyzes the surface of the text. Of the types of linguistically oriented literary criticism, discourse analysis is probably one of the most productive for preaching. It helps in two key ways. First of all, discourse analysis helps determine the parameters of the text. Certain recognizable literary devices serve as structural signals which indicate where the text begins and ends. This critical process can be helpful with some types of texts where form criticism and other methods previously mentioned cannot be employed. Second, discourse analysis helps identify the major concepts of the passage. In the same way that a sentence can be diagrammed grammatically, a larger unit of Scriptures can be analyzed and "block diagrammed" in such a way as to show its features, including a depiction of the major and minor concepts. Repetitions, parallel structures, and other similar phenomena serve as "signs" or "signals" which indicate the structures of a literary unit. That structure provides strong clues to the meaning of the passage. In this form, discourse analysis criticism serves as "diagram-writ-large." This critical approach is particularly helpful with texts that are didactic in nature because it can help interpreters identify the unifying theme of the passage and the major emphases that relate to it. Coincidentally, it can be helpful in preaching through a book of the Bible. One of the potential pitfalls of preaching through books of the Bible is that we can get bogged down in the minutiae that do not matter. It is best to use the major segments of the book as texts.

2. Reader Oriented Literary Criticism. While focusing on the "implied narrator," *narrative criticism* has provided strategies and techniques for analyzing the scheme and structure of the biblical narratives. The utilization of these techniques can prove helpful in providing a structure for narrative sermons. The "undulations" within the passage can help differentiate between the focus and the "asides" in the narrative. For example, frequently after a *repeated* word or phrase the next major thought of the passage will occur. Recognizing these signals can help avoid majoring on the verbal "carriers" of the passage so that the message focuses on the intended major movement of the text.

For example, what is to keep one from preaching a sermon from Genesis 37 entitled "Don't Tell Anybody Your Dreams!"? Such a sermon would be based on the fact that when Joseph told his brothers his dreams it brought him a lot of trouble. Most of us intuitively stay away from that kind of thing, but we have no formal technique to help us avoid such things in a passage where the result would be less obviously ludicrous. In the long narrative about Joseph's life, the phrase "But God was with him" recurs. Suppose the text for a sermon were the entire "Joseph narrative." The title of the message could be "When God Is with You," and the various emphases of the message would be the thrust of each section between the recurrences of the phrase.

Reader-response literary criticism, with its emphasis on a desired impact of the literature on the implied reader and, more importantly, on the modern reader, provides its major contribution to preaching at the point of preaching theory. It reminds us that preaching is more than the passing on of information. It is an event in which we are to serve as catalysts for change in the lives of our listeners as they discern the significance for themselves of the meaning of the text.

Canonical Criticism

Canonical criticism emphasizes the early Old Testament covenant community's and the early Christian church's corporate understanding of the Scriptures. Its focus is on the meaning of all Scripture for the church. Canonical criticism gives two key reminders to those who preach.

1. Canonical criticism emphasizes sermons to meet congregation's needs. Texts were accepted because they met the needs of the community at given moments in its history. All of the texts were retained and received because together they met the needs of the people. This can serve to remind us to derive message ideas from the needs of the corporate body to which we minister. Preachers can find the more pertinent passages of Scripture from which to preach to a given situation in the church by identifying a motif of Scriptures within the canon that is analogous to the present situation of the congregation. Suppose, for example, that a congregation needed to hear a message intended to point the church to faithfulness in worship. The preacher could select Hag. 1:1–10 as the text. Here the particular matter under discussion was the fact that the people were neglecting to rebuild the temple after the return from their exile. Consequently, this passage finds its way into many sermons connected with building campaigns. However, their neglect to rebuild the temple was only a symptom of their neglect of the larger need to worship God. Therefore, this text can be used to preach that truth.

2. *Canonical criticism reminds us of the wholeness of Scripture.* While we do not want to blur the distinctiveness of any particular passage of Scripture, we do want to remember that no single text contains the *entire* matter of what the Bible has to say on that subject. Canonical criticism can remind us to use the concepts of the analogy of Scripture and progressive revelation. This may call specifically for the use of some qualifying words in our statements in our sermons from particular texts.

An example may help. The concepts of righteousness and faith are brought together closely at least four times in the canon. In Hab. 2:4 the idea is that a righteous man should live faithfully, even in difficult times. Whereas that passage presumed that the one spoken about was already righteous and simply described faithfulness as his reaction to events, in Rom. 1:17 Paul was concerned with faith as the process by which the righteousness of God can become an attribute of a person. In Gal. 3:11 the emphasis was that the righteous will live by faith as opposed to living by the law of the Judaizers. In Heb. 10:38 the concept reverts back towards the Old Testament concept that life is the reward of God's people who remain faithful to him. It would be possible to preach a series of sermons with one sermon on each of these texts or to preach one sermon with multiple "points" based on these separate texts. The point is that the congregation hears the entire canon on the matter. As John D. W. Watts says, "Canonical interpretation will not allow the individual text to be lost in the larger whole, but it will also not allow it to be used without regard to the whole of Scripture."

Conclusion

Perhaps now all of us engaged in the classical disciplines of biblical studies and the practical discipline of preaching can join hands to bridge the chasm that too long has separated us. Hopefully, the biblical scholars feel that the result of their work should yield more than information concerning the time of the text, the history of the text, the form of the text, the variations of the text, the structures of the text, or the multiple uses of the text. Whatever results there are should be beneficial beyond the walls of the academic community. It is important to remember that the Bible is intended to be functional for the church.

Those of us who preach the texts of the Bible can understand that our people have neither the privilege nor the background to take advantage of the latest developments in biblical criticism. We can remind ourselves that the only way the Scripture can accomplish fully its purpose in their lives is for us to be faithful in using properly the latest disciplines of biblical studies in the preparation of biblical sermons.

▼

For Further Study

Allen, Ronald J. *Contemporary Biblical Interpretation for Preaching.* Valley Forge: Judson, 1984.

Bailey, Raymond, ed. *Hermeneutics for Preaching: Approaches to Contemporary Interpretations of Scripture.* Nashville: Broadman, 1992.

Black, David Alan, and David S. Dockery, eds. *New Testament Criticism and Interpretation.* Grand Rapids: Zondervan, 1991.

Culpepper, R. Alan. "A Literary Model." In *Hermeneutics for Preaching: Approaches to Contemporary Interpretations of Scripture,* edited by Raymond Bailey, 77–104. Nashville: Broadman, 1992.

Graves, Mike. "The Sermon as Symphony: The Role of Literary Forms in Composing the Sermon." Unpublished paper presented at the Academy of Homiletics. Washington, D.C., 1993.

Greidanus, Sidney. *The Modern Preacher and the Ancient Text: Interpreting and Preaching Biblical Literature.* Grand Rapids: Eerdmans, 1988.

Hirsch, E. D. *The Aims of Interpretation.* Chicago: University of Chicago Press, 1976.

Kaiser, Walter. *Toward an Exegetical Theology: Biblical Exegesis for Preaching and Teaching.* Grand Rapids: Baker, 1981.

Skinner, Craig. "Critical Interpretations." Unpublished paper presented at the Academy of Homiletics. Washington, D.C., 1993.

Watts, John D. W. "A Canonical Model." In *Hermeneutics for Preaching: Approaches to Contemporary Interpretations of Scripture,* edited by Raymond Bailey, 77–104. Nashville: Broadman, 1992.

Wells, C. Richard. "New Testament Interpretation and Preaching." In *Criticism and Interpretation,* edited by David Alan Black and David S. Dockery, 563–85. Grand Rapids: Zondervan, 1991.

Chapter Twenty-one

Shaping Sermons by the Literary Form of the Text

Grant Lovejoy

Under the Holy Spirit's inspiration, the biblical writers conveyed their message in the literary manner best suited for accomplishing God's purposes. The writers did not aim just to report the truth matter-of-factly; they also intended to declare God's word powerfully, persuasively. They chose a communication strategy to fit their message and the effect God wanted it to have on those who heard it. Consequently, instead of simply asking *what* a passage means, careful students of Scripture also ask *why* a passage was given and *how* the passage conveys its meaning. These three elements—a focused message, an intended outcome, and an appropriate strategy for communicating the message—also characterize sound preaching. Simply speaking, a sermon ought to say and do what a passage of Scripture says and does. A sermon is most likely to achieve that goal when it pays attention to the literary structure and dynamic of the biblical text.

Sometimes we can determine the literary dynamic simply by identifying the genre of the biblical book. We observe that the book is narrative, prophecy, wisdom, psalm, gospel, epistle, or apocalypse and go from there. Most of the time, however, simply labeling the genre of the biblical book falls short of our purposes. We also need to know the literary form of the particular passage with which we are working. Historical narratives, for instance, sometimes contain poetic material and epistles may contain hymn fragments. In fact, each major category of genre may include many subcategories (or forms) of literary genre. For the purposes of this chapter, "genre" will refer to the larger categories and "form" will refer to the particular literary characteristics of smaller units of Scripture (see Greidanus, 21–23). It is fortunate that preachers do not have to label and categorize each text's form before preaching from the text, since biblical scholars have been working on that task for years without coming to a consensus. The key for those who preach, as Mike Graves argues in an unpublished paper, is to understand the movement and mood of the text.

Why Shape Sermons by the Literary Form of the Text?

Preachers sometimes ask themselves, "Should I shape my sermons according to the literary form of the text? Is this worth the time and effort involved?" The answer to these questions is yes. At least four reasons encourage preachers to shape their sermons by the literary form of the text.

God Used a Variety of Literary Forms

An all-wise God thought some portions of his truth would be best conveyed through narrative, other portions via poetry, others via proverbs, and so forth. It stands to reason that we would follow his lead in communicating his message—not just in content, but in method as well. This does not mean that a sermon on a biblical poem must itself be a poem (as will be explained further below), but it does mean that we respect God's choice of communicative strategy.

Literary Form Is Related to Theological Content

Literary form and theological content cannot be as easily separated as some have thought. We may casually contrast content and method, as above, but we know we oversimplify the situation in the process. The form (or method) is part of the meaning. For much of Christian history, preachers have ignored the literary forms of Scripture when it came to developing the sermon. Preachers have taken a sermon text, extracted its theology, then poured that theology ("principles" or "timeless truths") into a sermon structure borrowed from ancient Greek rhetoric. Yet in doing that we have often lost important dimensions of the biblical message. The similes of Ps. 102:3–8 (NIV), for example, are essential to a full appreciation of its message.

For my days vanish like smoke;
my bones burn like glowing embers.
My heart is blighted and withered like grass;
I forget to eat my food.
Because of my loud groaning
I am reduced to skin and bones.
I am like a desert owl,
like an owl among the ruins.
I lie awake; I have become
like a bird alone on a roof.
All day long my enemies taunt me;
those who rail against me use my name as a curse.

Who can communicate the richness of Ps. 102:3–8 in a proposition—or even in a series of propositions? The poetic form is integral to the way the psalm conveys its message.

Following Literary Forms Helps Balance Information and Experience

Using clues from biblical form can help us strike a better balance between information and experience in our preaching. Scripture informs the mind, touches the heart, and challenges the will. In like fashion, good preaching gives the hearers something to know, something to feel, and something to do. Sometimes the inherent drama and urgency of the text gets lost in the making of "points," so we reach for a deathbed story to supply emotional appeal. In capable hands such external illustrations can be used responsibly and well. But it is ironic that we may search high and low for emotionally-charged illustrations to enliven a message when the passage being preached may be a narrative with high drama itself. Given a chance to tell its story *as a story* and not in an alien form, that narrative text can speak with a fine blend of information, vicarious audience participation, and challenge.

Following Literary Forms Gives Variety to Preaching

Variety in sermon form serves both the truth and the congregation. This chapter emphasizes how variety in sermon form serves the interests of biblical truth. But what we know about those who listen also encourages variety in sermon approach. Modern people expect variety and choices in every aspect of their lives. When the sermon's form remains stubbornly, and predictably the same week after week, people wonder why. Scientists studying the right brain-left brain phenomena have also given preachers reason to put more variety into their sermons. If researchers are right, some people who hear us will receive truth best through more cognitive, analytical, formally logical messages. The same congregation will also contain people who will be reached best by messages that move by a more intuitive, narrative logic, that employ an abundance of sensory language, and that are more emotional. No single sermon structure or style meets the broader needs of biblical truth or the congregation. Fortunately, simply by following the lead of the Bible, with its incredible diversity of literary genres and forms, we can be well on our way to better and more varied preaching.

Following Literary Form in Preaching

Shaping sermons according to the text's literary form has increasingly come to be regarded as a basic principle of homiletics. As valuable as the principle is, however, it has limitations—limitations well known to those who encourage the form-sensitive sermon.

Sermons Cannot Duplicate Literary Form

Sermons cannot be poems, proverbs, apocalypses or several other types of literature found in Scripture. Greidanus (20) puts it plainly: "Again, the goal of shaping the sermon according to the form of the text cannot be slavish imitation. One might speak instead of *respect* for the text" (his emphasis). Graves suggests that we speak of the "form-sensitive" sermon.

Form-Sensitive Preaching May Neglect the Hearers

The current focus on being biblical in form as well as content comes as a timely emphasis, but preachers should not consider it the whole truth. Sound homiletics keeps together the two indispensables of preaching: the biblical word and the contemporary world. If preaching lacks the biblical word, it has nothing substantial to say; if preaching fails to connect with the contemporary world, its speaking is irrelevant and ineffective. In a laudable effort to be thoroughly faithful to the text, preachers may forget that the biblical writers chose their approach with an ancient audience in mind. The ancient strategy may work marvelously today. In fact, it often does and should be the first option considered. But finally our sermons must speak to today's audiences. As Thomas G. Long points out, contemporary preachers speak in "an oral sermonic form, which is itself a genre with accompanying expectations and conventions" (*Preaching and the Literary Forms of the Bible*, 33). Violating congregational expectations of what a sermon is in order to imitate the text can be counterproductive.

Some Topics Require Multiple Texts

Though normally an asset, form-sensitive preaching's emphasis on working from a single complete text can be a limitation. Although faithful proclamation of complete units of Scripture should dominate our preaching, topics do arise which cannot be addressed accurately and faithfully from a single text. Exploring the doctrine of the Trinity or the biblical view of divorce and remarriage, for instance, takes us to many texts. The more texts used, the less possible it is for biblical form to influence the structure of the message significantly. On occasion it will also seem advisable to preach from less than a complete unit of Scripture. A pair of verses out of a psalm or a single statement taken from a discourse by Jesus may provide a sufficient basis for a solid sermon. The verses actually used should be interpreted in light of the larger literary and historical context, of course, but literary form will play a reduced role in shaping the message.

Five Questions for Developing the Message

In the trip from text to congregation, preachers can follow a fairly well-defined path. This route should not, however, be traveled as though we were taking part in a forced march. Nor should we conduct ourselves like tourists on a prepackaged itinerary who spill out of the bus, snap photos hastily, and pile back into the bus so they can hurry to "see" the next destination. We cannot hope to understand texts if we approach them in that manner. The process should be more like a walk accompanied by a friend who is a long-time resident of the area. We keep moving forward, but without such haste that we miss interesting and informative pauses along the way. We may even explore an occasional side path because the friend knows what lies down that trail. Eventually, of course, we must press onward. Upon arrival, however, we will have more than blurry photographic trophies; we will have actually seen and heard, smelled and felt and touched. More than that, we will have been taught by a wise guide. Perhaps we will have pondered our experience long enough to enable us to speak about it with the insight and power that comes only to the one who is a genuine witness.

In *Preaching and the Literary Forms of the Bible* (24–34), Thomas G. Long identifies five questions that arise at major turns in the path from text to sermon. Let's examine these questions.

What Is the Genre of the Text?

In identifying the genre of the text, we must usually do more than recognize the genre of the biblical book (narrative, prophecy, wisdom, psalm, gospel, epistle, apocalypse). Better commentaries, especially those written with an appreciation for literary analysis, will help identify the specific literary form of a given text. (See James Bailey and Lyle Vander Broek, *Literary Forms in the New Testament* for an overview of the literary forms used in the New Testament.)

What Is the Rhetorical Function of This Genre?

The point in identifying the genre of the text is to understand its rhetorical function. By "rhetorical function" we mean how it achieves its aim of persuading or influencing its readers. Long helpfully differentiates the literary features of the text from its rhetorical function: "The literary features are those elements of language and sequence that make the text what it is. The rhetorical dynamics are the effects that the literary features are intended to produce in a reader. Literary features are in the text; rhetorical dynamics, though caused by the text, are in the reader" (26). Once a portion of Scripture has been determined to be apocalyptic, for example, we can draw some conclusions about its rhetorical function. Apocalyptic literature seeks to encourage believers to hold to the faith in times of persecution. Knowing this about apocalyptic literature shapes how we understand and proclaim texts drawn from it.

What Literary Device Does This Genre Use to Achieve Its Rhetorical Effect?

Long's third question connects the first two. *How* does this particular genre use language to achieve the rhetorical aim? Every genre has its own methods. Long points out that a pun, for instance, aims to get a giggle or groan out of the reader by making a wordplay involving double meaning. Apocalyptic literature uses imaginative, symbolic language and employs numbers which have clearly-defined spiritual significance.

How Does the Text Embody These Characteristics and Dynamics?

This question focuses the first three questions on the text at hand. In rhetorical analysis of biblical texts, we look for features such as the following: repeated use of a word or phrase; exclamations; imperatives; connecting words such as "because," "therefore," "so that," "for," and "now"; pronouns, especially changes in person; parallelisms; questions; contrasts in thought, scene, or character; participial phrases; repetitions in thought; and opening and closing statements in the text. After identifying their presence in the text, we then can begin asking about their function. Repetition, for example, can give emphasis to key ideas, establish a dominant theme or motif, and add emotional force, among other things. Careful reflection will enable us to begin to discern the writer's intent. Good commentaries will fill in the gaps in our understanding of both what was expected in the genre and how this particular passage carries through or deviates from that expectation.

How May the Sermon Say and Do What the Text Says and Does?

Long's fifth question, about the way the sermon can say and do a portion of what the text says and does, reflects the fact that no sermon can capture everything in a text. A tedious, plodding sermon may exhaust the hearers but it can never exhaust the richness of the passage. Thus freed from the unrealistic burden of trying to tell everything the text says, preachers can focus on conveying the *main* idea of the text. Preachers need to be able to say in a single concise sentence what main idea from the text they intend to announce. If teachers of preaching agree on anything, it is this principle. The sermon needs an organizing concept. Whether called the sermon's "thesis," "proposition," "theme," "focus," or something else, a crisp declarative sentence capturing the essence of the message must emerge from our interaction with the text and congregation.

The central idea of the sermon is what the sermon intends to *say*. Along with it, the sermon needs a statement of rhetorical intent. That is, preachers need to be able to indicate what they hope the message will *do* in the lives of those who hear it. Normally the major objective of the sermon will grow out of the analysis of the rhetorical function of the text, but it may arise otherwise. The major objective serves as a guide for the further development of the message. Knowing what we want the sermon to do, we can include or exclude sermonic elements in light of our purpose. The statement of major objective never intends to dictate to God what he can do with the message. Nor does the major objective tell everything we hope to accomplish. Instead, the major objective stands as an expression of our desire to speak purposefully, with clear focus. God himself finally determines how he will use the message in the lives of those who hear it.

Having studied the text and identified what the central idea and major objective of the sermon will be, we turn next to the task of developing a form or structure for the message. Structure has to do with movement, sequence, arrangement. The message must begin somewhere and end somewhere else, hopefully at the accomplishment of the major objective. The question of structure is how to lead people on the journey that gets them from where they are when the sermon begins to where the text suggests they should be by the sermon's end. The message needs to unfold with a sense of progression. As mentioned above, sometimes we can simply appropriate the structure of the text. With a narrative text, the plot line of Scripture can provide the framework for the message. With an epistle, the flow of the writer's argument may serve very well as a guide to developing sermonic flow, as Lorin Cranford has suggested in a previous chapter of this book. We are wise to consider the structure suggested by the text before mulling over other possible strategies. More is said below about the structures best suited to various genres and forms of biblical literature.

With the general strategy of the sermon in mind, we can pursue the materials needed in order to flesh out the message. The first consideration should be what from the text needs to be proclaimed. The biblical content will likely consist of either historical background (prior events, customs, culture, geography) or linguistic material (word meanings, significance of grammar and syntax, literary features). This material may be explained in a straightforward fashion (a teaching style), or it may be incorporated into the message in a more indirect fashion (a poetic/narrative style), depending on the sermon's objective. (The recent trend among most homileticians has been away from a teaching style and toward a more narrative or poetic style, though Thomas Long and William Willimon, among others, have cautioned against jettisoning the teaching approach too quickly in favor of narrative.) In addition to the biblical content, the message normally will also include contemporary elements such as examples, comparisons, arguments, and suggestions about ways the hearers can put this truth to work in their own lives. The development of an introduction and conclusion completes the sermon.

Review: Basic Principles of Form-Sensitive Preaching

Before we turn to suggest strategies and structures for selected biblical genres and forms, we need to remind ourselves of some basic principles that come into play when we decide to shape sermons around the form of the text.

Respect the Literary Contours and Boundaries

For one thing, a commitment to following the literary form normally means the sermon text is a larger portion of Scripture: a whole psalm, an entire episode in a narrative, a full pericope (or more) from one of the Gospels. The sermon respects the literary contours and boundaries of the text as it seeks to be faithful to the message of the text.

Recognize the Flow of the Text

The message emphasizes the flow of thoughts within the text and avoids atomizing the text. Every portion of the text gets careful scrutiny during the process of preparation, but the sermon itself normally avoids giving the etymology of words, or grammatical data. Insights drawn from etymology and grammar are used, but used unobtrusively. After all, seeing the restaurant's kitchen can kill the appetite. The message seeks to speak *of* and *from* the text, not merely report *about* the text. Sermons are events, passionate attempts to change people's lives and eternal destinies. The message must capture the movement present in the text.

Capture the Mood of the Passage

In seeking to reproduce the impact as well as the truth of the text, the form-sensitive sermon gives careful attention to the mood of the message. Attention to mood reflects an awareness that Scripture both informs and moves us and that our sermons ought to do both as well. As Fred Craddock says it so memorably, sermons on the theme of freedom can range in mood from seventy-six trombones marching down Main Street to the sound of black women quietly singing "We Shall Overcome" beneath a jail window. Both sermons may speak of freedom, but the effect is different because the mood is different. We will need to choose imagery and language carefully, as well as pay careful attention to the delivery of the message, as we shape the mood of the sermon.

With this background in mind, we now turn to a discussion of strategies for selected literary dynamics in Scripture. Several factors suggest that we give extended attention to preaching from narrative texts: their abundance, their relative neglect (especially Old Testament narratives) among preachers, and the difficulty many preachers have when trying to move from a more deductive, propositional sermon style to the inductive movement of the narrative sermon. Following the section on narratives, we will look briefly at strategies for epistles and biblical proverbs. These discussions merely suggest a few possibilities. Fortunately, a number of good resources are available to help those who want further elaboration on these or other literary forms. (See the listing at the end of the chapter.) No one has worked out strategies suitable to every type of biblical literature. That task finally falls to each preacher in light of the congregation to which the sermon will be delivered.

Six Elements of Narrative

Biblical narratives come in a variety of lengths and complexities. They aim at a wide range of responses. Consequently, preachers cannot come to them with a one-size-fits-all approach. Still, they do have certain common features. The form-sensitive message recognizes that narratives have the basic elements of any story: setting, scene, characters, and plot (conflict, climax, and resolution). During the rhetorical analysis of the text, preachers will want to look for these elements and see how the biblical writer uses them.

Setting

Notice how the writer sets the scene in 2 Sam. 11:1, (NIV) : "In the spring, at the time when kings go off to war, David sent Joab out with the king's men and the whole Israelite army. They destroyed the Ammonites and besieged Rabbah. But David remained in Jerusalem." The last sentence has an ominous ring to it, hinting at trouble ahead. In its own introduction, a message on this episode can seek to retain the crisp phrasing and to hint that trouble is brewing in the midst of apparent success. Thus the scene and setting are established.

Characterization

Students of narrative texts will also want to pay attention to the ways biblical writers develop their characters. In Scripture, character development comes most frequently through what the characters do and say. The Bible seldom gives physical descriptions of its characters. Unlike modern writers, biblical writers say surprisingly little about their characters' motives and psychological states. Perhaps the silence aims to draw listeners into the story to fill in the gaps in description. The biblical writers' restraint should encourage restraint on our part, too, as we explore the inner states and motives of biblical characters. Those who attribute David's adultery with Bathsheba to a mid-life crisis on David's part have imposed a modern psychology on the biblical text.

Plot

The handling of plot sets form-sensitive sermons clearly apart from more traditional "three-points-and-a-poem" messages. Sermons shaped around rhetorical points seldom work to retain suspense in the message. The form-sensitive message, with its focus on mood and movement, tries to recreate through the sermon an experience of tension, suspense, and resolution like that found in the text. Accordingly, the narrative message lets the story unfold as a story rather than merely summarizing the plot in the introduction. Preachers working to create a viable narrative message must discern what the point of tension is in the biblical story, then be sure in developing the message that the sermon helps the hearers feel the tension. Hearers are most likely to feel the tension when they have identified with the biblical character who is caught in the conflict. The message will present the biblical person so as to help build bridges of shared value and shared experience between the hearers and the biblical characters. When this is done well, listeners find themselves thinking, "I've been there," or "I had to deal with the same situation," or "I've been afraid of that disaster coming my way, too." Once the identification has been established, then the sermon elaborates the plot with the realization that the hearers will experience the truth of the text vicariously.

Identification

In deciding upon a sermon strategy, preachers need to ask which of the biblical characters in the story they think their hearers will identify with most easily. It may be that different members of the audience will identify with different biblical characters. Preachers cannot dictate with whom hearers identify, but they can shape the message to encourage some identifications and discourage others. Deciding what identifications to encourage comes through prayerful consideration of both text and congregational need.

In the story of Jesus' healing of the paralytic brought by four friends (Mark 2:1–12), for example, we might (at least theoretically) encourage our congregation to identify (1) with the paralytic unable to help himself, (2) with the four friends who had faith that Jesus could heal and took action to get their friend to Jesus, (3) with those around the door who blocked the paralytic's access to Jesus, (4) with the owner of the home, who may have taken a very dim view of the uninvited crowd, as well as the most literal raising of the roof, (5) with Jesus, who received the man gladly and extended divine forgiveness and healing to him, or (6) with the teachers of the law who were incensed at Jesus' alleged blasphemy. Probably all six have been the focus of a sermon at one time or another!

Any sermon will tend to cast certain of these characters into the foreground, where they are more prominent, and leave others barely noticed in the background. Taking the text as a guide, we would likely leave the crowd and the homeowner in the deep background. The paralytic and his friends would be more prominent, enough so that some might identify with them. The most prominent figure in the story is Jesus, so he likely will be the dominant figure in a narrative message on this text. The teachers of the law, though they appear last in this story, are also important characters, especially when we realize that this episode is just one of a series of running conflicts between Jesus and Jewish leaders. If we were doing a series of messages through the Gospel of Mark, we would likely want to treat the scribes in a way that would foreshadow future clashes as well as depict their role in this story.

Preachers sometimes unwittingly insist on forcing their congregations to identify with the sinners in the story. When we do that, by implication we may be identifying ourselves with the virtuous characters or with God himself. A strong reaction may ensue when the preacher makes an identification resisted or resented by the hearers, as surely often happened when the Pharisees saw themselves in Jesus' parables. Reaction need not always be negative, of course; David's identification enabled him to come to repentance over his adultery.

Application

A related issue in preparing narrative sermons is whether the hearers' application of the message to themselves via identification is all the application the sermon should attempt. Those who would leave application to the hearers point out that narratives such as short stories, plays, novels, and movies shape values without making direct application. Judging from the Gospel accounts, they argue, Jesus frequently let his parables stand alone, without making further application for his audience. Furthermore, the Holy Spirit is at work applying the biblical message. The sermon can be trusted to his care, they insist.

Those who call for direct application point to biblical precedents as well. After all, Nathan did say, "You are the man!" Old Testament narratives do sometimes include evaluative statements, brief though they may be. Jesus elaborated on his parables at times in order to help his followers connect them with their own experience. Judging from the sermon summaries in the Book of Acts, apostolic preaching was quite pointed in application even when it had a large narrative component in the message. What is more, they argue, in actual practice the narrative sermon often falls short of the ideal; brief direct application gives a second opportunity in case the hearers somehow missed the thrust of the message. What we know about the way people restructure stories to fit their experience also gives credence to the idea of guiding the hearers in relating the stories to themselves. In most instances some direct application will be advisable. When the audience is well informed and the biblical material is very familiar to them, the hearers may be trusted to provide the unspoken word of application. (Harold Freeman, *Variety in Biblical Preaching*, discusses this issue in more detail.)

Form

A number of sermon forms can respect the unique features of a narrative text and convey its message to a contemporary congregation effectively. Those who have worked extensively with narrative sermons have discovered several basic patterns which can be adapted and used in preaching from narrative texts. We will briefly discuss six representative patterns.

A *pure narrative* could be considered the most elementary structure. As John Holbert describes it in *Preaching Old Testament* (42–43), the pure narrative sermon draws its structure from the plot of the text. The sermon focuses on retelling the biblical story without making explicit application or giving words of exhortation. The pure narrative message may elaborate on the details of the story, add color and drama within the bounds set by sound exegesis, and otherwise heighten the impact of the story, but according to Holbert it remains a story. The sermon does not explain the story; it retells it. The message begins where the story begins and the message ends where the story ends. Obviously this type of message has no direct application from the preacher to the hearers. Chapter 4 of Holbert's *Preaching Old Testament* (79–92) gives an excellent example of a pure narrative sermon titled "The Best Laugh of All." Holbert's paragraph-by-paragraph explanation of why he developed the sermon as he did enhances the usefulness of the chapter.

Running the story is a second form the narrative message can take. As described by Eugene Lowry in *How to Preach a Parable: Designs for Narrative Sermons* (38), running the story has some similarities to the pure narrative. For instance, both approaches require a fairly lengthy and involved biblical story to sustain the sermon. Both approaches develop the message along the same lines as the biblical plot and both emphasize retelling the story creatively and powerfully. Lowry, however, utilizes material from outside the biblical world in running the story, whereas Holbert's pure narrative approach stays within the confines of the biblical world. Lowry feels free to use allusions to contemporary life, illustrations, and other extra-biblical material as part of running the story. His focus is not so much on reproducing the story per se as on leading listeners through a sequence of experiences that commonly occur in biblical stories. He wants all his sermons to have a narrative-like sequence of initial conflict, escalation of the conflict, a redemptive word or event which brings resolution, and the experience of joy. (See Lowry's *The Homiletical Plot* for a full discussion of this sequence.)

The *framed narrative* is a third possible strategy. The framed narrative differs from the pure narrative in that the framed narrative has introductory and concluding comments that are not used in the pure narrative (Holbert, 43). These introductory and concluding comments prepare listeners for the story and then sharpen the focus of the story after it has been told. The comments thus constitute the "frame" for the story. Holbert insists that the concluding statements must not explain the story. The story must carry its own message. The conclusion of the frame narrative simply aims to "fo-cus the narrative for the congregation" (43).

Delaying the story, like Holbert's framed narrative, requires the preacher to prepare the hearers before taking up the biblical text. As described by Lowry (*How to Preach a Parable*, 38–39), delaying the story involves using the opening minutes of the sermon to give the biblical background of the text or, more often, to prepare people to listen afresh to a familiar story. Such preparation is es-pecially useful, Lowry claims, when the story is both familiar and brief. Unless the hearers have been readied, they respond to the text with a mental yawn brought on by the feeling that they al-ready know everything the text has to say. In delaying the story, the introduction may take a considerable portion of the message to impress a particular problem or need on the congregation. When the preacher turns to the text for an answer to the prob-lem, the congregation is ready to hear it.

Suspending the story is the reverse of delaying the story. The mes-sage follows the story line until it encounters the difficulty, then moves outside the text to resolve the difficulty (or at least address it more adaquately). Lowry describes suspending the story as a fine strategy when the text has an exegetical, moral, or theological dif-ficulty in it (39). Lowry points out that the sermon may need to "flash back" into biblical history for necessary background materi-al, "flash forward" to a later biblical text that clarifies or resolves the difficulty, or "flash out" to extra-biblical information that helps the sermon come to grips with the troublesome aspect of the text. The story raises an issue that is then developed in a more thematic or topical fashion from resources outside the text itself.

Alternating the story is a sixth narrative structure to consider. It too comes from Eugene Lowry (40). Alternating the story hop-scotches back and forth between the text and other material, often another story (biblical or extra-biblical) which has a similar plot. This strategy uses the supplied story as a recurring reinforcement of the text. The parallel story often gives the message a contemporary quality that strengthens its impact. The supplied story functions as an extended illustration. So, for example, the parable of the prodi-gal son will be told in combination with the story of another way-ward person who faced similar circumstances. The preacher tells the first portion of one of the stories, then the first portion of the other, then back for the second episode of the first story, and so forth. Using the same language in the two stories helps pull them together and also smooths transitions between them.

Imagination

When seeking to develop messages from narrative texts in particular, preachers often wonder about the use of their imagination in fleshing out the stories. To some people "imagination" is synonymous with "fanciful" or "imaginary." But in this case we speak of imagination as the capacity to create mental images of what is taking place in the text. We develop the images first for ourselves, then for those who hear our messages. Thomas Troeger's, *Imagining a Sermon* and Paul Scott Wilson's, *Imagination of the Heart* offer assistance to those interested in cultivating the homiletic imagination.

Some preachers have felt it helpful (adapting David Buttrick's camera metaphor in *Homiletic*) to think of themselves as directing the filming of a re-creation of the biblical event. When the tape rolls, what will the viewer see? A panoramic shot of Judean hills? A fishing boat pushing out into placid water? A bustling Jerusalem marketplace? If it is the marketplace, what sounds would be audible? The clatter of horses' hooves, haggling voices, children's laughter, or the buzzing of flies around sheep carcasses dangling from a hook? Since the sermon (unlike film) can also appeal to the senses of taste and smell, the sermon could describe the marketplace aromatically: fish drying in the sun, the muskiness of unwashed bodies, the perfumers' delicious samples. Then of course the imagination helps us picture the action that took place and the way the words were said, the awkward pauses or the too-fast rattling that tips off excuse-making. Though seldom taught in exegetical handbooks, this exercise of the preacher's imagination is an integral element in coming to an understanding of the text in service of preaching. The narrative message in particular requires it.

So the imagination is essential to preaching. But it must be disciplined by careful study of the text and the historical background of the text. "The biblical text is the control for the preacher's imagination" (Achtemeier, 66). It may be helpful to think in terms of what is clearly *provable* in the text; what is *probable* in light of what we know about the setting, and the customs and culture of the day; and what could be labeled as merely *possible*. Sticking with what is provable is the safest course, though at times we can feel confident in including what is probable. The market scene described above would be an example of material in the probable category that could be used judiciously if based on solid research. (Following Scripture's lead, we will show restraint in description.) The sermon should avoid including material that has no more basis than to say that it is not beyond the realm of possibility. The sermon can unobtrusively indicate a degree of uncertainty about probable material by saying something to the effect that, "If it was a normal day in the market . . ." Those who insist on speculating owe it to the hearers to identify the speculation as such: "Scripture does not tell us what happened. I wonder if perhaps it was something like this."

The completed form-sensitive sermon from a biblical narrative, then, will seek to preserve the movement and mood of the story. In so doing the message may follow the sequence in the text or may have a sequence better suited to the major objective of the sermon. The sermon will seek to develop identification between the hearers and the biblical characters so that the hearers can begin applying the message to themselves. As the preacher judges it necessary, the message may use comparison, allusion, and application along the way to strengthen the identification. The message will conclude crisply, with focus on the central idea of the sermon.

Strategies for Epistolary Texts

The epistles of the New Testament contain a wide variety of literary forms within them, as has already been mentioned. Compared to narrative texts, epistles tend to be more theologically dense, more argumentative, and more direct in their appeals for the readers to take specified courses of action. The writers of the epistles wrote to a specific situation, yet knew that their letters were being circulated for wider use. The epistles are written documents, but their writers understood that more people in the church were likely to hear the epistle read than to read it themselves. Epistles, therefore, often resemble sermons in significant ways. So we need not fear that epistles pose insuperable challenges for preaching. They already contain sermonic qualities.

In selecting a sermon strategy for an epistolary text, we again need to determine the central idea of the text, the major objective of the text, and the mood of the text. Beyond those concerns, we will want to identify the structure of the text and seek to understand what that structure was meant to accomplish. The structure of the text often provides an excellent basis for a sermon structure. A key step in grasping the flow of the text is identifying the relationships among the clauses and phrases of the text. By means of a syntactical diagram of the Greek text or even a sentence flow analysis of an English translation, we can identify the dominant and subordinate ideas of the text. If we want the sermon to follow the text in its emphases, we can make the major affirmations of the text the major affirmations or points of the sermon, while arranging the subsidiary ideas of the text under the major ideas that they support. Walter Kaiser's *Toward an Exegetical Theology* is but one of many resources available which demonstrate how to develop a syntactical diagram and use it to shape a classical rhetorical sermon structure, which is often a natural fit with epistolary texts.

For example, James 2:1–13 deals with the issue of favoritism in the church. The passage begins with a stern command: "My brothers, as believers in our glorious Lord Jesus Christ, don't show favoritism" (NIV). An illustration (vv. 2–3) and a series of arguments against showing favoritism (4–13) then follow. Through favoritism, James asserts, they position themselves as unjust judges (v. 4b). Additionally, favoritism contradicts God's own treatment of the poor (v. 5–6a). By their favoritism they ally themselves with ungodly people (vv. 6b–7) and violate the "royal law" of Scripture, thereby exposing their selective obedience (vv. 8–11). Finally, favoritism ignores the coming judgment of God, who loves mercy and expects his children to demonstrate it toward others (vv. 12–13). This basic framework could give order and sequence to a message on the text. As it stands, the text is quite didactic and direct in its application.

Following the principle of respecting the text's own strategy, we might formulate a message which announces the wrongness of favoritism, then vividly illustrates favoritism taking place within the church, and finally presents the series of arguments against favoritism. The preacher certainly would want to choose illustrations from the contemporary church and would want to polish the phrasing of each of the arguments. Indeed, the preacher might notice how the argument seems to begin and end with the theme of judgmentalism and adjust the message accordingly. Each argument could be elaborated from the text and connected with the hearers' own experiences of being treated with prejudice.

Throughout the message the preacher would want to present the demands of the text in light of the mercy and grace of God, as alluded to in verse 1 and mentioned more specifically in verses 5 and 13. James's reference to them as "brothers" (v. 1) and "my dear brothers" (v. 5) conveys a mood of love and mutuality that could be overlooked in the thicket of accusations and rhetorical

questions. However pointed the sermon becomes in rebuking favoritism, it needs also a clear note of love, a reassurance that the
relationship remains intact in spite of this word of correction.

Strategies for Proverbs

The Book of Proverbs gets little attention in most pulpits. Yet it
too is part of the canon and can speak powerfully to modern living.
The opening chapters of Proverbs contain extended discussion of
the importance of getting wisdom and the dangers of adultery. As
connected discourse, these blocks of material (and others like them
later in the book) can be developed sermonically somewhat along
the lines of epistolary material. The sermon can track the argument
of the text, being sensitive to the movement and mood of the text.
Beginning in chapter 10, though, the Book of Proverbs takes on a
different character, in that it offers epigrams instead of paragraph-
length discussions of topics. The "individual wisdom sentence," as
it is called in William McKane, *Proverbs* (10) poses a different challenge for the preacher. Though it is possible to collect several of
these sentences around a common subject matter and develop an
effective topical-biblical message, that approach does not capture
the essence of the literary form.

As Long (56–58) points out, the individual wisdom sentence
arises out of careful reflection on life. "A person of gifted discernment, the Sage" spots a thread of truth running through a series of
similar experiences. In pondering these experiences, the Sage develops a crisp, memorable way of stating that truth. In a very real
sense, behind every wisdom sentence lies a series of stories which,
taken together, prove the reality which the proverb states. Thus the
proverb has both future and past dimensions. The proverb aims to
embed itself in the hearer's memory for future use. But the proverb
also aims to evoke from the hearer's memory past incidents where
the truth of the proverb has been evident. The wisdom sentence
has the concrete, down-to-earth specificity of real life.

In preaching one of these individual wisdom sentences, then,
the preacher can try to respect its basic dynamic by creating an opportunity for the truth of the proverb to emerge once again
through a series of stories. Long (62) suggests a sermon structure
which uses the proverb as a symphonic element, as a recurring
theme. It will function as a refrain does between the stanzas of a
hymn. The majority of the message will be a series of brief, realistic

vignettes. The proverb will be used at the conclusion of each vignette as a way of reinforcing the truth of the text.

Suppose we took for our text Prov. 16:18: "Pride goes before destruction, a haughty spirit before a fall" (NIV). The text implies two pictures. The first shows someone smug and secure, looking with disdain on others; the second shows that arrogance brought low. In selecting stories which will allow the proverb's wisdom to shine forth, we can look both to Scripture and contemporary living. The sermon might describe Belshazzar's feast (Dan. 5:1–31), with a thousand goblets tinkling and the confident laughter of the mighty. Heady with wine and power, Belshazzar orders the sacred vessels from the temple in Jerusalem brought. He invites his guests, his wives, even his concubines to drink from these cups—cups holy to the God of Israel. Toast follows toast: "To the god of gold!" "To the god of silver!" "To the gods of wood, stone, and iron!" But never to the God of Israel, for had not Belshazzar's father vanquished him when he defeated the armies of Israel?

Suddenly the fingers of a human hand appear, writing on the plaster walls of the palace. The laughter stops; jaws fall slack and few dare even the barest of whispers. Belshazzar's smirk dies and his face grows pale. He is so frightened his knees knock together briefly, but then they lose strength even for that.

Belshazzar wonders what the writing means. None of the nobles can say. He summons the wisest men in all the kingdom, but none of them can interpret it. Finally someone remembers a Hebrew brought to Babylon years before. Belshazzar summons him. Daniel, prophet of the Most High God, arrives to interpret the dream. "You, O Belshazzar, have set yourself up against the God of heaven. Though you knew better, you praised gods of gold and silver, of iron and wood and stone and bronze, and yet you did not honor the God who holds your life in his hand. Therefore, hear the meaning of the message written on the wall: Your days, numbered. Your ways, found wanting. Your kingdom, divided and given to others." Gone—before he even realized what was happening. "Pride goes before destruction, a haughty spirit before a fall."

I think back to the day an intelligent, attractive woman wept quiet tears as she told a congregation something to this effect: "Last fall my husband announced that after thirty-seven years of marriage, we were through. I was shocked. We were Christians, active in our church. I had borne four children; I had been a model wife. I cooked the meals, cleaned the house, kept the books for his business, did everything he asked. I knew my husband would never leave me. We had seen others in the church divorce, but I had always said, 'Never me.' I realize now how I turned my back on my friends when they were going through their divorce. 'If only they had been the kind of wife I am,' I told myself, 'this wouldn't have happened to them.' They were failures, but I had a successful marriage." A long silence. She took a deep breath. "How arrogant I was! What an unlovely spirit I had! How could I have been so blind?" "Pride goes before destruction . . . ."

With each story, the text echoes again, "Pride . . . a haughty spirit . . . ." Along the way the sermon needs to offer a redemptive word, giving a distinctively Christian interpretation to the text. The good news could come through telling the story of someone like Simon Peter, who found a merciful God ready to pick up the shards of a pride-shattered world and make of them a new life.

Whatever literary form the text, the sermonic aim remains the same: to enable the Scripture to say and do once again what God wills so that those who hear it will respond in faith to him. The Word of God, active and piercing, does not rely on human ingenuity for its power. Yet God has ordained to do his saving work through preaching, which necessarily involves us in the process. In love and gratitude we seek to preach as faithfully and skillfully as possible. As the incarnation so clearly demonstrated, the Word can be both divine and human. With that encouragement, we prepare and preach, trusting that our frail and inadequate words are made sufficient by Christ.

▼

For Further Study

Achtemeier, Elizabeth. *Preaching from the Old Testament.* Louisville: Westminster/John Knox, 1989.

Bailey, James, and Lyle Vander Broek. *Literary Forms in the New Testament.* Louisville: Westminster/John Knox, 1992.

Buttrick, David. *Homiletic: Moves and Structures.* Philadelphia: Fortress, 1987.

Craddock, Fred B. *As One Without Authority.* 3d ed. Nashville: Abingdon, 1979.

———. *Preaching.* Nashville: Abingdon, 1985.

Freeman, Harold. *Variety in Biblical Preaching.* Waco: Word, 1987.

Graves, Mike. "The Sermon as Symphony: The Role of Selected New Testament Literary Forms in Sermon Composition." Unpublished Manuscript.

Greidanus, Sidney. *The Modern Preacher and the Ancient Text: Interpreting and Preaching Biblical Literature.* Grand Rapids: Eerdmans, 1988.

Holbert, John C. *Preaching Old Testament: Proclamation and Narrative in the Hebrew Bible.* Nashville: Abingdon, 1991.

Kaiser, Walter. *Toward an Exegetical Theology.* Grand Rapids: Baker, 1981.

Long, Thomas G. *Preaching and the Literary Forms of the Bible.* Philadelphia: Fortress, 1989.

Lowry, Eugene. *How to Preach a Parable: Designs for Narrative Sermons.* Nashville: Abingdon, 1989.

———. *The Homiletical Plot: The Sermon as Narrative Art Form.* Atlanta: John Knox, 1980.

O'Day, Gail R., and Thomas G. Long, eds. *Listening to the Word.* Nashville: Abingdon, 1993.

Troeger, Thomas H. *Imagining a Sermon.* Nashville: Abingdon, 1990.

Wardlaw, Donald M., ed. *Preaching Biblically: Creating Sermons in the Shape of Scripture.* Philadelphia: Westminster, 1983.

Wilson, Paul Scott. *Imagination of the Heart: New Understandings in Preaching.* Nashville: Abingdon, 1988.

Chapter Twenty-two

The Seeable Sermon

Calvin Miller

There is no authority in preaching that abounds with the same pulpit clout as the dramatic and adept use of Scripture. However, the second most authoritative implant in a sermon may be a well-placed illustration. When the preacher joins the power of the Bible to strong sermon images, the impact of this marriage can shake the congregation with Richter-scale force.

By using this sermonic technique even the most dingy exposition can be rewired and audience interest electrified. It is really a simple matter of learning how to use what I call *Image Paralleling* for the sake of transforming the audible word into the visual word. We have often too narrowly conceived of sermon illustrations as mere anecdotes. But the verb *to illustrate* comes from the Latin stem, *lustr,* "to cast light on" or "to clarify." The word really means to make it "easier to see." This can be done by adding stories to our sermons, but it may also be done by using other forms of clarifications such as definitions or quotes. While quotes can make the sermons more visual, they may only amplify its logic and argument. Beware this weakness. A quote used to support a quote can turn out to be only one more "hearable" reinforcement of some sermonic precept, while an illustration may create images that give the sermon visual force.

In the currency of our everyday communication, we tend to speak from a vast lexicon of mental pictures. Many of these derive from our acquaintance with novels, screenplays, and television programming.

"Lines, plots, images, and characters, by their very mention furnish us much of the script for living . . .

'My hometown was *Peyton Place*, pure *Harper Valley P.T.A'*.
'His life is *"Rags to Riches," "Prince and the Pauper"* stuff.'
'He has an *"Oedipus"* complex or, she a *"Cinderella"* complex.'
'This is an ant-and-grasshopper philosophy'.
'He's a *"rebel without a cause"'*.
'The whole situation is a *"comedy of errors"'*.
'That was a Phyrric victory'.
'Don't be so *Trafalgar'*.
'He met his *Waterloo* that time'.
'Well, if it isn't the *Lone Ranger'*.
'Life is certainly *Camelot*, when it's not the *Pit and the Pendulum*,' etc." (Miller, *Spirit, Word, and Story*, 165).

We truly are a picture-driven generation. We have been conditioned to see things before we hear them. In fact until we see things clearly, we will not hear them very well.

We live in the midst of a video revolution, where a culture groomed on "couch-potato" televiewing and cinema gluttonizing is demanding that all public speakers speak in pictures. To use the words of a sermon only to create audible arguments is a technique that went out just before silent movies came in. Neal Postman suggests that we are so gorged with video values that we have nearly *amused ourselves to death*. We may insist that the church needs to turn its people back to an era of hard-core, perceptual exegesis; but if we insist on speaking only with audible reason, void of illustrating images, we may soon be suffering from congregational abandonment.

Like Siddhartha facing his river with a fly rod, the sermonizer must fling the sermon text into the swim of the current video generation. Within this river lies a fast-paced flow of pictures that will have the audience snapping at the fly. These images will allow the preacher to reinforce Scripture power with the literary clout. In my book, *Spirit, Word, and Story*, I call this *paralleling*. Paralleling locks two powerful words together: the ancient audible Word of God gives the sermon authority while the later more visual words from the best images of our generation. "Seeable" sermon images are then born that allow those all-powerful, but sometimes obscure ancient words to live in light.

In this union is the wedding of two kinds of inspiration. First is the divine inspiration of the living and authoritative Word of God. Second is the word of human inspiration (with a lower case "i") that tells of that lesser genius that comes from people whose personalities and circumstances set them afire with creative and powerful insights. But visualizing the latter can illumine and make usable the former.

At the outset let us ask three questions. What is paralleling? What do we parallel with? And finally, what does it accomplish? First, the definition: paralleling is consciously setting the logic of the sermon side by side with light in the sermon. It is a contrived juxtaposition of truth and illumination. It is born in an honest admission that even the Prado at night holds no art. Light makes art real. Paralleling is the hanging of sermonic pictures and the arranging of homilectical track-lighting that brings the artistry of the sermon to light.

Keeping the art and the light together is best done, for me, by mentally arranging my sermon into parallel columns. In the first column is the truth of God's Word and in the second is the track-lighting of word pictures, stories, and other amplifying images. When I illustrate the technique below I will follow this double column technique. Many kinds of illustrations can exist in column two: other precepts and percepts (images) can be used, of course, but keep in mind that the danger in illustrating perceptual Bible truths entirely with other perceptual truths has the effect of creating only a gallery of lights, where some light fixtures seem to exist only to shine on other light fixtures. While the illumination may be good, no one will leave church taking the sermon's pictures with them. There have been no pictures.

The reason we go to the Prado is to see the pictures and not marvel at the lighting. Thus I generally do not allow myself to think of paralleling percepts with other percepts. Using precepts to speak to percepts can wonderfully strengthen the logical force of the sermon. This perceptual force should be allowed to occur naturally to make sermons reasonable. But *image force* makes the sermon as video as the video age it serves.

The second question, "What do we parallel with?" may be answered quickly: "With anything that illuminates or makes more visual—bits of movies, parts of plays, scraps of poems, quotations, commercials, and brief fictional vivisections from novels, television sitcoms, newspaper articles, editorial cartoons, comic strips, and so forth."

Having defined and described parallelling, let us finally ask, "What good is it? What purpose does it serve in the sermon?" Parallelling accomplishes these three things: (1) it transmutes precepts into concepts; (2) it brings the key precepts of the sermon (one of which should be the sermon's main point), from the "mind's ear" to the "mind's eye"; (3) it cements the pre-modern biblical image proposed by the text to a contemporary picture that the audience can understand.

Transmuting Precepts to Concepts

Precepts are maxims, commandments, or rules. The Bible is filled with these and we naturally want to preach these since they comprise the commandments and instructions of Scripture. They impart authority to preaching. They are the "shalts" and "shalt nots," the "repent and believes," the "go ye's," and "harkens" of the Word. Precepts follow the "thus sayeth the Lords" of our sermons. The use of the biblical precepts keeps God talking throughout our homilies. For all the bad press that preaching and preachers have gotten in recent years, preaching, in the minds of most people, still is seen as the way that God gets his turn to talk in human conversation. These ancient "thus sayeths" do give God his say in sermons. Therefore the various passages of Scripture which lace the homily together, from text to support, are really the most important elements of preaching, for when God quits talking in the sermon, the sermon as sermon ceases to exist.

Concepts are aggregate ideas. According to the dictionary, they are things "formed by mentally combining." Precepts call for recognition and obedience. Concepts challenge us toward idea formation and synthesis. Precepts draw an audience no closer to the speaker, since they do not call for reasoning, but for mutual celebration, agreement, or obedience. Concepts, on the other hand, are gatherings of similar ideas whose alluring power causes the preacher and the "preached to" to separate their minds and think through what has been said.

While their minds are separated in these times of thought, the listeners are really saying inwardly, "Now, let me see if your words are something I can assimilate into my world view." In any good sermon these times of separation are necessary to evaluate the strong content that every sermon should have. It is of course key that this separation be only intermittent. In far too many sermons the separation of the preacher's mind and the congregation's minds has become a way of life (although in this case the use of the term "way of life" may be an oxymoron).

Precepts become quickly defined. "Thou shalt not commit adultery" is usually memorized by church children long before they have any idea what adultery is. Therefore, merely repeating a precept in a sermon will only tell people what they have long known and probably agree with, however well or poorly they may be obeying it.

But precepts come alive when images are allowed to fill them with interest. Strong images almost demand that precepts are so true and vital that they must mesh with and become a part of our world view and belief system. In other words, they help these pictorial ideas to be conceptualized in our brain.

There is no double entendre suggested in calling to mind that the words *conceptualize* and *conception* are from the same root. When conception occurs, the whole world of perceptual genetics dies. At conception a growing, combining and expanding organism is established. In this tight little system of expanding life, all that will not be a growing, integrated part of the whole is expelled. In fact, spontaneous abortion or miscarriage is how life, itself reckons with an organism where stubborn, alien biology will not join this wholeness. Thus it is with conceptualizing. Precepts begin to combine into a life principle that adds bulk and intricacy and life to the sermon because great truths join together to form our worldviews. That which welds them into wholeness may be image.

In widely different arenas both Joseph Campbell and John Newport have demonstrated that various world cultures literally form their entire belief systems on myths or stories. The principle is so universal that we cannot deny the force that stories play in welding together the various precepts of what we believe as well. At the heart of all of our Christian precepts such as *Jesus Saves, Life in Christ, He came unto his own*, lie stories of the cross, the cradle, the Bath Qol. The precepts are fixed within us by images and stories.

To illustrate how paralleling changes precepts to concepts, consider in the left-hand column the biblical precept and in the right-hand column the image that transforms the precept into a concept:

"Honor your father and mother that your days may be long upon the earth" (Exod. 20:12).

"How sharper than a serpent's tooth to have a thankless child" (Shakespeare, *King Lear*, Act I, Scene iv, line 310).

This may seem like only paralleling a precept with a precept so that no concept is formed. But *King Lear* suggests a whole story about children who dishonor their aging parent. The quote from Exodus only says "don't dishonor" perceptually. The story of King Lear forms an image-driven concept of a particular parent who was dishonored. For audiences unfamiliar with *King Lear*, some of the story may need to be told to be sure that some conceptualizing does occur.

Remember that it is always legitimate to illustrate a biblical precept with a biblical story. Exodus 20:12 could just as easily be illustrated with the story of the two brothers in Luke 15; in this parable there are illustrated two very different ways of dishonoring a parent. But in addition to illustrating with Lear, a very contemporary film that many in the audience will have seen is *A River Runs Through It*. Here the simple precept takes on a clear concept of how the commandment is to be obeyed or disobeyed. Movies are especially good to induce an audience to visualize since they are born as images in our minds the first time we see them. Remember that while we usually say we "hear" a sermon (and a precept too for that matter), we generally say we "see" a movie and hence films by their very "seen" nature cause precepts to move easily into concepts.

Perry Edward Smith was one of the two shot-gun murderers of the Clutter family in Truman Capote's *In Cold Blood*. Smith's father abandoned him at a school when he was a child, promising that he would return to pick him up. He never came back. The child grieved ever after and lived in a kind of "bed-wetting" insecurity that would accompany him all his life. The night before he was hanged on the gallows at Lansing, Kansas, he was heard crying in his sleep, "Where are you been Daddy, I've been looking everywhere for you Daddy" (128). Thus the story conceptualizes the precept, with a more contemporary literary picture from which the concepts are built. In his powerful Beecher Lectures, Walter Brueggeman encourages the use of well-placed poems or fractions of poems. If Emily Dickinson is summoned forth to bear witness to Exod. 20:12, she might quote those few lines that honored her father at his passing, which plunged her into the scribbling of these beautiful and haunting lines (152):

I never lost as much but twice,
And that was in the sod:
Twice have I stood a beggar
Before the door of God!
Angels, twice descending,
Reimburse my store.
Burglar, banker, father,
I am poor once more.

Precepts tell us what we are to do, concepts help us to pictorialize how we are doing it.

Bringing the Key Precept from the Mind's Ear to the Mind's Eye

This part of paralleling deals largely with what those sermon adjectives make us see. Nouns identify what the sermon is about. They are the chief blocks of identification. Verbs are the doing words, they put the "shall" in the "shalts" of sermon authority. But adjectives are the spectacles of the sermon. If we forget them we shall find our audience squinting "to see" what we are talking about. So if we want to get the sermon out of the ear and into the eye we must make our precepts visual.

Consider the Exod. 20:12 precept in this second mode of paralleling: (First the precept will be presented, followed by Helmut Thielicke's visualization):

Honor thy father and mother that thy days may be long upon the earth (Exod. 20:12).

———

But he, the prodigal son, who sees his condition from inside. The world sees only the facade and what is in the show window of this botched-up life. But he hears the rattle of the invisible chains in which he walks . . . the bitter laughter goes up from the pigsty . . . and the very voice of the father's heart overtakes us in the far country and tells us that incredibly joyful news, "You can come home! You can comes home!" (Thielicke, 25-29).

———

There are any number of descriptive quotes that will add image to the precept, "Honor your father and mother." For instance,

"There are times when parenthood seems to be nothing but feeding the mouth that bites you," (Peter DeVries, quoted in Winokur, 212) or "The Jewish man with parents alive is a fifteen year-old boy and will remain a fifteen-year-old boy until they die" (Philip Roth, quoted in Winokur, 213) or that ever-popular bumper sticker: "Insanity is hereditary; you get it from your children."

But if the eye of the sermon is to be really all-seeing the adjectives must be ever abundant in the image that we are creating. The Thielicke quote does much better than the two or three proverbs which follow. Consider James E. Warren's highly adjectival rendering of the eye-holding image:

A lantern sent its cheerful rays
    Into the night,
Carried in my father's hand,
    A lovely sight.

Watching from the window pane
    I peeked to see
The amber lantern bob and glow
    And wink at me.

Country life was simple then . . .
    The nights were fair;
An old victrola medley danced
    Upon the air.

The stock was safe and bedded down,
    This I could tell . . .
The swinging lantern glowed again
    To say all's well.

Poets are not just word economists; they are really image economists. This means you can usually rely on them not only for the most carefully selected adjectives which will help you create the image, but you usually can rely on them for just the right adjective. Speaking of a prodigal who was slow to honor his mother, Ruth Bell Graham wrote (137):

She waited for the call that never came:
searched every mail for a letter, or a note, or a card,
that bore his name;
and on her knees at night,
and on her feet all day,
she stormed Heaven's Gate
in his behalf;

The prodigal had not returned
but God was God,
and there was work to do.

Such adjectival pictures help the listener see the sermon and
not merely hear it.

Paralleling Cements the Pre-modern Biblical Image to Contemporary Understanding

If sermons are going to be heard they must not sound like the
medieval text. "Honor thy father and mother" sounds like what
a slave in Goshen would have said to her parents in 1400 B.C. A
more modern parent would be a little less "Exodus" and a little
more "Rodney Dangerfield": "How come I don't get no respect
around here!" Paralleling brings the ancient text into contemporary application. Lois A. Cheney (126) reminds us that if children
are ever to show parents any respect, then parents must first
show children a little respect as well.

Once, a little boy said,
"Where is God?"
And his mother said,
"Eat your lunch."

And he grew older.

And he asked a teacher,
"Where is God?"
And the teacher said,
"Do your homework."

And he grew older.

And he asked a minister,
"Where is God?"
And the minister said,
"Go to church."

And he grew older.

He ate his lunches
And did his homework
And he went to church.

And pretty soon,
He didn't ask anymore

"Where is God?"

The number one criticism of sermons has to do with their relevance and application. Images must be *right-now*. Shifting the biblical precept or image into the contemporary mind is a matter of correlating the ancient text with recent images.

During a recent stay at Oxford I was offered the opportunity of visiting several Anglican churches. In most of them I found only sparse crowds, mostly older people. But in St. Aldgates I arrived fully ten minutes ahead of time but still far too late to get a seat. My wife and I sat on the floor along with several other congenial late arrivers. Just after the service started, two very fine, smiling young people vacated their seats, and in a very substitionary kind of atonement took our places on the floor. As the service progressed, the drama club of the church began to illustrate the text of the day. The text was on fatherhood, with a drama done in the style of the Broadway musical, *Godspell*. It was all so contemporary and "right now" that the young people around me moved in with high-intensity interest. They laughed and broke into applause with their approval. The service was full of good instruction, deep and exciting truths, punctuated with laughter, tears and an almost rapt attention.

What caused this service to be so packed with young people? The service told me all. David McInnes, their pastor, has found a way to weld the biblical text to contemporary living and then to apply this glorious wedding to right-now living. His hermeneutic was both contemporary and useable.

But somehow my explanation is too mechanistic. Beneath the hermeneutic lay something so numinous, it is beyond this or any essay to describe. The only hermeneutic which can explain this must come from John 3. When the wind blows, it proclaims itself, says Jesus, but its definition of power remains elusive. I only bring this up to remind ourselves that the key to full churches and rapt attention is not merely getting the text into contemporary image and useability. A proper hermeneutic is not the starting place. The starting place lies in such things as the pastor's spiritual neediness and his deep desire for union with Christ. Some of those who help him in the task of proclamation and worship should also hunger after the bedrock of a godly relationship. But if these inner principles can be wed to such procedural and systematic things as a contemporary and image-driven hermeneutic, then the matrix that makes such church attendance possible may be in place.

If we return to Exod. 20:12, "Honor thy father and mother," we might want to illustrate it with the biblical passage from Genesis 22.

Isaac spoke up and said to his father Abraham, "Father?" "Yes, my son," Abraham replied. "The fire and wood are here," Isaac said, "But where is the possible lamb for the burnt offering?" Abraham answered, "God himself will provide the lamb for the burnt offering, my son." And the two of them went on together.

Isaac's honoring of his father can be understood if we understand his willingness to be laid upon the wood and to be sacrificed. For it is not sacrifice of a teenage son unless the son willingly assists. The honor that Isaac gives to Abraham is obvious in his submission to whatever his father must have in mind. Thus even as he lays himself on the wood he is acting out his honor for his father.

The honor of the son for his aging parent might be obviously illustrated in Ella Wheeler Wilcox's celebration of her mother's passing and the tribute she pays her (558):

The queen is taking a drive today,
They have hung with purple the carriage way.
They have dressed with purple the carriage track,
Where the queen goes forth and never comes back.

Uncover your head! Lift your hearts on high!
For the queen in silence is driving by.

I remember a Mother's Day when pursuing the fifth commandment I paralleled Proverbs 31, the wife of noble character, with a sonnet I had written of my own mother so long ago (see next page).

What has been done here is to cement the biblical text to a (somewhat literary) illustration from my own time and life. The image opens upon a contemporary window of light on the ancient truth.

In this particular case the text is applied in terms of Exod. 20:12. Here then is how we honor our mother and father as I had done in writing the poem. Here also is spelled out the why of the hermeneutic. The "why" and "how" of honoring is brought into direct tangent with the listeners and what they each might do to apply it.

The answer is created by an image that inspired them "to see" what each of them might do to make the scriptural principle useable in their own lives.

She speaks with wisdom,
and faithful instruction is
on her tongue.

She watches over the affairs
of her household and does
not eat the bread of idle-
ness.

Her children arise and call her
blessed; her husband also,
and he praises her:

"Many women do noble things,
but you surpass them all."

Charm is deceptive, and beauty
is fleeting; but a woman
who fears the Lord is to be
praised.

Give her the reward she has
earned, and let her works
bring her praise at the city
gate.

Prov. 31:26–31

Three decades past I skipped
long beside

Her. Soul tired—I carried
grain and grumbled.

How tall she looked! How
large the fields! Her
stride

Was smooth. Attempting to
keep pace, I stumbled.

She sat the grain where all
the grass seemed dead,

And ran her fingers through
my tangled thatch.

"Some day the fields will
seem so small," she said.

"When you've grown large
the field will be no match."

"The fields are very big." I
said. "You'll see!"

She grinned and kissed my
immaturity.

Our shadows were El Greco-
esque as we

Trudged on across the endless
earthen sea.

She sleeps beneath those
fields where she stood
tall.

And I at last, can see, the
fields are small.

Miller, *If This Be Love,* 8.

Conclusion

Image paralleling then is the welding of biblical ideas, precepts and images with other kinds of stories to cement the truth of the sermon in the hearers' minds. Paralleling may not be just learning to write down the sermon's key illustrations and ideas in two columns but in literally learning to think in these double columns as we prepare the sermon. In *Spirit, Word and Story* (104), I describe this double-image process in this way:

When I Preach on:	I Can Support with Literature Quotes from:
Ruth and Boaz	*Romeo and Juliet*
David's faithless Absalom	*King Lear*
Job	*J.B.*
Adam	*Paradise Lost*
Cain and Abel	*East of Eden*
Paul	*Great Lion of God*
Liberalism	*The Closing of the American Mind*
Personal struggle	*Death of a Salesman*
Hell	*No Exit*

In this double mode of thinking through a sermon you are actually "seeing" your illustrated way through your sermon. But best of all you will be learning to preach in a mode that is constantly "synthesizing" or "drawing together." You will then be learning to preach in a conceptualizing mode that will foster the same response as those who hear you. For if you are consistent you learn to prepare a sermon in this interesting way and they will consistently expect to be interested in the sermons you have prepared. As they bring this same sense of expectation into worship the services will begin and end with a cathexis and strong rapport that will demonstrate the worthiness of paralleling as an important hermeneutical technique.

For Further Study

Capote, Truman. *In Cold Blood*. New York: Signet, 1965.

Cheney, Lois A. *God Is No Fool*. Nashville: Abingdon, 1969.

Dickinson, Emily. *Favorite Poems of Emily Dickinson*. New York: Avenel Books, 1978.

Graham, Ruth Bell. *Sitting by My Laughing Fire*. Minneapolis: World Wide Publishing, 1977.

Miller, Calvin. *If This Be Love*. San Francisco: Harper & Row, 1984.

———. *Spirit, Word, and Story*. Dallas: Word, 1989.

Thielicke, Helmut. *The Waiting Father*. New York: Harper Jubilee, 1959.

Warren, James E. "Childhood Relit." From *Poet's Treasury*, edited by Viola Jacobsen Berg. Winamac, Ind.: Redeemer Books, 1992.

Wilcox, Ella Wheeler. "The Queen's Last Ride." In *Best Loved Poems of the American People*. Edited by Hazel Selleman, 557–58. Garden City, N.Y.: Garden City Books, 1936.

Winokur, Jon, compiler. *The Portable Curmudgeon*. New York: NAL Books, 1987.

A Student's Glossary for
Biblical Studies

The need for a specialized glossary arises for the student who first encounters the overwhelming number of technical terms in biblical studies. The obvious gaps in dictionary help have been in the areas of language, grammar, history, and criticism. Terms have been chosen with the theological student in mind who tackles the Hebrew and Greek texts along with their allied disciplines. We have concentrated our effort on important definitions found both in this book and other primary tools for biblical interpretation.

In many cases an entry is accompanied by examples from the Bible. Recourse to Hebrew and Greek will clarify the examples; these are introduced by the abbreviations *Heb:* and *Gk:*, meaning an example from the Hebrew Old Testament (OT) and the Greek New Testament (NT) respectively. Illustrations applicable to both languages or of a general nature are introduced by *Ex:* (example). When an entry title contains more than one word or term, synonyms and alternate spellings are separated by a comma (Stich, Stichos); different parts of speech, such as a noun and an adjective, by a slash (Messiah/messianic).Unless otherwise indicated, the translation used is the NIV.

Accent/Accentuation. In the biblical languages, a matter of stressed sound or force of utterance. Also a mark used in written Hebrew and Greek to indicate the nature and place of the spoken accent.

Acrostic. In Hebrew poetry, an arrangement of successive words or phrases that begin with consecutive letters of the alphabet. There are a number of acrostics in the OT that are lost in translation. *Heb:* Pss. 111, 112, 119; Prov. 31:10–31; Lam. 1–4. There are no NT acrostics.

Ad Hominem. Latin, "to the man." An argument that is directed to one's prejudices rather than to one's intellect, or an argument that attacks the opponent rather than his arguments. *Gk:* the argument of Rom. 3:1–5 concludes, "I am using a human argument"; cf. Matt. 12:27.

Adjective/Adjectival. A word, phrase, or clause used to modify a noun or in some cases a substantive. In Hebrew and Greek, it agrees with the word modified (concord). *Heb:* "Abraham held a great feast" (Gen. 21:8). *Gk:* "I am the good shepherd" (John 10:11).

Adjunct. A modifier attached to the head of a phrase, or a secondary element (such as an adjective or adverb) that can be removed without the structural identity of the construction being affected. *Ex:* "I went home today" or "I went home," but not "I went today."

Adoptionism. A Christological heresy of Gnosticism, which holds that the human Jesus became divine or was possessed by the divine Christ at the time of his baptism; a form of docetism ascribed to Cerinthus in Asia Minor at the end of the first century A.D.

Adverb/Adverbial. A word, phrase, or clause used to modify a verb, adjective, or another adverb. In English, adverbs are usually formed with the suffix -ly. In Hebrew and Greek, many adverbs are formed with suffixes; other parts of speech and many clauses are used adverbially. *Heb:* "Agag came to him confidently" (1 Sam. 15:32). *Gk:* "Freely you have received, freely give" (Matt. 10:8).

A Fortiori. Latin for "from the stronger (reason or argument)." The conclusion drawn is inferred to be even more certain than the preceding.

Agape. A transliteration of one of the Greek words for "love" found in the NT. It is self-giving, self-sacrificing love preeminently found in God himself.

Aggadah. See haggadah.

Aleppo Codex. A Hebrew manuscript of the OT from the tenth century A.D., claimed to have been pointed (see pointing) by Aaron ben Asher, the most illustrious member of the Ben Asher family. Preserved, although with loss of a quarter of its folios, and adopted for a new critical edition of the OT by the Hebrew University.

Alexandrian Text. A NT text-type associated with Alexandria, Egypt; allegedly revised in the fourth century A.D. by the Egyptian bishop Hesychius. Its early form (called the neutral text by Westcott and Hort) includes the major witnesses Codex Sinaiticus and Codex Vaticanus. Also called Egyptian, Hesychian, or Beta text.

Allegory. An interpretation that assumes that a text has a secondary and hidden meaning underlying its primary and obvious meaning; a story that presents its true meaning through figures; it has been called a prolonged metaphor. Allegorical interpretation of the Bible was widespread in the early church (e.g., Origen and Augustine). Ex: interpreted allegorically, the Song of Solomon deals with the love of Christ for his church; cf. Gal 4:24. See typology.

Alliteration. Words or syllables that begin with the same sound. Alliteration is usually not retained when words are translated from one language to another. *Heb:* Ps. 122:6; Amos 5:5; Isa. 1:18–20. *Gk:* Rom. 1:29–30; 1 Pet. 1:4.

Allusion. In biblical studies, an implied or indirect reference to the OT in the NT by means of a common theme, word, or idea; a brief verbatim phrase that comes from the writer's vocabulary of faith, rather than an explicit quotation of the OT text. A less clear allusion is called an echo.

Amanuensis. A scribe or secretary hired to write from dictation; Paul frequently used an amanuensis (cf. Rom. 16:22; Gal. 6:11; Col. 4:18).

Ambiguous. A word or phrase that may have more than one meaning in a specific context. *Heb:* "Ahab served Baal a little; Jehu will serve him much" (2 Kings 10:18). *Gk:* "Destroy this temple, and I will raise it again in three days" (John 2:19).

Anachronism. An error in chronology by which events, circumstances, or customs are misplaced in time, generally too early. *Ex:* when Shakespeare refers to the striking of a clock in *Julius Caesar*, he introduces an anachronism. *Heb:* the reference to the Philistines in Gen. 21:32 has frequently been called an anachronism, as it is believed that these people did not settle the eastern Mediterranean coast until ca. 1200 B.C.

Anagogical/Anagogic Sense. Greek, "leading above." Mystical interpretation of the Scriptures popular in the Middle Ages that focused on references to the afterlife. *Ex:* an interpretation of the Promised Land in terms of heaven. See fourfold sense.

Analogue. That which corresponds to something else; in biblical studies, specifically an earthly analogy for something divine. *Ex:* shepherd, father, king.

Analogy. A comparison between two otherwise dissimilar things so that the one that is less known or understood is clarified by the other. *Gk:* Paul, who is fond of analogy, compares the love of a husband for his wife to that of Christ for the church (Eph. 5:25); 1 Cor. 14:6–8; 2 Tim. 2:3–7.

Analogy Of Faith. Latin, *analogia fidei*. Method of interpretation whose principle is that Scripture interprets Scripture; assumes that a passage is to be seen in the full context of Scripture and that the Bible has an underlying unity.

Analytical Lexicon. An alphabetically arranged list of all the major parts of speech, including nouns and verbs in their inflected forms, parsed and defined. Analytical lexicons are available for the Hebrew and Aramaic OT and for the Greek NT. Also called a parsing guide.

Anamnesis. Greek, "memory." Recalling to mind, especially the redemptive acts of God, for example, the commemoration of Christ's death in the Lord's Supper.

Antediluvian. Refers to the period of time before the Flood.

Anthropomorphism/Anthropomorphic. A description of God in human terms or with physical characteristics. *Ex:* "God saw" (Gen. 1:4), the "arm of the LORD" (Isa. 51:9), "the LORD smelled the pleasing aroma" (Gen. 8:21).

Anthropopathism/Anthropopathy. The attribution of human emotions or feelings to God. *Heb:* "the LORD's anger" (Exod. 4:14), "You do not delight" (Ps. 51:16). *Gk:* "the kindness and sternness of God" (Rom. 11:22).

Antilegomena. Greek, "the ones spoken against." The books that were not accepted by all circles into the NT canon or, more precisely, NT books that were disputed during the first three Christian centuries (see Eusebius, *Ecclesiastical History* 3.25). See homologoumena.

Antinomianism. In biblical ethics, the attitude and practice of unlimited moral license, based on the assumption that grace means freedom to sin; a misunderstanding of Christian liberty. *Ex*: Rom. 3:8; 6:1–2; Gal. 5: 13; 1 John 3:4–6. Also called libertinism.

Antithesis/Antithetical. Contrast; a figure of speech in which words, phrases, or clauses (parallelism) are contrasted by being balanced one against the other. *Heb:* "For the LORD watches over the way of the righteous, but the way of the wicked will perish" (Ps.1:6). *Gk:* "He was delivered over to death for our sins and was raised to life for our justification" (Rom. 4:25).

Antithetic Parallelism. In Hebrew poetry, the second line of a couplet contrasts with the thought of the first by means of a contradictory or opposing statement, thereby intensifying the thought of the first line. *Ex:* Prov. 10:1.

Antonym, Antonymy. A word that is approximately opposite in meaning and use to another. *Ex:* "bad" is an antonym of "good." *Heb:* "God called the light 'day,' and the darkness he called 'night'" (Gen. 1:5).

Aphorism. A short, pithy statement of a general truth; a maxim. *Heb:* Prov. 13:1; *Gk:* Gal. 6:7.

Apocalypse/apocalyptic. Greek, "to uncover," "unveil." A heavenly revelation disclosing the meaning and end of history. It concerns the overthrow of the present age and the establishment of God's rule. As a genre, a group of OT, intertestamental, and NT texts featuring vision, symbol, and historical determinism. *Ex*.: Daniel 7–12 (OT), Enoch (See Pseudepigrapha), and Revelation (NT).

Apocalypse, The. Another name for the Book of Revelation.

Apocrypha/Apocryphal, OT. A large group of Jewish writings outside the OT canon that were composed between 200 B.C. and A.D. 200. They are included in the Septuagint and the Latin Vulgate.

Apocrypha/Apocryphal, NT. A collective term for noncanonical literature produced by the early church that developed forms present in the NT, viz., gospels, acts, epistles, and apocalypses. By and large, spurious writings that served Gnostic tenets and rivaled NT documents in some communities of early Christianity.

Apocryphon. Greek, "hidden writing." A term used to describe a noncanonical, pseudonymous writing of the intertestamental or early church periods that qualifies for, but is not included in, the traditional collections of Apocrypha and Pseudepigrapha. *Ex:* the *Genesis Apocryphon* from Qumran.

Apodictic Law. A law that is stated in absolute terms; cf. casuistic law. *Heb:* the OT laws introduced by "you shall" (Exod. 20:3–17).

Apologia. Greek for "apology" or "defense." A reasoned verbal defense or explanation of one's conduct; also a rhetorical genre in the Second Sophistic. *Ex:* Christian apologies by Paul (Acts 26:1–29) and harassed believers (1 Pet. 3: 15).

Apophthegm. See apothegm.

A Posteriori. Latin for "from the latter (effect)." Argument from inductive reasoning; derived by reasoning from observed facts or experience; the opposite of *a priori*.

Apostolic Age. The earliest period of church history, coextensive with the activity of the apostles; generally dated A.D. 30 to A.D. 100, from the founding of the Jerusalem church to the death of the apostle John.

Apostolic Fathers. Conventional title given to the Greek church fathers immediately following the apostolic age; the collection of Greek patristic writings that date from the early second century A.D: the letters of Clement of Rome, Ignatius of Antioch, Polycarp, and Barnabas, the Shepherd of Hermas, the Didache, the fragments of Papias, and the letter to Diognetus.

Apostolicon. Greek for "that relating to an apostle." Used variously by the Greek church fathers to refer to an apostolic writing, a collection of epistles (Marcion's term for Paul's letters), or a lectionary of one of the NT epistles.

Apostrophe. A sign used in English and Greek to indicate the omission of one or more letters from a word. Also, a figure of speech in which a person (usually absent) or personified thing is addressed rhetorically, as if present and capable of understanding. *Heb:* "Hear, O heavens! Listen, O earth!" (Isa. 1:2). *Gk:* "Now you, if you call yourself a Jew" (Rom. 2:17).

Apothegm, Apophthegm. A short, pithy saying that expresses an important truth in a few words; a maxim. In form criticism, a technical term for a saying of Jesus set in a brief narrative context. *Ex:* Mark 2:23–28. Also called paradigm, pronouncement story, and chreia.

A Priori. Latin for "from the former (cause)." Argument from deductive reasoning; derived by reasoning from self-evident presuppositions; the opposite of *a posteriori.*

Aramaic. A branch of the northwest Semitic languages that is closely related to Hebrew. In the OT, Ezra 4:8–6:18; 7:12–26; Dan. 2:4b–7:28; and Jer. 10:11 are in Aramaic rather than Hebrew. Aramaic had become the common language of the Jewish people by NT times. See Aramaism, Masoretic text.

Aramaism. The insertion of an Aramaic word where a Hebrew or Greek word should have appeared, or a feature of NT language that reflects Aramaic influence. *Ex:* "Rabboni" (John 20:16). See semitism.

Archaism. The preservation (or insertion) of an earlier or more primitive word or expression.

Archetype. A manuscript that is not the immediate parent of another but is a remoter ancestor.

Argumentum E Silentio. Latin for "argument from silence." An interpretation based on the silence of the Scriptures, often on the assumption that because a biblical writer did not mention an event he was ignorant of it or it had not happened when he wrote. *Heb:* the scarcity of messages by Jeremiah during the reign of Josiah is used as an argument that he was not totally supportive of Josiah's reforms. *Gk:* the letters of Paul must have been collected after the writing of Acts since otherwise Luke would have referred to them.

Asceticism. A lifestyle designed to combat vice and develop virtue by self-denial and, in exaggerated forms, withdrawal from society.

Attributive. An adjective or other adjunct word that stands before the noun it qualifies. *Ex:* white bread. *Heb:* the attributive may also be expressed by the genitive relationship: "man of strength" = "strong man." *Gk:* the attributive may follow the noun when both have the article.

Authorized Version. See AV.

Autograph. The original manuscript in the author's own handwriting or dictated to an amanuensis by the author. No autographs of biblical texts have been discovered.

Autonomous Reason. The belief that the reason is free and able to discover truth without reference to higher authority.

AV. Abbreviation for Authorized Version; another name for the King James Version of the Bible. See KJV.

Babylonian Talmud. See Gemara.

B. C. E. Abbreviation of "Before the Common Era" (sometimes understood as "Before the Christian Era"). It is used as a "neutral" substitute for B.C. ("Before Christ").

BH. Abbreviation used to designate Kittel's *Biblica Hebraica*; third edition published 1937; sometimes abbreviated BH3, BHK.

BHS. Abbreviation of *Biblia Hebraica Stuttgartensia*, a complete revision of BH; published in its entirety in 1977.

Biblical Criticism. A term used loosely to describe all the methodologies applied to the study of the biblical texts.

Biblicism/Biblicist. Uncritical and extremely literal interpretation of the Scriptures.

Bibliography. An alphabetically arranged list of books and articles that are pertinent to a given subject.

Bibliolatry. Excessive reverence for the Bible that makes it into a sacred object, usurping the place of the God of the Bible who properly should be the object of reverence.

Byzantine Text. The NT text-type associated with Byzantium and the Greek East, found in the majority of later manuscripts and usually the majority reading of a passage. Probably revised at Antioch of Syria in the fourth century A.D. (Lucianic text). It is the basis of the Textus Receptus. Also called Syrian, Koine, Alpha, or Antiochene text.

CA., C. Abbreviation of the Latin word *circa*, "about," "approximately." *Ex*: David became king ca. 1020 B.C.

Chalcedon. The Council of Chalcedon (A.D. 451) adopted the formula that Christ is completely human and completely divine, his two natures being inseparable.

Canon. Greek, "measure," "norm." The books of the Bible that have been accepted as inspired and authoritative. The Jewish canon of the OT (39 books) and the NT canon (27 books) together form the Christian canon.

Canonical. Pertaining to the books or parts of the OT and NT that form the canon.

Canonical Criticism. Study of the biblical texts in their present form in the canon and of the process by which they were composed and transmitted.

Cardinal. Short for cardinal number (one, two, three, etc.). See ordinal.

Cartesian. Related to the philosophy of Renè Descartes that was essential to the rise of modern thought and scientific method. Descartes' *Discourse on Method* laid the foundation for a primary way in which modern thinkers have approached the discovery of new knowledge.

Casuistic Law. A law that is stated in conditional terms; the key word is "if"; sometimes called case law. *Heb*: "If a man has a stubborn and rebellious son" (Deut. 21:18–19). See apodictic law.

Catechesis/Catechetic. Oral instruction in one's faith or a collection of written materials used for this purpose. Form criticism proposes that catechetical needs were responsible for the formation of some of the Scriptures.

Catena. Latin, "chain." A commentary (lit., chains of comments) made up of strung-together quotations that accompanies biblical and theological writings. The device is found in various sources, such as the LXX, Qumran, and the church fathers. The word generally means a series of quotations, sayings, or stories. *Ex:* the chain of OT quotations in Rom. 9:25–29.

Catholic Epistles. Title assigned by Eusebius (*Ecclesiastical History* 2.23) to seven NT letters: James, 1–2 Peter, 1–3 John, and Jude. The term *katholikê* (Greek "universal") was apparently used in the sense "addressed to all the churches," although 2–3 John and 1 Peter have specific addresses. Also called General Epistles.

C. E. Abbreviation of "Common Era" (sometimes understood as Christian Era"). It is used as a "neutral" substitute for A.D. (*Anno Domini,* "in the year of [our] Lord").

Charisma/Charismatic. Greek for "gift," "a favor bestowed." A spiritual gift, an endowment of God's grace bestowed by the Holy Spirit. "Charismatic" refers to a person who claims spiritual gifts, or to behavior performed in the power of such gifts. *Gk:* "Now about spiritual gifts" (1 Cor. 12:1).

Chiasmus, Chiastic. An arrangement of the parallel members of a verse or literary unit to form an a-b-b'-a' arrangement (the first line corresponds to the fourth, the second to the third). Chiasmus is also called inverted or introverted parallelism: extended patterns appear in Hebrew and Greek. *Heb:* Ps. 30:8–10; Gen. 4:4b–5a. *Gk:* Rom. 10:9–10; 1 Cor. 1:24–25; Philemon 5.

Chiliasm/Chiliastic. From the Greek word "thousand." The belief that Christ will return to reign on earth for a thousand years (Rev. 20). Synonymous with Millennialism/ Millennial.

Christocentric. Centered on Jesus Christ; having Jesus Christ as the focal point, as in a theology or a hermeneutical method.

Christology/Christological. That part of theological study or confession relating to the person and work of Christ, especially the union in him of the human and the divine.

Circumlocution. A roundabout way of expressing something that could be stated more directly or in fewer words. *Heb:* The Hebrew language does not have a verb "to have," so the idea must be expressed by circumlocution: "We have an aged father" (Gen. 44:20) is literally, "There is to us an aged father." *Gk:* It is commonplace in the verb and genitive constructions dependent on the LXX.

Circumstantial Clause. The statement of the particular circumstances under which the action of the main clause takes place. *Heb:* "As the sun was setting, Abram fell into a deep sleep" (Gen. 15:12). *Gk:* The Greek participle performs this function in a wide variety of ways: temporal, causal, conditional, etc. "When God raised up [temporal participle] his servant, he sent him" (Acts 3:26).

CJ. Abbreviation of Latin *coniectura,* "conjecture." In textual criticism and in a critical apparatus, the conjectural reading of a manuscript. Also abbreviated conj.

Clause. A clause may compose all or part of a complete sentence; it consists of a subject and predicate. In terms of function in the sentence, clauses are of three types: main, subordinate and coordinate.

Codex (pl., codices). An ancient manuscript in book form, made of papyrus, parchment, or vellum. In earlier times, documents were written on scrolls or clay tablets; the codex became dominant in the second century A.D. among Christian scribes.

Cognate Language. A language that shares a common origin with another. Spanish and Italian are cognate languages sharing a common origin in Latin.

Cognitive Process. The process of learning or of thinking.

Colloquialism. A word or expression used in spoken and informal language rather than in written and formal language.

Commentary. A study of a book (or of several books) of the Bible that employs the critical insights of linguistic, historical, and theological disciplines.

Common Era. See C. E.

Common Sense Rationalism. A philosophical movement founded by Thomas Reid (1710–1796) which asserts certain basic reasonable principles by which everyone lives, and that any philosophy, however logical it may be, that does not conform to these principles is to be rejected.

Comparative Religion. A comparative historical and theological study of the various religions of the world with a particular interest in discovering their similarities and mutual relations.

Complex Sentence. A sentence composed of one main clause plus at least one subordinate clause. *Ex:* "When they heard this, they were amazed" (Matt. 22:22).

Composition. The art of putting together words and sentences in accordance with the rules of grammar and rhetoric; in grammar, the relationship between morpheme, word, phrase, clause, sentence, and discourse.

Composition Criticism. An alternative term for redaction criticism, used by some scholars to emphasize the compositional technique of a true author as opposed to a mere redactor or editor.

Compound-complex Sentence. A sentence composed of two or more main clauses plus at least one subordinate clause. *Ex:* "When Israel was a child, I loved him, and out of Egypt I called my son" (Hos. 11:1).

Compound Sentence. A sentence composed of two or more main clauses, often joined by a coordinating conjunction. *Ex:* "Gladness and joy will overtake them, and sorrow and sighing will flee away" (Isa. 35:10).

Conceptual Grid. A framework of presuppositions and concepts through which one views a text in the interpretive process. *Ex:* The *logos* doctrine of Greek philosophy (the rational principle of creation) was used by the early fathers to expound the church's Christology.

Concordance. An alphabetical listing of the principal words in a book, giving all or some of the places where the word occurs. *Ex: Young's Analytical Concordance.*

Consonantal Text. The Hebrew text of the OT as written originally without the use of vowel points. Any text that is made up of consonants only.

Condition/Conditional Clause. A type of adverbial clause that poses an "if "; also called a protasis. There are four conditional sentence structures in Greek. *Heb:* "If my head were shaved, my strength would leave me" (Judg. 16:17).

Contextualization. The act or practice of placing an element of language, culture, behavior, etc. in its linguistic, cultural, or social setting in order to interpret it properly. For the reading of a text, this involves preceding and following sections (the literary context or co-text), the historical situation of the writer, and the perspective of the reader.

Contextual Principle. The interpretive principle that Scripture should be read in context, that is, in its literary, historical, and social dimensions.

Coordinate/coordination. The linking of grammatical units of equal rank. Coordinate clauses occur in a compound sentence; they can be joined by a coordinating conjunction such as *or, but,* or *and.* See parataxis.

Copyist. In biblical studies, one who copies the Scriptures. See scribe.

Cosmogony. A theory regarding the creation and origination of the world or universe.

Cosmology. Study of the orderly system or character of the universe. The ancient Near East largely conceived of a three-tiered cosmology: the earth, the water below, and the heavens above.

Credo. A creed or brief, authoritative expression of religious beliefs. Gerhard von Rad argued that such passages as Deut. 6:20–24, 26:5b–9, and Josh. 24:2b–13 are creeds of the faith of ancient Israel.

Creedal. Of, or pertaining to, a creed or credo.

Critical Apparatus. The textual critical footnotes found in Hebrew and Greek editions of the OT and NT. These notes supply readings that support or differ from the printed text and give manuscript sources for comparative studies of the text.

Critical Text. A hypothetical reconstruction of a document based on available divergent recensions.

Criticism. From Greek *krisis,* "act of judging." A general term that refers to the art of making an intelligent judgment about some object of study. In biblical studies, the major areas of criticism include the following: canonical criticism, form criticism, grammatico-historical criticism, higher criticism, historical criticism, literary criticism, redaction criticism, religio-historical criticism, rhetorical criticism, source criticism, structural analysis, stylistic criticism, textual (lower) criticism, and tradition criticism.

Cult/cultic. The public worship practices of a people, involving established forms, rites, feasts, times, places, etc. When used in biblical studies, the word should not be confused with its popular connotation (Satan cult, etc.).

Dead Sea Scrolls. Writings of an Essene-like community that were discovered in 1947 near the Dead Sea. They have been dated between 168 B.C. and A.D. 233. They include the oldest OT manuscripts yet discovered.

Decalogue. From Greek "ten words." Another name for the Ten Commandments (Exod. 20:1–17; Deut. 5:6–21).

Deconstruction. A literary-critical method associated with Jacques Derrida (b. 1930) that relativizes the meaning of a text. This theory states that meaning arises out of the interaction of the reader and the text, thus ultimate meaning is continually deferred because every reader interprets differently.

Texts thereby "deconstruct" or subvert their own claims to self-evident meanings.

Deductive Method. The process of reasoning from the general to the particular, as opposed to inductive, which goes from the particular to the general. For biblical languages, a traditional method of pedagogy and grammar that introduces the learner to grammatical structure by rules and paradigms and then applies the principles learned to the reading of texts. By contrast, the inductive method begins with the text and leads the student to formulate grammatical structure by generalizing from examples encountered in reading.

Demythologize. To interpret those parts of the Bible considered to be mythological (i.e., where the supernatural, transcendent is described in terms of the mundane, this-worldly) by understanding the essential existential truths contained in the imagery of the myth. Rudolf Bultmann is particularly associated with demythologizing the Scriptures.

Denotative Meaning. The aspect of meaning that most closely relates to that portion of the nonlinguistic world to which the word refers. Also called referential meaning. *Ex*: the denotative meaning of "father" includes human, male, generation, and ancestor, whereas the connotative meaning suggests care, love, protection, and discipline.

Dependent Clause. Another name for a subordinate clause.

Determinism/Deterministic. Tending to see every factor as the result of one overarching cause that cannot be changed. Determinism in theology is usually associated with the idea of predestination.

Deus Ex Machina. Latin for "god out of the machine." In Greek drama a deity was lowered suddenly onto the stage by mechanical means to resolve the dilemma at hand or untangle the plot. The phrase is now applied pejoratively to contrived solutions by means of an artificial or improbable device.

Deuterocanon/Deuterocanonical. A term used by Roman Catholics to designate books or parts of books that are not found in the Hebrew Bible but are included in the Septuagint and accepted as inspired since the Council of Trent; others call these books the Apocrypha. Catholics refer to the Pseudepigrapha as the Apocrypha.

Deutero-Isaiah. The name given to the unknown author of Isaiah 40–55 (sometimes applied to Isaiah 40–66) by those who do not accept the unity of the Book of Isaiah.

Deuteronomist Historian. A designation given by many scholars to an unknown editor responsible for compiling the books of Deuteronomy, Joshua, Judges, 1–2 Samuel, and 1–2 Kings, ca. 550 B.C.

Deutero-Pauline. Name given to canonical letters of Paul whose authenticity is doubted by some scholars; usually ascribed to the work of a Pauline admirer who imitated the apostle's style. The list includes Ephesians, Colossians, 2 Thessalonians, 1–2 Timothy, and Titus.

Devotio Moderna. Pietistic approach to hermeneutics which emphasizes the role of the Holy Spirit as illuminator.

Devotional Study. Bible study which seeks personal truths or encouragement to live closer to God.

Diachronic. From Greek, "through time." A term used to refer to the developing or changing state of a language over a period of time. *Heb: ylk* became *hlk; Gk:* the dual number was dropped. See synchronic.

Dialect. One of a number of varieties of a language, especially as differentiated by geographical region or by social class. *Ex*: Ugaritic, Hebrew, and Aramaic are northwest Semitic dialects: Ionic, Doric, and Attic are classical Greek dialects.

Dialogue. A conversation between two or more persons. The character of biblical faith—the relationship of God and persons—makes dialogue an inevitable form of rhetorical expression. *Heb:* "Come now, let us reason together" (Isa. 1:18); Hab. 1–2 contains a dialogue between God and the prophet. *Gk:* "Then one of the elders asked me . . . I answered" (Rev. 7:13–14).

Diaspora. The dispersion or scattering of the Jewish people after the exile of 587 B.C., particularly the extended settlements following the conquests of Alexander the Great.

Didactic. That which is intended to teach or instruct. Much of the OT and NT is didactic in nature. *Ex*: the Sermon on the Mount.

Direct Equivalence. A theory of translation that believes only one English word should be used to represent each Hebrew or Greek word found in the OT and NT. See formal correspondence.

Discourse. A biblical passage displaying semantic and structural coherence, unity, and completeness, and conveying a message. From a linguistic viewpoint, discourse is marked by certain universals or restraints that give it structure. *Ex*: the Bread of Life discourse (John 6:25–59). See discourse analysis.

Discourse Analysis. The linguistic task of discovering the regular features of discourse structure, the way in which words, phrases, clauses, and especially sentences and whole compositions are joined to achieve a given purpose.

Docetism/Docetic. From Greek *dokein*, "to seem." A Christological heresy of Gnosticism, which asserted that Christ "seemed" to suffer, i.e., the death of the divine Christ was only apparent, not real. *Ex*: docetism is the target of the polemic in 1 John 5:6.

Documentary Hypothesis. A theory that explains the formation of the Scriptures, especially the Pentateuch, as being the result of combining a number of documents from different sources and time periods. See also source criticism, JEDP.

Doxology. From Greek *doxa*, "praise," "glory." An ascription of praise or glory to God or the persons of the Trinity, usually found at the end of a literary section. *Heb:* "Praise be to the LORD, the God of Israel, from everlasting to everlasting" (1 Chron. 16:36). *Gk:* "Oh, the depth of the riches of the wisdom and knowledge of God!" (Rom. 11:33).

DSS. Abbreviation of Dead Sea Scrolls.

Dualism. Any doctrine that asserts that there are two absolute powers or principles. Matter and spirit in Gnosticism are two ultimately opposed realms of being; biblical dualism is ethical in character, e.g., spirit versus flesh.

Dynamic Equivalence. A type of translation in which the message of the biblical text is conveyed to the reader with effect equivalent to that for the original reader; closer to a paraphrase, and contrasted with formal equivalence. Also called functional equivalence.

Ecclesiology. The branch of theology that is concerned with the nature of the church.

Eisegesis. Reading into a passage of Scripture the meaning one wishes to find in it. See exegesis.

Ekklesia. Greek for "church" or "assembly."

El. A Hebrew name for God in the OT. The word is the most general designation for deity and was also used by the Canaanites for the name of their chief god. Frequently combined with an adjective to create a name for God that expresses one of his attributes. See El Elyon.

El Elyon. A name of God, customarily translated as "God Most High." The name occurs thirty-one times in the OT (e.g., Gen. 14:18).

Elohim. A Hebrew name for God found 2,570 times in the OT; it is the plural of *Eloah.* In addition to being a proper name of God, it can also refer to gods in general. See El.

Enlightenment. Eighteenth-century movement that exalted reason and human freedom. Enlightenment thinkers recognized no higher authority than reason, refusing to accept supernatural revelation as authority. Among the great Enlightenment thinkers were Jean Jacques Rousseau, John Locke, and John Stuart Mill.

Epigraphy. The study of inscriptions written on durable materials such as stone.

Epiphany. A manifestation of God (Exod. 3; 19; Isa. 6; Ezek. l); also called theophany. Also, a feast celebrated on January 6 that commemorates the coming of the Magi as being the first manifestation of Jesus Christ to the Gentiles.

Epistemology. Greek, "study of knowing." The branch of philosophy concerned with the theory and grounds of knowledge, especially its limits and validity.

Epistle. Greek for "letter." A genre of Greco-Roman public correspondence applied to the NT letters; now distinguished from the latter as a technical term in literary criticism. See letter.

Epistolary. Of, or pertaining to, an epistle.

Epistolography. The study of Hebrew and Greek letter writing.

Eschatology. From Greek *eschatos,* "last." Strictly speaking, the study of events associated with the end of time; the term is drastically modified by some interpreters.

Eschaton. Greek for "the end," i.e., of the present world order.

Etymology. Study of the origin or derivation of a word.

Euphemism. A word substituted for another, usually for reasons of good taste or delicacy.

Excursus. A digression that gives an extended discussion of a matter not covered extensively in the main body of a text; often placed at the end of a text as an appendix.

Exegesis. The use of critical and scholarly methods to derive the meaning of a passage of Scripture; it is to be distinguished from exposition and eisegesis. It may also refer to the written product of such study.

Exegete. The person who practices or writes an exegesis.

Exposition. A method of elaborating the meaning of a text as determined by exegesis and showing its contemporary relevance or application without distorting or falsifying its original meaning; it is to be distinguished from exegesis.

Extrabiblical. Not found in the Bible; also used as another term for extracanonical.

Extracanonical. Books that were not accepted into the canon as part of the Scriptures; also called noncanonical or extrabiblical. See Apocrypha, Pseudepigrapha.

Figurative Language. See figure, figure of speech.

Figure, Figure Of Speech. The use of words in a way other than the ordinary or literal sense. Figurative language may be expressed by such devices as metaphor and simile. *Heb:* "all the trees of the field will clap their hands" (Isa. 55:12). *Gk:* "I am the bread of life" (John 6:35).

Formal Correspondence. Another term for formal equivalence.

Formal Equivalence. A type of translation in which the form and structure of the original are reproduced as nearly as possible, in contrast to dynamic equivalence. Also called formal correspondence. *Ex:* the NASB stresses formal equivalence, the Contemporary English Version dynamic equivalence, while the Living Bible is a paraphrase.

Form Criticism. The analysis of a text according to typical, identifiable literary forms by which the people of a given cultural context expresses itself linguistically.

Former Prophets. In the Hebrew Bible this is the designation of the books of Joshua, Judges, 1–2 Samuel and 1–2 Kings.

Formgeschichte. German name for the discipline known as form criticism.

Four Document Hypothesis. An elaboration of the two-source hypothesis on the relationship of the Synoptic Gospels made by B. H. Streeter. He postulated that behind Matthew and Luke lay four sources: M, the material unique to Matthew (written A.D. 60, Jerusalem); L, the material unique to Luke (written A.D. 60, Caesarea); Mark (written A.D. 66, Rome), and Q, the sayings source (written A.D. 50, Antioch).

Fourfold Sense. A theory of biblical interpretation on four levels formulated as early as John Cassian (ca. A.D. 425) that flourished throughout the medieval period. The four meanings of Scripture were (1) literal, (2) allegorical, (3) moral (or tropological), and (4) anagogical (mystical and eschatological); biblical exegesis for a thousand years exhibited the fourfold sense of each passage. See anagogical.

Gattung. German word for "kind" [of form]. See genre.

Gemara. A type of commentary on the Mishnah produced by rabbis in the third through sixth centuries A.D. It contains a variety of proverbs, tales, and customs that relate to rabbinic lore as well as direct expositions of the text. The Mishnah together with the Palestinian Gemara is called the Palestinian or Jerusalem Talmud; the Mishnah together with the Babylonian Gemara is called the Babylonian Talmud.

Genealogy. The history of the descent of a person or a family from earlier ancestors. Both the OT and NT contain extensive genealogical lists. *Ex:* 1 Chron. 1:1–9:44; Matt. 1:1–16.

General Epistles. Another name for the Catholic Epistles.

Genre. As applied to literature, this term denotes a distinctive group (or a structural scheme) with respect to style, form, and purpose; now being used in form criticism to replace the German term *Gattung.*

Geschichte. A German term for "history." See *historie.*

Gloss. (1) An added comment usually placed in the margins of an ancient text by the copyist. Sometimes glosses made their way into the text when later recopied. John 5:3b–4 is considered by many NT scholars to be such a gloss. (2) A marginal or interlinear commentary copied by students during lectures at medieval schools; the most famous collection of these notes was the *Glossa Ordinaria,* which became a standard work of reference.

Glossolalia. Greek, "tongue-speaking." The gift of speaking in tongues. See charisma.

Gnosis/Gnostic/Gnosticism. From Greek *gnosis,* "knowledge." A widespread and highly diverse religious movement with roots in Greek philosophy and folk religion. Its chief emphases are the utter transcendence of God, created matter as fallen and evil, and salvation by esoteric knowledge. The Gnostic heresy or Gnosticism is the developed system that emerged in the second century A.D. and is associated with the names of Marcion, Basilides, and Valentinius. Sources of information on Gnosticism are the church fathers—Tertullian, Irenaeus, Hippolytus, and Origen—and the Gnostic texts of Nag Hammadi. By convention some scholars refer to pre-Christian evidence as gnosis, reserving the term Gnosticism for the later heresy; other scholars prefer the terms incipient or proto-Gnosticism for pre-Christian and NT evidences.

Grammatico-Historical Criticism. This discipline makes use of many critical disciplines in order to shed light on the Scriptures and to understand them better. It studies the historical background together with grammatical, syntactical, and linguistic factors. It usually combines exegesis with exposition and is used largely in conservative circles.

Griesbach Hypothesis. A solution to the Synoptic problem proposed by J. J. Griesbach (1783), which holds that Matthew was the earliest Gospel, that Luke depended on Matthew, and that Mark later used the two, producing an abbreviated and conflated version (See conflation). Chief among contemporary advocates is W. R. Farmer; also called the two-gospel hypothesis.

Haggadah/Haggadic. From Hebrew "to narrate." The nonlegal sections of rabbinic literature, featuring imaginative exposition and explanatory narration of OT texts, enhanced by anecdotes and spiritual maxims. See Halakah, Midrash.

Halakah/Halakic. From Hebrew, "to walk." The Jewish oral laws of the Tannaim that supplemented or explained the laws of the OT: the legal portions of rabbinic literature as distinct from haggadah, emphasizing rules for conduct of life. These normative interpretations are preserved in various midrashim, the Mishnah, and the Talmud.

Harmony Of The Gospels. A rearrangement of the four Gospels on a chronological basis so that they present a unified, continuous life and ministry of Jesus; the earliest known example is Tatian's *Diatessaron. Ex:* A. T. Robertson, *A Harmony of the Gospels for Students of the Life of Christ.* See synopsis of the Gospels.

Hebraism. A word or idiom derived from the Hebrew language; in biblical studies it refers especially to any part of the Septuagint or NT Greek that shows the influence of Hebrew style and terminology.

Heilsgeschichte. A German word translated variously as "salvation history," "redemptive history," or "sacred history"; it interprets the Bible as the ongoing story of God's redemptive activity in history.

Hellenistic Age. The era of cultural unity in the Greek East brought about by the conquests of Alexander the Great. The period extends from the death of Alexander (323 B.C.) to the rise of the Augustan principate (31 B.C.).

Hellenize/Hellenization. The adoption or imposition of Greek language and culture; a tendency accelerated in Judaism during the Hellenistic age.

Hermeneutics. Theory and principles of interpretation; for writings, correctly understanding the thought of an author and communicating that thought to others. See exegesis.

Hexapla. From Greek for "sixfold." The first "parallel Bible," an OT edition compiled by Origen ca. A.D. 245 that contained in six parallel columns the Hebrew text, a Greek transliteration of the Hebrew text, and several Greek versions of the OT.

Higher Criticism. A type of biblical criticism that deals with matters such as historical background, authorship, date of writing, etc., as opposed to lower or textual criticism.

Historical Criticism. A term that is used loosely to describe all the methodologies related to biblical criticism. It was developed especially in the nineteenth century when it was believed that reality was uniform and universal and could be discovered by human reason and investigations. Also, it is used to mean the historical setting of a document (such as time, place, sources, etc.). The term is also used to describe an emphasis on historical, philological, and archaeological analysis of the biblical texts.

Historie. A German term used in contemporary criticism to denote that which is public and verifiable according to the methods of historiography. Its counterpart, *Geschichte*, refers to the significance of historical facts for faith, which is not open in the same way to historical scrutiny. See *Heilsgeschichte*.

History Of Religions School. An early-twentieth-century German school of interpretation that applied the principles of comparative religion to the study of early Christianity. It held that, as a religion of the Roman empire, Christianity was a syncretistic faith borrowing from mystery religions and Gnosticism. Chief proponents of this school were R. Reitzenstein (1861–1931) and W. Bousset (1865–1920). Also called religio-historical criticism.

Homiletics. The study of preaching as an art and a science.

Homologoumena. Greek, "ones agreed to." Books of the Bible that were received by all alike, i.e., undisputed books of the NT canon (see Eusebius, *Ecclesiatical History* 3.25). See antilegomena.

Hyperbole. Greek, "flung too far," an overstatement. A literary exaggeration for the purpose of emphasis without any intention of deception. *Heb:* "David [has slain] his tens of thousands" (1 Sam. 18:7). *Gk:* "It is easier for a camel to go through the eye of a needle than for a rich man to enter the kingdom of God" (Matt. 19:24).

Hypothesis. A conjectural explanation that has not yet been verified but leads to scientific understanding; a preliminary step towards a theory, which is more comprehensive and better grounded.

Idiom. An expression used in a language that is peculiar or unique to that language in grammatical construction or meaning. Hebrew and Greek are replete with idiomatic expressions. *Ex:* "As the Lord lives," "son of the bridal chamber."

Implied Author. An analytical framework in narrative criticism that depicts the implied author through clues in the text itself apart from the identity of the real author provided by historical reconstruction. Often the implied author is identical with the narrator in the text who tells the story. See literary criticism.

Implied Reader(s). In narrative criticism, a depiction of the readers implied by clues from the text alone, who may be distinguished from the real readers in both the original and contemporary settings. See literary criticism.

Imagery. Another designation for figurative language. See also figure, figure of speech.

Inerrancy/Inerrant. The doctrine that the Bible is free from error or mistake; its rationale usually is based on verbal inspiration and is restricted to the autographs, which would be free from textual corruption. The term *infallibility* properly means the Bible is incapable of error, not liable to deceive or mislead. Although the adjectives *inerrant* and *infallible* are often used synonymously, some scholars apply the word *infallible* only to what the Bible teaches, in order to avoid the connotation of historical and scientific accuracy in all matters implied in the word *inerrant*.

Infallibility/Infallible. See inerrancy.

In Media Res. Latin for "in the midst of things." For dramatic effect, a narrative account may take up a story not at its beginning but in the middle of later events.

Inscription. Engraved writing on durable materials such as stone, wood, or metal; the term includes graffiti but usually excludes coins (numismatics), papyrus, and parchment.

Intentional Fallacy. The error of studying a literary work in order to establish or assess the author's intention rather than concentrating on what the text actually says. Modern literary criticism tends to the view that a text's meaning is detached from the author's intention and control, hence literary-critical insights must be deliberately ahistorical.

Interlinear Bible. A Bible that contains an English translation written between the lines of the biblical text printed in Hebrew or Greek.

Intertestamental Period. The period between the completion of the writing of the OT Scriptures and the beginning of the NT era.

Ipsissima Verba/Ipsissima Vox. Latin, "the very words" or "the very voice." The exact words or language spoken or written by an individual and preserved without any change. Especially applied to the actual words of Jesus as preserved in the Gospels as distinct from sayings attributed to him by the early church; if the actual words are not preserved, one seeks the actual message or "the very voice."

Irony. A kind of humor, ridicule, or sarcasm in which the true meaning intended is the opposite of the literal sense of the words. *Heb:* "Woe to those who are heroes at drinking wine and champions at mixing drinks" (Isa. 5:22). *Gk:* "I am not in the least inferior to the 'super-apostles'" (2 Cor. 12:11); "We are fools for Christ, but you are so wise in Christ!" (1 Cor. 4:10).

JEDP. Terminology used in the documentary hypothesis to designate the documents identified by this method of analysis: J = Jahwist, dated ca. 950 B.C.; E = Elohist, dated ca. 850 B.C.; D = Deuteronomist, dated ca. 622 B.C.; P = Priestly, dated ca. 500–450 B.C. Proponents of this theory believe that J and E were combined ca. 750 B.C., to which D was added ca. 620 B.C., with P added in the postexilic period, giving the Pentateuch its final form as we know it by 400 B.C. This hypothesis was given its classical expression by Julius Wellhausen in 1878. See source criticism.

Jehovah. A pronunciation of Yahweh that began in medieval times out of a misunderstanding of the vowels of the name *Adonai* (Lord) written with the consonants JHVH by the Masoretes. This combination of vowels and consonants produces the hybrid "Jehovah" in English. However, the vowels were intended to instruct the reader to substitute the name *Adonai* for the sacred unpronounceable name.

Jerusalem Talmud. See Gemara.

Kairos/Kairotic. A term derived from Greek that describes a period of time that has special significance, cf. nodal points in *Heilsgeschichte*. The Exodus was a kairotic event for the ancient Israelites; the incarnation was a kairotic event for Christians.

Kenosis/Kenotic. From Greek *kenos*, "empty." A Christological term that refers to the self-limitation of Christ in the incarnation, derived from Phil. 2:5–11. *Gk:* "but made himself nothing [lit., emptied himself], taking the very nature of a servant" (Phil. 2:7).

Kerygma. Greek for "proclamation" or "preaching." A NT term for the act or content of apostolic proclamation of the gospel. The minimal points include (1) Jesus as the fulfillment of the OT promises, (2) his mission attested by mighty works, (3) his crucifixion, (4) resurrection, (5) ascension and promise of his Parousia, and (6) a call to repentance issuing in the forgiveness of sins and the gift of the Holy Spirit. *Ex:* Acts 2:14–39; 13:16–41; Rom. 1:1–6; 1 Cor. 15:1–8. In modern biblical theology and criticism, kerygma may refer to the content of what is preached or to the act of preaching.

Koine Greek. The "common" Greek dialect spread throughout the Greek East in the wake of Alexander's conquests, primarily through his armies; the lingua franca of the Hellenistic age. The NT is written in a Koine halfway between the vernacular of the papyri and the literary Koine of prose writers such as Josephus; the grammar and style owe much to the OT and can be described as Semitic or biblical Greek. See semitism.

Koine Text. Another name for the Byzantine text.

Koinonia. Greek for "sharing" or "fellowship." Descriptive of the church in the NT and in contemporary usage. *Gk:* Acts 2:42; 1 Cor. 1:9; 1 John 1:7.

Lament. A term used in form criticism to designate a particular literary form characterized by complaint or dirge; sometimes it is a funeral song. *Ex:* the Book of Lamentations.

Latinism. A word or idiom derived from Latin that appears in the NT. The majority of occurrences are loanwords from the areas of Roman administration, military, and coinage. *Gk: kolonia* (Acts 16:12); *kentyrion* (Mark 15:39); *denarion* (Matt. 20:9).

Latter Prophets. In the Hebrew Bible, the designation of the books of the major prophets and minor prophets as distinguished from the former prophets.

Law. A general designation of the requirements of God to be obeyed by the covenant people. Specifically, it is the designation of the first five books of the Hebrew Bible, also called the Torah. See apodictic law.

Lectionary. From Latin "reading." Compilation of portions of Scripture for reading in worship services of synagogues and churches. Ancient lectionaries form one source of witnesses to the text of the Greek NT.

Leningrad Codex. A Hebrew manuscript of the entire OT copied in A.D. 1008, a primary witness to the Ben Asher text. It forms the basis of *Biblia Hebraica* (BH) and *Biblia Hebraica Stuttgartensia* (BHS).

Letter. The letters of Paul are closest in form to the familiar private correspondence of the Hellenistic and Roman period. Their unique features include (1) apostolic greeting, (2) prayer report and thanksgiving, (3) an opening formula to the main body, which itself consists of doctrine and paraenesis, (4) a travelogue, and (5) a closing with Christian greetings. The distinction between letter and epistle has limited value because some NT letters have the characteristics of public correspondence.

Lexicon. The word is used most frequently in biblical studies to designate a dictionary of Hebrew words that are found in the OT or a dictionary of Greek words that are found in the NT. *Ex:* Brown, Driver, and Briggs, *Hebrew and English Lexicon of the Old Testament;* and Arndt, Gingrich, and Danker, *A Greek-English Lexicon of the New Testament and Other Early Christian Literature.*

Liberation Theology. A theological movement born in the Third-World in the 1960s that proposes the liberation of oppressed peoples from social, economic, and political tyranny as the dominant theme of the Bible. The OT Exodus from Egypt and the NT Sermon on the Mount are paradigm texts for liberation hermeneutics.

Linguistics. The scientific study of language developed as a discipline in the twentieth century; when the emphasis is historical, the term is equivalent to the older term *philology.*

Literal. The ordinary or basic meaning of a word or expression in contrast to a figurative meaning. See also figure, figure of speech.

Literal Translation. A translation based on exact word-for-word renderings that retain the word order of the original language as much as possible. An extremely literal translation from one language to another can be awkward, wooden, or unnatural. See formal equivalence.

Literary Criticism. A study of the literary characteristics of a text, especially its structure, style, vocabulary, point of view, repetition of words, and plot. Approaches to biblical narrative adopt an analytical distinction between the real author and readers and the implied author and readers depicted in the text.

Loanword. A foreign word used in a biblical text. There are, for example, Persian, Aramaic, and Greek loanwords found in the OT, and Aramaic and Latin ones in the NT. *Heb:* a Persian word, *pardes,* "orchard" (Song of Sol. 4:13). *Gk:* a Latin word, *phragellion,* "whip" (John 2:15).

Locus Classicus. A Latin term used for the passage of Scripture or other literature that is usually cited as the best illustration or explanation of a word or subject. *Ex:* John 3:16 is a *locus classicus* of the gospel; Exod. 21:24 is the *locus classicus* for the law of retaliation.

Logion (pl., Logia). Greek for "saying." A saying of Jesus, usually in contrast to a longer utterance such as a parable. *Gk:* "If anyone wants to be first, he must be the very last, and the servant of all" (Mark 9:35). The plural *logia* refers to a collection of sayings, particularly a sayings-source (Q) for the Gospels or the *logia* compiled by Matthew (according to Papias).

Lollards. A Dutch term meaning "mumblers"; followers of the dissident scholar and preacher, John Wycliffe. The Lollard movement grew in England during the fourteenth century but was persecuted severely in the early fifteenth century.

Lower Criticism. Another term for textual criticism.

LXX. Latin numerals for "seventy"; symbol for the Septuagint. According to tradition, it was fitting that, since seventy elders accompanied Moses up Mount Sinai (Exod. 24:1–9), seventy elders should translate the Torah into Greek. However, the *Letter of Aristeas* reasons that seventy-two were involved in the translation (six times twelve tribes).

Magic. A term used in biblical studies to describe a widespread belief in the ancient Near East that the gods could be activated or moved to work on behalf of a worshiper who brought offerings, performed prescribed rituals, or repeated certain incantations.

Magnificat. The name of Mary's hymn of praise at the announcement of Jesus' birth (Luke 1:46–55), derived from the opening word of the Latin text: *Magnificat anima mea Dominum*, "My soul praises the Lord."

Major Prophets. In the Hebrew Bible, the Books of Isaiah, Jeremiah, and Ezekiel. English Bibles (based on the Septuagint arrangement) add the Book of Daniel; in the Hebrew Bible Daniel is found in the section called Writings or Hagiographa.

Makarism. From Greek for "blessing." Another name for a beatitude (Matt. 5:3–10).

Manuscript. In textual criticism this refers to the handwritten document in the original language. Secondarily, it is used to describe any handwritten document. It is abbreviated MS (sing.) and MSS (pl.).

Maranatha. A primitive Aramaic formula of the early church; the phrase can be translated as a creedal declaration, "Our Lord has come" *(maran atha)*, or, more likely, an eschatological prayer, "Our Lord, come!" *(marana tha)*. Gk: 1 Cor. 16:22; cf. Rev. 22:20.

Masoretes. From Hebrew for "tradition." The Jewish scholars who added the vowel points to the Hebrew consonantal text.

Masoretic Text. The vocalized text of the Hebrew Bible, prepared by a group of Jewish scholars around A.D. 700 to preserve the oral pronunciation of the Hebrew words. See Masoretes.

Massoretes. See Masoretes.

Messiah/Messianic. A title from a Hebrew word meaning "to smear," "to anoint." Kings and priests were anointed, i.e., set apart for their service through an anointing ceremony. The term came to be applied to a member of the family of David who would appear to restore the kingdom of Israel. The NT presents Jesus as the Christ (Greek *Christos* or Messiah), the fulfillment of the messianic hopes of the OT.

Messianic Secret. The intentional concealment of Jesus' identity as the Messiah, particularly in Mark, by means of injunctions to silence following miracles (exorcisms and healings) and in training the twelve disciples. William Wrede argued that the secrecy motif was Mark's invention, created to explain how Jesus could be proclaimed as the Messiah when he never claimed as much in his lifetime. The biblical motif is better described as a "Son of God" secret.

Metalanguage. Language about language, the formal terms or grammatical language used to describe language itself. *Ex*: sentence, clause, adjective, alliteration, etc.

Metaphor. An implied comparison, the transfer of a descriptive term to an object to which it is not literally applicable; saying that one thing "is" another. *Heb:* "The LORD is my light and my salvation" (Ps. 27:1). *Gk:* "I am the gate for the sheep" (John 10:7). See parable, simile.

Methodology. The form and methods of study employed in a given discipline.

Metonymy. The use of one word (often an attribute) for another that it suggests, as the effect for the cause, the cause for the effect, the sign for the thing signified. *Heb:* "You prepare a table before me" (Ps. 23:5): "table" is a metonym for food. *Gk:* "This cup is the new covenant in my blood" (Luke 22:20); "cup" is a metonym for its contents.

Midrash (Pl., Midrashim). Rabbinic interpretation of the OT text, both the practice and genre of rabbinic exposition. Its content may be either halakic or haggadic, although the best known midrashim (expository commentaries) are haggadic in nature.

Millennialism/Millennial. From the Latin word "thousand." See chiliasm/chiliastic.

Minor Prophets. The twelve books of the prophets from Hosea to Malachi: the name originated with the rabbis.

Minuscule. Small letters joined together one after another with strokes. Also called cursive writing. Minuscules, the manuscripts of the Greek NT in this script, superseded the uncial manuscripts and now form the great bulk of extant copies, more than 2500 manuscripts.

Mishnah. A codification of the traditional oral law of the Tannaim as distinct from the written Torah of the Pentateuch. Committed to writing ca. A.D. 200 by Rabbi Judah Ha-Nasi (The Prince), it is the basic halakic document of Judaism, containing sixty-three tractates organized into six major divisions. See Talmud.

Mnemonic Device. A literary aid to memory such as an acrostic, catchword, or connected themes. *Heb:* the graded number in Amos' oracles against the nations—"for three crimes . . . and for four" (Amos 1:3, 6, 13; 2:1, 6). *Gk:* the arrangement of Jesus' genealogy into three sections of fourteen names, probably connected with the numerical value *(gematria)* of the name David in Hebrew: *dwd* = 14 (Matt. 1:1–17).

Modifier. A grammatical unit that limits or describes another word, phrase, or clause: usually it has an adjectival or adverbial function.

Modus Operandi. Latin term for "method of operation."

Monism. A philosophical viewpoint that views all reality as a unified whole or in organic connection.

Monograph. A scholarly, carefully documented study of a particular (usually limited) subject as opposed to an introduction or survey.

Monotheism. Belief in the existence of only one God.

Morphology. From Greek *morphe*, "form." A study of the forms (morphemes) that comprise the structure of words in a language. The phoneme is the basic meaningful element of speech; the morpheme the basic meaningful element of grammar. See syntax.

Motif. In literature, a salient feature of the work, especially the recurring theme or dominant feature. It is any repetition that helps unify a work by recalling its earlier occurrence and all that surrounded it. *Heb:* the appeal to return to God is the motif of Jeremiah 3–4. *Gk:* the theme of God's righteousness pervades Paul's exposition in Rom. 3:21–5:21.

MS/MSS. Abbreviations of manuscript/manuscripts.

MT. Abbreviation for Masoretic text.

Mystery Religions. The pagan cults of the Hellenistic age whose adherents gained the promise of redemption by initiation into the secret ceremonies (*Gk: mysterion,* "mystery") of the cults. The more important mystery religions were those of Isis and Osiris from Egypt, of Attis and Cybele from Phrygia in Asia Minor, of Adonis from Syria, of Mithras from Persia, and the Greek cult of Demeter at Eleusis. See History of Religions School.

Myth/Mythological. Popularly, a story that is untrue, imaginative, or fictitious. In biblical studies the word has been applied in a positive and functional way (though misunderstood because of association with its popular meaning) to literary forms that express transcendent realities and truths in this-worldly terms. *Ex:* Some scholars understand *hell* not as a literal place (by this definition of myth) but as the human condition of being separated from God.

NA^{27}. Abbreviation for the Nestle-Aland text of the Greek NT, 27th edition (1993). See Nestle-Aland Greek NT.

Nag Hammadi Codices. An extensive collection of fourth-century Christian and non-Christian Gnostic writings, discovered in 1946 at a site near the modern city of Nag Hammadi in upper Egypt. The twelve papyrus codices represent many literary forms as well as diverse forms of Gnosticism. The texts reinforce the view that Gnosticism has a non-Christian origin but does not predate the NT.

Narrative. A story told, a type of historical account basic to biblical literature organized around a series of events, generally in chronological order, that includes participants and attendant circumstances. *Ex:* the Pentateuchal narratives of creation and Israel's early history and the Gospel accounts of Jesus' ministry.

NASB. Abbreviation for the New American Standard Bible, a revision of the American Standard Version (ASV), first published in its entirety in 1970.

Natural Theology. A philosophical approach that seeks to discover and validate truth claims about God and religious matters from the standpoint of reason and the natural world. Natural theology builds its conceptual framework on the empirical data of the created order.

NEB. Abbreviation for the New English Bible, a translation by British scholars, first published in its entirety in 1970. See REB.

Nestle-Aland GK NT. A critical text of the Greek NT, first published in 1898 by Eberhard Nestle; the 22nd–25th editions (1956–63) were revised by Erwin Nestle and Kurt Aland. The 26th edition (NA^{26}, 1979) and the third edition of the United Bible Societies Greek NT (UBS^3, 1975) printed the same text with differences in punctuation and the critical apparatus. The 27th edition (referred to as NA^{27}, 1993) reproduces the text of NA^{26}.

NIV. Abbreviation for the New International Version, a translation by evangelical scholars from several countries, first published in its entirety in 1978.

NKJV. Abbreviation for the New King James Version, a modernization of the KJV, first published in its entirety in 1982.

NRSV. Abbreviation for the New Revised Standard Version, a revision of the RSV, published in 1989.

Numismatics. The study and collection of coins.

Ontology. Greek, "study of being." That branch of philosophy which is concerned with the fact and nature of ultimate reality or existence.

Oracle. A term used to mean any communication or message from God to humanity.

Oral Tradition. The preliterary stages of a written text; the assumption that a spoken message passed from generation to generation by word of mouth before taking a fixed written form. *Ex:* individual pericopes in the Gospels. See form criticism, tradition criticism.

Ordinal. Short for ordinal number (first, second, third, etc.). See cardinal.

Orthography. The correct writing of words and letters according to standard usage.

Pantheism. The belief that God is everything and that his attributes are expressed in the forces of the universe.

Palestinian Talmud. See Gemara.

Papyrus (Pl., Papyri). An Egyptian plant made into a writing material (hence called papyrus) by the ancient Egyptians and widely used by other ancient peoples. Sheets were formed by cutting the stems into long, thin strips that were placed in two crosswise layers and glued together by hammer blows.

Parable/Parabolic. A short, usually fictitious, narrative in which a moral or spiritual truth is taught; an extended metaphor. In the teaching of Jesus it takes the form of a story or anecdote, an aphorism, or a similitude. The primary meaning of the kingdom of God is spoken in parables. *Heb:* Isa. 5:1–7. *Gk:* Parable of the mustard seed (Matt. 13:31–32).

Paradigm. An example or pattern of a conjugation or declension, showing a word in all its inflectional forms. In form criticism, another name for apothegm.

Paradox. A statement that is self-contradictory or seemingly false or opposed to common sense, but which in fact may be profoundly true; e.g., the sovereignty of God does not preclude human freedom. Biblical language and faith are replete with such paradoxes. *Heb:* "Those who guide this people mislead them, and those who are guided are led astray" (Isa. 9:16). *Gk:* "For when I am weak, then I am strong" (2 Cor. 12:10).

Paraenesis/Paraenetic, Parenesis/Parenetic. In form criticism, used to describe a text containing a series of admonitions, usually ethical and eclectic in nature; a text that exhorts or gives advice. *Heb:* Prov. 1:8–19. *Gk:* 1 Thess. 4:1–12.

Parallel. A word, idea, or construction that is similar in all essential points to another. *Heb:* "For you have been my refuge, a strong tower against the foe" (Ps. 61:3). *Gk:* "He will give you another Counselor . . . the Spirit of truth" (John 14:16–17). See parallelism.

Parallelism. In Hebrew poetry, the relationship between two or more lines. Hebrew poetry is characterized by parallelism of thought rather than by rhyme. The types of parallelism that have been identified in Hebrew poetry include: synonymous, synthetic, antithetic, emblematic, inverted (chiastic), and climactic.

Paraphrase/Paraphrastic. Restatement of a text, passage, or literary composition, giving the meaning in words other than those of the original writer or speaker. Also, a free translation. Do not confuse with periphrasis. *Ex:* The Living Bible is a paraphrase rather than a translation. See dynamic equivalence.

Parataxis. Coordination of words, clauses, and/or sentences in series, without any other expression of their syntactical relationship; the opposite of hypotaxis or subordination. It is characteristic of Hebrew composition (copulative *waw*) and appears in sections of the NT influenced by Semitic style. *Gk:* copulative *kai* at the beginning of Mark's pericopes. See coordinate/coordination.

Parchment. A writing material prepared from the skins of animals. See vellum.

Parenesis. See paraenesis.

Parousia. Greek for "coming," "presence." Used in the NT as a common noun, e.g., "comforted us by the coming of Titus" (2 Cor. 7:6), but primarily as a technical term for the return of Christ. *Gk:* "Concerning the coming of our Lord Jesus Christ" (2 Thess. 2:1).

Parse/Parsing. A pedagogical exercise to aid in morphological analysis; to describe grammatically a part of speech by listing its inflectional modifications and/or its syntactic relationships in the sentence. *Heb:* The verb *'amar* is parsed as qal, perfect, third person, masculine gender and singular in number. *Gk:* the verb *lusomen* is future, active, indicative, first, plural. See analytical lexicon.

Parsing Guide. See analytical lexicon.

Participle. A verbal form that has characteristics of both noun and verb. In Hebrew it represents characteristic, continual, uninterrupted action. *Heb:* "The Spirit of God was hovering over the waters" (Gen. 1:2). The Greek participle is widely used as a substantive, adjective, and adverb in phrases and clauses. *Gk:* ". . . in God, who raised him from the dead and glorified him" (1 Pet. 1:21).

Parts of Speech. The major word classes into which the vocabulary of a language is divided. Traditional divisions in Hebrew and Greek grammar are based on meaning and function: they are noun, pronoun, adjective, verb, adverb, preposition, conjunction, and particle.

Pastoral Epistles. Since the eighteenth century a collective name for 1–2 Timothy and Titus, owing to their nature as pastoral instruction for church ministry.

Patriarchy. Greek for "rule of the father." The common form of social organization in tribal cultures where the father or male ancestry is supreme in the clan or family. *Ex:* the Israelite settlement of Canaan.

Patristics. From Latin *pater*, "father." The branch of theological study that deals with the writings and thought of the Greek and Latin church fathers; in a stricter sense, the major Christian fathers to the close of the eighth century A.D. Also called patrology.

Patrology. Another name for patristics.

Pentateuch. Greek name for the first five books of the OT.

Pericope. A designated portion or unit of Scripture; it may be quite brief or relatively long. Particularly, the self-contained literary units or sections of the Gospels. *Heb:* Ezek. 18:15–17 is a pericope. *Gk:* the healing of the paralytic in Capernaum (Mark 2:1–12).

Personification. A figure of speech in which some human characteristic is attributed to an inanimate or abstract object. *Heb:* "The land we explored devours those living in it" (Num. 13:32). *Gk:* "the stones will cry out" (Luke 19:40).

Pesher (Pl., Pesharim). Hebrew for "commentary." A unique form of haggadic midrash documents found among the Dead Sea Scrolls. The commentary form uses a formula, "this means," and fulfillment motif revealing the mystery of God's purpose. *Ex:* the Habakkuk commentary from Qumran (abbreviated 1QpHab).

Philology. Traditional term for the study of language history; in the widest sense, the study of literature, also linguistics; in classical usage, the study of ancient culture as revealed in history, language, art, literature, and religion.

Plenary Inspiration. From Latin, "full." The view that the Bible is inspired in all its parts. Frequently used synonymously with verbal inspiration.

Pointing. A term that refers to the vowels added by the Masoretes to the consonantal text of the OT (Hebrew was originally written without vowels) in order to preserve the pronunciation of the language at a time when it was in danger of being forgotten.

Polytheism. The belief in many gods. Most cultures of the biblical period espoused this religious practice.

Postapostolic Age. The period immediately following the apostolic age, ca. A.D. 100–150; also called subapostolic age.

Praxis. From Greek, "to practice." The practice of a discipline or skill; the application of theoretical understanding to the realities of life.

Preunderstanding. In hermeneutics, the inevitable assumptions and attitudes that one brings to the interpretation of a text. Its philosophical rationale maintains that everything is understood in a given context and from a given point of view.

Prolegomenon (pl., Prolegomena). An introduction to or preliminary remarks for a study. *Ex:* Julius Wellhausen, *Prolegomena to the History of Ancient Israel.*

Prophets. A class of people in OT times who received messages from God and transmitted them to the people. Also, the name of the third division of the Hebrew Bible.

Prose. The ordinary form of written or spoken language. It does not make use of the special literary forms of structure, meter, and rhythm that are characteristic of poetry.

Proselyte. A convert to a religious faith; in NT times it was used especially of a convert to Judaism.

Protasis. The subordinate or "if" clause that expresses the condition in a conditional sentence (apodosis). *Heb:* "If you fully obey the LORD . . . [protasis], the LORD your God will set you high above all the nations on earth [apodosis]"

(Deut. 28:1). *Gk:* "If you love me [protasis], you will obey what I command [apodosis]" (John 14:15).

Psalter. Another name for the Book of Psalms.

Pseudepigrapha. Greek, "falsely inscribed." When capitalized, the traditional name given to 65 documents of Jewish and Christian origin that were not included in the OT canon or in the Apocrypha. These books were written ca. 250 B.C.–A.D. 200. There are also pseudepigraphal writings connected with the NT.

Pseudonym/Pseudonymous. A fictitious name or a name of a well-known person from the past assumed by a writer who for various reasons prefers not to use his own name. *Ex:* The Wisdom of Solomon in the Apocrypha; many scholars classify the books of Daniel and 2 Peter as pseudonymous; many OT and NT pseudepigrapha, including the *Apocalypse of Moses* and the *Letter of Peter to Philip*.

Q. Siglum for the Synoptic sayings-source or the double tradition of Matthew and Luke; likely derived from the German word *Quelle*: "source." Used in source-critical research of nineteenth-century German scholarship. There is no agreement on the question whether Q was written or oral or on its origin, date, and contents. Although currently disputed, a source like Q remains integral to the two source hypothesis.

Qumran. First-century site, eight-and-a-half miles south of Jericho, on the western edge of the Dead Sea. Eleven caves near the Qumran community yielded the Dead Sea Scrolls.

Rabbi. The transliteration of Hebrew *rabbi,* "my master" or "my teacher." Originally a respectful term of address used in greeting experts in the law, it became a title in the first century A.D. for a member of the Tannaim. *Gk:* used in the Gospels as an honorary designation of Jesus (e.g., Mark 9:5; John 1:38; 6:25), also in its Palestinian Aramaic form, *rabboni* (Mark 10:51; John 20:16).

Real Author. See implied author.

REB. Abbreviation for the Revised English Bible, a revision of the NEB published in 1989.

Received Text. Another name for *textus receptus.*

Recension. An edition of an ancient text that involves a revision of an earlier text form.

Receptor Language. The language into which an original text is translated. In a translation from Greek to English, Greek is the source language, English the receptor language. Also called target language.

Redaction. See redactor.

Redaction Criticism. A study of how the Scriptures reached their final form from the earliest oral form, through a process of editing and composition, to their written form. Especially in the Gospels, the study of the editorial techniques and contributions of the Gospel writers. Also called composition criticism.

Redactor. One who edited a document at a later time to bring it up to date or who in some other way modified a text. One who collects and edits older and smaller units (it is generally assumed) of material into newer, larger compositions. The process of editing is called redaction. *Ex:* Mark as redactor of the earliest gospel tradition.

Regula Fidei. Latin for "rule of faith." The extension of the kerygma to creedal-type confessions used for catechesis and as criteria of orthodoxy in the early church.

Renaissance. Literally, "renewal," "rebirth." In history, the period which began in Italy in the fourteenth century and was marked by a rebirth of interest in classical art and literature.

Rhetoric. The art of persuasive speech or discourse, used especially of literary composition; skillful or artistic use of speech.

Rhetorical Criticism. A study of the structural patterns of a literary unit with attention given to various devices (such as parallelism, chiasmus, etc.) used in its composition. Special attention now focuses on the kinds of persuasion and topics of argumentation that are used by the biblical writers in comparison to forms of ancient rhetoric.

Rhetorical Question. An expression cast in the form of a question, not to elicit an answer but to make a stylistic point of emphasis. The expected answer is understood. A rhetorical question may be asked to introduce a subject which the speaker or writer wishes to discuss. *Heb:* "'Does Job fear God for nothing?' Satan replied" (Job 1:9). *Gk:* "How shall we escape if we ignore such a great salvation?" (Heb. 2:3).

RSV. Abbreviation for the Revised Standard Version, a revision of the RV and ASV in the light of the KJV and not a completely new translation; first published in its entirety in 1952. See NRSV.

RV. Abbreviation for the Revised Version, a British revision of the KJV; it was first published in its entirety in 1885.

Sacerdotalism. Latin for "priesthood." Religious practice governed by an official priesthood (a class distinguished from the laity) that mediates between God and man, being authorized to perform acts of ministry restricted to the priestly class itself.

Saga. A common narrative genre in the OT; it is a story that contains fundamental truths apart from historical consideration; it usually actualizes the event vividly. *Ex:* the story of Sodom in Genesis 19 is classified as a saga.

Salvation History. Translation of the German term *Heilsgeschichte.*

Samaritan Pentateuch. A Hebrew recension of the Pentateuch, retained and used in the Samaritan community during the Second Temple period; a pre-Masoretic textual tradition that was probably revised in the first century B.C. It differs significantly from the Masoretic text but preserves ancient and important readings.

Satire. Prose or poetry in which contemporary vices or follies are held up to ridicule; its popular adaptation in Horace and Juvenal is full of invective and sarcasm. *Ex:* Paul's satirical outburst against the intruders in the church at Corinth (2 Cor. 10–13).

Scribal Error. An obvious mistake made by a scribe in the copying of a document.

Scribe. Originally a secular office held by one who was skilled in the art of writing. In postexilic Judaism the scribes composed a class of professional interpreters and teachers of the Law. See amanuensis.

Scroll. Papyrus, parchment, or leather sheets joined together in rolls, usually 10–12 inches wide and up to 35 feet long. Writing was usually on one side only in vertical columns a few inches wide. The scrolls were read by rolling from left to right between two rollers. See codex.

Second Temple Period. A designation of the Hellenistic-Roman period from the viewpoint of the Jewish commonwealth, beginning with the subjugation of Palestine by Alexander in 332 B.C. and extending through the first Jewish revolt to the destruction of the Temple in A.D. 70.

Semantics. The science of the meaning of words. In biblical studies, especially the view that word meaning is not simply a listing of independent items but a study of fields wherein words interrelate and define each other.

Semitism. A word or construction derived from Hebrew or Aramaic, more specifically those features of the LXX and the Greek NT that reflect the influence of Hebrew (Hebraism) or Aramaic (Aramaism).

Sensus Plenior. Latin for the "fuller meaning" of a passage of Scripture intended by God but not clearly intended by the human author or understood by the original hearers or readers.

Septuagint. From Latin *septuaginta,* "seventy." Greek translation of the OT that (according to the *Letter of Aristeas*) was made by Jews of Alexandria, Egypt, around 250 B.C.; the word is frequently written as LXX. Strictly speaking, the term should apply only to the Pentateuch, but the name came to be used of the entire Greek translation of the OT.

Septuagintism. A word or idiom in the Greek NT that is due to the influence of the Septuagint; because of the influence of Hebrew on the Septuagint, many Septuagintisms are properly Semitisms. *Gk:* the use of *tou* with the infinitive after verbs (Luke 4:10; 9:51; Acts 3:12; 15:20).

Servant Songs. The designation of Isa. 42:1–4; 49:1–6; 50:4–9; 52:13–53:12 because these passages describe one who is a servant of the Lord. The designation was first proposed by Bernard Duhm in 1892.

Shekinah. From Hebrew, "to dwell." A way of referring to the divine presence of God that developed during the Intertestamental period. The word is not found in the Bible but is found in the Targums and rabbinic writings.

Shema. Hebrew, "hear." Taken from the first word of the passage, the title given to Deut. 6:4–9, Judaism's confession of faith, proclaiming the unity of God.

Siglum (Pl., Sigla). A letter (or letters), abbreviation, or symbol used to indicate a manuscript or source of an edited text. *Ex:* 1QpHab for the pesher-commentary on Habakkuk from Qumran cave 1 (See Dead Sea Scrolls); Q for the common tradition of Matthew and Luke not in Mark.

Simile. An explicit comparison (usually with the word "like") of two things that in their general nature are different from each other; cf. metaphor, which is an implied comparison. *Heb:* "I am like a moth to Ephraim" (Hos. 5:12); *Gk:* "They are like children sitting in the marketplace" (Luke 7:32).

Similitude. A parable form proper, a figurative story that compares an unknown reality (the kingdom of God in Jesus' use) to a known image, a typical circumstance, or event. The image depicts things that happen every day and general situations accessible to everyone. *Ex:* the parables of the lost sheep and the lost coin (Luke 15:4–10).

Sine Qua Non. Literally, "without which not." That indispensable or essential element without which something does not exist.

Sitz Im Leben. A German expression used in form criticism to describe the "situation in life," i.e., the cultural context out of which a certain form of literary expression arose, especially the community setting in which a form was developed and understood.

Sola Fides. Latin, "faith alone." Reformation principle of salvation or justification by faith alone apart from human merit.

Sola Scriptura. Latin, "Scripture alone." Reformation principle of authority for life and doctrine by Scripture alone apart from church tradition.

Source Criticism. A special aspect of literary criticism, an analytical methodology used in the study of biblical books to discover individual documents (or sources) that were used in the construction of a particular literary unit as we now have it. *Ex*: the source hypotheses postulated for the Synoptic problem.

Speech Act. A term used in the philosophy of language, associated with the insights of J. L. Austin and J. R. Searle, to refer to those utterances that perform an act as opposed to those that convey information; e.g., in saying "I bless you," the act of blessing occurs.

Structural Analysis, Structural Criticism, Structuralism. A study of the structure of the language to which the biblical texts conform in order to be intelligible; often concerned primarily with the sentence and smaller units. It has also been called stylistic criticism. In a wider sense, it examines the structural features of biblical narratives that can be analyzed in terms of underlying modes of expression inherent to all human thought. Interest in the author's purpose and historical dimensions of the text are minimal.

Subordinate Clause. A clause that is dependent on another clause for its meaning; it does not make sense when standing alone. It is usually introduced by a particle, conjunction, or adverb and can be a part of a main clause or a complex sentence. Also called dependent clause. *Heb:* "because of the evil you have done" (Jer. 4:4). *Gk:* "because of their lack of faith" (Matt. 13:58).

S.V. Abbreviation of Latin *sub voce*, "under the voice [i.e., utterance]" or *sub verbo*, "under the word." It means "look up the reference under the entry or heading named."

Synchronic. A term that refers to the static or fixed aspects of a language at a given point in time. *Heb:* Guttural letters do not take a daghesh forte in Hebrew. *Gk:* The use of the perfect tense in first-century Koine Greek. See diachronic.

Syncretism. The mingling of different religious beliefs through the influence of contact with other cultures. *Ex:* the fusion of traditional Greek cults and oriental beliefs in the mystery religions; the blending of Yahweh worship with Baal worship in Israel.

Synod. A formal assembly of church officials having authority to speak and to make decisions on behalf of the church.

Synonym. A word that has approximately the same meaning and use as another; e.g., "purpose" is a synonym of "intention." *Heb: ish* and *geber* are synonyms for "man." *Gk:* the word "good" renders *agathos, kalos* (Matt. 7:18), and *chrestos* (1 Cor. 15:33).

Synopsis of the Gospels. An edition of Matthew, Mark, and Luke (sometimes with John) arranged in parallel columns: the printed format preserves the full text of each Gospel in sequence. The first printed synopsis was made by J. J. Griesbach (1776). *Ex:* A. Huck and H. Greeven, *Synopse der drei ersten Evangelien;* K. Aland, *Synopsis of the Four Gospels.* See also harmony of the Gospels.

Synoptic Gospels. From Greek *synoptikos,* "seen together." The first three Gospels (Matthew, Mark, and Luke), which present a parallel or common view of the story of Jesus. The term harks back to the printed *Synopsis of the Gospels* by J. J. Griesbach (1776).

Synoptic Problem, The. How to account for the similarities and differences in wording, content, and sequence among the Synoptic Gospels. See also two source hypothesis, Griesbach hypothesis.

Syntax. From Greek *syntaxis,* "arrangement." A study of the arrangement of words to show their mutual relations in the sentence; sentence structures as opposed to morphology, the study of word structure.

Talmud. The name given to the combination of the Mishnah and the Gemara; the compilations of rabbinic teaching and interpretation made by the Amoraim during the third through sixth centuries A.D. in the academies of Babylonia and Palestine. These compilations are called the Babylonian Talmud, comprising some two and one-half million words, and the Palestinian or Jerusalem Talmud, a shorter version.

Tanak. Jewish name for the entire OT. It is a word composed of the first letters of Torah, Nebiim, and Ketubim, the three major divisions of the Hebrew Bible.

Tannaim/Tannaitic. Collective name given to the earlier generations of rabbis (ca. first two centuries A.D.) who were duly qualified to expound the Scriptures with authority; some 120 scholars dating from the last of the "pairs," Hillel and Shammai, to Judah Ha-Nasi, the compiler of the Mishnah. The word *tanna,* "teacher," or "transmitter," was later applied to students who successfully learned the traditions.

Targum. Aramaic for "translation." Usually refers to translations of parts of the OT into Aramaic that originated in the public reading of the OT in the synagogue and involved a certain amount of interpretative comment or paraphrase. *Ex:* the Targum of Onkelos (the Pentateuch) and the Targum of Jonathan (the Prophets).

Tautology. The needless repetition of an idea in different words; a statement true by virtue of its logical form alone. *Ex:* widow woman; it rained rain; God is divine.

Temporal. The expression of duration or point in time. There are a number of ways of expressing the temporal idea in Hebrew and Greek. In Hebrew the preposition *beth* can mean "while." *Heb:* "And while they were in the field" (Gen. 4:8). Greek primarily utilizes particles in case constructions or verbal phrases to express time. *Gk:* "When his family heard about this, they went" (Mark 3:21).

Text-type. A major grouping of biblical manuscripts, based on textual affinities, geographical proximity, and local recensions. The three primary text-types are Alexandrian, Western, and Byzantine or Lucianic.

Textual Criticism. The discipline that attempts to reconstruct the original text of the Bible as nearly as can be determined. The procedure involves reconstruction of the history of transmission and assessment of the relative value of manuscripts. The discipline is also called lower criticism.

Textual Evidence. The cumulative evidence of various manuscripts for a particular reading of the text.

Textus Receptus. The phrase means "received text." The text underlying the earliest printed editions of the Greek NT upon which the King James Version was based; a Byzantine text-type published in two main editions by Stephanus (1550) and Elzevir (1633). Also used to designate any standard text, such as the Ben Asher text of the OT.

Theocracy. Government by the immediate direction of God or through those who are his representatives. *Ex:* During the period of the Judges, Israel was a theocracy.

Theodicy. A vindication of the justice of God in permitting evil to exist. *Ex:* the Book of Job is a theodicy.

Theophany. A manifestation of God in a visible form. *Ex:* the burning bush (Exod. 3:1–5); the living creatures and throne (Ezek. 1:4–28). See epiphany.

Torah. The word properly means "instruction." The name of the first division of the Hebrew Bible composed of the first five books; it is also referred to as the Law.

Tractate. A treatise or essay; a book or section of the Mishnah or Talmud, e.g., the tractate *Pirke Aboth*.

Tradition Criticism, Tradition History. A study of the history of a tradition from its oral to its written stage. It is based on the belief that the material in the OT (and the NT to a lesser extent) passed through many generations by word of mouth before taking a fixed written form. This discipline is also called traditio-historical criticism, oral tradition, and in German *Uberlieferungsgeschichte*.

Translation. Transferring thoughts or writings from one language to another, while preserving the original meaning and intent of the author or speaker. Translation has also been used to describe the phenomenon of Enoch's (Gen. 5:24) and Elijah's (2 Kings 2:11) departing to be with God without experiencing death. See dynamic equivalence, formal equivalence.

Two Document Hypothesis. See two source hypothesis.

Two Source Hypothesis. The most widely-accepted solution to the Synoptic problem, developed in late nineteenth-century German scholarship. It postulates the priority of Mark; this earliest Gospel served as a major source for Matthew and Luke, and the latter two also used another common source, the sayings source, usually called Q. The hypothesis of Mark and Q (held in modified forms) now lacks critical consensus; also called the two document hypothesis. See four document hypothesis, Griesbach hypothesis.

Type/Typology. A method of biblical interpretation that sees persons, things, or events in the OT as foreshadowings or patterns ("types") of persons, things, or events in the NT, particularly as they occur within the framework of history as opposed to allegory. *Ex:* Joseph as a type of Christ.

UBS[4]. Abbreviation for United Bible Societies' text of the Greek NT, fourth edition (1993). See United Bible Societies Greek NT.

Ugaritic. Ancient semitic language of Ugarit in Syria.

Uncial. Early form of Greek, written entirely in capital letters. Any text or manuscript written in capital letters.

United Bible Societies Greek NT. A critical text of the Greek NT, now in its fourth edition (1993; referred to as UBS4). Since UBS3 (1975) this edition prints the same text as the 26th and 27th editions of Nestle-Aland; although its critical apparatus is more selective, the evidence cited is exhaustive for any variant listed.

Urevangelium. German for "primitive" or "original Gospel." The name assigned by G.E. Lessing to the lost Aramaic document that was the common source of the Synoptic Gospels. Also called *Urgospel*, primitive Gospel, or original Gospel.

Urgospel. Another name for *Urevangelium*.

Variant Reading. A term used in textual criticism to refer to differences in the wording of a biblical passage that are discovered by comparing different manuscripts of the passage. *Ex*: a comparison of the Masoretic text with the LXX reveals a number of variants between the two texts. The Dead Sea Scrolls have also revealed variants between the Masoretic text and these scrolls.

Vaticinium Ex Eventu. A Latin term that means "prophecy or prediction made after the event." A disputed principle of historical criticism that assumes that an event known to a biblical writer is turned into a prophecy by literary artifice. *Ex*: The Roman siege of Jerusalem known to Luke is placed back on the lips of Jesus as a prophecy (Luke 19:42–44; 21:20).

Vellum. A leather writing material made from calfskin; sometimes refers to a finer, more expensive product, but often synonymous with parchment.

Verbal Inspiration. The belief that every word in the Bible is inspired by God. A corollary of this view is inerrancy. Verbal inspiration should be distinguished from the dictation theory in that the former is generally held to involve both divine and human authorship (See paradox); frequently used as synonymous with plenary inspiration.

Vernacular. The language of ordinary daily speech in a certain locality or region, as opposed to literary language. It frequently does not follow strict grammatical rules of correct usage.

Version. A translation of the Bible from one language to another; frequently it is dependent on preceding translations. *Ex*: King James Version, Revised Standard Version, New International Version.

Vowel Points. See pointing.

Vulgate. A translation of the Bible into Latin by Jerome at the end of the fourth century A.D.; the "common" version of the medieval Catholic church. Jerome translated the OT directly from the Hebrew text current in his day; the NT is based on the Old Latin and underwent curious revision.

Wisdom. Wisdom was a phenomenon of ancient Near Eastern culture that observed human experience and benefitted from it in order to gain mastery of life. It has been described as a quality of mind that distinguished the wise man from others (he is often contrasted with the "fool" in the OT). His wisdom enabled him to use factual knowledge to make proper judgments involving everyday living and so he was able to live well and enjoy success. Wisdom was also considered to be a quality inherent in God. Wise living in Israel was associated with following the precepts and counsel of God. Wise men exercised significant influence in the royal courts as well as among the common people. See wisdom literature.

Wisdom Literature. The name given to a type of literature common to the ancient Near East. Job, Proverbs, and Ecclesiastes are the wisdom books of the OT, but wisdom writing is also found elsewhere in the OT. See wisdom.

Worldview. The framework through which one sees reality; the set of convictions by which one knows and interprets reality. A Christian worldview includes such things as belief in the supernatural and moral certainty. A modern worldview is skeptical of the supernatural and exalts reason. A post-modern worldview is morally relativistic and pluralistic in its approach to truth.

Writings, The. The third division of the Hebrew Bible; also called the Hagiographa or Ketubim. See Torah.

Yahweh, Jahweh. The name for God found most frequently in the OT; it occurs approximately 6,823 times. It is the suggested pronunciation of the Hebrew tetragram. The word is usually translated as "The Lord" but sometimes as "Jehovah" (based on a misunderstanding of the combination of the consonants of YHWH and the vowels of *Adonai*). Most English versions use "LORD" for Yahweh, "Lord" for Adonai; cf. Exod. 4: 10.

▼

A Student's Guide to Reference Books and Biblical Commentaries

There is no end to the writing of books on the Bible. They are to the Bible student what wrenches are to a mechanic—the tools of the trade; likewise, they should be purchased for a specific use. We recommend that the student become acquainted with a book before buying it. The question to ask is, Will (or can) I use it? To that end we have compiled a selected bibliography to guide the Bible student in the use of reference books and commentaries. We offer two rules-of-thumb: (1) use it first (spend time in the library); (2) be selective and balanced. The great Manchester scholar, T. W. Manson, once said that any discipline could be mastered by use of no more than a hundred books—the right books, of course.

To guide the student we have marked several entries with either an asterisk (*) or dagger (†). We do not intend thereby to suggest that these books alone should be consulted, rather that these are basic and representative of two poles of scholarship: the more popular, introductory level, and the more critical, technical level.

*. . . books marked by asterisk are expository, more popular, and meaningful for beginning students.

†. . . books marked by dagger are linguistic, more technical, and intended for advanced students.

Reference Books

Bibliography. For a fuller discussion of commentaries and exegetical tools in general we note the following guides:

*Carson, D. A. *New Testament Commentary Survey.* 4th ed. Grand Rapids: Baker, 1993.

Childs, B. S. *Old Testament Books for Pastor and Teacher.* Philadelphia: Westminster, 1977.

†Danker, F. W. *Multipurpose Tools for Bible Study.* Rev. and exp. ed. Minneapolis: Augsburg Fortress, 1993.

†Fitzmyer, J. A. *An Introductory Bibliography for the Study of Scripture.* 3d rev. ed. Subsidia Biblica 3. Rome: Biblical Institute, 1990.

France, R. T. *A Bibliographic Guide to New Testament Research.* 3d ed. Sheffield: JSOT, 1979.

*Longman, Tremper III. *Old Testament Commentary Survey.* 2d ed. Grand Rapids: Baker, 1995.

Martin, R. P. *New Testament Books for Pastor and Teacher.* Philadelphia: Westminster, 1984.

Stuart, Douglas. *A Guide to Selecting and Using Bible Commentaries.* Dallas: Word, 1990.

One-Volume Reference. The beginning student will find the following single volumes from Broadman Press to be a dependable reference trio that is generously illustrated:

Dockery, David S., ed. *Holman Bible Handbook.* Nashville: Broadman, 1992.

Butler, Trent C., ed. *Holman Bible Dictionary.* Nashville: Broadman, 1991.

Brisco, Thomas V. *Holman Bible Atlas.* Nashville: Broadman, forthcoming.

Bible Dictionary. The multivolume works should be consulted for standard essays on a given biblical topic.

Achtemeier, P. J., ed. *Harper's Bible Dictionary.* San Francisco: Harper & Row, 1985.

†Bromiley, G. W., ed. *International Standard Bible Encyclopedia.* 4 vols. Rev. ed. Grand Rapids: Eerdmans, 1979–86.

*Douglas, J. D., ed. *The New Bible Dictionary.* Rev. ed. Downers Grove, Ill.: InterVarsity, 1984.

†Freedman, D. N., ed. *The Anchor Bible Dictionary.* 6 vols. Garden City, N.Y.: Doubleday, 1992.

Bible Atlas. Chronological data, maps, charts, and photographs of the Bible lands are available in the following student atlases:

Aharoni, Yohannon, and Michael Avi-Yonah. *The Macmillan Bible Atlas.* Rev. ed. New York: Macmillan, 1977.

Beitzel, Barry. *The Moody Atlas of Bible Lands.* Chicago: Moody, 1985.

Paterson, John H., Donald J. Wiseman, John J. Bimson, and J. P. Kane, eds. *New Bible Atlas.* Downers Grove, Ill.: InterVarsity, 1985.

Biblical Word Studies. In addition to the standard lexicons of Hebrew and Greek, the student should consult the following sets for extended treatments of individual words:

†Botterweck, G. J., Helmer Ringgren, and H.J. Fabry, eds. *Theological Dictionary of the Old Testament.* 7 vols. of 12 to date. Grand Rapids: Eerdmans, 1974–.

*Brown, Colin, ed. *New International Dictionary of New Testament Theology.* 4 vols. Grand Rapids: Zondervan, 1975–78.

†Kittel, Gerhard, and Gerhard Friedrich, eds. *Theological Dictionary of the New Testament.* Translated by G. W. Bromiley. 10 vols. Grand Rapids: Eerdmans, 1964–78.

*Van Gemeren, William A., et al., eds. *New International Dictionary of Old Testament Theology.* 3 vols. Grand Rapids: Zondervan, forthcoming.

Biblical Commentaries

By way of suggested reading, we have marked a handful of commentaries for each book of the Bible. Again, we do not intend by these selections to endorse all the interpretations set forth in them. We value them because they are sound and helpful, not because they are always right. The following list features representative approaches to the biblical text. A given text should be studied, if possible, in the original language. By way of general approach, the student should consult available volumes on each biblical book from the following series:

Anchor Bible (Doubleday)

Expositor's Bible Commentary (Zondervan)

Hermeneia (Fortress)

Interpretation (John Knox)

International Critical Commentary (T. & T. Clark)

New American Commentary (Broadman)

New Century Bible (Eerdmans)

New International Commentary on the Old and New Testament (Eerdmans)

New Interpreter's Bible (Abingdon)

Tyndale Old and New Testament Commentaries (InterVarsity and Eerdmans)

Word Biblical Commentary (Word)

For brief exposition and helpful general articles, we recommend the following single volume commentaries:

Murphy, Roland E., Raymond E. Brown, and Joseph A. Fitzmyer, eds. *The New Jerome Biblical Commentary.* Englewood Cliffs, N.J.: Prentice Hall, 1990.

Wenham, G. J., J. A. Motyer, D. A. Carson, and R. T. France, eds. *New Bible Commentary.* 4th ed. Downers Grove, Ill.: InterVarsity, 1994.

Genesis

Atkinson, David. *The Message of Genesis 1–11.* Bible Speaks Today. Downers Grove, Ill.: InterVarsity, 1990.

Baldwin, Joyce G. *The Message of Genesis 12–50.* Bible Speaks Today. Downers Grove, Ill.: InterVarsity, 1986.

*Bruggemann, Walter. *Genesis.* Interpretation. Atlanta: John Knox, 1982.

Cassuto, Umberto. *A Commentary on the Book of Genesis.* 2 vols. Jerusalem: Magnes, 1961–64.

Driver, S. R. *The Book of Genesis.* 5th ed., enl. Westminster Commentaries. London: Methuen, 1948.

Hamilton, Victor P. *The Book of Genesis: Chapters 1–17.* New International Commentary on the Old Testament. Grand Rapids: Eerdmans, 1990.

———. *The Book of Genesis: Chapters 18–50.* New International Commentary on the Old Testament. Grand Rapids: Eerdmans, 1995.

Keil, C. F., and F. Delitzsch. *The Pentateuch.* Translated by James Martin. 3 vols. Biblical Commentary on the Old Testament. Edinburgh: T. & T. Clark, 1865.

*Kidner, Derek. *Genesis.* Tyndale Old Testament Commentaries. Downers Grove, Ill.: Inter-Varsity, 1967.

Leupold, H. C. *Exposition of Genesis.* Grand Rapids: Baker, 1956.

Rad, Gerhard von. *Genesis: A Commentary.* Rev. ed. Translated by J. H. Marks. Old Testament Library. Philadelphia: Westminster, 1973.

Skinner, John. *A Critical and Exegetical Commentary on Genesis.* 3d ed. International Critical Commentary. New York: Scribner's Sons, 1930.

†Westermann, Claus. *Genesis 1–11: A Commentary.* Translated by John J. Scullion. Minneapolis: Augsburg, 1984.

†———. *Genesis 12–36: A Commentary.* Translated by John J. Scullion. Minneapolis: Augsburg, 1984.

†———. *Genesis 37–50: A Commentary.* Translated by John J. Scullion. Minneapolis: Augsburg, 1984.

†Wenham, Gordon J. *Genesis 1–15.* Word Biblical Commentary. Waco: Word, 1987.

†———. *Genesis 16–50.* Word Biblical Commentary. Dallas: Word, 1994.

Exodus

†Cassuto, Umberto. *A Commentary on the Book of Exodus.* Translated by I. Abrahams. Jerusalem: Magnes, 1967.

†Childs, Brevard S. *The Book of Exodus.* Old Testament Library. Philadelphia: Westminster, 1974.

Clements, Ronald E. *Exodus.* Cambridge Bible Commentary. Cambridge: Cambridge University, 1972.

*Cole, R. A. *Exodus.* Tyndale Old Testament Commentaries. Grand Rapids: Eerdmans, 1973.

Davidman, Joy. *Smoke on the Mountain.* Philadelphia: Westminster, 1954.

Durham, John I. *Exodus.* Word Biblical Commentary. Waco: Word, 1987.

Ellison, H. L. *Exodus.* Daily Study Bible. Philadelphia: Westminster, 1982.

Fretheim, Terence E. *Exodus.* Interpretation. Louisville: John Knox, 1991.

Hyatt, J. P. *Exodus.* New Century Bible. London: Oliphants, 1971.

Keil, C. F., and F. Delitzsch. *The Pentateuch.* 3 vols. Translated by James Martin. Biblical Commentary on the Old Testament. Edinburgh: T. & T. Clark, 1865.

Noth, Martin. *Exodus*. Translated by J. Bowden. Old Testament Library. Philadelphia: Westminster, 1962.

*Ramm, Bernard. *His Way Out: A Fresh Look at Exodus*. Glendale, Calif.: Regal Books, 1974.

Sarna, Nahum M. *Exodus Shemot*. JPS Torah Commentary. Philadelphia: Jewish Publication Society, 1991.

Leviticus

*Harrison, R. K. *Leviticus*. Tyndale Old Testament Commentaries. Downers Grove, Ill.: InterVarsity, 1980.

†Hartley, John E. *Leviticus*. Word Biblical Commentary. Dallas: Word, 1992.

Keil, C. F., and F. Delitzsch. *The Pentateuch*. Translated by James Martin. 3 vols. Biblical Commentary on the Old Testament. Edinburgh: T. & T. Clark, 1865.

*Knight, G. A. F. *Leviticus*. Daily Study Bible. Philadelphia: Westminster, 1981.

Levine, Baruch A. *Leviticus Va-yikra*. JPS Torah Commentary. Philadelphia: Jewish Publication Society, 1989.

Mays, James L. *The Book of Leviticus, The Book of Numbers*. The Layman's Bible Commentary. Vol. 4. Richmond: John Knox, 1963.

Milgrom, Jacob. *Leviticus 1–16*. Anchor Bible. New York: Doubleday, 1991.

Noth, Martin. *Leviticus*. Translated by J. E. Anderson. The Old Testament Library. Philadelphia: Westminster, 1977.

Snaith, Norman H. *Leviticus and Numbers*. New Century Bible. London: Thomas Nelson, 1967.

†Wenham, G. J. *The Book of Leviticus*. New International Commentary on the Old Testament. Grand Rapids: Eerdmans, 1979.

Numbers

†Ashley, Timothy R. *Numbers*. New International Commentary on the Old Testament. Grand Rapids: Eerdmans, 1993.

Budd, Philip J. *Numbers*. Word Biblical Commentary. Waco: Word, 1984.

†Gray, George Buchanan. *A Critical and Exegetical Commentary on Numbers*. International Critical Commentary. Edinburgh: T. & T. Clark, 1903.

Greenstone, Julius H. *Numbers, with Commentary*. Philadelphia: Jewish Publication Society of America, 1939.

Harrison, R. K. *Numbers*. Wycliffe Exegetical Commentary. Grand Rapids: Baker, 1993.

*Huey, F. B. *Numbers*. Bible Study Commentary. Grand Rapids: Zondervan, 1981.

Keil, C. F., and F. Delitzsch. *The Pentateuch*. Translated by James Martin. 3 vols. Biblical Commentary on the Old Testament. Edinburgh: T. & T. Clark, 1865.

Mays, James L. *The Book of Leviticus, The Book of Numbers*. The Layman's Bible Commentary. Vol. 4. Richmond: John Knox, 1963.

Milgrom, Jacob. *Numbers Ba-midbar.* JPS Torah Commentary. Philadelphia: Jewish Publication Society, 1990.

Noth, Martin. *Numbers: A Commentary.* Translated by James D. Martin. Old Testament Library. Philadelphia: Westminster, 1968.

Riggans, Walter. *Numbers.* Daily Study Bible. Philadelphia: Westminster, 1983.

Snaith, Norman H. *Leviticus and Numbers.* New Century Bible. London: Thomas Nelson, 1967.

*Wenham, Gordon J. *Numbers.* Tyndale Old Testament Commentaries. Downers Grove, Ill.: InterVarsity, 1981.

Deuteronomy

Brown, Raymond. *The Message of Deuteronomy.* Bible Speaks Today. Downers Grove, Ill.: InterVarsity, 1993.

Christensen, Duane L. *Deuteronomy 1–11.* Word Biblical Commentary. Dallas: Word, 1991.

———. *Deuteronomy 12–34.* Word Biblical Commentary. Dallas: Word, forthcoming.

Clements, R. E. *God's Chosen People: A Theological Interpretation of the Book of Deuteronomy.* London: SCM Press, 1968.

Craigie, Peter C. *The Book of Deuteronomy.* New International Commentary on the Old Testament. Grand Rapids: Eerdmans, 1976.

†Driver, S. R. *A Critical and Exegetical Commentary on Deuteronomy.* International Critical Commentary. New York: Scribner's Sons, 1902.

Keil, C. F., and F. Delitzsch. *The Pentateuch.* Translated by James Martin. 3 vols. Biblical Commentary on the Old Testament. Edinburgh: T. & T. Clark, 1865.

Mayes, A. D. H. *Deuteronomy.* New Century Bible. London: Oliphants, 1979.

*Merrill, Eugene H. *Deuteronomy.* New American Commentary. Nashville: Broadman, 1994.

Miller, Patrick D. *Deuteronomy.* Interpretation. Louisville: John Knox, 1990.

Payne, David F. *Deuteronomy.* Daily Study Bible. Philadelphia: Westminster, 1985.

†Rad, Gerhard von. *Deuteronomy.* Translated by Dorothea Barton. Old Testament Library. Philadelphia: Westminster, 1966.

Smith, George Adam. *The Book of Deuteronomy.* Cambridge Bible for Schools and Colleges. Rev. ed. Cambridge: Cambridge University, 1918.

*Thompson, J. A. *Deuteronomy.* Tyndale Old Testament Commentaries. Downers Grove, Ill.: InterVarsity, 1974.

Wright, G. E. "Deuteronomy: Introduction and Exegesis." In *The Interpreter's Bible.* Vol. 2. Nashville: Abingdon, 1953.

Joshua

†Boling, Robert G. *Joshua: A New Translation with Notes and Commentary.* Anchor Bible. Garden City, N.Y.: Doubleday, 1982.

Bratcher, Robert G., and Barclay M. Newman. *Translator's Handbook on the Book of Joshua.* New York: United Bible Societies, 1983.

*Bright, John. "Joshua: Introduction and Exegesis." In *The Interpreter's Bible.* Vol. 2. Nashville: Abingdon, 1953.

†Butler, Trent C. *Joshua.* Word Biblical Commentary. Waco: Word, 1983.

Cohen, Arthur. *Joshua and Judges: Hebrew Text and English Translation, with an Introduction and Commentary.* Soncino Books of the Bible. London: Soncino, 1950.

Gray, John. *Joshua, Judges and Ruth.* New Century Bible. London: Thomas Nelson, 1967.

Hamlin, E. John. *Inheriting the Land: A Commentary on the Book of Joshua.* International Theological Commentary. Grand Rapids: Eerdmans, 1983.

Keil, C. F., and F. Delitzsch. *Joshua, Judges, Ruth.* Translated by James Martin. Edinburgh: T. & T. Clark, 1887.

†Soggin, J. Alberto. *Joshua: A Commentary.* Translated by R. A. Wilson. Old Testament Library. Philadelphia: Westminster, 1972.

*Woudstra, Marten H. *The Book of Joshua.* New International Commentary on the Old Testament. Grand Rapids: Eerdmans, 1981.

Judges and Ruth

Atkinson, David. *The Message of Ruth.* Bible Speaks Today. Downers Grove, Ill.: Inter-Varsity, 1985.

*Auld, A. Graeme. *Joshua, Judges and Ruth.* Daily Study Bible. Philadelphia: Westminster, 1984.

†Boling, Robert G. *Judges.* Anchor Bible. Garden City, N.Y.: Doubleday, 1975.

Campbell, Edward F. *Ruth.* Anchor Bible. Garden City, N.Y.: Doubleday, 1975.

*Cundall, Arthur Ernest, and Leon Morris. *Judges and Ruth.* Tyndale Old Testament Commentaries. Grand Rapids: Eerdmans, 1968.

Davis, Dale Ralph. *Such a Great Salvation: Expositions of the Book of Judges.* Grand Rapids: Baker, 1990.

Gray, John. *Joshua, Judges and Ruth.* New Century Bible. London: Thomas Nelson, 1967.

Hubbard, Robert L. Jr. *The Book of Ruth.* New International Commentary on the Old Testament. Grand Rapids: Eerdmans, 1988.

Keil, C. F., and F. Delitzsch. *Joshua, Judges, Ruth.* Translated by James Martin. Edinburgh: T. & T. Clark, 1887.

†Moore, George F. *A Critical and Exegetical Commentary on Judges.* International Critical Commentary. New York: Scribner, 1895.

†Soggin, J. Alberto. *Judges: A Commentary.* Translated by John Bowden. Old Testament Library. Philadelphia: Westminster, 1981.

Wilcock, Michael. *The Message of Judges.* Bible Speaks Today. Downers Grove, Ill.: InterVarsity, 1992.

First and Second Samuel

Ackroyd, Peter. *The First Book of Samuel.* Cambridge Bible Commentary. Cambridge: Cambridge University, 1977.

————. *The Second Book of Samuel.* Cambridge Bible Commentary. Cambridge: Cambridge University, 1977.

†Anderson, A. A. *2 Samuel.* Word Biblical Commentary. Dallas: Word, 1989.

*Baldwin, Joyce G. *1 and 2 Samuel.* Tyndale Old Testament Commentaries. Downers Grove, Ill.: InterVarsity, 1988.

*Brueggeman, Walter. *First and Second Samuel.* Interpretation. Louisville: John Knox, 1990.

Caird, George B. "The First and Second Books of Samuel: Introduction and Exegesis." In *The Interpreter's Bible.* Vol. 2. Nashville: Abingdon, 1953.

†Driver, S. R. *Notes on the Hebrew Text and the Topography of the Books of Samuel.* 2d ed. Oxford: Clarendon, 1913.

†Hertzberg, H. W. *I and II Samuel.* Old Testament Library. Translated by John Bowden. Philadelphia: Westminster, 1964.

Mauchline, John. *1 and 2 Samuel.* New Century Bible. London: Oliphants, 1971.

McCarter, P. Kyle. *1 Samuel.* Anchor Bible. Garden City, N.Y.: Doubleday, 1980.

————. *2 Samuel.* Anchor Bible. Garden City, N.Y.: Doubleday, 1984.

*Payne, D. F. *I & II Samuel.* Daily Study Bible. Philadelphia: Westminster, 1982.

Smith, H. P. A *Critical and Exegetical Commentary on the Books of Samuel.* International Critical Commentary. Edinburgh: T. & T. Clark, 1904.

First and Second Kings

Auld, A. Graeme. *I & II Kings.* Daily Study Bible. Philadelphia: Westminster, 1986.

Brueggemann, Walter. *1 Kings; 2 Kings.* Atlanta: John Knox, 1982.

†DeVries, S. J. *1 Kings.* Word Biblical Commentary. Waco: Word, 1985.

†Gray, John. *I & II Kings: A Commentary.* 2d ed. Old Testament Library. Philadelphia: Westminster, 1970.

Hobbs, T. R. *2 Kings.* Word Biblical Commentary. Waco: Word, 1985.

*House, Paul R. *1, 2 Kings.* New American Commentary. Nashville: Broadman, 1995.

†Montgomery, James A. *A Critical and Exegetical Commentary on the Books of Kings.* 2d ed. Edited by H. S. Gehman. International Critical Commentary. Edinburgh: T. & T. Clark, 1951.

Slotki, I. W. *Kings: Hebrew Text and English Translation, with an Introduction and Commentary.* Soncino Books of the Bible. London: Soncino, 1950.

Wifall, Walter. *Court History of Israel: A Commentary on First and Second Kings.* St. Louis: Clayton, 1975.

*Wiseman, Donald J. *1 & 2 Kings*. Tyndale Old Testament Commentaries. Downers Grove, Ill.: InterVarsity, 1992.

First and Second Chronicles

†Braun, Roddy. *1 Chronicles*. Word Biblical Commentary. Waco: Word, 1986.

Dentan, Robert C. *The First and Second Books of the Kings; The First and Second Books of the Chronicles*. Layman's Bible Commentary. Vol. 7. Richmond: John Knox, 1964.

†Dillard, Raymond B. *2 Chronicles*. Word Biblical Commentary. Waco: Word, 1987

Francisco, Clyde T. "First and Second Chronicles." In the *Broadman Bible Commentary*. Vol. 3. Nashville: Broadman, 1970.

Keil, C. F. *Books of the Chronicles*. Translated by Andrew Harper. Clark's Foreign Theological Library. Edinburgh: T. & T. Clark, 1872.

Myers, Jacob M. *I Chronicles*. Anchor Bible. Garden City, N.Y.: Doubleday, 1965.

————. *II Chronicles*. Anchor Bible. Garden City, N.Y.: Doubleday, 1965.

*Selman, Martin J. *1 Chronicles*. Tyndale Old Testament Commentary. Downers Grove, Ill.: InterVarsity Press, 1994.

*————. *2 Chronicles*. Tyndale Old Testament Commentary. Downers Grove, Ill.: InterVarsity Press, 1994.

Thompson, J. A. *1, 2 Chronicles*. New American Commentary. Nashville: Broadman, 1994.

*Williamson, H. G. M. *1 and 2 Chronicles*. New Century Bible. Grand Rapids: Eerdmans, 1982.

Ezra and Nehemiah

†Blenkinsopp, Joseph. *Ezra-Nehemiah: A Commentary*. The Old Testament Library. Philadelphia: Westminster, 1988.

*Breneman, Mervin. *Ezra, Nehemiah, Esther*. New American Commentary. Nashville: Broadman, 1993.

Clines, David J. A. *Ezra, Nehemiah, Esther*. New Century Bible. Grand Rapids: Eerdmans, 1984.

Fensham, Charles F. *Books of Ezra and Nehemiah*. New International Commentary on the Old Testament. Grand Rapids: Eerdmans, 1982.

Holmgren, Fredrick Carlson. *Ezra and Nehemiah: Israel Alive Again*. International Theological Commentary. Grand Rapids: Eerdmans, 1987.

Keil, C. F. *Ezra, Nehemiah and Esther*. Translated by Sophia Taylor. Biblical Commentary on the Old Testament. Edinburgh: T. & T. Clark, 1873.

*Kidner, Derek. *Ezra and Nehemiah*. Tyndale Old Testament Commentaries. Downers Grove, Ill.: InterVarsity, 1979.

Myers, Jacob M. *Ezra, Nehemiah*. Anchor Bible. Garden City, N.Y.: Doubleday, 1965.

†Williamson, H. G. M. *Ezra, Nehemiah*. Word Biblical Commentary. Waco: Word, 1985.

Esther

Anderson, Bernhard W. "Esther: Introduction and Exegesis." In *The Interpreter's Bible.* Vol. 3. Nashville: Abingdon, 1954.

*Baldwin, Joyce G. *Esther: An Introduction and Commentary.* Tyndale Old Testament Commentaries. Downers Grove, Ill.: InterVarsity, 1984.

*Breneman, Mervin. *Ezra, Nehemiah, Esther.* New American Commentary. Nashville: Broadman, 1993.

†Clines, D. J. *Ezra, Nehemiah, Esther.* New Century Bible. Grand Rapids: Eerdmans, 1984.

Coggins, R. J., and S. Paul Re'emi. *Israel Among the Nations: A Commentary on the Books of Nahum and Obadiah and Esther.* International Theological Commentary. Grand Rapids: Eerdmans, 1985.

Keil, C. F. *Ezra, Nehemiah, and Esther.* Translated by Sophia Taylor. Biblical Commentary on the Old Testament. Edinburgh: T. & T. Clark, 1873.

†Moore, Carey A. *Esther.* Anchor Bible. Garden City, N.Y.: Doubleday, 1971.

Job

*Anderson, Francis I. *Job.* Tyndale Old Testament Commentaries. Downers Grove, Ill.: InterVarsity, 1976.

*Bennett, T. Miles. *When Human Wisdom Fails: An Exposition of the Book of Job.* Grand Rapids: Baker, 1971.

†Clines, David J. A. *Job 1–20.* Word Biblical Commentary. Dallas: Word, 1989.

Davidson, A. B. *The Book of Job.* Cambridge Bible for Schools and Colleges. Cambridge: Cambridge University, 1918.

Delitzsch, Franz. *The Book of Job.* Translated by Francis Bolton. 2 vols. Biblical Commentary on the Old Testament. Edinburgh: T. & T. Clark, 1866.

†Dhorme, Edouard. *A Commentary on the Book of Job.* Translated by Harold Knight. London: Thomas Nelson, 1967.

†Driver, S. R., and G. B. Gray. *A Critical and Exegetical Commentary on Job.* International Critical Commentary. Edinburgh: T. & T. Clark, 1921.

*Ellison, H. L. *From Tragedy to Triumph.* London: Paternoster, 1958.

Gordis, Robert. *Book of Job: Commentary, New Translation and Special Studies.* New York: Jewish Theological Seminary, 1978.

†Habel, Norman C. *Book of Job: A Commentary.* Old Testament Library. Philadelphia: Westminster, 1985.

Hartley, John E. *The Book of Job.* New International Commentary on the Old Testament. Grand Rapids: Eerdmans, 1988.

†Rowley, H. H. *Job.* New Century Bible. London: Thomas Nelson, 1970.

Psalms

Alexander, J. A. *Psalms, Translated and Explained.* 6th ed. 3 vols. New York: Scribner, 1869.

Allen, Leslie C. *Psalms 101–150.* Word Biblical Commentary. Waco: Word, 1983.

Anderson, Arnold A. *The Book of Psalms*. 2 vols. New Century Bible. London: Oliphants, 1972.

Briggs, C. A., and E. G. Briggs. *A Critical and Exegetical Commentary on the Book of Psalms*. 2 vols. The International Critical Commentary. Edinburgh: T. & T. Clark, 1906–7.

Craigie, Peter C. *Psalms 1–50*. Word Biblical Commentary. Waco: Word, 1983.

†Dahood, Mitchell. *Psalms*. 3 vols. Anchor Bible. Garden City, N.Y.: Doubleday, 1966–70.

Delitzsch, Franz. *A Biblical Commentary on the Book of Psalms*. Translated by D. Eaton. 3 vols. New York: Funk and Wagnalls, 1883.

*Kidner, Derek. *Psalms*. 2 vols. Tyndale Old Testament Commentaries. Downers Grove, Ill.: InterVarsity, 1973.

Knight, G. A. F. *Psalms*. 2 vols. Daily Study Bible. Philadelphia: Westminster, 1982.

Kraus, Hans-Joachim. *Psalms 1–59*. Translated by Hilton C. Oswald. Minneapolis: Augsburg, 1988.

————. *Psalms 60–150*. Translated by Hilton C. Oswald. Minneapolis: Augsburg, 1989.

*Mays, James L. *Psalms*. Interpretation. Louisville: Westminster/John Knox, 1994.

*Leupold, H. C. *Exposition of Psalms*. Columbus, Ohio: Wartburg, 1959.

Mowinckel, Sigmund. *The Psalms in Israel's Worship*. Oxford: Basil Blackwell, 1962.

Perowne, J. J. Stewart. *The Book of Psalms: A New Translation with Introduction and Notes*. 2 vols. 8th ed. Cambridge: Deighton Bell, 1892.

Tate, Marvin E. *Psalms 51–100*. Word Biblical Commentary. Dallas: Word, 1990.

†Weiser, Artur. *Psalms*. Translated by Herbert Hartwell. Old Testament Library. Philadelphia: Westminster, 1962.

Proverbs

Delitzsch, Franz J. *Biblical Commentary on the Proverbs of Solomon*. Translated by M. G. Easton. Clark's Foreign Theological Library. Edinburgh: T. & T. Clark, 1874–75.

*Garrett, Duane A. *Proverbs, Ecclesiastes, Song of Songs*. New American Commentary. Nashville: Broadman, 1993.

*Kidner, Derek. *Proverbs*. Tyndale Old Testament Commentaries. Downers Grove, Ill.: InterVarsity Press, 1964.

†McKane, William. *Proverbs, A New Approach*. Old Testament Library. Philadelphia: Westminster, 1970.

Oesterley, W. O. E. *Book of Proverbs with Introduction and Notes*. Westminster Commentaries. London: Methuen, 1929.

*Rylaarsdam, John Coert. *Proverbs, Ecclesiastes, and the Song of Solomon*. Layman's Bible Commentary. Vol. 10. Richmond: John Knox, 1964.

Scott, R. B. Y. *Proverbs, Ecclesiastes.* Anchor Bible. Garden City, N.Y.: Doubleday, 1965.

†Toy, Crawford Howell. *Critical and Exegetical Commentary on the Book of Proverbs.* International Critical Commentary. New York: Scribner's Sons, 1899.

Whybray, R. Norman. *Proverbs.* New Century Bible. Grand Rapids: Eerdmans, 1995.

Ecclesiastes

Barton, George Aaron. *Critical and Exegetical Commentary on the Book of Ecclesiastes.* International Critical Commentary. New York: Scribner, 1908.

†Crenshaw, James L. *Ecclesiastes: A Commentary.* Old Testament Library. Philadelphia: Westminster, 1987.

Delitzsch, Franz J. *Commentary on the Song of Solomon and Ecclesiastes.* Translated by M. G. Easton. Clark's Foreign Theological Library. Edinburgh: T. & T. Clark, 1877.

*Eaton, Michael A. *Ecclesiastes.* Tyndale Old Testament Commentaries. Downers Grove, Ill.: InterVarsity, 1983.

*Garrett, Duane A. *Proverbs, Ecclesiastes, Song of Songs.* New American Commentary. Nashville: Broadman, 1993.

Gordis, Robert. *Koheleth: The Man and His World.* Texts and Studies of the Jewish Theological Seminary of America. Vol. 19. New York: Jewish Theological Seminary of America, 1951.

Kaiser, Walter C. *Ecclesiastes: Total Life.* Chicago: Moody Press, 1979.

*Kidner, Derek. *The Message of Ecclesiastes.* Downers Grove, Ill.: InterVarsity, 1976.

Leupold, H. C. *Exposition of Ecclesiastes.* Columbus, Ohio: Wartburg, 1952.

†Murphy, Roland. *Ecclesiastes.* Word Biblical Commentary. Dallas: Word, 1992.

Rylaarsdam, John Coert. *Proverbs, Ecclesiastes, and the Song of Solomon.* Layman's Bible Commentary. Vol. 10. Richmond: John Knox, 1964.

Whybray, R. N. *Ecclesiastes.* New Century Bible. Grand Rapids: Eerdmans, 1989.

Song of Solomon

*Carr, G. Lloyd. *Song of Solomon.* Tyndale Old Testament Commentaries. Downer's Grove, Ill.: InterVarsity Press, 1984.

Delitzsch, Franz J. *Commentary on the Song of Solomon and Ecclesiastes.* Translated by M. G. Easton. Clark's Foreign Theological Library. Edinburgh: T. & T. Clark, 1877.

*Garrett, Duane A. *Proverbs, Ecclesiastes, Song of Songs.* New American Commentary. Nashville: Broadman, 1993.

†Gordis, Robert. *Song of Songs and Lamentations: A Study, Modern Translation and Commentary.* New York: KTAV, 1974.

Gledhill, Tom. *The Message of the Song of Songs.* Bible Speaks Today. Downers Grove, Ill.: InterVarsity, 1994.

Harper, Andrew. *Song of Solomon: With Introduction and Notes.* Cambridge Bible for Schools and Colleges. Cambridge: Cambridge University, 1902.

†Murphy, Roland. *Song of Songs.* Hermeneia. Philadelphia: Fortress, 1990.

Pope, Marvin H. *Song of Songs: A New Translation with Introduction and Commentary.* Anchor Bible. Garden City, N.Y.: Doubleday, 1977.

Rylaarsdam, John Coert. *Proverbs, Ecclesiastes, and the Song of Solomon.* Layman's Bible Commentary. Vol. 10. Richmond: John Knox, 1964.

Isaiah

Alexander, J. A. *Commentary on the Prophecies of Isaiah.* New York: Scribner, Armstrong and Co., 1875.

Clements, Ronald E. *Isaiah 1–39.* New Century Bible. Grand Rapids: Eerdmans, 1980.

Delitzsch, Franz. *Biblical Commentary on the Prophecies of Isaiah.* 2 vols. Edinburgh: T. & T. Clark, 1877.

Kaiser, Otto. *Isaiah 1–12: A Commentary.* 2d ed. Translated by John Bowden. Old Testament Library. Philadelphia: Westminster, 1983

———. *Isaiah 13–39: A Commentary.* Translated by John Bowden. Old Testament Library. Philadelphia: Westminsteer, 1974.

Leupold, H. C. *Exposition of Isaiah.* Grand Rapids: Baker, 1968.

*Motyer, J. Alec. *The Prophecy of Isaiah: An Introduction and Commentary.* Downers Grove, Ill.: InterVarsity, 1993.

Muilenberg, James. "Isaiah 40–66: Introduction and Exegesis." In *The Interpreter's Bible.* Vol. 5. Nashville: Abingdon, 1953.

Oswalt, John N. *Book of Isaiah, Chapters 1–39.* New International Commentary on the Old Testament. Grand Rapids: Eerdmans, 1986.

Scott, R. B. Y. "Isaiah 1–39: Introduction and Exegesis." In *The Interpreter's Bible.* Vol. 5. Nashville: Abingdon, 1953.

Skinner, John. *The Book of the Prophet Isaiah.* 2 vols. Cambridge Bible for Schools and Colleges. Cambridge: Cambridge University, 1905–1906.

Smith, G. A. *The Book of Isaiah.* Expositor's Bible. New York: Funk & Wagnalls, 1900.

†Watts, J. D. W. *Isaiah 1–33.* Word Biblical Commentary. Waco: Word, 1985.

†———. *Isaiah 34–66.* Word Biblical Commentary. Waco: Word, 1987.

†Westermann, Claus. *Isaiah 40–66: A Commentary.* Translated by D. M. G. Stalker. Old Testament Library. Philadelphia: Westminster, 1969.

Whybray, R. N. *Isaiah 40–66.* New Century Bible. London: Oliphants, 1975.

*Wright, G. Ernest. *Isaiah.* Layman's Bible Commentary. Vol. 11. Richmond: John Knox, 1964.

*Young, E. J. *The Book of Isaiah.* 3 vols. Grand Rapids: Eerdmans, 1965–1972.

Jeremiah and Lamentations

Bright, John. *Jeremiah.* Anchor Bible. Garden City, N.Y.: Doubleday, 1965.

Brueggemann, Walter. *To Pluck Up, to Tear Down: A Commentary on the Book of Jeremiah 1–25.* International Theological Commentary. Grand Rapids: Eerdmans, 1988.

————. *To Build, To Plant: A Commentary on Jeremiah 26–52.* International Theological Commentary. Grand Rapids: Eerdmans, 1991.

†Carroll, Robert P. *Jeremiah: A Commentary.* Old Testament Library. Philadelphia: Westminster, 1986.

Clements, R. E. *Jeremiah.* Interpretation. Atlanta: John Knox, 1988.

†Craigie, Peter C., Page Kelley, and Joel F. Drinkard Jr. *Jeremiah 1–25.* Word Biblical Commentary. Dallas: Word, 1991.

Davidson, Robert. *Jeremiah.* 2 vols. Daily Study Bible. Philadelphia: Westminster, 1985.

Driver, S. R. *The Book of the Prophet Jeremiah.* London: Hodder and Stoughton, 1906.

Gordis, Robert. *Song of Songs and Lamentations: A Study, Modern Translation and Commentary.* New York: KTAV, 1974.

Habel, Norman C. *Concordia Commentary: Jeremiah, Lamentations.* St. Louis: Concordia, 1968.

*Harrison, R. K. *Jeremiah and Lamentations.* Tyndale Old Testament Commentaries. Grand Rapids: Eerdmans, 1979.

Hillers, Delbert R. *Lamentations.* Anchor Bible. Garden City, N.Y.: Doubleday, 1972.

Holladay, W. L. *Jeremiah 1: A Commentary on the Books of Jeremiah, Chapters 1–25.* Hermeneia. Philadelphia: Fortress, 1986.

————. *Jeremiah 2: A Commentary on the Books of Jeremiah, Chapters 26–52.* Hermeneia. Philadelphia: Fortress, 1989.

*Huey, F. B. *Jeremiah, Lamentations.* New American Commentary. Nashville: Broadman, 1993.

Hyatt, James Philip. *Jeremiah, Prophet of Courage and Hope.* New York: Abingdon, 1958.

†McKane, William. *A Critical and Exegetical Commentary on the Book of Jeremiah.* International Critical Commentary. Edinburgh: T. & T. Clark, 1987.

Skinner, John. *Prophecy and Religion.* Cambridge: Cambridge University Press, 1922.

†Thompson, John A. *The Book of Jeremiah.* New International Commentary on the Old Testament. Grand Rapids: Eerdmans, 1980.

Ezekiel

Allen, Leslie C. *Ezekiel 20–48.* Word Biblical Commentary. Dallas: Word, 1990.

Brownlee, William H., and Leslie C. Allen. *Ezekiel 1–19.* Word Biblical Commentary. Dallas: Word, 1986.

Cooke, G. A. *A Critical and Exegetical Commentary on the Book of Ezekiel.* International Critical Commentary. Edinburgh: T. & T. Clark, 1936.

*Craigie, Peter C. *Ezekiel.* Daily Study Bible. Philadelphia: Westminster, 1983.

Davidson, A. B., and A. W. Streane. *The Book of the Prophet Ezekiel.* Cambridge Bible for Schools and Colleges. Cambridge: Cambridge University, 1900.

†Eichrodt, Walther. *Ezekiel.* Translated by Cosslett Quinn. Old Testament Library. Philadelphia: Westminster, 1970.

Ellison, H. L. *Ezekiel, the Man and His Message.* Grand Rapids: Eerdmans, 1956.

Greenberg, Moshe. *Ezekiel 1–20.* Anchor Bible. Garden City, N.Y.: Doubleday, 1983.

Keil, C. F. *Biblical Commentary on the Prophecies of Ezekiel.* Translated by James Martin. Edinburgh: T. & T. Clark, 1875.

Skinner, John. *The Book of Ezekiel.* Expositor's Bible. London: Hodder & Stoughton, 1909.

*Taylor, John B. *Ezekiel.* Tyndale Old Testament Commentaries. Downers Grove, Ill.: InterVarsity, 1969.

Wevers, John W. *Ezekiel.* New Century Bible. London: Thomas Nelson, 1969.

†Zimmerli, Walther. *Ezekiel: A Commentary on the Book of the Prophet Ezekiel.* Translated by R. E. Clements, et al. 2 vols. Hermeneia. Philadelphia: Fortress, 1979–83.

Daniel

Anderson, Robert A. *Signs and Wonders: A Commentary on the Book of Daniel.* International Theological Commentary. Grand Rapids: Eerdmans, 1984.

*Baldwin, Joyce G. *Daniel.* Tyndale Old Testament Commentaries. Downers Grove, Ill.: InterVarsity, 1978.

Charles, R. H. *A Critical and Exegetical Commentary on the Book of Daniel.* Oxford: Clarendon, 1929.

†Collins, John J. *Daniel: A Commentary on the Book of Daniel.* Hermeneia. Minneapolis: Fortress, 1993.

Driver, S. R. *The Book of Daniel.* Cambridge Bible for Schools and Colleges. Cambridge: Cambridge University, 1901.

†Goldingay, John. *Daniel.* Word Biblical Commentary. Dallas: Word, 1989.

Hartmann, Louis F., and Alexander A. Di Lella. *The Book of Daniel.* Anchor Bible. Garden City, N.Y.: Doubleday, 1978.

Lacocque, Andre M. *The Book of Daniel.* Translated by David Pellauer. Atlanta: John Knox, 1979.

Leupold, H. C. *Exposition of Daniel.* Columbus, Ohio: Wartburg, 1949.

Montgomery, James Alan. *A Critical and Exegetical Commentary on the Book of Daniel.* International Critical Commentary. New York: Scribner's Sons, 1927.

Porteous, Norman. *Daniel.* Old Testament Library. Philadelphia: Westminster, 1965.

Russell, D. S. *Daniel.* Daily Study Bible. Philadelphia: Fortress, 1981.

*Wallace, Ronald S. *The Message of Daniel.* Bible Speaks Today. Downers Grove, Ill.: InterVarsity, 1979.

*Young, Edward J. *The Prophecy of Daniel: A Commentary.* Grand Rapids: Eerdmans, 1949.

Minor Prophets

*Craigie, Peter C. *Twelve Prophets*. 2 vols. Daily Study Bible. Philadelphia: Westminster, 1984.

Eiselen, F. C. *The Minor Prophets*. Whedon's Commentary on the Old Testament. New York: Eaton and Mains, 1907.

Keil, C. F. *The Minor Prophets*. Translated by James Martin. 2 vols. Biblical Commentary on the Old Testament. Edinburgh: T. & T. Clark, 1888.

*McComiskey, Thomas E, ed. *The Minor Prophets: An Exegetical and Expository Commentary*. 3 vols. Grand Rapids: Baker, 1992–95.

Smith, George Adam. *The Book of the Twelve Prophets*. 2 vols. Expositor's Bible. London: Hodder & Stoughton, 1903.

Hosea

Andersen, Francis I., and David N. Freedman. *Hosea*. Anchor Bible. Garden City, N.Y.: Doubleday, 1980.

Cheyne, T. K. *Hosea*. Cambridge Bible for Schools and Colleges. Cambridge: Cambridge University, 1884.

Harper, W. R. *A Critical and Exegetical Commentary on Amos and Hosea*. International Critical Commentary. Edinburgh: T. & T. Clark, 1905.

*Hubbard, David Allan. *Hosea*. Tyndale Old Testament Commentaries. Downers Grove, Ill.: InterVarsity, 1989.

*Limburg, James. *Hosea-Micah*. Interpretation. Atlanta: John Knox, 1988.

†Mays, James L. *Hosea*. Old Testament Library. Philadelphia: Westminster, 1969.

*Snaith, Norman Henry. *Amos, Hosea, and Micah*. Epworth Preacher's Commentaries. London: Epworth, 1956.

†Stuart, Douglas. *Hosea-Jonah*. Word Biblical Commentary. Waco: Word, 1987.

Vawter, Bruce. *Amos, Hosea, Micah: With an Introduction to Classical Prophecy*. Old Testament Message. Vol. 7. Wilmington, Del.: Michael Glazier, 1981.

Ward, James M. *Hosea: A Theological Commentary*. New York: Harper & Row, 1966.

†Wolff, Hans Walter. *Hosea: A Commentary on the Book of the Prophet Hosea*. Translated by Gary Stansell. Hermeneia. Philadelphia: Fortress, 1974.

Joel

Allen, Leslie C. *Books of Joel, Obadiah, Jonah, and Micah*. New International Commentary on the Old Testament. Grand Rapids: Eerdmans, 1976.

Driver, S. R. *The Books of Joel and Amos*. The Cambridge Bible for Schools and Colleges. Cambridge: Cambridge University, 1915.

*Hubbard, David Allan. *Joel & Amos*. Tyndale Old Testament Commentaries. Downers Grove, Ill.: InterVarsity, 1989.

Smith, J. M. P., W. H. Ward, and J. A. Bewer. *A Critical and Exegetical Commentary on Obadiah and Joel*. International Critical Commentary. Edinburgh: T. & T. Clark, 1911.

†Stuart, Douglas. *Hosea-Jonah.* Word Biblical Commentary. Waco: Word, 1987.

Thompson, John A. "The Book of Joel: Introduction and Exegesis." In *The Interpreter's Bible.* Vol. 6. Nashville: Abingdon, 1956.

*Watts, John D. W. *The Books of Joel, Obadiah, Jonah, Nahum, Habakkuk, and Zephaniah.* Cambridge Bible Commentary. Cambridge: Cambridge University, 1975.

†Wolff, Hans Walter. *Joel and Amos.* Translated by Waldemar Janzen, et al. Hermeneia. Philadelphia: Fortress, 1977.

Amos

Andersen, Francis I., and David Noel Freedman. *Amos.* Anchor Bible. Garden City, N.Y.: Doubleday, 1989.

Cripps, Richard S. *A Critical and Exegetical Commentary on the Book of Amos.* 2d ed. London: S.P.C.K., 1955.

Driver, S. R. *The Books of Joel and Amos.* Cambridge Bible for Schools and Colleges. Cambridge: Cambridge University, 1915.

Harper, W. R. *A Critical and Exegetical Commentary on Amos and Hosea.* International Critical Commentary. Edinburgh: T. & T. Clark, 1905.

*Hubbard, David Allan. *Joel and Amos.* Tyndale Old Testament Commentaries. Downers Grove, Ill.: InterVarsity, 1989.

*Limburg, James. *Hosea-Micah.* Interpretation. Atlanta: John Knox, 1988.

†Mays, James L. *Amos.* Old Testament Library. Philadelphia: Westminster, 1969.

Paul, Shalom M. *Amos.* Hermeneia. Minneapolis: Fortress, 1991.

Snaith, Norman Henry. *Amos, Hosea, and Micah.* Epworth Preacher's Commentaries. London: Epworth, 1956.

†Stuart, Douglas. *Hosea-Jonah.* Word Biblical Commentary. Waco: Word, 1987.

Vawter, Bruce. *Amos, Hosea, Micah: With an Introduction to Classical Prophecy.* Old Testament Message. Vol. 7. Wilmington, Del.: Michael Glazier, 1981.

†Wolff, Hans Walter. *Joel and Amos.* Translated by Waldemar Janzen, et al. Hermeneia. Philadelphia: Fortress, 1977.

Obadiah

Allen, Leslie C. *Books of Joel, Obadiah, Jonah, and Micah.* New International Commentary on the Old Testament. Grand Rapids: Eerdmans, 1976.

*Baker, David W., T. Desmond Alexander, and Bruce K. Waltke. *Obadiah, Jonah, Micah.* Tyndale Old Testament Commentaries. Downers Grove, Ill.: InterVarsity, 1988.

Coggins, R. J., and S. Paul Re`emi. *Israel Among the Nations: A Commentary on the Books of Nahum and Obadiah and Esther.* International Theological Commentary. Grand Rapids: Eerdmans, 1985.

*Limburg, James. *Hosea-Micah.* Interpretation. Atlanta: John Knox, 1988.

†Stuart, Douglas. *Hosea-Jonah.* Word Biblical Commentary. Waco: Word, 1987.

Thompson, J. A. "The Book of Obadiah: Introduction and Exegesis." In *The Interpreter's Bible*. Vol. 6. Nashville: Abingdon, 1956.

†Watts, John D. W. *Obadiah: A Critical Exegetical Commentary*. Grand Rapids: Eerdmans, 1969.

†Wolff, Hans Walter. *Obadiah and Jonah: A Commentary*. Translated by Margaret Kohl. Minneapolis: Augsburg, 1986.

Jonah

Allen, Leslie C. *Books of Joel, Obadiah, Jonah, and Micah*. New International Commentary on the Old Testament. Grand Rapids: Eerdmans, 1976.

*Baker, David W., T. Desmond Alexander, and Bruce K. Waltke. *Obadiah, Jonah, Micah*. Tyndale Old Testament Commentaries. Downers Grove, Ill.: InterVarsity, 1988.

Fretheim, Terence. *The Message of Jonah: A Theological Commentary*. Minneapolis: Augsburg, 1977.

*Limburg, James. *Hosea-Micah*. Interpretation. Atlanta: John Knox, 1988.

Smart, James. "Jonah: Introduction and Exegesis." In *The Interpreter's Bible*. Vol. 6. Nashville: Abingdon, 1956.

Snaith, Norman Henry. *Notes on the Hebrew Text of Jonah*. London: Epworth, 1945.

†Stuart, Douglas. *Hosea-Jonah*. Word Biblical Commentary. Waco: Word, 1987.

*Watts, John D. W. *The Books of Joel, Obadiah, Jonah, Nahum, Habakkuk, and Zephaniah*. Cambridge Bible Commentary. Cambridge: Cambridge University, 1975.

†Wolff, Hans Walter. *Obadiah and Jonah: A Commentary*. Translated by Margaret Kohl. Minneapolis: Augsburg, 1986.

Micah

Allen, Leslie C. *Books of Joel, Obadiah, Jonah, and Micah*. New International Commentary on the Old Testament. Grand Rapids: Eerdmans, 1976.

*Baker, David W., T. Desmond Alexander, and Bruce K. Waltke. *Obadiah, Jonah, Micah*. Tyndale Old Testament Commentaries. Downers Grove, Ill.: InterVarsity, 1988.

Cheyne, T. K. *Micah*. Cambridge Bible for Schools and Colleges. Cambridge: Cambridge University, 1882.

Copass, Benjamin A., and E. L. Carlson. *Study of the Prophet Micah: Power by the Spirit*. Grand Rapids: Baker, 1950.

†Hillers, Delbert R. *Micah: A Commentary on the Book of the Prophet Micah*. Hermeneia. Philadelphia: Fortress, 1984.

King, Philip J. *Amos, Hosea, Micah: An Archaeological Commentary*. Philadelphia: Westminster, 1988.

*Limburg, James. *Hosea-Micah*. Interpretation. Atlanta: John Knox, 1988.

†Mays, James L. *Micah*. Old Testament Library. Philadelphia: Westminster, 1976.

Smith, Ralph L. *Micah-Malachi*. Word Biblical Commentary. Waco: Word, 1984.

Snaith, Norman Henry. *Amos, Hosea, and Micah.* Epworth Preacher's Commentaries. London: Epworth, 1956.

Vawter, Bruce. *Amos, Hosea, Micah: With an Introduction to Classical Prophecy.* Old Testament Message. Vol. 7. Wilmington, Del.: Michael Glazier, 1981.

†Wolff, Hans Walter. *Micah the Prophet.* Translated by Ralph D. Gehrke. Philadelphia: Fortress, 1981.

Nahum and Habakkuk

Achtemeier, Elizabeth. *Nahum-Malachi.* Interpretation. Atlanta: John Knox, 1986.

*Baker, David. *Nahum, Habakkuk, and Zephaniah.* Tyndale Old Testament Commentaries. Downers Grove, Ill.: InterVarsity, 1988.

Coggins, R. J., and S. Paul Re`emi. *Israel Among the Nations: A Commentary on the Books of Nahum and Obadiah and Esther.* International Theological Commentary. Grand Rapids: Eerdmans, 1985.

Davidson, A. B. *Books of Nahum, Habakkuk and Zephaniah.* Cambridge Bible for Schools and Colleges. Rev. ed. Cambridge: Cambridge University, 1920.

Garland, D. David. "Habakkuk." In *The Broadman Bible Commentary.* Vol. 7. Nashville: Broadman, 1972.

*Maier, W. A. *The Book of Nahum.* St. Louis: Concordia, 1959.

†Roberts, J. J. M. *Nahum, Habakkuk, Zephaniah.* Old Testament Library. Louisville: Westminster/John Knox, 1990.

Robertson, O. Palmer. *The Books of Nahum, Habakkuk, and Zephaniah.* New International Commentary on the Old Testament. Grand Rapids: Eerdmans, 1990.

†Smith, Ralph L. *Micah-Malachi.* Word Biblical Commentary. Waco: Word, 1984.

Watts, John D. W. *The Books of Joel, Obadiah, Jonah, Nahum, Habakkuk, and Zephaniah.* Cambridge Bible Commentary. Cambridge: Cambridge University, 1975.

Zephaniah

Achtemeier, Elizabeth. *Nahum-Malachi.* Interpretation. Atlanta: John Knox, 1986.

*Baker, David. *Nahum, Habakkuk, and Zephaniah.* Tyndale Old Testament Commentaries. Downers Grove, Ill.: InterVarsity, 1988.

Berlin, Adele. *Zephaniah.* Anchor Bible. Garden City, N.Y.: Doubleday, 1994.

Davidson, A. B. *Books of Nahum, Habakkuk and Zephaniah.* Cambridge Bible for Schools and Colleges. Rev. ed. Cambridge: Cambridge University, 1920.

Kapelrud, A. S. *The Message of the Prophet Zephaniah.* Oslo: Universitesforlaget, 1975.

†Roberts, J. J. M. *Nahum, Habakkuk, Zephaniah.* Old Testament Library. Louisville: Westminster/John Knox, 1990.

Robertson, O. Palmer. *The Books of Nahum, Habakkuk, and Zephaniah.* New International Commentary on the Old Testament. Grand Rapids: Eerdmans, 1990.

†Smith, Ralph L. *Micah-Malachi*. Word Biblical Commentary. Waco: Word, 1984.

*Watts, John D. W. *The Books of Joel, Obadiah, Jonah, Nahum, Habakkuk, and Zephaniah*. Cambridge Bible Commentary. Cambridge: Cambridge University, 1975.

Haggai

Achtemeier, Elizabeth. *Nahum-Malachi*. Interpretation. Atlanta: John Knox, 1986.

*Baldwin, Joyce G. *Haggai, Zechariah, Malachi*. Tyndale Old Testament Commentaries. Downers Grove, Ill.: InterVarsity, 1972.

Coggins, R. J. *Haggai, Zechariah, Malachi*. Old Testament Guides. Sheffield: JSOT, 1987.

Mason, Rex. *Books of Haggai, Zechariah and Malachi*. Cambridge Bible Commentary. Cambridge: Cambridge University, 1977.

Meyers, Carol L., and Eric M. *Haggai and Zechariah 1–8*. Anchor Bible. Garden City, N.Y.: Doubleday, 1987.

†Petersen, David L. *Haggai and Zechariah 1–8: A Commentary*. Old Testament Library. Philadelphia: Westminster, 1984.

Redditt, Paul L. *Haggai, Zechariah, Malachi*. New Century Bible. Grand Rapids: Eerdmans, 1995.

†Smith, Ralph L. *Micah-Malachi*. Word Biblical Commentary. Waco: Word, 1984.

Verhoef, Pieter A. *Books of Haggai and Malachi*. New International Commentary on the Old Testament. Grand Rapids: Eerdmans, 1986.

Zechariah

Achtemeier, Elizabeth. *Nahum-Malachi*. Interpretation. Atlanta: John Knox, 1986.

*Baldwin, Joyce G. *Haggai, Zechariah, Malachi*. Tyndale Old Testament Commentaries. Downers Grove, Ill.: InterVarsity, 1972.

Coggins, R. J. *Haggai, Zechariah, Malachi*. Old Testament Guides. Sheffield: JSOT, 1987.

*Leupold, Herbert Carl. *Exposition of Zechariah*. Columbus, Ohio: Wartburg, 1956.

Mason, Rex. *Books of Haggai, Zechariah and Malachi*. Cambridge Bible Commentary. Cambridge: Cambridge University, 1977.

†Meyers, Carol L., and Eric M. *Haggai and Zechariah 1–8*. Anchor Bible. Garden City, N.Y.: Doubleday, 1987.

†. *Zechariah 9–14*. Anchor Bible. Garden City, N.Y.: Doubleday, 1993.

Petersen, David L. *Haggai and Zechariah 1–8: A Commentary*. Old Testament Library. Philadelphia: Westminster, 1984.

Redditt, Paul L. *Haggai, Zechariah, Malachi*. New Century Bible. Grand Rapids: Eerdmans, 1995.

†Smith, Ralph L. *Micah-Malachi*. Word Biblical Commentary. Waco: Word Books, 1984.

Malachi

Achtemeier, Elizabeth. *Nahum-Malachi.* Interpretation. Atlanta: John Knox, 1986.

*Baldwin, Joyce G. *Haggai, Zechariah, Malachi.* Tyndale Old Testament Commentaries. Downers Grove, Ill.: InterVarsity, 1972.

Coggins, R. J. *Haggai, Zechariah, Malachi.* Old Testament Guides. Sheffield: JSOT, 1987.

*Kaiser, Walter C. Jr. *Malachi: God's Unchanging Love.* Grand Rapids: Baker, 1984.

Mason, Rex. *Books of Haggai, Zechariah and Malachi.* Cambridge Bible Commentary. Cambridge: Cambridge University, 1977.

†Smith, Ralph L. *Micah-Malachi.* Word Biblical Commentary. Waco: Word, 1984.

Redditt, Paul L. *Haggai, Zechariah, Malachi.* New Century Bible. Grand Rapids: Eerdmans, 1995.

Verhoef, Pieter A. *Books of Haggai and Malachi.* New International Commentary on the Old Testament. Grand Rapids: Eerdmans, 1986.

Matthew

Blomberg, Craig L. *Matthew.* New American Commentary. Nashville: Broadman, 1992.

Broadus, John A. *Commentary on the Gospel of Matthew.* American Commentary. Philadelphia: American Baptist Publication Society, 1886.

Bruner, Frederick Dale. *Matthew 1–12: The Christbook.* Dallas: Word, 1987.

———. *Matthew 13–28: The Churchbook.* Dallas: Word, 1990.

*Carson, D. A. "Matthew." In *The Expositor's Bible Commentary.* Vol. 8. Grand Rapids: Zondervan, 1984.

†Davies, W. D., and Dale Allison. *A Critical and Exegetical Commentary on the Gospel According to St. Matthew.* 2 vols. to date. International Critical Commentary. Edinburgh: T. & T. Clark, 1988–1991.

*France, Richard T. *The Gospel According to St. Matthew.* Tyndale New Testament Commentaries. Rev. ed. Grand Rapids: Eerdmans, 1987.

Garland, David E. *Reading Matthew: A Literary and Theological Commentary on the First Gospel.* New York: Crossroad, 1993.

Gundry, Robert H. *Matthew: A Commentary on His Handbook for a Mixed Church Under Persecution.* 2d ed. Grand Rapids: Eerdmans, 1994.

†Hagner, Donald A. *Matthew 1–13.* Word Biblical Commentary. Dallas: Word, 1993.

†———. *Matthew 14–28.* Word Biblical Commentary. Dallas: Word, 1993.

Hendriksen, William. *Exposition of the Gospel According to Matthew.* New Testament Commentary. Grand Rapids: Baker, 1973.

Hill, David. *The Gospel of Matthew.* New Century Bible. London: Oliphants, 1972.

McNeile, A. H. *The Gospel According to St. Matthew: The Greek Text with Introduction, Notes, and Index.* London: Macmillan, 1915.

Morris, Leon. *The Gospel According to Matthew.* Pillar New Testament Commentary. Grand Rapids: Eerdmans, 1992.

Mounce, Robert H. *Matthew.* Good News Commentary. New York: Harper & Row, 1985.

Mark

Anderson, Hugh. *The Gospel of Mark.* New Century Bible. London: Oliphants, 1976.

Brooks, James A. *Mark.* New American Commentary. Nashville: Broadman, 1991.

*Cole, R. A. *The Gospel According to St. Mark.* Rev. ed. Tyndale New Testament Commentaries. Grand Rapids: Eerdmans, 1989.

†Cranfield, C. E. B. *The Gospel According to St. Mark.* 3d ed. Cambridge Greek Testament Commentary. Cambridge: Cambridge University, 1966.

Guelich, Robert. *Mark 1–8:26.* Word Biblical Commentary. Dallas: Word, 1989.

Gundry, Robert H. *Mark: A Commentary on His Apology for the Cross.* Grand Rapids: Eerdmans, 1993.

Hooker, Morna. *A Commentary on the Gospel According to St. Mark.* Black's New Testament Commentaries. London: A & C Black, 1992.

*Lane, William L. *The Gospel of Mark.* New International Commentary on the New Testament. Grand Rapids: Eerdmans, 1974.

Mann, C. S. *Mark.* Anchor Bible. Garden City, N.Y.: Doubleday, 1986.

Nineham, D. E. *The Gospel of St. Mark.* Pelican Commentaries. Baltimore: Penguin, 1964.

Swete, H. B. *The Gospel According to St. Mark.* 3d ed. London: Macmillan, 1909.

†Taylor, Vincent. *The Gospel According to St. Mark: The Greek Text with Introduction, Notes, and Indexes.* 2d ed. New York: St. Martin's, 1966.

Luke

Arndt, W. F. *The Gospel According to St. Luke.* Bible Commentary. St. Louis: Concordia, 1956.

Bock, Darrel L. *Luke.* 2 vols. Baker Exegetical Commentary. Grand Rapids: Baker, 1994.

*Caird, G. B. *The Gospel of St. Luke.* Pelican Commentaries. Baltimore: Penguin, 1963.

Creed, J. M. *The Gospel According to St. Luke: The Greek Text with Introduction, Notes, and Indexes.* London: Macmillan, 1930.

Ellis, E. E. *The Gospel of Luke.* Rev. ed. New Century Bible. London: Oliphants, 1974.

Evans, Craig A. *Luke.* New International Biblical Commentary. Peabody, Mass.: Hendrickson, 1990.

†Fitzmyer, Joseph A. *The Gospel According to Luke.* 2 vols. Anchor Bible. Garden City, N.Y.: Doubleday, 1981–85.

Geldenhuys, J. N. *Commentary on the Gospel of St. Luke.* New International Commentary on the New Testament. Grand Rapids: Eerdmans, 1951.

Godet, Frederic. *A Commentary on the Gospel of St. Luke.* Translated by E. W. Shalders. New York: Funk and Wagnalls, 1887.

†Marshall, I. Howard. *Gospel of Luke: Commentary on the Greek Text.* New International Greek Testament Commentary. Grand Rapids: Eerdmans, 1978.

Nolland, John. *Luke 1–9:20.* Word Biblical Commentary. Dallas: Word, 1989.

―――. *Luke 9:21–18:34.* Word Biblical Commentary. Dallas: Word, 1993.

―――. *Luke 18:35–24:53.* Word Biblical Commentary. Dallas: Word, 1993.

Plummer, Alfred. *A Critical and Exegetical Commentary on the Gospel According to St. Luke.* International Critical Commentary. Edinburgh: T. & T. Clark, 1914.

*Stein, Robert A. *Luke.* New American Commentary. Nashville: Broadman, 1993.

John

†Barrett, C. K. *The Gospel According to St. John: An Introduction with Commentary and Notes on the Greek Text.* 2d ed. Philadelphia: Westminster Press, 1978.

Beasley-Murray, George R. *The Gospel of John.* Word Biblical Commentary. Waco: Word, 1987.

†Brown, Raymond E. *The Gospel According to John.* 2 vols. Anchor Bible. Garden City, N.Y.: Doubleday, 1971.

*Bruce, F. F. *The Gospel of John.* Grand Rapids: Eerdmans, 1983.

*Carson, Donald A.*The Gospel According to John.* Pillar New Testament Commentary. Grand Rapids: Eerdmans, 1991.

Dodd, C. H. *The Interpretation of the Fourth Gospel.* Cambridge: Cambridge University, 1953.

Morris, Leon. *Commentary on the Gospel of John.* Rev. ed. New International Commentary on the New Testament. Grand Rapids: Eerdmans, 1994.

Schnackenburg, Rudolf. *The Gospel According to St. John.* 3 vols. Herder's Theological Commentary on the New Testament. New York: Crossroad, 1968–82.

Turner, G. A., and J. R. Mantey. *The Gospel According to John.* Evangelical Commentary. Grand Rapids: Eerdmans, 1964.

Westcott, B. F. *The Gospel According to St. John: The Authorized Version with Introduction and Notes.* London: John Murray, 1881.

Acts

†Barrett, C. K. *A Critical and Exegetical Commentary on Acts 1–14.* International Critical Commentary. Edinburgh: T. & T. Clark, 1993.

†Bruce, F. F. *The Acts of the Apostles: The Greek Text with Introduction and Commentary.* 3d ed. Grand Rapids: Eerdmans, 1990.

―――. *Commentary on the Book of Acts.* Rev. ed. New International Commentary on the New Testament. Grand Rapids: Eerdmans, 1988.

Carter, C. W., and Ralph Earle. *The Acts of the Apostles.* Evangelical Commentary. Grand Rapids: Zondervan, 1959.

Haenchen, Ernst. *The Acts of the Apostles: A Commentary.* Translated by R. McL. Wilson, et al. Philadelphia: Westminster, 1971.

Lake, Kirsopp, and H. J. Cadbury. *The Beginnings of Christianity, Part I: The Acts of the Apostles.* Vol. 4: *English Translation and Commentary.* London: Macmillan, 1933.

*Longenecker, Richard N. "Acts." In *The Expositor's Bible Commentary.* Vol. 9. Grand Rapids: Zondervan, 1981.

*Marshall, I. H. *The Acts of the Apostles.* Tyndale New Testament Commentaries. Grand Rapids: Eerdmans, 1981.

Neil, William. *Acts.* New Century Bible. London: Oliphants, 1973.

Polhill, John B. *Acts.* New American Commentary. Nashville: Broadman, 1992.

Rackham, R. B. *The Acts of the Apostles.* 12th ed. Westminster Commentaries. London: Methuen, 1939.

Stagg, Frank. *The Book of Acts.* Nashville: Broadman, 1955.

*Stott, John R. W. *The Message of Acts.* Bible Speaks Today. Downers Grove, Ill.: InterVarsity, 1990.

Romans

Barrett, C. K. *A Commentary on the Epistle to the Romans.* Rev. ed. Black's New Testament Commentary. Peabody, Mass.: Hendrickson, 1993.

*Bruce, F. F. *The Letter of Paul to the Romans.* Rev. ed. Tyndale New Testament Commentaries. Grand Rapids: Eerdmans, 1985.

†Cranfield, C. E. B. *A Critical and Exegetical Commentary on the Epistle to the Romans.* International Critical Commentary. 2 vols. Edinburgh: T. & T. Clark, 1975–79.

†Dunn, James D. G. *Romans 1–8.* Word Biblical Commentary. Dallas: Word, 1988.

†————. *Romans 9–16.* Word Biblical Commentary. Dallas: Word, 1988.

Fitzmyer, Joseph A. *Romans.* Anchor Bible. Garden City, N.Y.: Doubleday, 1993.

Gifford, E. H. *The Epistle of St. Paul to the Romans.* London: John Murray, 1886.

Godet, Frederic. *Commentary on St. Paul's Epistle to the Romans.* Translated by A. Cusin. New York: Funk & Wagnalls, 1883.

*Johnson, Alan F. *Romans: The Freedom Letter.* Rev. ed. 2 vols. Everyman's Bible Commentary. Chicago: Moody, 1985.

Käsemann, Ernst. *Commentary on Romans.* Translated by G. W. Bromiley. Grand Rapids: Eerdmans, 1980.

Moo, Douglas J. *Romans.* 2 vols. Wycliffe Exegetical Commentary. Chicago: Moody, 1991-forthcoming.

Morris, Leon.*The Epistle to the Romans.* Pillar New Testament Commentary. Grand Rapids: Eerdmans, 1988.

Sanday, William, and Arthur C. Headlam. *A Critical and Exegetical Commentary on the Epistle to the Romans.* 5th ed. International Critical Commentary. Edinburgh: T. & T. Clark, 1902.

Thomas, W. H. Griffith. *St. Paul's Epistle to the Romans: A Devotional Commentary.* Grand Rapids: Eerdmans, 1946.

First Corinthians

Barrett, C. K. *A Commentary to the First Epistle to the Corinthians.* Harper's New Testament Commentaries. New York: Harper and Row, 1968.

*Bruce, F. F. *1 and 2 Corinthians.* New Century Bible. London: Oliphants, 1971.

Conzelmann, Hans. *1 Corinthians: A Commentary on the First Epistle to the Corinthians.* Translated by James W. Leith. Hermeneia. Philadelphia: Fortress, 1975.

†Fee, Gordon D. *The First Epistle to the Corinthians.* New International Commentary on the New Testament. Grand Rapids: Eerdmans, 1987.

Findlay, G. G. "St. Paul's First Epistle to the Corinthians." In *The Expositor's Greek Testament.* Vol. 2, Edited by W. R. Nicoll. London: Hodder and Stoughton, 1900.

Godet, Frederic L. *Commentary on the First Epistle of St. Paul to the Corinthians.* Translated by A. Cusin. 2 vols. Edinburgh: T. & T. Clark, 1886.

Hering, Jean. *The First Epistle of Saint Paul to the Corinthians.* Translated by A. W. Heathcote and P. J. Allcock. London: Epworth, 1962.

Moffatt, James. *The First Epistle of Paul to the Corinthians.* Moffatt's New Testament Commentary. London: Hodder and Stoughton, 1938.

*Morris, Leon. *The First Epistle of Paul to the Corinthians.* Rev. ed. Tyndale New Testament Commentaries. Grand Rapids: Eerdmans, 1985.

†Robertson, Archibald, and Alfred Plummer. *A Critical and Exegetical Commentary on the First Epistle of St. Paul to the Corinthians.* International Critical Commentary. 2d ed. Edinburgh: T. & T. Clark, 1914.

Second Corinthians

*Barnett, Paul.*The Message of 2 Corinthians.* Bible Speaks Today. Downers Grove, Ill.: InterVarsity, 1988.

Barrett, C. K. *A Commentary on the Second Epistle to the Corinthians.* Harper's New Testament Commentaries. New York: Harper & Row, 1973.

Beasley-Murray, G. R. "2 Corinthians." In *The Broadman Bible Commentary.* Vol. 11. Nashville: Broadman, 1971.

Bruce, F. F. *1 and 2 Corinthians.* New Century Bible. London: Oliphants, 1971.

†Furnish, Victor F. *II Corinthians.* Anchor Bible. Garden City, N.Y.: Doubleday, 1984.

Harris, Murray J. "2 Corinthians." In *The Expositor's Bible Commentary.* Vol. 10. Grand Rapids: Zondervan, 1976.

Hering, Jean. *The Second Epistle of Saint Paul to the Corinthians.* Translated by A. W. Heathcote and P. J. Allcock. London: Epworth, 1967.

Hughes, Philip E. *Paul's Second Epistle to the Corinthians*. New International Commentary on the New Testament. Grand Rapids: Eerdmans, 1962.

*Kruse, Colin G. *The Second Epistle of Paul to the Corinthians*. Tyndale New Testament Commentaries. Downers Grove, Ill.: InterVarsity,1987.

†Martin, Ralph P. *2 Corinthians*. Word Biblical Commentary. Waco: Word, 1986.

Plummer, Alfred. *A Critical and Exegetical Commentary on the Second Epistle of St. Paul to the Corinthians*. International Critical Commentary. Edinburgh: T. & T. Clark, 1915.

†Thrall, Margaret E. *A Critical and Exegetical Commentary on the Second Epistle to the Corinthians*. Vol. 1. International Critical Commentary. Edinburgh: T. & T. Clark, 1994.

Galatians

Betz, H. D. *Galatians: A Commentary on Paul's Letter to the Churches in Galatia*. Hermeneia. Philadelphia: Fortress, 1979.

†Bruce, F. F. *The Epistle to the Galatians: A Commentary on the Greek Text*. New International Greek Testament Commentary. Grand Rapids: Eerdmans, 1982.

†Burton, E. D. *A Critical and Exegetical Commentary on the Epistle to the Galatians*. International Critical Commentary. Edinburgh: T. & T. Clark, 1921.

Cole, R. A. *The Epistle of Paul to the Galatians*. Rev. ed. Tyndale New Testament Commentaries. Grand Rapids: Eerdmans, 1989.

Dunn, James D. G. *The Epistle to the Galatians*. Black's New Testament Commentaries. Peabody, Mass.: Hendrickson, 1994.

Fung, R. Y. K. *The Epistle to the Galatians*. New International Commentary on the New Testament. Grand Rapids: Eerdmans, 1988

*George, Timothy. *Galatians*. New American Commentary. Nashville: Broadman, 1994.

*Hansen, G. Walter. *Galatians*. IVP New Testament Commentary. Downers Grove, Ill.: InterVarsity, 19

Lightfoot, J. B. *St. Paul's Epistle to the Galatians*. 19th ed. London: Macmillan, 1926.

Longenecker, Richard N. *Galatians*. Word Biblical Commentary. Dallas: Word, 1990.

Ephesians

Abbott, T. K. *A Critical and Exegetical Commentary on the Epistles to the Ephesians and to the Colossians*. International Critical Commentary. Edinburgh: T. & T. Clark, 1897.

†Barth, Markus. *Ephesians*. 2 vols. Anchor Bible. Garden City, N.Y.: Doubleday, 1974.

*Bruce, F. F. *The Epistles to the Colossians, to Philemon, and to the Ephesians*. New International Commentary on the New Testament. Grand Rapids: Eerdmans, 1984.

*Caird, G. B. "The Letter to the Ephesians." In *Paul's Letters from Prison*. New Clarendon Bible. Oxford: Clarendon, 1976.

Lincoln, Andrew T. *Ephesians*. Word Biblical Commentary. Dallas: Word, 1990.

Mitton, C. L. *Ephesians*. New Century Bible. London: Oliphants, 1976.

†Robinson, J. A. *Saint Paul's Epistle to the Ephesians: A Revised Text and Translation, with Exposition and Notes*. 2d ed. London: Macmillan, 1904.

Westcott, B. F. *Saint Paul's Epistle to the Ephesians: The Greek Text with Notes and Addenda*. London: Macmillan, 1906.

Philippians

Beare, F. W. *The Epistle to the Philippians*. Harper's New Testament Commentaries. New York: Harper & Brothers, 1959.

*Bruce, F. F. *Philippians*. Good News Commentary. New York: Harper & Row, 1983.

Caird, G. B. "The Letter to the Philippians." In *Paul's Letters from Prison*. New Clarendon Bible. Oxford: Clarendon, 1976.

Collange, J. F. *The Epistle of Saint Paul to the Philippians*. Translated by A. W. Heathcote. London: Epworth, 1979.

Fee, Gordon. *Philippians*. New International Commentary on the New Testament. Grand Rapids: Eerdmans, 1995.

†Hawthorne, Gerald F. *Philippians*. Word Biblical Commentary. Waco: Word, 1983.

Lightfoot, J. B. *St. Paul's Epistle to the Philippians*. London: Macmillan, 1894.

*Martin, Ralph P. *The Epistle of Paul to the Philippians*. Rev. ed. Tyndale New Testament Commentaries. Grand Rapids: Eerdmans, 1987.

———. *Philippians*. New Century Bible. London: Marshall, Morgan and Scott, 1976.

†O'Brien, Peter T. *The Epistle to the Philippians: A Commentary on the Greek Text*. New International Greek Testament Commentary. Grand Rapids: Eerdmans, 1991.

Robertson, A. T. *Paul's Joy in Christ*. Revised by W. C. Strickland. Nashville: Broadman, 1959.

Silva, Moisés. *Philippians*. Wycliffe Exegetical Commentary. Chicago: Moody, 1988.

Colossians and Philemon

*Bruce, F. F. *The Epistles to the Colossians, to Philemon, and to the Ephesians*. New International Commentary on the New Testament. Grand Rapids: Eerdmans, 1984.

Caird, G. B. "The Letter to the Colossians" and "The Letter to Philemon." In *Paul's Letters from Prison*. New Clarendon Bible. Oxford: Clarendon, 1976.

Harris, Murray J. *Colossians & Philemon*. Exegetical Guide to the Greek New Testament. Grand Rapids: Eerdmans, 1991.

Lightfoot, J. B. *St. Paul's Epistles to the Colossians and Philemon: A Revised Text with Introductions, Notes and Dissertations*. 3d ed. London: Macmillan, 1879.

Lohse, Edward. *Colossians and Philemon: A Commentary on the Epistles to the Colossians and Philemon.* Translated by W. R. Poehlmann and R. J. Karris. Hermeneia. Philadelphia: Fortress, 1971.

*Martin, R. P. *Colossians and Philemon.* New Century Bible. London: Oliphants, 1974.

Melick, Richard R. *Philippians, Colossians, Philemon.* New American Commentary. Nashville: Broadman, 1991.

†Moule, C. F. D. *The Epistles of Paul the Apostle to the Colossians and Philemon.* Cambridge Greek Testament Commentary. Cambridge: Cambridge University, 1957.

†O'Brien, Peter T. *Colossians, Philemon.* Word Biblical Commentary. Waco: Word, 1982.

Robertson, A. T. *Paul and the Intellectuals.* Revised and edited by W. C. Strickland. Nashville: Broadman, 1959.

Schweizer, Eduard. *The Letter to the Colossians.* Translated by Andrew Chester. Minneapolis: Augsburg, 1982.

Wright, N. T. *The Epistles of Paul to the Colossians and to Philemon.* Tyndale New Testament Commentaries. Grand Rapids: Eerdmans, 1986.

First and Second Thessalonians

*Best, Ernest. *A Commentary on the First and Second Epistles to the Thessalonians.* Harper's New Testament Commentaries. New York: Harper & Row, 1972.

†Bruce, F. F. *1 & 2 Thessalonians.* Word Biblical Commentary. Waco: Word, 1982.

Findlay, G. G. *The Epistles to the Thessalonians.* Cambridge Greek Testament for Schools and Colleges. Cambridge: Cambridge University, 1904.

Frame, J. E. *A Critical and Exegetical Commentary on the Epistles of St. Paul to the Thessalonians.* International Critical Commentary. Edinburgh: T. & T. Clark, 1912.

Hendriksen, William. *Exposition of I and II Thessalonians.* New Testament Commentary. Grand Rapids: Baker, 1955.

Hiebert, D. E. *The Thessalonian Epistles: A Call to Readiness.* Chicago: Moody, 1971.

Hogg, C. F., and W. E. Vine. *The Epistles to the Thessalonians with Notes Exegetical and Expository.* London: Pickering & Inglis, 1914.

Lightfoot, J. B. *Notes on the Epistles of St. Paul.* London: Macmillan, 1895.

*Marshall, I. Howard. *1 and 2 Thessalonians.* New Century Bible. Grand Rapids: Eerdmans, 1983.

†Milligan, George. *St. Paul's Epistles to the Thessalonians.* London: Macmillan, 1908.

Morris, Leon. *The First and Second Epistles to the Thessalonians.* Revised edition. New International Commentary on the New Testament. Grand Rapids: Eerdmans, 1991.

*———. *The Epistles of Paul to the Thessalonians.* Revised edition. Tyndale New Testament Commentaries. Grand Rapids: Eerdmans, 1987.

Wanamaker, Charles A. *The Epistles to the Thessalonians.* New International Greek Testament Commentary. Grand Rapids: Eerdmans, 1990.

First and Second Timothy and Titus

Barrett, C. K. *The Pastoral Epistles.* New Clarendon Bible. Oxford: Clarendon, 1963.

Bernard, J. H. *The Pastoral Epistles.* Cambridge Greek Testament for Schools and Colleges. Cambridge: Cambridge University, 1899.

Dibelius, Martin, and Hans Conzelmann. *The Pastoral Epistles.* Translated by P. Buttolph and A. Yarbro. Hermeneia. Philadelphia: Fortress Press, 1972.

*Fee, Gordon D. *1 and 2 Timothy, Titus.* Good News Commentary. New York: Harper & Row, 1984.

Guthrie, Donald. *The Pastoral Epistles.* Tyndale New Testament Commentaries. Grand Rapids: Eerdmans, 1957.

*Kelly, J. N. D. *A Commentary on the Pastoral Epistles.* Harper's New Testament Commentaries. New York: Harper and Brothers, 1963.

†Knight, George. *The Pastoral Epistles.* New International Greek Testament Commentary. Grand Rapids: Eerdmans, 1992.

Lea, Thomas D. and Hayne P. Griffin Jr. *1, 2 Timothy, Titus.* New American Commentary. Nashville: Broadman, 1992.

Lock, Walter. *A Critical and Exegetical Commentary on the Pastoral Epistles.* International Critical Commentary. Edinburgh: T. & T. Clark, 1924.

Mounce, William. *The Epistles of 1 and 2 Timothy and Titus.* New International Commentary on the New Testament. Grand Rapids: Eerdmans, forthcoming.

Oden, Thomas C. *First and Second Timothy and Titus.* Interpretation. Louisville: John Knox, 1989.

†Simpson, E. K. *The Pastoral Epistles: The Greek Text with Introduction and Commentary.* London: Tyndale Press, 1954.

Hebrews

Attridge, Harold. *The Epistle to the Hebrews.* Hermeneia. Philadelphia: Fortress, 1989.

Brown, Raymond. *Christ Above All: The Message of Hebrews.* Bible Speaks Today. Downers Grove, Ill.: InterVarsity, 1982.

*Bruce, F. F. *The Epistle to the Hebrews.* Revised edition. New International Commentary on the New Testament. Grand Rapids: Eerdmans, 1988.

Davidson, A. B. *The Epistle to the Hebrews.* Handbooks for Bible Classes. Edinburgh: T. & T. Clark, 1882.

Delitzsch, Franz J. *Commentary on the Epistle to the Hebrews.* 2 vols. Edinburgh: T. & T. Clark, 1872.

†Ellingworth, Paul. *The Epistle to the Hebrews.* New International Greek Testament Commentary. Grand Rapids: Eerdmans, 1993.

Guthrie, Donald. *The Letter to the Hebrews.* Tyndale New Testament Commentaries. Grand Rapids: Eerdmans, 1983.

Hagner, Donald A. *Hebrews.* Good News Commentary. San Francisco: Harper & Row, 1983.

Hering, Jean. *The Epistle to the Hebrews*. Translated by A. W. Heathcote and P. J. Allcock. London: Epworth, 1970.

*Hughes, P. E. *A Commentary on the Epistle to the Hebrews*. Grand Rapids: Eerdmans, 1977.

Kistemaker, Simon J. *Hebrews*. New Testament Commentary. Grand Rapids: Baker, 1984.

†Lane, William L. *Hebrews 1–8*. Word Biblical Commentary. Waco: Word, 1987.

†———. *Hebrews 9–13*. Word Biblical Commentary. Dallas: Word, 1991.

Moffatt, James. *Critical and Exegetical Commentary on the Epistle to the Hebrews*. International Critical Commentary. Edinburgh: T. & T. Clark, 1924.

Montefiore, Hugh. *A Commentary on the Epistle to the Hebrews*. Harper's New Testament Commentaries. New York: Harper & Row, 1964.

Nairne, Alexander. *The Epistle to the Hebrews*. Cambridge Greek Testament for Schools and Colleges. Cambridge: Cambridge University, 1917.

Westcott, B. F. *The Epistle to the Hebrews*. 3d ed. London: Macmillan, 1920.

James

Adamson, James B. *The Epistle of James*. New International Commentary on the New Testament. Grand Rapids: Eerdmans, 1976.

†Davids, Peter H. *Commentary on James*. New International Greek Testament Commentary. Grand Rapids: Eerdmans, 1982.

Dibelius, Martin. *James*. Revised by Heinrich Greeven. Hermeneia. Philadelphia: Fortress, 1976.

Hiebert, D. Edmond. *The Epistle of James: Tests of a Living Faith*. Chicago: Moody, 1979.

Hort, F. J. A. *The Epistle of St. James: The Greek Text with Introduction, Commentary as far as Chapter IV, Verse 7, and Additional Notes*. London: Macmillan, 1909.

Laws, Sophie S. *A Commentary on the Epistle of James*. Harper's New Testament Commentaries. New York: Harper & Row, 1980.

Martin, Ralph P. *James*. Word Biblical Commentary. Waco: Word, 1988.

†Mayor, Joseph B. *The Epistle of St. James: The Greek Text with Introduction, Notes, and Comments*. London: Macmillan, 1897.

*Mitton, C. Leslie. *The Epistle of James*. Grand Rapids: Eerdmans, 1966.

*Moo, Douglas J. *The Letter of James*. Tyndale New Testament Commentaries. Grand Rapids: Eerdmans, 1985.

Robertson, A. T. *Studies in the Epistle of James*. Revised and edited by H. F. Peacock. Nashville: Broadman, 1959.

Ropes, James Hardy. *A Critical and Exegetical Commentary on the Epistle of St. James*. International Critical Commentary. Edinburgh: T. & T. Clark, 1916.

First and Second Peter and Jude

†Bauckham, Richard J. *Jude, 2 Peter*. Word Biblical Commentary. Waco: Word, 1983.

†Beare, F. W. *The First Epistle of Peter: The Greek Text with Introduction and Notes.* 3d ed. Oxford: Basil Blackwell, 1970.

Bigg, C. A. *A Critical and Exegetical Commentary on the Epistles of St. Peter and St. Jude.* International Critical Commentary. Edinburgh: T. & T. Clark, 1901.

Davids, Peter H. *The First Epistle of Peter.* New International Commentary on the New Testament. Grand Rapids: Eerdmans, 1990.

Goppelt, Leonhard. *A Commentary on I Peter.* Edited by Ferdinand Hahn. Translated by John E. Alsup. Grand Rapids: Eerdmans, 1993.

*Green, Michael. *The Second Epistle General of Peter and the General Epistle of Jude.* Rev. ed. Tyndale New Testament Commentaries. Grand Rapids: Eerdmans, 1987.

*Grudem, Wayne A. *The First Epistle of Peter.* Tyndale New Testament Commentaries. Grand Rapids: Eerdmans, 1988.

Hort, F. J. A. *The First Epistle of St. Peter, I.1–II.17.* London: Macmillan, 1898.

*Kelly, J. N. D. *A Commentary on the Epistles of Peter and Jude.* Harper's New Testament Commentaries. New York: Harper and Row, 1969.

Mayor, J. B. *The Epistle of St. Jude and the Second Epistle of St. Peter: Greek Text with Introduction, Notes and Comments.* London: Macmillan, 1907.

Michaels, J. Ramsey. *1 Peter.* Word Biblical Commetnary. Waco: Word, 1988.

†Selwyn, E. G. *The First Epistle of St. Peter: The Greek Text with Introduction, Notes and Essays.* 2d ed. London: Macmillan, 1947.

Wand, J. W. C. *The General Epistles of St. Peter and St. Jude.* Westminster Commentaries. London: Methuen, 1934.

First, Second, and Third John

†Brown, Raymond E. *The Epistles of John.* Anchor Bible. Garden City, N.Y.: Doubleday, 1982.

Brooke, A. E. *A Critical and Exegetical Commentary on the Johannine Epistles.* International Critical Commentary. Edinburgh: T. & T. Clark, 1912.

Dodd, C. H. *The Johannine Epistles.* Moffatt New Testament Commentary. London: Hodder and Stoughton, 1946.

Findlay, George G. *Fellowship in the Life Eternal: An Exposition of the Epistles of St. John.* London: Hodder and Stoughton, 1909.

Law, Robert. *The Tests of Life: A Study of the First Epistle of St. John.* Edinburgh: T. & T. Clark, 1909.

*Marshall, I. Howard. *The Epistles of John.* New International Commentary on the New Testament. Grand Rapids: Eerdmans, 1978.

Plummer, Alfred. *The Epistles of St. John.* Cambridge Greek Testament for Schools and Colleges. Cambridge: Cambridge University, 1986.

†Smalley, Stephen S. *1, 2, 3 John.* Word Biblical Commentary. Waco: Word, 1984.

*Stott, John R. W. *The Epistles of John.* Revised edition. Tyndale New Testament Commentaries. Grand Rapids: Eerdmans, 1988.

Westcott, B. F. *The Epistles of St. John: The Greek Text with Notes.* Introduction by F. F. Bruce. 4th ed. Grand Rapids: Eerdmans, 1966.

Revelation

†Beckwith, I. T. *The Apocalypse of John: Studies in Introduction with a Critical and Exegetical Commentary.* New York: Macmillan, 1919.

Beasley-Murray, G. R. *The Book of Revelation.* New Century Bible. London: Marshall, Morgan & Scott, 1978.

Caird, G. B. *A Commentary on the Revelation of St. John the Divine.* Harper's New Testament Commentaries. New York: Harper & Row, 1966.

Charles, R. H. *A Critical and Exegetical Commentary on the Revelation of St. John.* 2 vols. International Critical Commentary. Edinburgh: T. & T. Clark, 1920.

*Johnson, Alan F. "Revelation." In *The Expositor's Bible Commentary.* Vol. 12. Grand Rapids: Zondervan, 1981.

Ladd, G. E. *A Commentary on the Revelation of John.* Grand Rapids: Eerdmans, 1972.

Minear, Paul S. *I Saw a New Earth: An Introduction to the Visions of the Apocalypse.* Cleveland: Corpus Books, 1968.

Morris, Leon. *The Book of Revelation.* Revised edition. Tyndale New Testament Commentaries. Grand Rapids: Eerdmans, 1986.

Mounce, Robert. *The Book of Revelation.* New International Commentary on the New Testament. Grand Rapids: Eerdmans, 1977.

*Newport, John P. *The Lion and the Lamb.* Nashville: Broadman, 1986.

†Swete, H. B. *The Apocalypse of St. John: The Greek Text with Introduction, Notes and Indexes.* 3d ed. London: Macmillan, 1908.

▼

Index